Intifada

The Palestinian Uprising Against Israeli Occupation

**Edited by Zachary Lockman
and Joel Beinin**

A MERIP Book

South End Press
Boston, MA

Copyright © 1989 by Middle East Research and Information Project
Suite 119
1500 Massachusetts Ave., NW
Washington, DC 20005

Cover and interior graphic design by Kamal Boullata
Cover photograph by George Azar
Photograph credits: George Azar (p. 25 top, p. 141 top, p. 180 top right
and bottom, p. 248, p. 315), Rick Reinhard (p. 2 top, p. 25 bottom, p. 98, p.
99 top, p. 140 top, p. 141 bottom, p. 180 top left, p. 248 top, p. 249, p. 302,
p. 303, p. 314) and John Tordai (p. 2 bottom, p. 3, p. 24, p. 99 bottom, p. 140
bottom, p. 181, p. 248 bottom).
Text design and production by the South End Press collective
Manufactured in the U.S.A. on recycled, acid-free paper
First edition, second printing

Library of Congress Cataloging-in-Publication Data
Intifada: the Palestinian uprising against Israeli occupation
edited by Zachary Lockman and Joel Beinin
p. cm.
"A MERIP book"
Includes bibliographies.
    1. West Bank—History—Palestinian Uprising, 1987-
2. Gaza Strip—History—Palestinian Uprising, 1987-
I. Lockman, Zachary, 1952-   . II. Beinin, Joel, 1948-
    DS110.W47I57 1989   956.95'3—dc20   89-11595
    ISBN 0-89608-365-9
    ISBN 0-89608-363-2(pbk)

South End Press, 116 Saint Botolph Street, Boston, MA 02115
98 97 96 95 94 93 92 91 90   2 3 4 5 6 7 8 9

Table of Contents

Preface

This book is a project of the Middle East Research and Information Project, better known as MERIP. At its inception in 1970, MERIP sought to put the question of US policy in the Middle East and support for popular struggles there on the agenda of the broad movement opposing the US war in Indochina. MERIP's main project has been publishing a bi-monthly magazine, originally called *MERIP Reports* but now known as *Middle East Report*. *Middle East Report*'s editorial agenda gives priority to analyzing the political economy and popular struggles of the contemporary Middle East and US policy in the region. It has become one of the most respected sources of information about the Middle East published in English and has played an important role in reorienting both scholarship and political discourse on the Middle East in this country. Its audience includes political activists, church and community groups, government officials, journalists, university students and scholars in North America, Europe and the Middle East. Subscriptions are available from MERIP, Suite 119, 1500 Massachusetts Ave., NW, Washington, DC 20005, and cost $20 for one year (overseas mail additional).

The enthusiastic reception of *Middle East Report*'s coverage of the Palestinian intifada encouraged the editors to consider producing a book on the subject. Several chapters of this book originally appeared as articles in *Middle East Report*. Some have been revised or updated; others have been left essentially unchanged. To the eyewitness accounts and analyses of the uprising itself we have added historical background, a discussion of the uprising's impact on Israel, an analysis of organizing and activism in the US around Palestinian-Israeli peace issues, a selection of resistance poetry by Palestinians and Israelis, a list of the martyrs of the first year of the intifada and other important documents. We hope that the information and analysis contained in this book will help both the general public and activists acquire a deeper understanding of the struggles now underway in the West Bank, Gaza and Israel and thereby contribute to building the US movement for peace in the Middle East.

Our first thanks must go to those whose contributions make up the text of this book, and especially those engaged in the ongoing struggle in the occupied territories and Israel who, despite adverse circumstances, put aside more immediate concerns to write and/or revise their contributions. Kamal

Boullata has given generously of his extraordinary talents by planning the book's graphic design and choosing the poems to be included; his efforts are greatly appreciated. We are particularly grateful for the photographic contributions of George Azar, Rick Reinhard and Tordai which enliven this book. Thanks are also owed to our editors, Steve Chase and Todd Jailer, and their comrades at South End Press for their flexibility, responsiveness and enthusiastic contribution to this partnership. Joe Stork and Martha Wenger, editor and assistant editor respectively of *Middle East Report*, gave considerable time and energy to this project despite being already overworked by their regular tasks in the MERIP office. The board of directors and editorial committee of MERIP authorized this project and delegated us to carry it out. We hope we have been faithful to their charge.

This book is dedicated to the Palestinian people struggling for national liberation and to those Israelis who have struggled in solidarity alongside them to build a future of peaceful coexistence, self-determination and social justice for both peoples.

Zachary Lockman
Joel Beinin

August 1989

Part 1

Introduction

Intifada

the land of Palestine shook
until the very stones loosened

and were gathered up by you
as other children, innocent, have picked flowers

your rocks blossomed blood-red
against a conspiracy of years

of having your every breath, heartbeat observed constrained
until you could not breathe, every gasp a battle

the way you suffocate under a veil
of teargas, chambers of death
your own homes, streets, gardens

you said you have had enough
and started an earthquake

drawing down a shower of hailstones
against a sinful nation

the occupation officers have hit a stone, been struck
by the steadfast hardness
of a people willing
to die on their feet
rather than live on their knees

you love your lives enough
to struggle
against the constraints

bound, as you have been
all your lives

you are loosening the bonds now
casting off what has kept you down
you are bound for glory
shaking, shaking until you are free.

—Peter Boullata

## Chapter 1

Intifada and Independence

Edward W. Said

I

The Palestinian uprising *(intifada)* on the West Bank and Gaza is said to have begun on December 9, 1987. A month earlier, an Arab summit meeting in Amman had resolved the usual moral support for the cause of Palestine, although the various kings and presidents had also indicated that their primary interest was not Palestine but the Iran-Iraq war. This partial demotion of Palestine was gleefully noted by commentators in the United States, led by the usual "experts" (Daniel Pipes, Thomas Friedman *et al.*) ever ready to portray Yasir Arafat as a bumbling scoundrel, grinning his way from one failure to another. What seems to have escaped "expert" and official Israeli notice was that the occupied territories had already had twenty years of a regime designed to suppress, humiliate and perpetually disenfranchise Palestinians, and that the likelihood of an outside force actually improving the situation had gradually disappeared. Instead the situation for Palestinians had gotten worse, and their sense of embattled loneliness, even abandonment, had increased. Capitulation was impossible. An intensification of resistance therefore seemed required, and with it greater discipline, more determination and enhanced independence of method, planning and action.

In discussing the unfolding intifada (note that this is the only Arabic word to enter the vocabulary of twentieth-century world politics) we are in fact talking about two dynamics, one internal to Palestinian life under Israeli domination, the other external, in which the Palestinian exile presence has interacted dialectically with regional and international powers. Consider first the internal situation. Alone of the territories occupied by Israel in 1967, the West Bank and Gaza remained in an unforgiving limbo of local repression and frozen political process. Sinai was returned to Egypt by 1982, while the Golan Heights and East Jerusalem were formally annexed by Israel, a change in status which, while hardly welcomed by the Syrians and Palestinians who lived in those places, nonetheless at least represented a new dynamic. In the meantime, more settlements were established in the West Bank and Gaza, more land was expropriated. After municipal elections on the West Bank (not in Gaza) in the spring of 1976 overwhelmingly returned pro-Palestine Liberation Organization (PLO) candidates, the officials were summarily dismissed. Whenever leaders emerged they were either imprisoned, killed or maimed by Israeli Jewish terrorists, or simply expelled.

And always, the expropriations of land, the increasingly tight control over water, the perpetual encroachments of Jewish settlements pressed down on Palestinians in the territories, which after 1967 became known as "administered" territories and were later renamed "Judea and Samaria." The Camp David accords, as interpreted by the Israelis and the United States, opened no avenue of independence, only a series of pointless negotiations with phantom Palestinian "inhabitants" from the occupied territories who could never be identified or promised anything. There were occasional, and quite unsuccessful, attempts to empower collaborationist Palestinians (e.g. the Village Leagues) who would perhaps be more amenable to doing the Israeli wish, but those never acquired anything like the credibility needed to swing a critical mass of Palestinians behind them. After a time they were dropped and forgotten.

Although it was frequently referred to as a benign occupation, the Israeli presence on the West Bank and Gaza hurt more and more people as time passed. Students were forced to endure the extended closing of schools and universities. Workers who depended for their livelihood on intermittent piecework inside Israel faced daily reminders of their subservient status: they were paid less than Jewish workers, had no union to support them, were required to be kept under lock and key any time they stayed overnight inside the Green Line. Some were burned alive as a consequence, many others referred to themselves as "slaves." There was a proliferation of over a thousand laws and regulations designed not only to enforce the subaltern, rightless position of Palestinians under Israeli jurisdiction, but also to rub their noses in the mud, to humiliate and remind them of how they were doomed to less-than-human status. Books by the thousands were banned. The colors of the Palestinian flag were outlawed; even the word "Palestine" could earn its user a jail sentence. Administrative detentions were common, as were the dynamiting of houses, torture, collective punishments and harassments, complete with rituals of dehumanizing behavior forced upon unarmed Palestinians. Yet Palestinians on the West Bank and Gaza were required to pay Israeli taxes (but had no one to represent them), to submit to the increasingly cruel whims of settlers who did what they wanted with impunity, to face their alienation from their own land. To plant a tree required a permit.

To hold meetings required a permit. Entry and exit required permits. To dig a well required a permit—one that was never given.

None of these horrific things went completely unnoticed. A fair number of Israelis, including veteran advocates of Palestinian rights like Uri Avneri and Matti Peled, protested them, and the Israeli press, notable for its independence by and large, recorded them. Various groupings—the Israeli League for Human and Civil Rights chaired by the unflagging Professor Israel Shahak, the small bands of peace activists sometimes including Peace Now, a handful of writers, academics, intellectuals, Knesset members—signalled the world that outrages were taking place. But the massive political, economic and military support of the United States enabled things to go on as usual. The outrages continued (in fact they increased) and with them, the powerful propaganda and justifying rhetoric of those whom Noam Chomsky has called "the supporters of the moral degeneration and eventual destruction of Israel" went forward unabated. By the early months of the first Reagan administration it became clear that there was nothing Israel might do, from unmercifully punishing Palestinians under its rule to invading countries all around it, that the United States would not support. Aid levels increased tremendously, so that aside from the direct budgetary support that Israel (uniquely of all the countries that receive US foreign aid) was assured of—all delivered at the beginning of the fiscal year—in amounts that approached one-third of the total US foreign aid budget ($3 billion in 1988), there were other kinds of unprecedented and blanket deals made. A strategic partnership was devised between the two countries; Israel was accorded favored-nation trading status; previous debts were forgiven; a huge variety of intelligence, military and political liaisons were established; US taxes were waived on Israeli securities, bonds and funds. Tom Dine, the head of American Israel Public Affairs Committee, noted in early 1987 that the United States (and especially the Congress) had never been more pro-Israeli.

People in the United States who had made a practice of speaking up for human rights everywhere in the world, particularly in countries within the Soviet sphere, simply said nothing about the appalling situation created by the Israeli occupation. Yet, in contrast to the US media's shameless pandering to the Israeli lobby,[1] the alternative sources of information continued to monitor the internal situation. Here mention must be made of local groups such as al-Haq/Law in the Service of Man, a group of Palestinian lawyers; the West Bank Data Project, funded by the Ford Foundation and directed by Meron Benvenisti; the Alternative Information Center in Jerusalem; and Raymonda Tawil's Palestine Press Service. The courageous and objective efforts of these and other groups to record and occasionally contest human rights abuses from murder to land expropriation made it impossible to pretend that no one knew what was going on in the name of democratic, freedom-loving Israel.

By the second Reagan administration a sizeable body of Israeli revisionist historical research had exposed the much longer record of Zionist attitudes and practices toward the Palestinians. As the truth about 1947-49 came to light—thanks to the efforts of Tom Segev, Simha Flapan, Benny Morris, Avi Shlaim and others—the remarkable coincidence between their research and the testimony of three generations of Palestinians became clear. More to the point, there emerged a perceptible continuity between Zionist theories and actions before as well as after 1967. The occupation, for all its deliberate and programmatic humiliation of Palestinians, its bare-knuckled attempts to rob a whole people of nationhood, identity and history, its systematic assault on civil institutions and vulnerabilities, could be seen as extending the logic of earlier Zionists like Herzl, Jabotinsky and Ben-Gurion into the present. Far from revealing a defensive strategy of self-protection against extermination and annulment, this logic instead showed a political and state philosophy relentlessly on the offensive, spurning Arab overtures for peace, attacking civilians undeterred by compassion or understanding, pretending all along that Israel was engaged in a fight for its survival. In this context, the protestations of Israel's idealistic friends that Zionism's early spirit was being corrupted and betrayed by Israeli occupation methods sounded both indecent and unconvincing.

It was the terrible force of these realities that Palestinians under occupation resisted. The stone-throwing children of the intifada starkly represented the very ground of the Palestinian protest: with stones and an unbent political will standing fearlessly against the blows of well-armed Israeli soldiers, backed up by one of the world's mightiest defense establishments (the Israeli military procurement mission in the United States had a yearly budget of $25 million for *administration* alone), bankrolled unflinchingly and unquestioningly by the world's wealthiest nation, supported faithfully and smilingly by a whole apparatus of intellectual lackeys. The occupation had lasted for twenty years without a single change for the better. Life was more difficult. Israelis were less interested in peace and coexistence. The United States, the other Arabs, even putative allies like the Soviet Union seemed paralyzed by that mixture of foregone hypocrisy and benevolent hand wringing that always contributed to sustaining the occupation still longer.

The time had come, therefore, to start trying to change realities from the bottom up. On the 18th of December 1987 the well-known Syrian poet Nizar Qabbani produced his brilliant ode to *atfal al-hajara* ("children of the stones"), and in characterizing their dazzling gesture of revolt also pinned down the cafe-haunting, nouveau-riche merchants, commission-agents, polygamous princes, intellectuals and rulers whose exploits in London and Cannes had in fact produced the *jil al-khiyana* ("generation of treason") that surrounded and still continued to exploit the Palestinian cause.

But the intifada also has its antecedents in the external, that is exile, situation of those dispossessed and dispersed Palestinians who were driven from their lands in 1948 and 1967. By 1969 the Palestine Liberation Organization and its constituent groups had emerged as a mobilizing force not only for Palestinians but for a whole generation of Arabs—intellectuals, young people, politically influential activists for whom the fall of Abdel Nasser and his unionist style of Arab nationalism had to be replaced with a political vision more capable of implementation and defense after the disasters of 1967. An early motto of the Palestinian movement was the ideal of establishing a unitary secular democratic state in all of Palestine; this attracted much attention in the Arab world first because of its intrinsic merits as a notion that rose above the crippling inhibitions imposed on whole populations by Zionism on the one hand and small-scale state nationalisms in the Arab world on the other. Also implied in the secular democratic state concept was a political and social program that would liberate people from the legacy of imperialism, in which partitions, makeshift state boundaries, and top-heavy national security states produced neither the true independence nor the political actualities for which earlier generations had so strenuously fought.

In the period 1969-74 Palestinians had disastrous encounters with Arab state authority in Jordan but principally in Lebanon. This revealed the defensiveness of the existing regimes as well as the uncritical fidelity to ethnic or resurgent religious nationalism. The secular state idea was slowly abandoned. At the 1974 Palestine National Council (PNC) meeting a new notion was put forward, espoused first by the Democratic Front and then adopted by Fatah, and Arafat in particular. Palestinian nationalism had to be recuperated immediately by a Palestinian national authority; thus, as the PNC resolutions began to put it, any portion of land liberated from Israeli occupation should go directly under the independent jurisdiction of a Palestinian "national authority." That same year Arafat came to the UN to offer his peace plan, having earlier in the year gained an Arab summit consensus that the PLO was "the sole legitimate representative of the Palestinian people."

Thus a new trajectory was established toward the idea of partitioning Palestine, although the word "partition" was never uttered and the program of a two-state solution was frequently both unclear and diverted. The PLO remained committed to "liberation" at the same time that the highest Palestinian authority—the PNC—had begun to speak of political (as opposed to "military" or "armed struggle") measures in furtherance of its national objectives; while it remained explicitly fixed on the complete liberation of Palestine, the PLO seemed to indicate a preference for the political independence of a Palestinian state. In time the liberation idea slipped from sight except as a historical *cum* rhetorical gesture; for after all, most Palestinians were not from the territories occupied by Israel in 1967 and their loss had to find a commemorative place somewhere in the concrete actualities of Palestinian life. Moreover, the UN General Assembly, the non-aligned movement, the socialist bloc, the Islamic conference and others had begun to show accelerating interest in Palestinian statehood, inalienable rights and so on. So while the international context showed a clear improvement in the Palestinian national status and pointed it toward a Palestinian state in a part of Palestine alongside Israel, some Palestinians, some Arab states, Israel and the United States engaged in furious battle in which civil war (Lebanon), invasion (Israel's massive interventions in Lebanon, from the early 1970s until the great campaign of 1982), inter-Arab imbroglios (the aftermath of Camp David, the contest with Syria's Hafez al-Assad from 1976 to the present) and Palestinian insurrections (1983-85) were all aimed ultimately at curtailing and perhaps even capturing the still potent symbol of "Palestine," which remained the central foreign policy issue of the Arab world. During this period, it was the PLO, particularly Fatah and Yasir Arafat, that provided the focus for the gradually emerging and finally unmistakable double-sided idea that Palestinians had to arrive at their vision of their own future *on their own,* and that this vision, while theirs, had also (and somehow) to conform to the international consensus (or "international legality," the phrase of choice in 1988).

Any history of the period, then, would have to concentrate on the relentless and unevenly matched fight between Israel and its supporters on the one hand and Palestinian nationalism and its supporters on the other. At issue were not just the political claims to self-determination of the latter, but the very idea of Palestine itself. The military contours of this fight had immense scope. Thus, for example, when Israel invaded Lebanon in full force in 1982, producing not only the horrors of the siege of Beirut but also the massacres of Sabra and Shatila (described with oxymoronic doublespeak by the Israeli commission of inquiry as showing the "indirect responsibility" of the Israeli army in charge), it was openly admitted by Israeli spokesmen that: a) the real battle was for the West Bank and Gaza, and the PLO had to be destroyed utterly because of its representative status; and b) because it had become internationally "responsible"—having observed a UN-monitored truce on the Israeli-Lebanese border for eleven months before June 1982—the PLO had to be attacked. Similarly, Israel's US-supported attacks on Tunis (October 1985) and its assassination of Abu Jihad in his home there (April 1988) showed the almost limitless extent to which Israel would go in combatting any independent Palestinian force.

The hard Likud line, always reinforced with astonishing complaisance by the Reagan administration whose perennial "green light" was never turned off, was challenged by some significant defections. New configurations appeared within Israel expressing all sorts of doubts about Israeli policy in Lebanon (the southern part of whose territory continues to be occupied as I write), the occupied territories and the Third World generally, in which support for discredited regimes was, it seemed, a vital order of business for the Israeli military-industrial complex. Similarly, in Western Europe and the United States, where support of Israel had traditionally been one of the cornerstones of postwar liberal and Jewish public opinion, a decreasingly friendly questioning of Israeli policy proceeded apace. Important symbols in the erosion of the wholesale approval of Israel were Arafat's meetings with the Pope, the slow but sure support given Palestinian positions by the European Community and the mounting authority of Jews critical of Israeli policy (among whom Nahum Goldmann, Pierre Mendes-France, Philip Klutznick and Bruno Kreisky were early leaders).

However, it was the Reagan administration's active cooperation with Israeli intransigence and hostility to Palestinian aspirations, human rights and life itself that characterized the environment external to Palestine. Some of the milestones were the moral permissiveness which—from Alexander Haig to George Shultz—the United States accorded Israel's adventures outside its borders; the astounding additions to the US dole to Israel after one or another of that country's particularly horrific exploits ($450 million added immediately after Sabra and Shatila, $180 million on the very day in December 1988 when Reagan admonished the Israelis about the expulsion and killing of Palestinians); the almost grotesque congruence between Israeli and US positions on "terrorism" which became the watchword of US policy in the second Reagan administration. Surveying all this, we can say with Christopher Hitchens that the complete "Israelization" of US foreign policy had occurred, so that by the penultimate year of Reagan's tenure Israel had become the main strategic ally of the United States east of the English Channel.

The horrendous cost to Palestinian civilians—most of them refugees— can scarcely be tallied even at this point. Over 20,000 Palestinians and Lebanese were killed by Israeli troops in the summer of 1982 alone. How many more in the occupied territories and elsewhere were punished by Israel—the reports of torture were internationally known at least since the mid-1970s—through imprisonment, expulsion, maiming, killing, loss of property and freedom, is difficult to say, but the inadequate figures that now exist are awful enough. They show something like a ratio of 100 Palestinians killed for every Israeli killed (this in the midst of an appallingly mindless chorus led by Israel about the scourge of Palestinian "terrorism") and, according to Alexander Cockburn, something on the order of one out of every sixty-six Palestinians imprisoned, roughly ten times the average for blacks under the South African regime. Proportional to the population, more Palestinians have been killed by Israeli soldiers during the intifada than US soldiers during the Korean and Vietnam wars. All of this was part of an orchestrated campaign to exterminate Palestinians as a political presence in Palestine. To Begin they were "two-legged vermin;" to General Eytan they were "drugged roaches in a bottle;" to Shamir they were "grasshoppers;" to the more polite, Palestinians were "the Arabs of Judea and Samaria;" to the *New York Times* they were simply "Arabs."

Even so, the Palestinian political line grew clearer and clearer. This is a major irony. In the United States, Arafat and the PLO were remorselessly and repeatedly attacked by a supine media and an Israeli-dominated policy elite for terrorism, extremism, rejectionism and hostility to democracy; in the Arab world, attacks on Arafat (culminating in a whole mutinous movement within Fatah ranks in 1983, eagerly financed by Syria) were fueled by charges that he was a capitulationist who had conceded too much to his enemies and given up armed for political struggle (the distinction in the Palestinian context was fatuous, but it had great emotional staying power nonetheless). The PNC for its part stayed on course. In 1984 it was convened in Amman despite enormous Syrian pressure. Once again the partitionist idea—with Jordanian confederation—was implicitly accepted. A new alliance was forged with Jordan in 1985 and 1986, precisely to accommodate Palestinian nationalism to the international consensus, now unambiguously upheld by Gorbachev's Soviet Union. All the Arab states, with the exception of Syria and Libya, had come around to the two-state view, although few actually said it publicly. Then came the criminal war of the Beirut refugee camps, sponsored by Syria between 1985 and 1988; Arafat and his forces were being constantly pressured by Syria and its pocket insurgents. Threats from the United States (which had attacked Libya in 1981 and 1986, as it was to do in 1989), the deepening Palestinian gloom in the West Bank and Gaza, the indifference of the Arabs, the endless Lebanese crisis, the rise of an anarchical Islamist movement, the hemorrhaging effect of the Iran-Iraq war, the ceaseless enterprise of the Israeli-US axis (as symbolized throughout 1986 and 1987 by Iran-contra and the campaign against Nicaragua), the absence of reliable Arab and strategic allies: all these took a severe toll on the Palestinian drive led by the PLO.

It remains impressive, I think, that the Palestinian center acquired more, not less, authority from its constituents. In April 1987 a PNC meeting in Algiers stressed that an international conference and negotiations were the desired means to end the dispute with Israel. Jordan had already defected from its alliance with the PLO, the result (said Palestinians) of US pressure. At regular intervals, but with sharper clarity after 1984, Arafat stated his willingness to meet with Israelis, to negotiate a peaceful settlement and to end the longstanding conflict. His remarks were either not reported or they were scorned. Meanwhile the situation on the West Bank and Gaza kept getting worse. Talk of "transfer" became widespread. Rabbi Kahane, with his explicitly racist but unimpeachably frank claim that Israel couldn't be both Jewish and democratic, attracted attention, indeed grew more popular. Isolated incidents (the moronically criminal hijacking of the *Achille Lauro* in 1985, the Rome and Vienna airport massacres) were treated as "trends," whereas the global assault on Palestinian rights (especially in the United States, Lebanon and the occupied territories) was pooh-poohed. When it finally erupted, the intifada was treated by the media (and the Israelis) as a problem of law and order; the historical and political context was denied and unreported.

A number of occurrences in the United States stand out as small but noteworthy parts of the international background to the intifada. In early 1988 a group of Palestinians in Los Angeles, legal residents all, were threatened with expulsion under the McCarran-Walters Act. Alex Odeh, a Palestinian citizen of the United States, had been assassinated in the same area less than three years before, yet none of his assailants were apprehended. During the previous winter Congress passed the Grassley Amendment (in effect, a bill of attainder) invidiously pointing the finger at the PLO, alone among all the world's organizations, as "terrorist" and closing the Palestine Information Office in Washington while threatening the PLO's UN observer mission with termination. The Los Angeles deportation threat and the Grassley Amendment were fought and ultimately defeated, but they showed the depth of the official US hatred of the Palestinians, how far the government was willing to go in forgiving Israel everything it did while punishing Palestinians for their mere existence, how arrogantly the administration dismissed the Arab position, and Arab humanity itself.

Despite all the protestations about freedom of the press, public discussion of the Palestinian people remained at a remarkably low and degraded level. Aside from "terrorism," a notion never carefully defined or even reflected upon, Palestinians were confined in such basically condemnatory terms as extremists (as opposed to moderates, who never seemed in evidence), rejectionist (Israel was routinely referred to in terms indicating morality and flexibility), and faction-ridden (despite the fact that the overwhelming preponderance of the PLO stood behind the centrist consensus). Among "dovish" Zionists in the West and Israel (chief among them Yehoshafat Harkabi, Arthur Hertzberg and Abba Eban) Palestinians were referred to in the scandalously racist framework of "a demographic problem," the suggestion being that too many Palestinians were a threat to Israel's Jewishness (or "purity," as the more honest of this group put it). In all such instances I am reminded of W.E.B. Dubois's answer to the question posed to blacks in this country: "How does it feel to be a problem?" It is, he says, "a very strange experience." For in fact the entire tenor of Zionist and Western discourse about the Palestinians has been to reduce us to so problematic, eccentric and unthinkable a level as to make our every effort to appear to be human only a confirmation of our dehumanized, permanently subaltern status. This has been the conceptual coefficient of the war against Palestinians led in the West by the supporters of Israel.

Faced with such an array of pressure, real threats and actual punishment, the Palestinian national will was mobilized and, by the end of 1987, had reached the threshold of pain it could no longer endure. The shadow line had to be crossed; whether or not the crossing actually took place on December 9, that quickly became the date when, as the Palestinian journalist Makram Makhoul reported, fear was forbidden and the stones were taken up. From now on there was to be no turning back, as the Palestinian sense of irreversibility took hold: the occupation had to end, political independence had to be declared, the sacrifice had to be made. After King Hussein had withdrawn his faltering and unpopular claims to the West Bank in late July 1988, the die was cast. A PNC meeting would have to be convened, the Palestinian claims had to be put forward, not in vague terms but in the accents of a movement bent upon national statehood.

II

The nineteenth session of the Palestine National Council which I attended (November 12-15, 1988), formally entitled the "intifada meeting," was momentous and, in many great and small ways, unprecedented. Held in Algiers, there were fewer hangers-on, groupies and "observers" than ever before. Security was tighter and more unpleasant than during the 1987 PNC session, also held in Algiers; Algeria had just brutally suppressed its own intifada, so the presence of several hundred Palestinians and at least 1,200 members of the press was not especially welcomed by the Ben Jadid government, which paradoxically needed the event to restore some of its tarnished revolutionary lustre. This was also to be the shortest PNC meeting ever held. Barely three and a half days long, it accomplished more by way of debate, discussion, resolutions and announcements than any Palestinian meeting in the post-1948 period. Above all, this PNC secured for Yasir Arafat the certainty of his place in Palestinian and world history for, as one member put it, "We're not only living through a Palestinian revolution; it's also Abu Ammar's [Arafat's *nom de guerre*] revolution."

None of the approximately 380 members came to Algiers with any illusion that Palestinians could once again get away simply with creative ambiguity or with solid affirmations of the need to struggle. The intifada's momentum and its success in creating a clear civil alternative to the Israeli occupation regime now necessitated a definitive statement by the PNC of support for the intifada as an end-to-occupation and relatively nonviolent movement. This required an unambiguous claim for Palestinian sovereignty on whatever Palestinian territories were to be vacated by the occupation. There also had to be an equally unambiguous statement on peaceful resolution of the conflict between Palestinian Arabs and Israeli Jews based on UN Resolutions 181 (partition), 242 and 338. In short, the PNC was asking of itself nothing less than emphatic transformation: from liberation movement to independence movement. Jordan's recent withdrawal of claims to the West Bank made the need for transformation urgent and compelling.

If you live in the United States, participating in Palestinian discussions, debates and soul-searching reappraisals is particularly poignant. Palestinians meet rarely enough, given the widespread dispersion of our five million people, and the fact that we have no center, no territorial sovereignty of our own, makes our distance from most other Palestinians, in the midst of a US society whose government's hostility to us seems limitless, a continuously frustrating experience. Tunis serves the role of occasional headquarters, but since Abu Jihad's assassination Arafat's presence has necessarily been fitful and erratic. Yet most of us in the PNC made at least one trip there; many documents and drafts went via fax, express mail or the telephone. And the date of the PNC kept getting postponed; it was definitively set by late October, not without trepidation, since Algeria's internal volatility remained high.

PNC members were to be quartered in bungalows adjacent to the enormous meeting hall set in a conference-*cum*-vacation center built by Ben Bella in 1965, approximately thirty miles west of Algiers. Four of us travelled together overnight to Paris from New York, transferred from de Gaulle to Orly airport and arrived in Algiers at 2 pm on November 11. Ibrahim Abu-Lughod and I were driven to one bungalow, only to find it already occupied; a second choice turned up the same situation, so we settled for a downtown hotel, which came to mean no hot food and hardly any sleep for three and a half days, as we commuted back and forth at the craziest hours. Despite jet lag, we went back to the conference center late that Friday night to call on Arafat, who seemed involved in three concurrently running meetings. He was confident but looked tired. Everyone knew that this was his step first to articulate, then to persuade everyone to take, then finally to choreograph politically. He handed me the Arabic draft of the declaration of statehood and asked me to render it into English. It had been drafted by committee, then rewritten by the poet Mahmoud Darwish, then, alas, covered with often ludicrously clumsy insertions and inexplicable deletions. Later, Darwish told me that the phrase "collective memory" had been struck by the Old Man because, we both opined, he took it for a poetic phrase. "Tell him it has a serious and even scientific meaning," Darwish implored me, "maybe he'll listen to you." He didn't, and I didn't listen to Arafat when he wanted other phrases from other contexts inserted.

Nobody was to see these texts until much later, and indeed perhaps the oddest part of this PNC—with its obsessive postmodern rhetorical anxieties—was how the two main documents (the declaration of statehood and the political resolutions) were discussed in public debates for hours on end without a piece of paper before us. After the opening ceremonies on Saturday the PNC divided itself into two committees, the Political and the Intifada. Arafat had the texts memorized, and Nabil Sha'ath, adroit chairman of the Political Committee, had them before him. All significant discussion about what we were doing took place in the riveting atmosphere of that committee, with speaker after speaker sounding off on what was after all the most significant political moment in Palestinian life since 1948. Words, commas, semicolons and paragraphs were the common talk of each recess, as if we were attending a convention of grammarians.

The heart of the discussions occurred in the speeches given late Sunday and mid-afternoon on Monday by George Habash and Abu Iyad (Salah Khalaf), the first an opponent of the by-now well-known substance of the political program, the second Arafat's key supporter and one of the main leaders of Fatah. Habash's express reservations concerned the clear acceptance of 242 and 338, resolutions unfriendly to us not just because they treat us only as "refugees" but also because they contained an implicit prenegotiating recognition of Israel. This, Habash said, was going too far too soon; there had been agreement that such tough issues as recognition, 242, borders, etc. would be handled at the international conference. Why, Habash asked, was it so necessary to go forward on everything *before* the conference? He spoke passionately and clearly, saying without hesitation that he and the Popular Front wished to remain within the PLO, no matter the outcome or the disagreements. To which, in a meandering and yet always fascinating speech, Abu Iyad responded by saying that decisions had to be made now, not only in the face of the discouraging realities of the Israeli elections but because our people needed an immediate, concrete statement of our goals. What clinched it for me as I listened to Abu Iyad was the logic of his thesis that decisive clarity was needed from us principally for ourselves and our friends, not because our enemies kept hectoring us to make more concessions.

Arafat remained throughout the debate, occasionally intervening, and yet maintaining his office, so to speak, from his seat in the house; an endless stream of secretaries, delegates, messengers and experts came to him, yet he seemed attuned to every phrase uttered in the hall. He had told me early on that he had planned the proclamation of independence to occur shortly after midnight, November 15, after a whole night's debate on November 14. By about 9:30 pm on Monday, November 14, the political program had been passed by a large majority in the Political Committee, and immediately afterwards the whole PNC was reconvened in plenary session. Habash and his supporters fought each sentence almost word by word on the crucial 242/338 paragraph, which was voted on in different forms half a dozen times. The somewhat garbled paragraph that resulted shows the effect of these battles in its ungainly phraseology, although the actual substance remains unmistakable. At one point Arafat stood up and recited the entire program from memory, indicating (as the chair hadn't done) where the clause, sentence and paragraph breaks occurred, so that there could be no mistake about meaning, emphasis, conclusion. For the first time in PNC history, voting by acclamation wasn't going to be enough; Habash insisted on precise tallies, which emerged to his disadvantage, 253 for, 46 against, 10 abstaining. There was a sad nostalgia to what he represented, since by voting against him we were in effect taking leave of the past as embodied in his defiant gestures. The declaration ceremonies that closed the meetings were jubilant, and yet somehow melancholy.

About this break with the past there could be no doubt. Every one of the great events in December 1988—Arafat's meeting in Stockholm with five leading US Jews, his speech at the UN in Geneva and the press conference that followed, his explicit recognition of Israel, the beginning of a US-PLO dialogue—was made possible by the PNC's decisions and the break with the past. To declare statehood on the basis of Resolution 181 was first of all to say unequivocally that a Palestinian-Arab state and an Israeli state should coexist together in a partitioned Palestine. Self-determination would therefore be for two peoples, not just for one. Most of us there had grown up with the reality (lived and remembered) of Palestine as an Arab country, refusing to concede anything more than the exigency of a Jewish state, won at our expense in the loss of our land, our society and literally uncountable numbers of lives. A million and a half of our compatriots were under brutal military occupation (as we met, the entire population of Gaza, 650,000 people, was under total curfew), fighting tanks and fully-armed soldiers with rocks and an unbending will. For the first time also, the declarations were implicitly recognizing a state that offered us nothing except the empty formulas of Camp David or the openly racist threats of population "transfer."

The declaration of statehood spelled out principles of equality, mutuality and social justice far in advance of anything in the region. Call them idealistic if you will, but better that than the remorseless sectarianism and xenophobia with which Palestinians have had to contend for these five decades. Then too the *principle* of partition was asserted, not the territories specified in the 1947 UN resolution. All of us felt that since Israel had *never* declared its boundaries, we could not declare ours now; better to negotiate the question of boundaries with Israel and a confederal relationship with Jordan directly with both than to spell them out fruitlessly in advance. There was no doubt, however, that we were in fact discussing the territories occupied in 1967.

Secondly, there was absolute clarity in speaking of a peaceful settlement to the conflict. "Armed struggle" does not appear in the binding resolutions. Central to the resolutions is a long and awkward sentence endorsing the international peace conference based on "UN Resolutions 242 and 338." The language surrounding acceptance of the UN resolutions is a statement of the obvious, not a reservation about acceptance. For example, representation by the PLO on an equal footing with other parties, the aegis of the Security Council, the *implementation* of 242 and 338, the centrality of the Palestinian-Israeli conflict, the inalienable rights of the Palestinian people: all these are mentioned as the *context,* the history, the Palestinian interpretation of what we were accepting. This was especially necessary since 242 and 338 say literally nothing about the political actualities of the Palestinian people, which in 1967 seemed scarcely evident, except as the detritus of the Arab-Israeli June war.

Thirdly, the rejection of terrorism in all its forms (also asseverated in the Declaration) makes an emphatic distinction between resistance to occupation (to which Palestinians are entitled according to the UN Charter and international law) and indiscriminate violence whose aim is to terrorize civilians. Note that no all-purpose definition of terrorism exists today, one that has validity and impartiality of application internationally. Yet the PNC took a step that is unusual in its attempt to make distinctions between legitimate resistance and a proscribed indiscriminate violence by states or by individuals and groups. Also note that Israel has always arrogated to itself the right to attack civilians in the name of its security. These facts highlight the courage of what was ventured in the Palestinian statement.

Finally and most importantly, all the resolutions, however they are read, clearly intend willingness to *negotiate* directly. There are no disclaimers about the "Zionist entity" or about the legitimacy of Israeli representatives. All of the relevant passages about peace, partition and statehood in the 1964 Palestinian National Covenant are flatly contradicted by the 1988 PNC resolutions, which gives their statement added, not lesser, force. All the refusals, attacks and insults heaped on the Council's results, both by Israel and the usual array of US "experts," signify consternation; clearly, the more Palestinians take responsible and realistic positions, the less acceptable they become, not just because Palestinians want peace but because official Israel does not know what to do when peace is offered. There is a dispiriting continuity here between the early days of Israel's existence when Ben-Gurion refused peace with the Arabs and the all-out rejection trundled out today by Likud and Labor alike.

The point is not that the Council documents are perfect and complete, but that they must be interpreted as everyone in Algiers intended—as a beginning that signals a distinct break with the past, as an assertion of the willingness to make sacrifices in the interests of peace, as a definitive statement of the Palestinian acceptance of the international consensus. A few days before the Algiers meeting, Sharon appeared on Italian television vociferating loudly about the need to kill Arafat. That no comparable sentiment was expressed about Israeli leaders anytime in Algiers is a fact that furnishes its own eloquent comment on the real difference now between Israeli and Palestinian leaders. These are dangerous times for Palestinians; the occupation will get worse, and assassinations and full-scale political war will intensify. For once, however, the record is unmistakable as to who is for peace, who for bloodshed and suffering. But the Palestinian campaign for peace must be joined, since sitting on the sidelines is no longer any excuse.

What is difficult either to understand or condone is how the US media—quite unlike that of the rest of the world—has internalized the rejectionism promulgated by the Israeli and US establishments. Far from reading the texts as they were meant to be read, commentators persisted in suggesting that whatever was said in the texts could not by definition be enough. On November 20 a major *New York Times* editorial accused the Palestinians of "gamesmanship and murkiness" in Algiers. The egregious A.M. Rosenthal ranted (November 18) about "a cynical continuation of the Arab rejectionism of Israel," and the equally improbable George Will (*Washington Post,* November 20) said that for Israel the Algiers meeting was the equivalent of a "Final Solution." Why is Israel itself not asked whether it is willing to coexist with a Palestinian state, or negotiate, or accept 242, or renounce violence, or recognize the PLO, or accept demilitarization, or allay Palestinian fears, or stop killing civilians, or end the occupation, or answer any questions at all? Perhaps the US media will someday break their silence, as Palestinians and the rest of the world already have.

III

What so dramatically transpired after the Algiers PNC was also a direct result of the intifada, which in 1989 continues bravely in its second year. But if the political victories of the Palestinian people have been duly noted and even celebrated internationally, the more profound social and moral achievements of this amazingly heroic anticolonial insurrection require fuller acknowledgement.

People do not find the courage to fight continually against as powerful an army as Israel's without some reservoir, some deeply and already present fund of bravery and revolutionary self-sacrifice. Palestinian history furnishes a long tradition of these, and the inhabitants of the West Bank and Gaza have provided themselves generously from it. Yet what is new is the focused will, the creative and voluntary nature of the people themselves. There has been no easy resort to weapons, for example, and no exercise in noisy (if noble-sounding) rhetoric. Instead the leaflets of the intifada have been concise, concrete and, above all, implementable; each was a *nida'* ("an appeal") and neither an order nor a pronouncement. Above all, what is most impressive is the sense that the intifada demonstrated of a collectivity or community finding its way together. The source of this is the organic nationhood that today underlies Palestinian life. For the first time Palestinians exposed themselves to it, allowed themselves to be guided by it directly, offered themselves to its imperatives. Instead of individuals and private interests, the public good and the collective will predominated. Leaders were never identified. Personalities were submerged in the group.

The intifada therefore accomplished a number of unprecedented things. In my opinion, the future of the Middle East as a whole is going to be influenced by them, and Palestine and Israel will never be the same again because of them. In the first place, collaborators with the occupation were encircled and gradually rendered ineffective, as the entire mass of people under occupation came together in a bloc that opposed occupation. Even the class of merchants and shopkeepers played a major role in this transformation. Secondly, the old social organizations that depended on notables, on family, on traditional hierarchy—all these were largely marginalized. A new set of institutions emerged and, in fields like health, education, food and water supply and agriculture, these provided an *alternative* social organization to that dominated by the occupation regime. In short, the new alternative social situation that emerged was national, independent and the first step in the appearance of the Palestinian state announced formally in Algiers on November 15. Thirdly, the role of women was substantially altered. The Palestinian woman had been seen essentially as a helper, a housewife, a secondary person in a male-dominated society, as is the case throughout the Arab and Muslim world. During the intifada, however, women came to the fore as equal partners in the struggle. They confronted Israeli (male) troops; they shared in decision-making; they were no longer left at home, or given menial tasks, but did what the men did, without fear or complexes. Perhaps it would be still more accurate to say that because of the intifada the role of men was altered, from being dominant to becoming equal.

These are momentous changes and, as I said, they will surely have an effect throughout the Middle East as the twentieth century approaches its end. In the meantime, however, 1989 presents a more concrete challenge. In the immense and understandable wave of euphoria that swept the Palestinian and Arab world as the US-PLO dialogue began, a number of other things are worthy of concern and attention. The new Israeli government is composed of men whose hostility not just to Palestinian aspirations but to Palestinians as human beings is undying. Men like Rabin, Sharon, Netanyahu, Arens and Shamir are the inheritors of a tradition of uncompromising brutality and lying, in which *all* means are justified so long as the end—Israeli ascendancy at the expense of Palestinian life itself—can be assured. Under the influence of these men, the level of protests and of repression in the occupied territories increased significantly during the last six weeks of 1988. On the other hand, the media has either been banned from reporting the facts or, as appears to be the case with the *New York Times,* has deliberately chosen to downplay the ugliness of what is taking place. To fire into a funeral procession and kill six people, to shoot at a group of men observing a moment of silence and kill three, to maim children, to put whole cities like Nablus and Gaza under twenty-four hour curfew for several consecutive days, to humiliate and beat people at random, to destroy houses—all these are sickening examples of an Israeli policy of escalated violence against Palestinians, with insufficient or no notice taken by the influential mainstream Western media.

What *has* captured media attention is the process of negotiation by which, for instance, Yasir Arafat pronounced certain phrases and then received US recognition. Since that time Palestinian spokesmen have been on television, have been interviewed by the radio, have been quoted extensively by newspapers. All of that discussion has been political. What has been left out has been the paradox by which Palestinian moderation has been met with increasing Israeli intransigence and actual violence. I myself agree with the policy articulated and voted upon by the PNC. I am a member and I voted enthusiastically for a realistic and above all clear policy. I certainly do not advocate any retreat from what we decided to do politically in order to gain the independence of the State of Palestine. But what surprises and worries me is that those of us who live outside the occupied territories have had to minimize a good part of the moral claim on which we stand when, because of the limited opportunities offered us, we neglect to speak in detail about what is happening to our people on the West Bank and Gaza, about what is being done to them by Israel but also about what, heroically, they are doing for themselves.

Here is where the difficult and crucial role of detail becomes important. The struggle for Palestine has always been, as Chaim Weizmann once said, over one acre here, one goat there. Struggles are won by details, by inches, by specifics, not only by big generalizations, large ideas, abstract concepts. Most of what the world now knows about daily life during the intifada is the result of a) what the Palestinians under occupation have experienced minute by minute; and b) what has been reported about those experiences and achievements, first by Palestinians and then by international agencies like the United Nations and Amnesty International, and by concerned citizens' groups in Israel, Europe and North America. Those of us Palestinians and Arabs who live outside Palestine—in exile or dispersion—have not been afforded enough time to testify to the daily details of life under occupation; we have therefore not impressed on the awareness or the conscience of the world what our people are suffering and how cruelly Israel has treated their aspirations. These details are what our struggle is all about: why, for example, should a Palestinian farmer require a permit to plant a new olive tree on his land, whereas a Jewish settler can do what he wishes on land expropriated from the Palestinian? This policy of persecution and discrimination is what we have contested, and still do contest. It is more important a fact of our political lives than negotiating with a US ambassador in Tunis.

I am deeply concerned that in the glamorous search for recognition and negotiations we will lose the moral and cultural detail of our cause, which is a cause after all and not just a sordid game to control images, or to say the right phrases, or to meet and talk with the right people. The United States has been supplying the Israeli army with the bullets that kill Palestinian men, women and children. It is up to us—Palestinians and supporters of Palestinian rights—to formulate a policy that deals directly with *this* United States, as well as the other United States, represented by the many people who support Palestinian self-determination. Neither can be neglected. Most important of all, we cannot neglect to register and attest to the suffering and the greatness of the Palestinians under Israeli occupation, which this remarkable collection of essays does so well. Only by pursuing these two tracks will we become partners in the common struggle, and not onlookers or mere passive observers. Thus will the inside and outside become one.

New York
January 9, 1989

## Part 2

Eyewitness to the Uprising

Those Who Pass Between Fleeting Words

O those who pass between fleeting words
Carry your names, and be gone
Rid our time of your hours, and be gone
Steal what you will from the blueness of the sea
And the sand of memory
Take what pictures you will, so that you understand
That which you never will:
How a stone from our land builds the ceiling of our sky.

O those who pass between fleeting words
From you the sword—from us the blood
From you steel and fire—from us our flesh
From you yet another tank—from us stones
From you teargas—from us rain
Above us, as above you, are sky and air
So take your share of our blood—and be gone
Go to a dancing party—and be gone
As for us, we have to water the martyrs' flowers
As for us, we have to live as we see fit.

O those who pass between fleeting words
As bitter dust, go where you wish, but
Do not pass between us like flying insects
For we have work to do in our land:
We have wheat to grow which we water with our bodies' dew
We have that which does not please you here:
Stones or partridges
So take the past, if you wish, to the antiquities market
And return the skeleton to the hoopoe, if you wish,
On a clay platter
We have that which does not please you: we have the future
And we have things to do in our land.

O those who pass between fleeting words
Pile your illusions in a deserted pit, and be gone
Return the hand of time to the law of the golden calf
Or to the time of the revolver's music!
For we have that which does not please you here, so be gone
And we have what you lack
A bleeding homeland of a bleeding people
A homeland fit for oblivion or memory
O those who pass between fleeting words
It is time for you to be gone
Live wherever you like, but do not live among us
It is time for you to be gone
Die wherever you like, but do not die among us
For we have work to do in our land
We have the past here
We have the first cry of life
We have the present, the present and the future
We have this world here, and the hereafter
So leave our country
Our land, our sea
Our wheat, our salt, our wounds
Everything, and leave
The memories of memory
O those who pass between fleeting words!

—Mahmoud Darwish

The West Bank Rises Up

Penny Johnson and Lee O'Brien with Joost Hiltermann

Ramallah's landscape this February 21, 1988 vibrates with the overtones of a war zone. Residents have dismantled the ancient stone wall across the street for a series of barricades. The smoke of a burning tire rises in the clear early afternoon air over nearby al-Am'ari refugee camp and army flares light the camp at night. The camp's main entrance has been sealed by a wall of cement-filled barrels. Helicopters chop the air overhead; sirens of ambulances and army jeeps pierce the air on streets that are virtually deserted this afternoon, ordinarily a busy time of day.

In camps and villages, even the winter nights are the scenes of sharp confrontation. In the village of 'Abbud, settlers from the nearby Neve Tsuf settlement descended on the village at about 10 pm on February 27, told the villagers in fluent Arabic to come out of their homes and not to be afraid, and fatally shot two residents, Ahmad and Riad Barghuti.

In Ramallah, we shop between 8 and 11 am. The sounds of the shop shutters closing signals a possible demonstration or march; otherwise, an uneasy quiet prevails through the afternoon and evening. Marches are launched on Friday from mosques and Sunday from the churches, Christians and Muslims and non-believers participating in them all. These places of worship are simply the (relatively) safest and most convenient places for people to gather.

In early February, villages in the north like Ya'bad, 'Arraba and Tubas were surrounded by row after row of self-made barricades; for a moment the army had lost control. Such temerity and defiance of authority was quickly punished by hundreds of soldiers who raided Ya'bad and 'Arraba at dawn one day beating and detaining people, and smashing villagers' household possessions.

February 22, in Kafr Na'ma, a village near Ramallah: the army stays away as about 1000 men, women and children march through the village to the cemetery to mourn twenty-year-old 'Abdulla 'Atiya, shot dead in Ramallah two days earlier. The village is decorated with scores of homemade Palestinian flags; at the graveside, when a minute of silence is declared for all the fallen, several family members slowly raise their arms and make the familiar V-sign. The whole crowd repeats their gesture as hail and driving rain whirl around them.

"Abnormal Routine"

In the occupied West Bank people walk with their eyes lowered to the ground. This posture is not to avoid the attention of the incessant military patrols or to avert one's eyes from witnessing their physical violence and harassment which are, still somehow shockingly, often carried out in full view. (A street scene, February 12, in Ramallah: after a small demonstration, soldiers detain a young man, cover his head with a makeshift hood, and beat him. One red-haired soldier, with a fresh face and wire-rim glasses like a bright college student, repeatedly returns to kick the prisoner. Soldiers shout at people staring silently from the windows of their houses: "Go away." When the watchers don't vanish quickly, soldiers hurl stones at the windows.) Neither do the downcast eyes indicate a population weary after twelve weeks of an uprising that has left over 100 dead, many hundreds injured, and thousands detained. The collective mood is almost electrifyingly high.

Rather, people look down to spot the latest statement from the Unified National Leadership of the Uprising, often found in the streets or tucked under a windshield wiper or door. For the first time in many years, words have a direct bearing on individual and collective action. People shape their daily lives around the announcements of general strikes, demonstrations from churches and mosques, and "assignments" to different sectors of the population. In mid-February, people rejoiced as "Communique no. 7" came out on schedule, despite an army raid on an 'Issawiyya print shop suspected of producing the statements.

Ask almost anyone in the occupied territories about this "uprising" and they will say, "It's something new." In fact, it is part of the complex dynamic in the Palestinian national movement since 1982 in the occupied territories, with characteristics both new and old.

We live and work in the West Bank, and our experiences form the basis of this description of events there. As residents, rather than as journalists, we have also experienced this "new life." "Interruptions"—curfews, detentions of neighbors and colleagues, sit-ins and merchant's boycotts—comprise our daily schedule. We participate in the charged atmosphere and emotions of this time; although this is not always conducive to critical distance, we try here to identify main trends of the uprising.

We do not document what a delegation from the US Physicians for Human Rights recently called an "uncontrolled epidemic of violence by the army and police," as the media have provided a wealth of such material. We only note here that the scope of this brutality is hard to appreciate from the individual accounts, as is its collective effect of erasing any protective barriers that previously stood between the army and settlers on one hand and Palestinians on the other.

Rather, we wish to concentrate on the movers of the uprising—the Palestinians under occupation. From our arbitrary vantage point in Ramallah during the last two weeks of February 1988, we view the new life of the population after nearly three months of the uprising.

This new "abnormal routine" is a fundamental achievement of the uprising. In the first phase, from December 9 to the end of 1987, the protests and demonstrations in the camps of Gaza and in several camps in the West Bank, especially Balata, moved like a paradigmatic "prairie fire," sparked by the rising toll of dead. Local organizers and organization were vital, but coordinated leadership was still missing.

The first statement from the Unified National Leadership of the Uprising appeared in the West Bank on January 8. Many date the origin of coordinated leadership, the second phase, even earlier, pointing to the demonstrations that arose all over East Jerusalem on December 19, 1987. Two days later, on December 21, Palestinian leaders inside Israel called a general strike that was completely effective in the West Bank and Gaza as well. This second stage decisively marked the uprising as more than an upsurge in the "cycle of violence." Any reference here to the Israeli occupation is now marked "Before Uprising." No one knows what "After Uprising" will bring. The problems are truly formidable, but there is a palpable sense, among both Palestinians and Israelis, that things will never be the same.

Weakness Into Strength

Perhaps any popular rebellion seems inevitable after it happens. As a Birzeit University academic puts it, "Any political scientist can write a quick paper on the roots of the uprising: it's all there."

And so it is. Yet after nearly twenty-one years of military occupation, the question remains, why now? The occupation seemed entrenched. The notion that occupier and occupied existed in an "uneasy equilibrium," as

Meron Benvenisti put it, was one of the most powerful myths of the post-1982 period, one that encapsulated the mood of those bleak years.

Neither the Israeli military nor political establishment seriously contemplated any major internal threat from the Palestinian population. For the soldiers stationed in the occupied territories, harassment—not security—was paramount. The chief of staff, General Dan Shomron, told Israeli defense correspondents that the army "had been taken by surprise by the scope and intensity of the rioting that swept through the West Bank and Gaza...."[1]

Some of the same factors that led to the entrenchment of the status quo contributed to its undoing. Since 1982 and the PLO withdrawal from Lebanon, hope for an external political solution has steadily dwindled. The Arab summit in Amman in November 1987 and the Reagan-Gorbachev meeting in early December helped dispel any remaining illusions of progress through summitry, Arab consensus or state visits to Washington. (On the positive side, the reconciliation of Palestinian organizations at the April 1987 meeting of the Palestine National Council in Algiers was probably an important factor in the unified leadership that coalesced in December.) While the official Israeli-Palestinian "problem" remained gridlocked, a new dynamic stemming from the grassroots began to emerge in the occupied territories.

Minister of Economics and Finance Gad Ya'acobi described one side of this dynamic when he attacked the "delusion of the status quo" and frankly noted "a creeping process of de facto annexation."[2] Meanwhile, the economic downturn in the Arab world, the coming of age of the first generation born under occupation and the "iron fist" policy launched in August 1985 all contributed to the Palestinians' growing militance.

A crucial linchpin of the occupation—the strategy of "normalization"—was beginning to weaken. Shlomo Gazit, the Coordinator of Affairs for the Occupied Territories for the first seven years of the occupation, once wrote that his goal was to create a situation where the Arabs "have something to lose." Israeli efforts in this direction—from Dayan's 1967 "open bridges" policy to the 1987 opening of the Cairo-Amman Bank—sought, with varying degrees of success, to construct the appearance of normal economic, social and community life, while enormous demographic and economic transformations took place. The intensification of settlements, confiscation and repression since 1983 finally overwhelmed any Palestinian sense of having something to lose.

The spark for the uprising is in itself of no special significance: a bizarre and bloody collision on the road leading to Gaza when an Israeli truck swerved and crashed into a car, killing four Gazans: the news spread quickly that the collision was deliberate, revenge by a relative of an Israeli settler stabbed in Gaza. The immediate backdrop is more relevant: an autumn of episodic but escalating confrontation between the Israeli army and settlers on one hand and Palestinian civilians and militants on the other.[3]

Communities Rise Up

At a Birzeit University rally on December 20, 1987, students, many of whom had not yet really entered the "field" of the uprising, intoned the names of Palestinian refugee camps in the West Bank and Gaza: Balata, Jabalya, Shati'. The new and extremely popular clandestine Voice of Jerusalem radio station—"a Palestinian Arab broadcast for the liberation of land and man [sic]"—daily peppered its broadcasts (before it was jammed in early February) with odes to places ("O, Hebron") and dramatic readings of names of towns, camps and villages, down to the tiniest Jerusalem suburb or remote village. Communities—refugee camps, villages and towns—provided a strong social base for the uprising. Part of this is Palestinian tradition and a strong local sense of identity; part is embedded in the dynamic of the uprising, which took its initial flavor and momentum from the explosive mixture of the special oppression and politicization of camp residents.[4]

In the December phase, the uprising was primarily a war of the camps versus the army. In Khan Yunis or Dayr al-Balah, the camp was in flames while the adjacent town remained relatively quiet. Both town and camp dwellers have similar socioeconomic profiles (workers in Israel, for example) and presumably similar nationalist sentiments. Later, the uprising moved from community to community and, by mid-January, West Bank villages became locales for resistance. Similarly, it spread from one strata of society to another.

An image comes to mind: a small group of Israeli leftist women, accompanied by a few foreigners and Palestinians from Nablus women's organizations, enters one of the main roads to Balata on December 17, carrying a wreath in memory of three Balata residents killed on December 11, one a teenage girl. An army jeep blocks the way but some delegates manage to slip by the jeep and turn the corner into another world. At least a thousand people, primarily young men and older women, are tightly pressed together, a wooden coffin draped with the flag is raised high, other Palestinian flags flutter in the wind, shouts of "Allahu akbar" [God is great] echo in the streets. The courage of Balata residents and their organization in the enclosed world of the camp was evident, as the army chased the demonstrators down a narrow street to an alley to a graveyard and to the main street again. After the Israelis left, they imposed a curfew.

Privilege is relative. It could be defined as living in Ramallah instead of Balata. The roll call of deaths by army gunfire from December 9-20 included thirteen from Gaza, four from Balata and one from Nablus. (Eleven are seventeen years old or younger.) On December 21, the day of the first all-Palestine general strike since 1939, the deaths of two Palestinians from Tubas and one from Jenin foreshadowed the remarkable role of West Bank village communities.

Ramallah and other towns, including Jerusalem, have found their own forms of struggle, from successful commercial strikes to marches and violent demonstrations. The dynamics of community still operate as the network of resistance has spread. The active resistance of youth and youthful workers has moved outwards to encompass other parts of society, although roles, degree of participation and victimization vary.

Generations of Occupation

Two Birzeit students accompanying an NBC crew to their closed campus in late January encountered a barricade in the road near the small village of Abu Qash "manned" by a boy so young he had to stand on his tiptoes to look in the car window and check out the passengers. "Go back, go back," he commanded imperiously, "we are all on strike."

Stories like this abound in West Bank living rooms, as Palestinian society reflects on the role of its youth in the current uprising. "Our generation failed," a dignified middle-aged woman told a visiting church delegation on Christmas day. "It is the children now who show us how to fight."

The international media tends to portray an undifferentiated image with a new label, *shabab* (colloquial Arabic for "guys" or "youths"): a young man, *kaffiya* masking his face, rock or flag in hand, confronting an Israeli patrol. This collective profile of bitterness and defiance ignores this generation's optimism and confidence. The "generation of occupation" stands at the center of the uprising, but it in no way stands apart from the rest of society or from the PLO. The society itself is youthful: 46 percent of West Bankers and 48 percent of Gazans are under age fourteen, and the number of persons aged twenty-five to thirty in the West Bank has doubled in a decade.[5]

The experience of Israeli occupation, and this generation's response to it, has created both striking and subtle changes in society and politics. Young people are not so much in rebellion—either against their families or against Palestinian leadership—as they are acting as a collective dynamo.

In the Ramallah-area village of al-Mazra'a al-Sharqiyya at the end of January, for example, young men of the village rather than elders greeted the medical team from the Union of Palestinian Medical Relief Committees. They had made arrangements to set up a temporary clinic. The young men, dressed in jeans, sneakers and thin jackets despite the blustery day, enthusiastically called out the names of the patients and counselled them to be at ease; they were "responsible" and would make sure the doctors would see them. These role reversals surface in many situations during the uprising: entering Balata or Jalazun or even a government hospital, any visitor encounters youths who are "responsible."

The very momentum of defiance has undermined two decades of assumptions and political realities. In Ramallah, a middle-aged professional woman, after watching demonstrations on television for a month, eagerly joins a group of young boys building a roadblock; in a Gaza hospital, a 100-year-old woman, her hand broken by soldiers, toothlessly murmurs defiance to the applause of other beating victims in surrounding beds.

The unprecedented popular mobilization has not been contingent upon the achievement of concrete political goals. Villagers in Ya'bad tell visitors the uprising will continue "until freedom;" a shopkeeper in Ramallah, who probably hasn't sold an appliance in months, swears he is striking "to end the occupation." The momentum of defiance is sustained by people's awareness of the new dynamics emerging on the ground, where Palestinian action now determines the Israeli reaction in an unprecedented fashion.

Street Facts

Israeli policy toward the Palestinians has always contained a large element of denial: denial of rights, denial of legitimacy, denial of voice. Not surprisingly, the initial Israeli response to the uprising was to deny: 1) that it was an uprising; 2) that "normal" measures were insufficient to control it; and 3) that it articulated the feelings of the majority of the population. On December 15, when four people were killed in Gaza's massive demonstrations, Chief of Staff Shomron announced that "although the area is not entirely quiet, the situation is already under control. Under no circumstances will we allow a small minority of inciters to rule over the vast majority, which is in general pragmatic and wants to live quietly."[6]

But the Israelis arrested 1,200 people in three weeks in December. The Israeli Defense Forces (IDF) deployed more troops in the Gaza Strip alone than it used to occupy the West Bank and Gaza in 1967.[7] Troops used tear gas and rubber bullets as well as live ammunition, and Defense Minister

Yitzhak Rabin gave his military commanders the power to deport "troublemakers," order administrative detentions, declare curfews and close schools.[8]

A month into the uprising, despite these harsh measures, an organized leadership emerged and protests spread to cities and villages throughout Palestine. This stage heralded something new in Palestinian resistance. Israeli pronouncements were suddenly acknowledging the conflict as one of physical control of the streets and ideological control of the political agenda. On both counts, the Israelis were having a surprisingly hard time holding their ground. Was Rabin betraying some panic when he insisted that "Gaza and Hebron, Ramallah and Nablus are not and will never become Beirut, Sidon and Tyre"? "Here we shall fight," he declared, "united and with all our strength, and it is great, against every force that tries by violent means to undermine our full control of Judea, Samaria and the Gaza Strip."[9]

Rabin's now famous "force, power and blows" announcement came out of this new context. "We will make it clear who is running the territories," said Rabin. "We are adamant that the violence shall not achieve its political aims."[10] That morning scores of Israeli troops had rampaged through the streets of Ramallah, beating shopkeepers and young men behind the "bloody wall" and forcing stores open. TV viewers later saw Rabin standing in front of stores in Ramallah's main square, saying: "You have seen most of the shops are open, so the announcements that called for strikes were not received by part of the population."[11] But strikes spread throughout all the occupied territories. Over the next month, dispirited soldiers patrolled Ramallah, seemingly too tired from fighting demonstrators to use the heavy crowbars they carried to open shops. By the beginning of February, patrols had given up altogether trying to force open stores. Rabin announced the policy of closing shops had been a mistake, and the general daily strike had become another fact of life under occupation—but one determined by the Palestinians themselves, not the occupiers. The "war of the shops," at least this first phase, was won.

The new dynamics of the uprising have redefined other familiar scenarios of occupation. The curfew has become the most effective technique for military control, as it generally ensures quiet while in effect. But in Gaza curfews now signify that the IDF is unable to enter a particular camp or area. Their efficacy is further blurred against the days of general strike, when Palestinians willingly recreate curfew conditions.

Curfews also symbolize another major setback for the Israelis—the participation of East Jerusalem Palestinians in the uprising and their open insistence that East Jerusalem is occupied territory. On January 23, authorities invoked emergency powers in East Jerusalem and imposed a curfew for the first time since 1967. The violent clashes since then have dispelled the myth of a unified city.

Increased Israeli violence and collective punishment often serve to popularize resistance, involving new sectors of Palestinian society by force. Women and girls in the Gaza camp of al-Shati' tell of battling troops who come to arrest their husbands and sons. They point proudly to fourteen-year-old Maryam, whose arm and leg were broken trying to protect her father. In Ramallah's Old City, women attacked a patrol with pots and pans in an attempt to release a detained youth. Outside Ramallah prison, three different women claimed an arrested youth, explaining, "They are all our sons."

Shopkeepers play an important role in maintaining momentum by their strict adherence to the daily and general strikes. Shops close at 11 am (or 6 pm in East Jerusalem) after three hours of business, as a matter of routine. In Ramallah, the merchants' committee patrols the streets, checking on closed shops in particular and the army's activities in general. Shop owners appear generally to have followed the call by the national leadership to desist from paying the much-resented value-added tax (VAT); in fact, many have been unable to pay because of their low cashflow. Civil Administration sources report a decline in taxes collected since the beginning of the uprising. The authorities have responded by making import and export licenses, as well as travel permits, contingent on proof of payment of taxes.[12] At the same time they lowered the amount of money that can be brought in across the bridge from an unlimited amount to NIS 600 in an effort to undercut any outside financial support for the strike.[13]

Israeli-made products are more rare in shops as the leadership's call for a boycott has widened. Shop owners are having difficulties paying Israeli suppliers, but banks have hesitated to enforce debt repayment because of the Israeli economy's great dependence on markets in the occupied territories. The large number of bounced checks has become a regular topic of concern in the economic pages of Israeli newspapers.

On February 6, the Unified National Leadership called on Palestinians collaborating with the authorities or employed in the Civil Administration, including the appointed mayors, to resign. A news broadcaster with the Israeli Arabic-language television program reportedly resigned after he received threats. Four municipal council members in Ramallah, al-Bireh and Dayr Dibwan, all appointed by the Israeli authorities in 1986, formally resigned during the second week of February without stating their reasons. Names of collaborators appeared on Ramallah walls in mid-February; late at night, army patrols could be seen carefully blacking out the names.

The most dramatic case of popular vengeance against a collaborator occurred in the village of Qabatya during the last week of February. During a demonstration by townspeople, a small boy threw a stone at the house of

Muhammad Ayad, an alleged informer for Shin Bet, Israel's internal security service. Ayad responded by opening fire on the crowd, killing a child. Villagers stormed the house several times; thirteen were wounded by gunfire. When Ayad's ammunition was exhausted, villagers entered the house and killed him with an ax. They dragged his body to the street, where virtually the entire village spat on it, including his relatives. His body was then hung on an electricity pylon, topped by two Palestinian flags. The next day, at a gathering in the mosque, four other collaborators handed their guns over to the *mukhtar* (the village leader), and formally apologized to the village. (Qabatya has been cordoned off ever since, and many residents seized.)

Local Leadership

From the hilly neighborhoods of Nablus, voices ring out, chanting the names of PLO organizations, then join together in the rallying call of "Allahu akbar"; a demonstration is underway.

The call is instructive: the leadership of the uprising rests firmly with local supporters of PLO organizations—Fatah, the Popular Front, the Democratic Front and the Palestine Communist Party (which unlike the guerrilla groups operates only in the occupied territories and only recently gained official representation in the PLO leadership). In Gaza, one must include the Islamic Jihad, which works in coordination with the PLO. The call of "Allahu akbar" is usually less a mark of Muslim revivalist politics than a unifying thread in Palestinian society.

It is common knowledge, and common sense, that the clandestine Unified Leadership consists of representatives of all the groups in the Palestinian national movement. The PLO and its constituent organizations have built an infrastructure of support and leadership in the occupied territories, recruiting and mobilizing among key sectors of Palestinian society such as students, workers, women and professionals. The pattern of politicization in the 1980s, particularly among the "generation of occupation," has increased affiliation along organizational lines. Crystallized into the Unified Leadership, the local PLO has coordinated and steered the uprising.

"Local" is a more operative word than "new." While firmly adhering to the slogan that the PLO is the sole legitimate representative of the Palestinian people, activists here have taken the initiative on the ground. The voice of this leadership is communal and anonymous; clandestine leaflets have replaced the press conferences of former days. In the process, some traditional nationalist leaders have been overwhelmed by events; "spokespeople" like journalist Hanna Siniora and Bethlehem Mayor Elias Freij have been relegated to clearly marginal roles.

Local activists have learned the lesson of anonymity after twenty years of Israeli arrests and expulsions. Their role does not call for visibility. Their immediate aim is not to open negotiations with the Israelis but to sustain the momentum of the uprising, to create a context in which the PLO's demand for an international peace conference will be heard and to help set the agenda for any such conference.

In each leaflet, the Unified Leadership enumerates specific demands and calls for specific actions. Distribution of the communiques is no longer a major problem: they are now headline news in the Israeli media. Communique no. 9, the *Jerusalem Post* dutifully reported on March 2, called for Palestinians serving in the Civil Administration and police to resign and urged the overthrow of the Israeli-appointed municipal councils.

The communique gives each day of the week ahead a particular focus: Friday and Sunday are for demonstrations after mosque and church services; Thursday is the Day of Return to the Land, urging people to take part in agricultural work; Sunday is Flag Day; Tuesday (March 8) is Women's Day; Wednesday is Martyrs' Day, with general protests to mark the beginning of the fourth month of the uprising.

By meticulously observing the various calls by the Unified Leadership, Palestinians have underscored the committee's legitimacy. Clearly the reconciliation between the various PLO factions during the April 1987 PNC in Algiers enhanced coordination between the various blocs in the occupied territories and boosted popular morale. A number of local groups have issued calls for mass action in conjunction with the Unified Leadership. In the village of al-Ram, for instance, landlords called on other landlords in the area to follow their example and not collect rents from striking shopkeepers. In Jerusalem, merchants from Ramallah and al-Bireh held their own press conference in January, vowing to strike until the end of occupation and enumerating the demands stated in the Unified Leadership communiques.

The level of coordination behind the uprising and in particular its "invisibility" clearly frightens the authorities. Military analyst Hirsh Goodman's alarm is typical as he imagines "the silent, shadowy figures moving between Gaza, the West Bank and East Jerusalem, spreading fear and hatred, forcing their children out of school to assemble at predetermined confrontation points, giving crash courses on how to make a Molotov cocktail and how best to burn a bus."[14]

Born of the Uprising

In a driving rain on February 17, about sixty women, three Palestinian flags bravely raised at the fore, marched to the municipality of al-Bireh, chanting slogans against the Israeli-appointed mayor, against army brutality, against Israeli schemes for "autonomy." "Let Shultz stay home with his wife," shouted one middle-aged matron to wide approval, referring to the US secretary of state's upcoming visit.

During the political turmoil of the winter and spring of 1982, the municipalities and other nationalist institutions were the focus both of Israeli repression and Palestinian mobilization. The nationalist mayors, dismissed that spring, had a commanding role. Universities, though closed, were centers of protest. Petitions circulated from professional associations and nationalist institutions. The National Guidance Committee, banned that year, still devised strategies.

Today, the 1982 leaders are silent or marginal, and the nationalist institutions that were their base are grappling to find a suitable role in the fluid environment of the uprising. While PLO leadership remains a constant, there are important changes in the makeup of that leadership and in its organizational expression.

Generational and even class relations are visibly shifting. Institutions with the largest resources, like universities, are floundering, and intellectuals and professionals to date seemingly marginal. By contrast, a bare, cold hall in Ya'bad is full of life, as the local popular committee meets with visitors in the wake of an army raid in the early morning hours of February 7. The popular committee—young men, chainsmoking, with faces alive and powerful—comprises known village activists from the worker's union and youth groups in particular, but it is nonetheless a new formation, born of the uprising.

A general strike marked the three-month anniversary of the uprising on March 9, designated the Day of the Martyrs. The events of that day are telling because they are not extraordinary: two more young men killed by army gunfire in the villages of Silwad and Turmus 'Ayya. The day before was International Women's Day. Village women marched together with Ramallah matrons, teenagers with their grandmothers, 500 strong, through the streets of Ramallah in an impressive silent march. Looking down the side streets, we saw women running to join the procession, which was eventually dispersed by tear gas and rubber bullets when it reached the center of town. The women had decided that no stones would be thrown; the youths adhered to their direction during the march, another sign that this uprising rests on the self-organization of an entire society.

On March 9, 1988 no workers went to their jobs in Israel. The success of labor boycotts, including the total boycott in Gaza during the first month of the uprising, contrasts sharply with the failure of Palestinian nationalists in the early years of the occupation to stop the flow of Palestinian labor to Israel. It is another of the "reversals" that characterize the uprising.

These reversals are a partial answer to the important question "What can the uprising achieve?" Looking at an uncertain future, we can only say that the ground has decisively shifted. The uprising is not an "event" with an endpoint, but a new stage in the relations between occupier and occupied.

## Chapter 3

Uprising in Gaza

Anita Vitullo

One year before the Palestinian mass uprising began, the writing was on the walls—the grey cement walls of refugee camp houses in Gaza, where you could read the anguish Gaza camp residents felt at the spectacle of the Amal militia bombarding Palestinians in the camps in Lebanon. These attacks forged a real unity among Palestinian factions there and carried Palestinians here into street demonstrations—as much against Amal's assault as against Israel's "iron fist."

Israeli military authorities must have sensed then that resistance was about to escalate; when demonstrations became irritatingly frequent, they increased punitive measures and violence against Gaza Strip residents, particularly against boys between thirteen and twenty years old.

On December 4, 1986, the Israeli army shot dead two Birzeit University students on campus. Both young men happened to live in the Gaza Strip, and their deaths set off demonstrations that grew from their home towns to encompass most of the camps and schools in Gaza in the days that followed.

Israeli authorities tried to contain the protests by arresting hundreds of boys and young men, picking them up off the streets, from their schoolyards and classrooms and homes, and taking them to police stations, military headquarters and the central prison in Gaza. When the demonstrations still continued, a second wave of arrests targeted ex-prisoners and known activists. An army camp on the edge of Gaza City was hastily converted to hold the overflow of young detainees. By the end of December 1986, authorities had detained more than 250 men of all ages in the four room-sized cells inside the army camp.

Palestinians in Gaza quickly dubbed the camp "Ansar II," after the notorious POW camp Israel had set up in south Lebanon. The Hebrew press reported widely on the inhuman conditions, regular beatings and sadistic treatment by soldiers, disregard for prison rules and regulations, arbitrary arrests and releases, and lack of legal rights. Gaza lawyers and popular organizations regularly appealed for better conditions, and detainees went on hunger strike several times.

Ansar II became an institutional symbol of Israeli policy toward youth in the Gaza Strip. Israel's now-famous beating policy began here, quietly and out of sight, within the barbed wire perimeter of Ansar II. There soldiers and military police practiced clubbing young Palestinians already handcuffed and under arrest. As the first year of Ansar II wore on, the kinds of injuries suffered by the detainees became more serious; by October and November, teenaged boys had to be hospitalized, and several of them underwent surgery to repair injuries caused by soldiers' guns, clubs and boots.

How effective was this Israeli policy in curbing stone-throwing and strike organizers? Dr. Haydar 'Abd al-Shafi', who directs the Red Crescent here, pointed at the writing on the wall: "The kids are drawing different conclusions. They are becoming more daring, and they are not running away."

Turning Up the Heat

In late January 1987, military authorities decided to use deportation to intimidate activists. Muhammad Dahlan, twenty-six, accused of leading a pro-Fatah youth organization, Shabiba, was expelled to Jordan and then to Egypt, where he was immediately arrested.

Demonstrations and school strikes nevertheless persisted in February, March and April. In a demonstration in Khan Yunis, a fifteen-year-old boy, his school bag still strapped to his back, was shot and killed by an Israeli soldier as he fled, terrified from soldiers chasing him in an army jeep. An Israeli army investigation called the shooting "per standing orders." Gaza's rage grew even more fierce.

On a hot summer day in August 1987, someone walked up to an Israeli army jeep stuck in traffic on Gaza's main street and shot twice at point-blank range, killing Lieutenant Ron Tal. He was commander of military police in Gaza, in charge of guarding detainees inside Ansar II and to and from military courts.

In response, Israeli authorities imposed unprecedented collective punishment measures on Gaza's half-million residents: for three days no one was permitted to enter or leave the Strip; Gaza City residents could not even go outside their homes, and the area where the incident took place was sealed off for one week. The Palestinians were simmering, especially because the harsh travel ban came during the major Muslim feast of al-Adha.

Israeli military authorities attributed the assassination to the Islamic Jihad. This growing Muslim revivalist organization had turned from attacking "communist" Palestinian nationalists to joining with nationalists against the Israelis.

In two separate but similar incidents on October 1 and 6, Israeli forces ambushed and killed seven men from Gaza, reported to be members or close associates of the Islamic Jihad. Three had escaped from Gaza prison in May and had remained in hiding in the Strip.

In the first attack, a well-known Gaza businessman and a local engineer, both unarmed, were shot on the spot when they attempted to pass through a roadblock. The two were apparently gunned down by accident, perhaps because they happened into an ambush set up for escaped prisoner Misbah al-Suri. Ten days later, Israeli officials said al-Suri had also died in the shooting. The long delay in disclosing this led to speculation that al-Suri had only been injured in the attack and was killed after being interrogated about his fellow escapees.

In the second incident, four Palestinians and a high-ranking Israeli prison official were killed in a shootout in a residential area of Gaza City. A small cache of weapons was found in the cars of the four men, which authorities said were to be used in a military operation against an Israeli target.

Late that night, military authorities descended on the homes of the families of those killed. Without informing them of their sons' deaths, they carried out searches and arrested family members. Three weeks later, Israeli authorities bulldozed their homes.

The ambush slayings sparked demonstrations throughout the territories beginning at the Islamic University, where two of the men had studied, and spreading to many towns and camps. General strikes and demonstrations shut down Gaza and the West Bank for more than a week. Al-Ittihad, the Israeli Communist Party's Arabic-language newspaper, used the word "insurrection" to describe the popular response. One Palestinian was killed and more than forty injured in a week of protest.

The size and scope of the demonstrations indicate how the popular reputation of the Islamic Jihad had grown in the last year, with the group claiming responsibility for several daring military operations against Israeli soldiers and settlers.

Israel attributed the Jihad's growth to Shaykh 'Abd al-'Aziz 'Awad, a popular teacher at Gaza's Islamic University who had spent time in Israeli and Egyptian prisons. Shaykh 'Awad was arrested on November 15 and ordered deported on the ground that he was the "spiritual leader" of the Islamic Jihad and responsible for its new cooperation with Fatah.

The tragedy of the shootouts was followed shortly by another killing. This time a seventeen-year-old girl was shot by a settler in her schoolyard in

Dayr al-Balah. Settlers said the girls had been throwing stones, but Intisar al-'Attar, wearing the scarf and long coat of Islamic dress, was running away when she was shot in the back. The settlers did not stop to aid the girl, and continued on their way without even reporting the shooting. A ballistics test of Israeli settler weapons resulted in the arrest of a schoolteacher for the shooting, but an Israeli judge released him after several days of intense campaigning by settlers.

With no protection from vigilante settlers, Palestinians fell to their own devices to make Gaza off-limits to Israelis: youths threw stones at cars with yellow Israeli license plates, and on December 7 an Israeli merchant from Tel Aviv was stabbed to death in Gaza's main square. Although Palestinians rushed to aid the man, no one cooperated with military interrogators, who arrested scores of people and clamped a curfew on the area.

Twenty-four hours later, on December 8, an Israeli army tank transporter drove into a line of cars of Arab workers who had just passed the Erez military checkpoint at the northern entrance to the Gaza Strip. Four workers were crushed to death and seven were seriously injured in the accident, witnessed by hundreds of laborers returning from jobs in Israel. Three of the dead men were from nearby Jabalya refugee camp. Their funerals that night turned into a huge demonstration of 10,000 camp residents, who charged that the accident was a retaliation for the murder of the Israeli merchant the day before.

The next day, several leaders of popular and professional institutions in Gaza held a press conference in West Jerusalem with the Israel League for Human Rights to discuss the deteriorating economic and security situation. While they were speaking, reports came in of more demonstrations in Jabalya camp and the shooting death of a twenty-year-old man, the first martyr on what was the first day of the Palestinian mass uprising—an explosion that came as a surprise to everyone but the Palestinians under occupation.

"Everyone here has a demonstration inside his heart"

The uprising might have started any place, but it began in Gaza's Jabalya refugee camp—whose 50,000 residents now proudly refer to their home as *mu'askar al-thawra* ("camp of the revolution").

Gaza Strip residents fueled the uprising with demonstrations that sometimes numbered in the tens of thousands, waving flags and carrying symbolic coffins, chanting every variety of nationalist slogan and vowing to revenge the latest martyr. Youths controlled whole neighborhoods in the cities and closed off the entrances to their camps with stone barricades, garbage and burning tires. When soldiers entered, residents pelted them with stones, debris and, occasionally, petrol bombs. Local shopkeepers closed down and laborers who worked in Israel refused to go to their jobs. Israeli officials refer to the demonstrations as "riots" and defend their repression as necessary to preserve "law and order." To the contrary, the protests showed restraint and rationality, which stemmed from a Gaza Strip-wide sense of community and of purposeful resistance. Demonstrations were not "peaceful" but neither did they turn Palestinians into mindless mobs. Youths stripped one Israeli down to his underwear in front of Shifa Hospital, but then let him run back to his fellow soldiers. A young Palestinian took another soldier's rifle away from him, broke it in two, then handed it back.

The power of Palestinians came from their sheer numbers and open defiance of Israeli authority. "We were waiting to do such an uprising," said one young resident. From another: "Everyone here has a demonstration inside his heart."

Demonstrators chose targets carefully, setting afire military vehicles and Israeli buses, attacking police stations, smashing Israeli bank windows and even storming an Israeli army outpost in the middle of Jabalya. On days of total strike, when transportation was also supposed to halt, even cars bearing Gaza's distinctive grey license plates might come under a hail of stones. Yet there were no attacks on any of a dozen Israeli resort settlements and no Israeli fatalities or even serious injuries from the several million stones that must have been tossed.

On some days Gaza was so "hot" that the sky was black with the smoke of burning tires and tear gas wafted in all directions. Experienced eyes often compared the street fighting and the air of anarchy apparent in Gaza to Beirut, a vision West Bankers saw only on television news clips. The scenes of the lopsided war in the sandy Strip and, at least for one brief moment, victory over the hated occupiers, left many observers breathless and asking, "Have you been to Gaza?"

Travel was limited to crews of foreign TV networks who plastered their cars with Arabic and English "Press" signs, and to military vehicles buzzing about pretending to have some control over a population they thought they knew so well. Even veteran Palestinian taxi drivers who had driven the Jerusalem-Gaza route for twenty years refused to enter the Strip on total strike days.

Gaza's Palestinians, the majority of whom have lived in refugee camps for forty years, knew there would be a terrible price to pay for their open defiance of Israeli rule. Authorities tried to confront every protest with live ammunition, then found there were too many people and too many incidents to deal with. Troops were doubled, then tripled and eventually increased to five times the usual number, including the crack Givati and Golani brigades.

In the first six weeks, the death toll was highest in Gaza: twenty-seven Palestinians representing every camp and city in this tiny area were killed, and at least 200 suffered gunshot injuries. Five boys, aged thirteen to sixteen, were among those killed. Families of two of the victims said they were killed at close range after they had been wounded. Many deaths were from head wounds, although Israeli soldiers were equipped with a new sniper gun which made killing avoidable. In the second six weeks, only two Gazans died from bullet wounds, one from month-old injuries, but fourteen died from tear gas and three boys, all age fifteen, were beaten to death by soldiers in separate incidents in February.

By mid-January tents were set up in Ansar II detention camp in Gaza City to hold 800 detainees; another 400 youths were sent north into Israel, to Atlit military prison, where conditions were equally appalling. Still more were held in police stations and military headquarters.

Gaza lawyers could not speak to their clients, sometimes they could not even locate them before their court appearances. They could not bring defense witnesses or even make a line of argument in their favor. There was no possibility of refuting the testimony of soldiers. Release on bail was never granted. All Gaza lawyers declared a strike in mid-December, saying they could not defend their clients until the beatings in prison stopped and conditions improved and until some minimum standards were introduced into the trial procedures. (West Bank lawyers joined their strike two weeks later.) The Israeli kangaroo court system proceeded undeterred. Trials went on without the presence of defense attorneys, resulting in high fines and sentences of four to five months for demonstrating and three to five years for throwing petrol bombs.

The focus of the Palestinian uprising remained on the Gaza Strip until mid-January 1988, when the authorities imposed long curfews on all eight Gaza Strip refugee camps. No one was allowed outside; food and water shortages added to the people's misery. Soldiers fired tear gas into homes and dropped tear gas into courtyards by helicopter.

Soldiers were stationed at the entrances and patrolled inside the vast camps at night, marking their way by painting four-foot-high Hebrew letters on the walls for "school," "mosque" and the names of neighborhoods. All the while they made arrests, searched houses and beat residents, young and old, using gunbutts, clubs and boots. One day in Jabalya camp, 100 people used their precious hour-long break in the curfew to seek medical treatment in the camp's United Nations Relief and Works Agency (UNRWA) clinic for injuries inflicted when soldiers broke into their homes and beat them.

Reports of food and medicine shortages during the long curfews on Gaza camps brought a tremendous outpouring of emergency relief from Palestinian institutions inside Israel and the West Bank. Trucks of food, milk and clothing came from the Galilee and the Golan, and from women's groups and other charitable organizations in the West Bank. Israel's attempt to starve out an already poor and very young refugee population reminded Palestinians of blockades on Beirut and the camps in Lebanon.

According to Israeli journalist Yehuda Litani, Israelis think of Gaza as a "horror," which is why Foreign Minister Shimon Peres could suggest a staged Israeli withdrawal early in December. The "Gaza First" idea has been tossed around by Israeli officials for the last ten years, as they ponder what to do with 600,000 landless Palestinians. People in Gaza reject the notion of partitioning Gaza from the West Bank. As in the West Bank, popular committees evolved and brought a measure of local government to neighborhoods and camps—organizing strike schedules for shopkeepers, assisting with the injured and directing demonstrations. Developments in Gaza, such as the lawyers' strike, became models for the more sophisticated West Bank. Gaza health and professional associations sent a petition reminding the International Committee of the Red Cross of its duty to be "more outspoken" against the "unbridled savagery" Gaza's population was witnessing.

In December underground leaflets from both the Islamic Jihad and the Popular Front for the Liberation of Palestine called for continued mass action. Then the major PLO factions together with the Islamic Jihad issued what became an extremely successful series of leaflets giving a semblance of leadership to the uprising. The older Islamic fundamentalist movement, the Muslim Brothers, periodically issued their own statements—for example, calling for strike action to commemorate Gaza's first occupation by Israel in 1956. But the Brothers lost favor with Gazans during the uprising. (See Chapter Twelve.)

Palestinians in Gaza hear the latest weekly communiques of the Unified Leadership broadcast by outside radio stations—Monte Carlo and al-Quds (until it was jammed by Israel)—making actual distribution of the leaflets unnecessary. Gaza residents often observed spontaneous general strikes for days at a time in response to local incidents. Huge demonstrations of 10,000 throughout Gaza greeted the news of a raid by three Palestinian commandos near Israel's Dimona nuclear reactor. And thousands of Gazan women with young children jammed Palestine Square in the center of Gaza City celebrating International Women's Day for the first time.

A surreptitious "National Information Committee" published daily press releases in English providing details of neighborhood incidents and political commentary and delivered them to Gaza's only hotel, which served as the headquarters for foreign correspondents.

Israel closed down the main press office in Gaza for one year and a second office for one month. Three Gaza journalists were arrested and their press equipment confiscated, a human rights worker was summoned for interrogation and another, 'Adli al-Yazuri, whose younger brother Basil was murdered by soldiers in December, was sentenced to six months detention without trial. The telephones of lawyers and physicians, the main source of information for people outside of Gaza, were also mysteriously cut for weeks at a time. And two leading lawyers were imprisoned.

By early March, it seemed as if the barbed wire around the notorious Ansar II prison camp had been extended to encompass all of the Gaza Strip in one giant prison. Despite the repressive measures dished out by the Israeli military authorities, though, the Gaza Strip today is filled with a sense of hope, confidence and visible unity.

Update: November 1988

The assassination in Tunis of Khalil al-Wazir (Abu Jihad), Fatah's second-in-command—by all accounts the work of an Israeli terror squad that infiltrated the PLO compound by using the identity cards of Lebanese fishermen kidnapped at sea—sent a wave of deep grief throughout the occupied territories. Official Israeli reports claimed that Abu Jihad was the remote-control "main organizer" of the Palestinian uprising; no doubt it was believed his murder would break the spirit of the people under occupation. Residents of Gaza, where Abu Jihad had once lived, regarded him with special affection. They were in the streets of one neighborhood or another almost non-stop for days after his death was announced.

Demonstrations ranged from the silent raising of Palestinian and black flags to burning tires in the street to marches by tens of thousands carrying funeral wreaths and pictures of the popular leader. The Gaza home of the Wazir family became a central organizing spot for street protests. A public call was made to change the name of Gaza's main street, al-Wahda, to Abu Jihad Street.

Israel's reaction to the renewed mass protests was unrestrained: soldiers shot freely at people in the streets, causing the bloodiest three-day period of the uprising. The mourning for Abu Jihad coincided with the beginning of the Muslim holy month of Ramadan, and mosques became a focus for Israeli military attention. In Gaza and Dayr al-Balah, two main mosques were attacked by soldiers on the second day of mourning and worshippers were beaten and teargassed. A sixty-three-year-old man lost an eye when a rubber bullet hit him in the face.

Besides the free use of gunfire and the siege of mosques, military authorities also began breaking other "rules," by arresting public figures and women, who had been considered off-limits up until then, and interfering with the merchants' strike. In an effort to break the Gaza lawyers' strike which had been going on since December, Israel announced unilaterally that the strike was over and then, to drive the point home, detained the deputy head of the Gaza Lawyers' Association and subjected him to ninety-six hours of interrogation. When he refused to call off the strike, his detention was extended without trial to six months. The head of the Gaza Medical Association, forty-five-year-old Dr. Zakariya al-Agha, was subjected to similar forms of intimidation: he was arrested for ninety-six hours and then held in detention for six months. Other prominent Gaza figures, including Red Crescent director Dr. Haydar 'Abd al-Shafi' and Yusra al-Barbari, the seventy-year-old head of the Gaza Women's Association, were summoned for interrogation. In another ploy to break the commercial strike, the military told Gaza shopkeepers that they had to pay a series of heavy taxes—a value-added tax, income tax, municipal taxes and various fines—if they wanted to open their businesses during the busy shopping month of Ramadan. Just seven days later, in a typical turnabout, the authorities announced that all Gaza shops were free to open without restrictions until the end of Ramadan in mid-May.

The Muslim Brothers called for a total protest strike in Gaza the following day. Almost simultaneously, Israeli authorities announced that new identity cards would be issued to Gaza residents, and that everyone over the age of sixteen would be required to participate in a personal "interview" with Israeli soldiers. The new ID cards, bright orange and color-coded by area of residence, were issued only to those who had paid the taxes and fines that were imposed during the intifada. The order was part of an elaborate plan to re-impose the Israeli civil administration on the Palestinians and thus end their boycott of its authority. At first, the Unified National Leadership urged the people not to apply for the new cards. But when soldiers began imposing curfews street by street and pulling people out of their houses to confiscate their old ID cards, most Gaza residents were forced to comply with the authorities.

Israel punished Burayj camp for boycotting the payment of electricity bills by imposing a twenty-day curfew and cutting off electricity and water supplies. As a further insult, an Israeli officer was appointed to rule over Burayj residents.

During Ramadan, when Muslims fast from dawn to dusk, Israeli forces placed many Gaza camps under curfew for weeks at a time, making it impossible for residents to buy even the barest essentials. Shati', Jabalya and Burayj were subjected to saturation tear-gas bombing by tanks and helicopters, raising to sixteen the number of residents of these camps who died after exposure to tear gas (usually in their own homes) during the first year of the intifada.

In an unprecedented action, Israeli troops arrested four women, including a mother of nine children, for six months' detention without trial. This was the first time that administrative detention had been used against women in Gaza. The four women had been active in the Women's Work Committees; three were kindergarten teachers in Shati' camp and the fourth, Tahani Abu Dagga, operated a small cookie factory in 'Abasan. Tahani, four months pregnant at the time of her arrest, suffered a miscarriage in prison and received no medical attention. Several weeks later her lawyer succeeded in getting her released on medical grounds. A few months later a fifth woman from Shati' was also sentenced to six months' detention without trial. The fact that Shati' camp women were subject to arbitrary arrest along with men was seen as an attack on this camp in particular and on organized protest by by Palestinian women in general.

An independent team of Israeli physicians that visited Gaza medical facilities in May released a report on June 9 which provided further evidence of Israeli human rights violations. The team, sponsored by the Israeli Citizens' Rights Movement (CRM), documented cases of women who had suffered spontaneous abortions after being teargassed, of people with serious wounds from rubber bullets, of physical torture during interrogations and of arrested hospital patients who were denied emergency surgery. This was the first investigation of human rights abuses in the occupied territories by Israeli physicians. Shortly after the report was released, two infants in Jabalya camp each lost an eye after being hit by rubber bullets in separate incidents.

The Israeli physicians' report eventually led to new orders threatening disciplinary action against Israeli soldiers who fired tear gas into enclosed areas like houses and schools. But Palestinians reported no decrease either in the use of tear gas in general or in the practice of firing it into houses. No Israeli soldier was ever reported to have been disciplined for violating the new regulations.

Despite the high level of violence to which Palestinians had grown accustomed during the uprising, especially brutal acts could still bring people into the streets in protest. In August a series of catastrophes raised the level of tension and anger in Gaza to a new peak. On August 10, three Gaza workers were burned to death while locked in their hut, next to the construction site where they worked in the Israeli town of Or Yehuda, near Tel Aviv. Two Israeli Jews were subsequently arrested for arson but few Israeli government officials joined the town's mayor in strongly condemning the murders. In at least two other Israeli neighborhoods, racist thugs beat up garbage collectors and other workers from Gaza, along with their Jewish employers. Two months later a forty-seven-year-old Gazan worker was beaten to death by Jews at a construction site in Lydda.

Like the incident which marked the beginning of the uprising in December 1987—the death of four Gaza workers killed when an Israeli truck crushed their car—the arson attack provoked an immediate popular response. This time, after heavy gunfire and curfews on camps failed to dissuade Palestinians from three days of intense street protests, the Israeli military authorities imposed a curfew on the entire Strip and barred journalists from the area. This was the second total curfew imposed on Gaza in eight months, a method which was to be employed repeatedly during the remainder of 1988. During the curfew Israeli soldiers carried out an unprecedented physical assault on Gaza homes, sending scores of men, women and children to the hospital, some with loss of eyesight and use of limbs. In some communities, all men aged twelve to forty-five were ordered out of their homes at 2 am and beaten, arrested or assigned the degrading task of removing stones and tires from the streets.

Among the dead in Gaza during these three days were a fifty-two-year-old man shot by soldiers for allegedly throwing stones at them, a twenty-year-old who died after multiple beatings, and a twenty-eight-year-old man who was reportedly writing graffiti on a wall. Two days later the army demolished his family's home in Mughazi camp, the first time a family had been punished in this way after a son had been killed.

Israel utilized the curfew to deport four Gaza residents to South Lebanon. The four men—a physician who had been in prison since 1986 and three former prisoners who had been released in the 1985 prisoner exchange—had been under expulsion orders since July 8 for alleged political activity. Like the Gazans expelled two weeks earlier, these men were also denied last visits with their families.

Almost immediately, Israel announced plans to expel another twenty-five people, the largest group ever to be banished from their homeland by military order. Ten of the men were Gaza residents, including a journalist, university lecturers and a fifty-four-year-old former political prisoner who is the oldest person that has been threatened with deportation in recent years. A few months later, an Israeli army review committee recommended that two of the men, a farmer and a fruit seller, not be expelled because the evidence against them was "insufficient." But General Yitzhak Mordechai, chief of the southern command which includes the Gaza Strip, rejected the recommendation.

The use of live ammunition against unarmed prisoners in a large new internment camp in the Negev desert, dubbed Ansar III, deeply shocked

Palestinians. The incident began when detainees refused orders to clean soldiers' quarters, insisting that such work violated the Geneva Conventions. As punishment, the prisoners were forced to sit in the hot desert sun for hours, and when they returned to their tents without permission they were attacked. Two detainees were shot dead at close range by the commander of the army-run prison camp—one of them was a Gaza resident who had bared his chest to the commandant in defiance—and more than seventy were injured by tear gas. Israeli human rights groups demanded an investigation but the army condoned its actions in Ansar III as "necessary."

In late August, in what General Mordechai described as an effort to "crush the popular committees," the Israeli army launched a massive wave of arrests in the Gaza Strip. With the banning of the popular committees, a grassroots network of community organizations and relief committees that had developed in the course of the uprising, activists became subject to arrest, lengthy prison terms and even deportation. Several hundred people from Gaza city, Shati' and Jabalya whom the Israelis claimed were active in thirty-seven popular committees were arrested. In Jabalya, schoolboys under ten years of age were reportedly beaten and interrogated by soldiers demanding the names of members of a pro-Fatah youth group in the camp. More than a hundred young men from Jabalya were arrested in house-to-house searches. Dozens of Palestinians were wounded by gunfire during demonstrations provoked by the army sweeps.

Previous waves of arrests in Gaza had little effect on the strength of the uprising. This wave, widely publicized on Israeli television, seemed to be designed at least in part to reassure an Israeli public facing general elections that the uprising could be contained. In what Palestinians interpreted as an Israeli effort to split their ranks and weaken the PLO, in this period the Israeli authorities and media also began to focus on Hamas, the Arabic acronym of the Islamic Resistance Movement.

In early September, Israeli soldiers added to their armaments a lightweight but lethal new plastic bullet and a freer shoot-to-punish policy. Suddenly Gaza's hospitals were filled with residents, including small children, wounded by the new ammunition. Injury rates returned to the high levels characteristic of the first two months of the uprising, when demonstrations had been massive, intense and widespread, in contrast to the more sporadic (though persistent) street protests of the months that followed. According to UNRWA, a thousand Gazans were wounded by gunfire in October and November alone, and double that number from beatings and tear gas despite the relatively small number of demonstrations.

The massive repression in Gaza was in large part responsible for the decline in the number of street protests in late autumn. Jabalya and Shati' camps have been under curfew for almost half a year. As a "reward" for their compliance, preparatory schools were re-opened in Gaza, but Israeli security forces have regularly opened fire on schoolchildren throwing stones on their way home from classes (at least three children have been killed in such incidents in recent months). In October, a three-year-old child was shot in front of his home in a Gaza City slum, the youngest Palestinian to die from Israeli gunfire during the entire occupation. From Ansar II detention camp in Gaza City, where 1200 detainees are held, prisoners have been taken to hospital with serious head injuries, and even a broken back, as a result of soldiers' clubbings.

During the mid-November Palestine National Council meeting in Algiers, all refugee camps in the entire Gaza Strip were put under curfew for a week, the borders were sealed, journalists were barred, electricity and telephone lines were cut, and the night-time curfew imposed in all of Gaza since the spring continued to be in effect. But with the irrepressibility for which Gaza has become known and admired since the intifada began, residents from the Egyptian border in the south to the northernmost town celebrated the declaration of an independent Palestinian state by chanting from their homes, in a community chorus, the slogan of Palestinian defiance: "Allahu Akbar!" On that day, high-flying fireworks could be seen erupting from Jabalya camp, the place where the intifada had begun in December 1987. A statement issued in the name of the "Popular Organizations and Independent Personalities in the Gaza Strip" expressed approval for the PNC's decisions. Among the Gaza community leaders who signed the statement were many who had been repeatedly summoned for interrogation or detained without trial over the previous year. Israel's brutal repression had not been able to crush the intifada.

## Chapter 4

Gaza Diary

Melissa Baumann

February 7, 1988

Morning

"Welcome to Gaza" the sign reads, but the streets are not inviting. The long road into town is nearly deserted, its shops and shanties locked shut; only a few men gather sporadically for coffee or a cigarette. Beyond, the camps stretch toward the sea like a giant junkyard, people and goods cast off on this spit of land.

At the start of a two-day general strike, it's unwise to be on the street. Soldiers are everywhere, visible and not.

A small contingent guards the gate to Shifa Hospital. Hundreds of casualties have passed through its wards; soldiers have teargassed and abducted its patients. Soon, a young man running from the army will turn to face a soldier, bare his chest and say "shoot me." The soldier will comply. Everyone will talk about it.

"You are journalists," Madame 'Aliya says from behind the desk at Marna House, an edifice that is walled in with poinsettia and orange trees. She smiles and shuffles a stack of media business cards. "I have them all. You must sign in. I have to turn in three copies to the military every morning."

The forbidden but ubiquitous cracked map of Palestine hangs on the wall. In the office cupboard are a few rubber bullets and tear gas canisters—souvenirs of current history. The fine print on the canisters reads "Made in Pennsylvania, USA, January 1988."

'Aliya is anxious to tell stories. She descends from one of Palestine's wealthiest landowners; now a widow, she runs this guest house, and her son nearby runs a supermarket.

"Do not feel sorry for us," she says, waving her cigarette in the air. "We are not starving people. We do not want your food. And we are not afraid. No one is afraid of their guns anymore."

She is reminded of the beatings that ostensibly displaced bullets. "Yes, with a bullet one can die and it's finished. But to be humiliated like this—it's horrible."

A phone call informs us there is shooting on 'Umar al-Mukhtar, one of Gaza's main streets. The grapevine is astounding; word travels at lightning speed. Another phone call summons Dr. Agha, head of the local Arab Medical Association. He runs through the litany of medical needs in Gaza's eight camps: emergency supplies and equipment as well as antidotes for chronic malnutrition, gastroenteritis, and respiratory and stress diseases. Duty over momentarily, he contemplates what violence—physical and structural—is doing to his child.

"Imagine—every house always has someone in prison. The other day my five-year-old daughter was drawing. I went over to see what it was. She was drawing wheels of fire, and blocked streets empty of people."

W., our guide and a human rights field worker, appears and we drive out onto the street, which smells of burning tires. The sea is not far off, a simple but grand surprise of nature beyond Gaza's clutter. We have come for a view of Ansar II, the detention center. It crouches on the shore, nearly hidden among the dunes, with several watchtowers, barbed wire fences and a conspicuous heavily guarded gate. Outside the gate, across the road from the soldiers, sit small circles of families vigilant for their sons, brothers, fathers among the 1,200 crammed inside.

Between Ansar II and the sea, scores of fishing boats lie scattered aimlessly, their upended hulls cracked and peeling. W. tells us that since the uprising began on December 9, 25,000 fishermen's families have been banned from their livelihood. The reason: security. All the same, men saw and hammer the skeleton of a boat, repairing it for a new season.

On a concrete jetty, children watch waves crash into geysers. We drive near them and are immediately swarmed by ten-year-olds flashing the "V" sign and smiling. Far down the beach a circle of horses gallop gracefully. Their riders wear helmets.

Back at the hotel we pick up L.—a student leader at Birzeit, under town arrest in Gaza these last two months—and R., a French journalist. Next stop: 'Ali 'Arab Hospital, a routine check on the latest casualties. On the way talk turns to the PLO, to political Islam. In recent months, all agree, Islamic Jihad has satisfactorily toed the nationalist line; the Muslim Brothers has not.

"We don't judge according to religion," says W. "We judge according to the value of your nationalism, which you can show in many ways. You can lower the price of your vegetables, give help to the injured—or you can carry a gun."

In the halls of 'Ali 'Arab, a private church hospital of seventy beds, medical staff press toward us urgently. "What are we to do?" asks the diminutive nurse matron, leading us to the intensive care ward to view one of the worst cases. A young man lies on an operating table, naked to the waist, a bandage swathed around his head. His body is bloated, stamped with giant purple bruises. An uncle, an elegant blue-eyed man with a silver mustache, Arab headdress and British Mandate English, steps forward.

"The soldiers put him in a hole and beat him," he said. "Can you believe the savagery?"

Before we can answer we are rushed out to the parking lot, where an ambulance has just shrieked to a halt. Two stretchers are unloaded: boys clubbed on the head this morning. One of them will die. As we watch, stunned, the old man—once a farmer, now living in Jabalya, Gaza's largest camp—comes toward us. He invites us to his home tomorrow morning—to hear another piece of history.

"If you gave me $1 million," he says, "or a big building in Egypt, I would say 'no.' I want to look at a Palestinian sky, to breathe the air of my home, to eat the greens from my land."

Evening

At dusk, W.'s friend H. drives us along the shore road toward Jabalya, still under curfew. Across a rough but verdant pasture we reach H.'s home, a small farm set like a boulder in the middle of this field, stopping just short of the sea. We pull up in a courtyard full of goats, and a tin door swings open, revealing H.'s mother in traditional dress, agitated. She steps toward her son, who is halfway out of the car, and waves her hands in the air. As we leave she tells him, "Come home soon."

Night has fallen when we reach the camp and have been handed over to H.'s cousin, a Jabalya resident. We follow him through the maze—60,000 people in a few square kilometers, alleyways strewn with cans, old shoes, spent refrigerators and tea kettles, many paths lined with an open sewer trench. Street lights are rare, so the houses—cement, wood and tin—glow from the inside, if at all. There is no sound—aside from an occasional baby's cry or dog's bark.

At the UNRWA clinic, havoc rules. The army may arrive at any moment, perhaps to raid its patients. It has been a heavy day for beatings: thirty-five casualties treated here and fourteen passed on to Shifa.

"Because they cut our phone lines we have a new system to call for help," says Dr. Samir Badri. "People shout from rooftop to rooftop, and eventually the cry reaches us."

The army is late. We don't wait for them, and instead follow our guide toward his home in Block 2. This happens to be the block of someone we are seeking: Fathi Ghabin, an artist once imprisoned for painting the Palestinian flag. We are determined to find him. But we get no farther than our guide's home; there is a quick exchange by the lighted doorway between him and his family while we wait in the shadows. H. has fled with the car; the army got dangerously close. As we set off into the blackness again, our failure to find Fathi makes his presence in our memories even more painful to us.

Our guide walks on the opposite side of the street from us; he has brought his small boy along for cover, the ruse of an evening stroll, as absurd as that is under these conditions. We are left on a deserted corner, under a street lamp, assured that a car will come for us soon. Arriving first is a group of men who, discerning our predicament, wait with us till we flag down someone leaving the camp. I wonder what will become of the people we leave behind.

At Shifa, the soldiers are gone, so we are snuck in. A surgeon, K., leads us through the wards to survey "the accidents." We reach a room full of young men, and the doctor ticks off three patients—one comatose, another with broken wrists, a third with trampled knees but smiling triumphantly. "Assaulted by the army, all of them," the doctor says—no accidents, these.

In a women's ward a fifteen-year-old girl in a red spring dress and lavender scarf sits up to speak. Her scarf carries the scent of tear gas. She tears at the sheet as she tells how soldiers invaded her home while she was cooking, beat her, and then tried to force her to sign a statement saying she had stabbed one of them. She refused, so they dragged her behind a jeep to a place where dozens of boys were being beaten. The soldiers said they would stop the beatings if she signed. She did not.

Upstairs a 102-year-old man from Jabalya sits upright, with hoary whiskers, missing teeth, and a worn gold prayer cap, energy belying his age. With an unsteady hand he offers everyone a cigarette.

The soldiers tried to bring a burning tire into his house, he says, and his family resisted. They were all beaten. He is not sure where they are. Raising his hands to God, he bursts into tears. Someone touches him on the shoulder, and we leave.

The night ends in the doctor's living room: an overstuffed velour sofa set, a coffee table and side tables with decorative china, the ancestral photograph (K.'s father, owner of a 7-Up factory, one of Gaza's few industrial plants) on the wall.

Dr. K. does his best to welcome us, but he is conspicuously uneasy in his own home. His outpouring is only a little startling—"In Gaza you just touch a person and he will talk for days," the doctor affirms. "I am sorry for my English," he continues. "We are prevented from speaking with people. There was an Arab doctors' conference in Cairo—we couldn't go. And the government limits the number of Palestinian doctors here."

He pauses slightly, seeming to dredge for the ultimate affront. "I once said to an Israeli soldier, 'It is better to die than to live in this situation.' And the Israeli soldier said: 'What situation?' "

February 8

Morning

The morning's task: to find the old man from Jabalya in the orange groves, near the main entrance to the camp. We drive slowly, searching, but the neat rows of trees yield nothing. We circle and retrace our tracks several times. Still nothing, and no one to ask.

It is still quiet: only a few stragglers in the street, an occasional family propped against a wall, laundry drying on scruffy bushes.

Quickly lost, we run into a gang of boys who crowd around when the car stops. After a brief interrogation, they assign the smallest one in their midst to accompany us to the clinic, a reference point in this labyrinth. About ten years old, he climbs into the back seat and points his finger to the east.

We don't get far. An army jeep rounds the bend ahead, and lumbers towards us. About twenty feet away it stops, we stop. A soldier comes to the car window, about nineteen, solemn and dutiful, careful not to reveal a crack of doubt about his mission. "You must leave," he says. "This is a closed military zone."

"Since when?" we ask.

"This is a closed military zone. You must get permission from the military commander's office if you want to be here."

Two jeeps—one in front, one behind—escort us out of the camp. When we pass a throng of young children on the road, we discharge our young guide, by now discernably anxious, and hope the army does not identify him.

Back at the hotel, W. meets us, ready to take us wherever we can go without getting evicted. We decide on UNRWA headquarters. There we find Dr. Ayyub, deputy field health officer, a man clearly juggling his work as a health official and his mission as a patriot.

"We are hungry for peace and land," he says, in an office plastered with maternal and child health care diagrams. "All the time I make lists for new first aid equipment, but why, when I don't accept this place as it is—to be a ghetto?

"We don't need better housing, better this, better that—we need land," he continues. "We have no guns, no aircraft, but by our solidarity we can do something, and the PLO should follow us on the inside.

"I grew up in a tent and I don't mind living in one again. My village is Masmiya, near Jaffa. I am against any solution that will not return me to this village."

We agree to reunite this afternoon for a trip to Burayj, the camp where Dr. Ayyub grew up and his family still lives.

Most of the Gaza Lawyers' Association has assembled to meet us, to brief us on chronic and recent human rights violations. We meet in the law library, where the association's ten members spend a lot of time lately; they have been on strike since mid-December, protesting the charades of both civil and military courts.

"By striking, we're calling attention to these illegal trials going on," says Sharabil al-Za'im, group spokesman, a contemplative man dressed for court in lawyer's greys. "And we're calling for the release of all detainees in Gaza and the West Bank."

The lawyers have a host of complaints to file against the territories' legal system; grievances are solicited around the table.

They can't appear in any civil court inside the Green Line. In Gaza's court system, they cannot see their clients until a confession is extracted, often twenty days after arrest. During the trial, the prosecutor's files are withheld from them. At any time the military government can declare a lawyer a security threat and ban him or her from court.

And the success rate of a Palestinian defense attorney? The lawyers confer. "About three cases in 20 years. Reduced sentences."

Afternoon

On the way to Burayj, Dr. Ayyub driving, we pass a boy grazing goats in a pasture littered with rusted-out cars. Across the street are the well-irrigated fields and cubist white residences of an Israeli settlement, part of a land grab that has already eaten up more than 30 percent of Gaza.

The doctor takes us past legions of soldiers at Burayj's gate; their encampment is just down the road. Soon we meet another barrier: stones, smoldering tires and barbed wire strung across the street—residents' strategy to "liberate" their camp, keep soldiers out. We are allowed to pass; two boys clear stones and peel back the wire. We leave the car at the UNRWA clinic, and follow the doctor further into the camp.

We go into a home for an affidavit of sorts, another dum-dum bullet case. The room where they seat us is covered with colorful straw mats and floral cushions—a set-up for quick disassembly. On cue, the wounded young man lifts his shirt to reveal a scar on his abdomen and starts his recitation—performances staged again and again until enough people hear them. "He was helping a ten-year-old boy to the clinic in December," Dr. Ayyub translates, "and was shot once, through the back."

Coffee and chocolates arrive; the story continues. Suddenly people stir at the doorway, and rush outside in response to an ominous drone on a megaphone. Curfew. We must be out of the camp in fifteen minutes; all others must be inside.

People walk quickly: parents seek their children, a young girl rushes to buy food. No one knows how long the curfew will last.

At a cross street we see a pending showdown. To our left, distant behind a thick veil of smoke, the shabab ready themselves with stones; to our right, soldiers cradle their guns. We take a detour, and find ourselves amid a crowd of people bringing chairs from the street into a courtyard. There has been a funeral, we learn, for a sixteen-year-old boy whose battered body was found tossed in the camp cemetery. Funerals are forbidden in Gaza.

In ten minutes the camp is nearly dead. We stop briefly outside one house painted with blue hands to ward off evil. The doctor disappears down the street with the shopkeeper who lives here. He returns in five minutes with a sack of frozen fish; the shopkeeper, with half his shop's merchandise on his back, is laughing.

One more stop: a rescue mission. We go to the home of the doctor's parents: a tiny courtyard full of orange peels, a dank living room where his mother, in white veil and embroidered dress, sits on a pile of old quilts. From another room appears an elfin boy in early adolescence, docile but anxious. "My nephew doesn't want to stay here tonight," the doctor says. "We'll take him to Gaza."

On the way back by the sea we get a brief glimpse of peace: a family circle on the beach, a boy stretched out on the sand.

The doctor takes us to his garden, an urban Eden. Almond, lemon, henna, fig, mango and banana trees grow in abundance. The doctor leads us through the greenery to his prize plant: a cactus transplanted from his village. As we sit down to coffee, Samar, his feisty three-year-old, pulls up marigolds.

The doctor has four children and two wives, one of whom wants thirteen children. He confides his approval, in spite of UNRWA's efforts at birth control.

"We will sacrifice one or two kids to the struggle—every family," he says. "What can we do? This is a generation of struggle."

February 9

W. calls us from his home, apologizing for not being able to accompany us today. "I have a 1 pm appointment at the military office," he says. "They want to discuss my work." He tells us, of course, there is nothing we can do; he will see us when he can.

Madame 'Aliya is even less reassuring: "They will take him to Ansar II, give him several beatings, and release him after a while."

More bad news—the Information Committee's press release, dated yesterday, reads:

> All men aged 14-60 were summoned by the military authorities from Block 2 in Jabalya and were systematically beaten without exception. Many required medical attention and were taken either to the local clinic or to the hospitals in Gaza.

We fear for Fathi, the artist, and the old man we never found among the orange trees.

So we try a different tack, and visit Yusra al-Barbari, founder of the Palestine Women's Union. Since 1964 this white-haired firebrand-samaritan has run literacy programs, sewing and knitting workshops, nurseries and kindergartens, and health projects in the Strip. She also pays home visits to women whose men have been killed, detained or deported. She has been especially busy lately.

"This is not all that new," she says. "Palestine has revolted since 1917, since the Balfour Declaration. I remember when I was four years old—my father owned a sesame oil factory here—there had been riots in Nazareth against the British. Palestinian women in Gaza held a meeting to gather donations, and gave me a wooden box to collect them.

"In primary school we submitted a petition, 'Down with Balfour.' I wasn't sure what it meant. And in 1936, I remember, all Palestinians went on strike for six months.

"The British," she continues, "imposed curfews, demolished homes, killed many. I remember in the old city of Gaza the army used to come knock on doors—Indian and Australian soldiers of empire—just like the Israelis. Once when an Israeli military governor came here to see us," she recalls, "he said he wanted to bring presents for our girls. I told him, 'The best present would be if you were the last military governor of this district.' "

An older woman shepherds us off down the street where tea is served. We sit silently for several minutes, with the shades drawn.

"I am Arafat's cousin," the woman says finally, her face wan and tired. "I live here with just my sister. Our mother died this last year; they would not let her out to see her three sons. Now we are locked in, no permission to come or go."

She realizes there is little we can do. "I am sorry to make you sad," she says quietly.

There is nowhere to go, or so it seems. Jabalya, Burayj and the Beach Camp are closed off; someone made it into Khan Yunis this morning, but who knows what will become of them. We decide to try Nusayrat, the camp opposite Burayj.

The long road into camp looks deserted; a family picnics in a field near the orange groves. We stop by a sign saying "Town Council;" in front of the sign, a group of men huddles together. We ask about the army—where are they, who has been hurt? "No trouble today," they tell us, "but who knows—at any moment...."

We drive farther into the camp, zigzagging around gaping holes. Everywhere we go people stare, and children begin to follow the car, slowed as it is by the construction. "PLO! Israel no!" they shout, or "We give our blood to Palestine!" Soon, fifty or more are in our wake, laughing, skipping, running. I wonder if ten years from now, five, three, or one, they will find such an audience—or if they will need one.

## Chapter 5

The Significance of Stones: Notes from the Seventh Month

Joe Stork

Visitors to the West Bank and Gaza get a very immediate, sensory grasp of the significance of stones. In the West Bank, the main cities and towns and many larger villages lie along the ridge of hills and plateaus running north to south and forming a sort of geological spine between the Mediterranean coastal plains and the Jordan rift valley. It is a land made in equal measure of stone and soil. The inhabitants and their ancestors have used the stone to hold the soil to the hillsides in order to provide rooting ground for their olive and fruit trees. The hill country of the West Bank is a subtly sculptured landscape of terraces that testify to uncounted generations of unobtrusive settlement, rows of rough stones piled patiently and mended every several seasons.

The occupiers of the last twenty-one years have quarried the same stone to build their fortress suburbs that stand over this land. These constructions do not blend; they dominate. They are no more a part of this landscape than the many tent encampments set up outside towns and large villages to garrison the tens of thousands of troops now needed to confront the stones.

It is fitting that this uprising has reclaimed these stones to sling at the army, and to barricade the roads against their armored vehicles. The road winding up to the small village of Kafr Na'ma, west of Ramallah, the day we visited, is broken for about thirty yards with rocks, some the size of small boulders. Our perspective staring out of the dusty windshield straight ahead gives a sharp, three-dimensional intensity and separateness to each stone. In the late morning light each rugged chunk has its own specific gravity, balancing one another as if this were a belt of asteroids separating us from them, visitors from inhabitants, city folk from country and, at crucial times, army from people.

Gaza's terrain is flat and sandy. Here the youngsters find their weapons in the cinderblocks that their parents have used for forty years to build their shelters in the camps. The word intifada has a connotation of "throwing off" which the translation "uprising" only partially captures and which perfectly suits the militant form the Palestinian youth have chosen for their war of independence. The chief target for this "throwing off" is the Israeli military occupation. In the process, though, the youth have also thrown off the Palestinian leadership embodied in the older generation of "personalities" and notables. They have thrown off the unequal relations that had characterized the role of the outside PLO leadership. They have thrown off the condescension and complacency of King Hussein and other rulers throughout the region.

Changing Gears

"How long can this go on?" is the question not just outsiders but people here in the West Bank and Gaza ask. And the response they are finding within themselves suggests that it could be for a very long time. The dynamic of resistance and rebellion has spread to include almost all sectors and generations of Palestinian society. As this insurrection has spread, so has it changed.

Any impression that it is waning seems decidedly mistaken. True, Israeli military tactics and large-scale arrests have helped diminish the spectacular confrontations of early 1988. Western media coverage has diminished as well, its short attention span further discouraged by Israel's campaign to choke off major media access to Palestinian views and experiences. But the uprising, Palestinians here insist, is a whole spectrum of activities. Only part of it is militant demonstrations and Molotov ambushes of military patrols. It is the impressive discipline of the merchants' strike, now more than half a year old. It is the agricultural self-help committees, the day-care centers and the "alternative schools" that the women's committees and other long-standing mass organizations have set up. The present stage of the uprising reminded us of an engine: after ignition and the loud energy of transforming a state of rest into a state of motion, it has now passed into a higher, quieter gear.

This quiet side of the uprising gets stated forcefully each day at noon as the metal shop shutters come down and the bustling streets suddenly empty and fall eerily silent. Street confrontations, some of them, have taken on an almost ritualistic quality. At a Ramallah intersection shortly after noon we see schoolgirls, most not yet teenagers, quickly throw up a barricade of stones and burning tires on their way home from school. Just a long block away, in the center of town, teams of three or four Israeli paratroopers (red berets) were patrolling the main market area, and on the roof of the tallest building military spotters with binoculars and radios scanned the streets.

The girls are not quiet; they shout their sing-song PLO rhymes. Some older boys join their brigade. After they're sure they've attracted the soldiers' attention, they move up a side-street hill and pull more rocks into the road, between them and where they expect the soldiers to come from. We move up with them. Even we had already learned to distinguish the loud pop of tear gas and rubber bullet canisters from the sharp crack of "live" ammunition; soon the air starts to irritate our eyes and lungs. Within a few minutes we've run between some houses and gardens to circle back down and around behind the soldiers who are now commandeering male passers-by to pull the barricade down and douse the burning tires. Some schoolgirls in their uniforms nonchalantly walk by. We're sure we recognize some who had just been building the barricade not ten minutes earlier.

Another day we are walking through one of the narrow streets of the casbah of Nablus, where the intifada hours of business are 8 to 11 am rather the usual 9 to 12. It is about 10:30, and the small shops and passageways are crammed with shoppers and sellers. We stop at a small shop to meet Abu Farid. (See the profile of Abu Farid in Chapter Ten.) Suddenly we hear nationalist chants accompanied by some small makeshift percussion instruments. Down the narrow street comes a team of seven young men, their heads completely wrapped with kaffiyas except for small eye-slits. One in front carries a very large Palestinian flag hung from a long pole. He and another lad are carrying small hatchets which they brandish theatrically. Abu Faris identifies them, with a smile, as "Fatah's strike force." The Israeli military spokesmen say the "strike forces" are thugs, enforcing the strikes and other Palestinian actions on a reluctant populace, but this was not the sense we got. All are draped in black tunics, in some cases a plastic trash bag with arm and head holes. They are reminding the merchants of the approaching hour of closing. After they pass, vendors bellow out prices to sell off their produce: "Two-and-a-half shekels before the cannon fires."

Just after 11, all the shops now shut, we wander out to a street on the perimeter of the old city, and into half a dozen soldiers. After inspecting our press credentials, the ranking officer tells us we are not allowed back in the old city. We circle around to another entrance. All but one of the back streets leading out of the old city has been sealed with concrete-filled tin drums stacked three high across the road, just like the entrances to the refugee camps. Inside, by the Great Mosque, what bustled noisily twenty minutes earlier is now very still. A jeep patrol this time finds us and orders us out of what is now a closed military area. Not five minutes later, the same jeep commander finds us still walking away, apparently not fast enough, and now orders us out of Nablus altogether. When we observe that these restrictions don't speak well of the democracy Israel claims it practices, Captain Eli replies, "Yes, but this is not my country. Not yet, anyway."

Balata, just outside Nablus, is the largest refugee camp on the West Bank. Here, with its crowded, congested alleys and confined rage, was where the uprising happened first in the West Bank, the day after it had started in Gaza. Our escort, Hamid, a nineteen-year-old in nondescript jeans and tee-shirt, rattles off the names of the seventeen neighborhoods of the camp: Haifa, Sabra, Damur....The streets have been renamed for Balata residents killed by the Israelis. There have been quite a few of these since the December 10 and 11 demonstrations that started the uprising in the West Bank and left four dead. Hamid refers to the alley-wise kids of Balata as "geniuses" for their ability to stay out of the clutches of the Israelis and the Palestinian informers who work for them. The uprising has not been good for some collaborators. Hamid tells us a story which may be apocryphal but captures the mythic stature that the particulars of this uprising have taken on. The head collaborator of the camp, the mukhtar, had outlived many assassination attempts over the past several years. Recently, while he was away in Amman, some young men managed to break into his well-fortified home and in the bathroom they hung a portrait of Arafat and a noose. When he returned home and entered his bathroom, he had a heart attack and died on the spot.

Jalazun, a large camp of 6,000 north of Ramallah, was under curfew for five solid weeks in March and April. Kamal tells us how the collaborators used to function there. He estimates that they were once about twenty in number. In return for informing on political activities and activists in the camp, they would be allowed to extort "fees" for securing permits, licenses and the like. To go to Egypt last year, Muhammad had to pay almost $600 in permit fees, including some $120 to the Palestinian collaborators.

In many camps and villages, collaborators have gone to the mosque to turn in their sidearms and renounce their traitorous behavior. Those who haven't, we are told, remain isolated and fearful. "Now they just sit in their houses all day doing nothing," we heard in the village of Idna. In other cases they have left for the relative anonymity of Jerusalem. Even in the case of collaborators, it seems that people have largely counted on unspoken—certainly unenforced—moral suasion to get such people to rupture their ties with the military regime. This seems to be especially the case in those villages, like Idna, where nearly everyone is related in some close or far degree to every one else. "Now is not the time to have wars between ourselves," one villager in Idna told us. "The intifada is more important."

Not Spontaneous

People in villages, camps and neighborhoods have been helping one another, especially those victimized by the army—a house destroyed, a husband or father seized and arrested. Most of the Palestinian casualties of this uprising, those shot dead, severely beaten, incarcerated without charge or trial, come from the camps and the poorer neighborhoods of towns and villages. We sat in many of their homes, we spoke with their mothers and sisters, their husbands and children. Our most difficult moment, probably, was in the Gaza hospital where we visited Huda Munir, the nine-month-old girl from Jabalya camp whose left eye had been destroyed by a rubber bullet. Her grandmother could not contain her anger at us; for her we were part of that world that allows Israel to get away with such outrages.

We also spoke with doctors, engineers, other professionals, people of property—people who tend to find some conservative accommodation with authority. They, too, now found themselves in a posture of confrontation with the military regime. Some are now doing their first prison stints—six months, renewable, without charges—in the sweltering desert concentration camp of Ansar III. We spoke with lawyers and human rights activists who are fighting as best they can the arbitrary rule of the occupying army. The army has imprisoned some 10,000 Palestinians since December, mostly for "thought crimes."

People have set up local committees to handle distribution of foodstuffs in curfew and siege conditions, to organize guard duty in villages, to promote local agricultural projects. Women working in one Ramallah neighborhood committee told us that one of their first steps was to conduct a house-to-house survey to learn special needs—elderly or infirm, number of school-age children, professional and manual skills that might be needed. One project was to compile people's blood types; this proved immensely useful as casualties mounted in the spring. They also collected donations to build up a fund for community needs.

Many of these projects, like the intifada gardens that are everywhere, are brand new, emblems of the uprising's scope and breadth. But their rapid appearance owes to the last dozen years of "training" in student organizing efforts. This is what one Popular Front cadre meant when he described the uprising as "not planned, but not spontaneous."

There is, of course, a strong streak of competition that characterizes relations among the four major political organizations—Fatah, the Popular Front, the Democratic Front and the Palestine Communist Party. Each has its "grassroots" organizations. Only in the case of the women's organizations has there been a serious effort at unifying or at least coordinating activities.

The women's committees and the Medical Relief Committee have nearly a decade of organizational experience. Medical Relief, for instance, was started by five doctors in 1979. Today it has a membership of some 800 health professionals, according to founder Mustafa Barghuti, including 315 physicians. In 1982, its mobile clinics saw 2,000 patients; in 1987 the figure was 50,000, and 28,000 during the first five months of the uprising.

The rivalry between the organizations to enlist new recruits seems muted, at least by contrast with the situation in the trade union movement a few years ago. The main competition for recruits, we were told, is in the dense refugee camps. Some of the fiercest rivalry, apparently, occurred in the first few months of the uprising. Perhaps not surprisingly the Communists and the Democratic Front, whose platforms and ideologies are very close and who therefore compete most directly for the same constituency, were most heatedly at odds. The situation seems to have improved, largely by popular demand, though many here worry that rivalry may again reach destructive proportions. "It is our national disease," one young university teacher said.

By some accounts, the main competition in the current phase comes chiefly from Fatah, whose broad street support has in the past seemed to exempt it from the need to work through such grassroots organizing. Now, in the new conditions created by the uprising, some activists affiliated with the other organizations say Fatah is trying to muscle in with its greater material resources and its weight of popularity without doing the hard, slogging organizing work that the others have put so much time and effort into. On the other hand, Fatah has very impressively mobilized youth and students through its Shabiba organization. Fatah thus provides a focus and channel for popular energies that otherwise might go untapped, or that would be under the diffuse direction of the Muslim Brothers or other "Islamist" (Muslim fundamentalist) elements.

Leadership Composition

This is the scene in the West Bank, as we could discern it. In Gaza, the left groups and Islamic Jihad, along with Fatah, comprise a regional Unified Leadership. In Gaza both the Communists and the Islamists have more militant reputations for confronting the Israelis in the streets than their counterparts in the West Bank. The impression we got was that the Islamists were going off on their own a bit in places where they were particularly strong, such as Khan Yunis, calling demonstrations and the like. On the West Bank the Islamist current seems more diffuse and lacking cohesion and organizational competence.

Related to the dynamics between the various organizations and tendencies is the unevenness of the mobilization process. The neighborhood and village committees tend to be concentrated in the central part of the West Bank (Ramallah-Jerusalem-Bethlehem and the camps and villages in these districts) and in Gaza. In Balata and Nablus, for instance, local organizers told us that the frequency and duration of curfews and sieges and the constant threat of army attacks had kept them occupied with more pressing duties. One young activist in Balata even used the word "luxury" to refer to the committees that had so impressed us further south. The disparity, though, may also reflect the relative strength and organizing history of the left organizations in the central region and in Gaza, and the prominence of Fatah in the north. The most organized villages seemed to be those where at least two, and often all four, of the major organizations have a presence, in just about every case going back several years before the uprising.

The structure of the uprising's leadership is not publicly known or widely discussed, and secrecy has doubtless been one factor behind its success. The Unified National Leadership appears to be located physically in the Jerusalem/Ramallah area, if several seizures of freshly printed leaflets are any indication. All that is known is that each of the four major organizations is represented, probably by one delegate each who rotate frequently. This is one reason the military regime has resorted to indiscriminate, mass arrests. One military raid came to the home of a Gaza man who had died two years ago. These roundups—one human rights lawyer characterized the tactic as "trolling"—have probably nabbed a few high-level cadres, but have clearly failed to put the Unified Leadership out of business.

In the cities, camps and villages the cadres of the major organizations are responsible for interpreting and implementing the *bayanat* (communiques) of the Unified Leadership. The composition of this local leadership thus reflects the balance of political forces in that area. In Gaza, the Islamic Jihad is represented; in Nablus, it seems, the higher committee consists essentially of the local Fatah leadership. Both in Nablus and Gaza there have been instances where the local leadership has issued its own directives elaborating the instructions of the Unified Leadership for local conditions. This local leadership appears to be fairly unstructured. We encountered one village where local Communist Party cadre said there was a village "higher" committee consisting of one representative from each of the major organizations. From what we could ascertain, though, this local leadership generally functions more informally.

This means that the left organizations have almost equal weight with Fatah at the key juncture of the Unified Leadership. Their weight on the ground is variously distributed, though generally speaking it is greatest in the central Ramallah-Jerusalem-Bethlehem area. The uprising has provided opportunities for these groups to extend their influence. One undisputed achievement of the past seven months has been the quantum extension of mass organizing. Yet the uprising has also engaged massive numbers of people who remain politically unorganized. The Palestinian street by and large belongs to Fatah. One of the most interesting questions today is how the insights and organizational experience of the left groups will influence the street in any long-lasting way, and reciprocally how the weight of Fatah (and the Islamists) in the street will inform the decisions of the Unified Leadership.

Dual Power

Although there have been occasional lapses (reflected in the simultaneous appearance of more than one "genuine" communique), the requirements of consensus decision-making have kept the leadership's demands realistic, things that people can accomplish. It is unrealistic to demand that all Palestinians stop working in Israel immediately. Instead, there are total strike days, once or twice a week, when people should not travel to Israel to work. This enables the Palestinians to retain the initiative.

The clandestine Unified Leadership represents legitimate political authority today in the West Bank and Gaza. It is precisely this protracted condition of dual power which constitutes the uprising's main achievement, and the main target of the Israeli military regime. This dual power is manifest everywhere—the merchants' strikes, the tax resistance, the local organizing. The existing Palestinian police force is no more than a vestigial attachment to the regime. The Israelis have literally had to reconquer villages, often more than once, using hundreds and in some cases many hundreds of troops. In May, when Maj. Gen. Amram Mitzna, the commander in the West Bank, was asked if there were "still any so-called liberated villages," he replied that there were still "a few villages, which I would not call liberated, but places that we enter more infrequently."

Perhaps the most impressive evidence of the authority of the Unified Leadership has been the widespread unity and discipline around methods and tactics, and in particular the decision not to take up arms. In the first six months, anyway, the Palestinians have largely maintained the political initiative. The military regime was unable to force its will on the merchants, and has given up this front. There is now talk of abandoning the different color license plates marking off Gaza and West Bank vehicles, so as to make it less easy for the young stonethrowers to discriminate against Israeli ones.

Of course, this would remove one small tool the occupiers had invented to establish such discrimination for their own purposes.

The military can command that the schools open or close, but they cannot determine which serves their purpose: when open, they provide points of assembly for demonstrations and the like; when closed, the children take up subversive subjects such as Palestinian history and geography in the classes set up by the local committees. Likewise, the prisons have long served as schools for militants who are more skilled and organized when they leave than when they entered. So the tactic of mass arrests also has a "downside" from an Israeli point of view. Not that it is a "mistake." Rather, it illustrates the dilemma Israel faces in trying to impose its rule on a thoroughly hostile population.

The Israeli military regime sees as its main task to beat down these efforts at establishing a parallel, competing political authority. This is why the soldiers shut down the agricultural committee in Bayt Sahur and arrested the local agronomist and civil engineer who had helped organize it. This is why the military regime closed down the Society for the Preservation of the Family in Ramallah. This is why military patrols shoot to shreds makeshift Palestinian flags that youths hang from utility wires. This is a struggle for political control, not matters of military security. Avishai Margalit has accurately translated the military regime's commitment "to restore law and order" as a determination "to erase the smile from the face of Palestinian youth."

The Israelis still enjoy an enormous capacity to enforce their rule, of course. The Unified Leadership had declared Sunday, June 19, as a day to boycott totally the military administration: no permits, no licenses, no paying taxes, no contact at all. That day outside the Ramallah district headquarters there were exceptionally long lines of Palestinians. Israel Radio crowed about how this showed the limits of the Unified Leadership's authority. It did, but it also showed the limits of Israeli authority. For several days before, military checkpoints in the Ramallah area stopped cars and liberally confiscated licenses and IDs, and told their owners they would have to appear that Sunday to reclaim them. In such ways the military regime drives home what all Palestinians are well aware of: that they are not yet capable of throwing off the control that the IDs represent.

The Israelis set up the same sort of contest when they decreed that all Gaza residents would have to get new IDs of a different color. The Unified Leadership fell into the political trap by calling on Gazans to boycott this order. When we visited Gaza, Palestinian friends told us that most Gaza City residents had gotten the new IDs; those who did not were mainly people who were wanted for questioning anyway. It was now the turn of Jabalya camp. On Sunday, June 12, we walked over to the Gaza military administration headquarters around 6:30 am. An enormous line of men, five to eight wide, stretched back up the road and then around the corner for several more blocks—perhaps two to three thousand. Back at the corner there were clusters of men around makeshift street corner photo studios, getting their Polaroid portraits, and others around men with old typewriters perched on stools or chairs filling out requisite forms. Some of the men in line told us the soldiers had brought them in buses a few hours earlier from Jabalya. Most of them faced a long day in the sun, and even at this early hour it was clear that tempers were short. There were surges forward that moved down the line like a wave. As the crowd spilled out into the roadway, a military jeep would roar up the road along the edge to force them back into some semblance of a line. When the soldiers saw us, this became a "closed military area." We moved around for a while longer, and eventually left. After we got a few blocks away, out of sight, we heard the loud pop of rifles firing tear gas and rubber bullet canisters. We later learned that there were a number of injuries, but no fatalities. Again, the Israelis had imposed their military and administrative will, but had they convinced these thousands of men that their future lay with the occupation and its new, red identity cards?

The Gaza ID issue nevertheless points up a real problem for the uprising leadership. "You cannot ask people to do things they cannot do," said one activist who was critical on this matter. "Now the people read the bayanat. They do the things they can do and they leave the rest. But if you accumulate ten or a dozen setbacks like this, you will lose the people."

Virtually everyone we spoke with saw the present phase as one of consolidation of the achievements of the first six months, a transition to a new phase of struggle. All characterized the coming period as one of "civil disobedience," meaning the severance of all links to the military authority and the Israeli economy. At issue, though, is how complete the rupture should be, and in what time frame. Popular Front cadres argue that groundwork has been laid, that key sectors of the population are ready to make a radical break. It would be an error of historic proportions, they say, to remain in this transition stage for very long and risk wasting the enthusiasm and determination that the uprising embodies.

Most other cadres feel that much more patient, low-profile organizing needs to be done, that the Palestinians need to choose carefully the time and circumstances for the next upsurge of activity. The Palestinian leadership and organizations cannot provide the material support for a campaign of total civil disobedience at this time. Such a step now would be irresponsible. The Popular Front people argue that this errs on the side of caution, that the only way to establish the conditions for a total break with the military regime is to precipitate situations that build up people's capacity to endure and to do without. Others respond that people's limits are already being tested, especially in the villages and camps where days and weeks of curfews, sieges and beatings take a steady toll while feeding resistance.

Declaring Independence

Most Palestinians will not hesitate a minute if you ask what they think they have achieved. In the first place, they say, it has had a profound impact on their own lives, on the way they see the world, on the way they relate as individuals to one another. The uprising has done a lot to bring Palestinians together, to close the gap of experience between Gaza and the West Bank.

There is enthusiasm for breaking down the patterns of consumption that has helped make the occupied territories such a large market for Israeli manufactures, an enthusiasm for doing without and for sharing. There is a kind of euphoria that tends to minimize the problems and difficulties they face, that exaggerates the effectiveness of their popular authority against Israeli repression. But it seems undeniably true that the uprising has completely marginalized pro-Hashemite elements, leaving absolutely no basis for the "Jordanian option" favored by Washington and the Labor party.

Besides their own Palestinian society, they see the greatest impact on their adversary, Israel. The uprising has deepened the crisis of the occupation and raised its costs across the board. We encountered some very creative efforts by Palestinian leftists to link up with Israeli opponents of the occupation—for instance, having weekly tours for Israelis to different West Bank villages or camps, and encouraging Israeli groups to "adopt a village" or camp and be responsible for providing material aid when needed and for protesting army sieges, curfews and the like. In the immediate aftermath of the Beita incident in early April (see Chapter Six), a joint Palestinian-Israeli Committee for Beita was formed to head off the campaign of the Israeli right and the settlers' movement to raze the village and expel all its inhabitants. "Beita was a very close thing," one of the Palestinian organizers told us. "[The settlers] came very close to precipitating an atrocity that would have had a very bad effect." Palestinian morale would have suffered greatly, and the intifada might have degenerated into violent outbursts that would have led to more atrocities and more mass expulsions. The function of the joint committees and the programs bringing Israelis into contact with the Palestinians is not only protective; it is also part of a strategy to combat Palestinian anti-Jewish chauvinism, and to force Israelis to confront the settler movement and isolate it.

We found a surprising degree of unity among people from all tendencies regarding Palestinian demands. The Unified Leadership has lately issued several specific lists of immediate demands, such as release of prisoners and pulling troops out of populated areas. We heard no criticism of those demands from the Palestinian side; the Israeli government rejects them out of hand.

With respect to more ultimate goals, we also found remarkable Palestinian unanimity around the two-state formula. Even before the now-famous memorandum of PLO spokesperson Bassam Abu Sharif surfaced in mid-June, when we asked what would be the most important contribution the PLO leadership outside could make to the uprising, the most frequent response we heard was this: to state unambiguously that the PLO accepts a two-state arrangement, Palestinian and Israeli, as the basis for a political resolution of the fundamental conflict. The one organizational demurral, not surprisingly, comes from Popular Front cadres, who somewhat tepidly endorse this as an "interim" solution. "Interim to what?" we heard others scoff, who saw this reluctant endorsement as an important step in the Popular Front's move away from its rejectionist position.

Most of the people we spoke with endorsed the contents, and certainly the gist, of the Abu Sharif document, though they were critical of its clumsy debut. "I want them to say it very clearly, not in the manner of Arafat," said Birzeit University teacher Azmy Bishara. "Not because this will change Israeli policy any time soon," Bishara continued, "but for one reason: because it's a golden opportunity for saying to the Arab world and the rest of the world that this is what we Palestinians want: no more, but no less. Not what Jordan wants, not what Syria wants, but what the Palestinians want. The Palestinians of the West Bank and Gaza have given the PLO leaders another opportunity to change their strategy, to stand apart from Syria, from Jordan, from the rest. It is a chance for the Palestinians to declare their independence from the Arab states as well as from Israel."

Since we left in late June, 1988, the confrontations and casualties have escalated again. To complement Defense Minister Rabin's policy of "force, might and beatings," Israel's military regime has embarked on a widespread campaign of sieges, curfews and economic restrictions—collective punishments outlawed by the Geneva Conventions—to try to smother the uprising.

Bayt 'Umar, a village south of Jerusalem, was chosen for "model" treatment: the military command summoned some fifty farmers and told them they would not get the usual permits to market their produce—mainly plums, now ready to harvest—in Gaza, Tel Aviv and Jordan. The *mukhtar* (village leader) says this will cost Bayt 'Umar about $5 million, or 90 percent of its annual income. "Bayt 'Umar looks harsh," says Clinton Bailey, an Israeli-American "expert" on Arab affairs at Tel Aviv University who advises the defense ministry, "but when you are confronted with an overall uprising and a challenge to government, you have to decide how to deal with it." For

Bailey, options are limited: "Your choice is to either club them over the head or get the society itself to come to some kind of *modus vivendi*."

Israeli and US commentators lament that "the quality of life" has become hostage to the uprising, at the insistence, of course, of the Palestinians. For most Palestinians "quality of life" is not something that can be measured exclusively by indices of purchasing power. Even General Amram Mitzna, the West Bank commander, acknowledged in June that there has been an "irreversible" rise in political self-confidence. Yet in practically the same breath Mitzna asserted that "we want the Palestinians not just to fear when they see an Israeli soldier, but to respect an Israeli soldier."

We found the observation of one Palestinian activist to provide the best summary of the present stage. "The main question," he said, "is now this: how much violence can the Israelis deploy, and how much can the Palestinians endure? If the Israelis could use all the means of violence at their disposal, they could surely wipe out the uprising. If the Palestinians could endure any level of violence it would just be a matter of time before they won their independence. There is an equilibrium here we must work to preserve, and to change in the Palestinians' favor, by limiting the Israeli recourse to violence and providing support that will enable the Palestinians to survive."

Chapter 6

Beita

Ellen Cantarow

Before April 6, 1988, Beita (pronounced BAY'tah, pop. 7,500) was known, when it was known at all, for its fine olive crops and its beauty. It is a white, stony little place whose narrow, unpaved streets twist and turn precipitously up terraced hills that burgeon with olive trees. The rusty hiccoughing of donkeys, the muezzin's call to prayer from the little stone mosque at the village's summit and the occasional drone of a tractor are about the only sounds you hear on warm days like the ones of my visit here in September 1988. Like most of the northern West Bank, Beita is Fatah territory. But even after April 6, 1988, journalists didn't discuss its politics. "Militant" and "fiery" were used about villages like the Communist Party stronghold Salfit, to Beita's south, or Qabatya to its north, where, in February of 1988, a collaborator was axed to death. Of Beita they wrote "lost in the hills" and "sleepy."

With its women carrying jerrycans of water on their heads and its little storefront where men sit fingering their worry beads and sipping coffee, Beita looked to me at first like one of Giovanni Verga's villages. The only thing that struck a very different note—a sign of the nine-month-old intifada (literally, "the shaking-off" or "shuddering")—was the wall-writing I saw everywhere: "The cruelty and violence of the army will only increase our struggle," signed, "Fatah." "Yes to national unity under the leadership of the PLO. No to attempts at division," signed, "Unified National Leadership." "Yes to civil disobedience." "Strike the 17th and 26th." And my favorite: "We salute you, castle of steadfastness," also signed Unified National Leadership.

My borrowed Peugeot with its blue plates—blue is for Arabs; yellow is for Israelis; to drive with yellow plates into a village like Beita in the heat of the intifada is to court stoning by the children—struggled up narrow, stony paths past a dog sleeping in the dust and under two tattered Palestinian flags hanging from electricity wires. I counted three demolished houses before my attention was diverted by an inspection detail of small, rough boys who pulled up on either side of me on donkeys. I stopped, explained through my translator where I wanted to go, and got escorted at a canter to a high point in the village near the mosque.

The Salih house in Beita was like dozens I've visited in the West Bank over the past nine years—a little, iron, painted gate, a tiny courtyard, a goat tied in an alcove beside cement stairs that mounted steeply to a scrubbed but barren set of small rooms on the first floor. I came with Hafiz Barghuti, a journalist from a large and important family near Ramallah, an hour and a half to the south. There are trade-unionist Barghutis and medical Barghutis; during the days of clan rule in Palestine the family members were effendis— landowners.[1]

The Mother's Story

This particular Barghuti had lived several years in Italy. His Italian was better than his English, my Italian was adequate, so we hobbled along with each other in that language, which made our hostesses and the children believe, firmly and approvingly, that I was Italian. (I didn't disabuse them: being from the United States doesn't get you high marks in these parts.) A child brought me a chair; instead I chose the little, lean cot by the window and instantly regretted it. The sun beat down on my shoulders, my pants were damp against my thighs and sweat trickled down my sides. I wondered how the three women sitting opposite me—Munira Salih's two sisters and her mother—could stand the September heat wave in their long, heavy dresses.

An unwritten rule of Israeli occupation in the territories seems to be: those who are punished will be punished for their punishment. This was the case, for example, in the southern town of Halhul where I did my first West Bank reporting in 1979. In the course of a high-school students' demonstration against the Camp David accords in April of that year, two of Halhul's teenagers were murdered either by a soldier or by a settler from nearby Kiryat Arba (it was never established which; there was no conviction) and a twenty-three-hour-a-day thirty-day curfew was levied on the hapless town.

The Salih's story was this: a settler from Elon Moreh had shot and killed twenty-one-year-old Musa, the son of the oldest woman and the brother of the two younger ones. Of the countless settler depredations in the region, this one was the most dramatic. Musa's sister, Munira, was shown her brother's body in the presence of his murderer. In her grief and rage she picked up a rock and struck and severely injured him. For this act Munira, wife of Taysir Da'ud, mother of three and four months pregnant with her fourth, was jailed, convicted of "aggravated assault" and sentenced to seven months in prison. After Munira's arrest the army came into the village and demolished the house Taysir's father had built for the couple six years earlier.

Munira's mother is a tall, spare, dark woman in her sixties. She has a hawklike nose and a pale, vertical line of blue tattooing in the middle of her lower lip, a traditional decoration of older countrywomen here. Her two other daughters have her dark, aquiline leanness and so, their mother told me, does Munira.

"Munira's youngest is sick because he misses his mother. And the next-littlest keeps crying, 'I want my mother,'" she said. Munira would get out of prison in three months, by which time her child would be born. Every two weeks the mother went to visit the daughter; the prison authorities allowed her the usual half-hour conversation through bars. When I asked about Musa she began a long lamentation: "I raised him all by myself; his father died when he was seven months old. He was always the best in his class; he was in his second year at Najah University. He played the flute. If he was a moment late coming home from university, I'd be going in the streets asking about him." At any sign of "trouble" in the village—demonstrations or clashes with the army—she would take Musa to the neighboring village where she was born. "I dreamed of seeing him walking hand and hand with his wife through the streets of this village," wept his mother, "but now he's lying in his grave! If your house has been demolished, you might rebuild it. If you lose your money, you might regain it. But if you lose your son...."

A child clinging to his grandmother's legs burst out crying. "Shhh!" said Barghuti. The child cried even harder when Barghuti shushed him again. "*Ma'alish*—never mind!" I said. This journalism business was a super-added tax on a family already visited with Biblical punishments. I said I would do what I could to publicize the family's case; I would try to return. "*Ahlan wa sahlan*—welcome," said Munira's mother in a hollow voice. "Your daughters have your eyes," I said as I was turning to leave. She kissed me then on both cheeks: "You are a nice person." "Ciao! Ciao..." called one of the older children enthusiastically as we walked down the road.

Someone had thrown orange drink at the windshield and side window of the Peugeot. No doubt one of the little boys from earlier. American freelance filmmakers staying at my East Jerusalem hotel said they had literally been disarmed by Beita children, a tough lot. "It was, like, creepy, man," said the group's producer. "They were outta control when they saw our cameras. They started throwing stones. The adults couldn't do anything about them, it was like *Lord of the Flies*." I poured water over the windshield and wiped off the orange drink. A vast assortment of journalists, writers and filmmakers from all over Western Europe and the United States had pounced on Beita immediately after its April tragedy. Little, if any, material aid had resulted from all the voyeurism.

Breakfast in the Grass

In the dozens of US news accounts about Beita, the name of the Palestinian Antigone, Munira Da'ud, was never mentioned. Instead, the media lit on a Jewish girl, fifteen-year-old Tirza Porat, accidentally killed April 6 by the same man who had killed Musa Salih. Overnight, Tirza became an international martyr. She was from a Jewish settlement, Elon Moreh, located near the West Bank's largest city, Nablus. Elon Moreh is a stronghold of Gush Emunim—Bloc of the Faithful—the religious-nationalist spearhead of settlements since 1967. On April 6, with other Elon Moreh teenagers, she had gone picnicking in the Palestinian hills. This seemed a rash thing to do at the height of the intifada, but then these children believe in manifest destiny: all of Eretz Yisra'el, from the ocean to the river Jordan, for the Jews.

The teenagers settled down for breakfast at a spring near Beita. With the group were two armed bodyguards, one of them twenty-six-year-old Roman Aldubi. This was a man, as it would happen, of such extremism and violent tendencies that the Israeli army had banned him the year before from entering Nablus, where he had been a party to the killing of a Palestinian child, 'Aysha Bahash, in her father's bakery.

From a distance, some farmers who had been tending their land saw the teenagers and the armed men and became alarmed. They sent one of their number running into Beita a kilometer away, and very soon after word of the settlers went out over the village mosque's loudspeaker. More villagers, among them Musa Salih, rushed to the aid of their neighbors near the spring. At some point the villagers threw stones at the settler-teenagers to drive them away. Instead of running away with his group, Aldubi began running towards the farmers. He fired his gun, hitting Musa Salih in the head.

Accounts vary about what happened next, but several facts seem clear. During the course of the next hour or so, the group, surrounded by Beitans, moved from the spring to the village itself. Villagers and some of the teenagers tried to keep Aldubi from shooting again. Nevertheless, he killed another villager and critically wounded a third. And he killed Tirza Porat.

The first Israeli reports screamed that Tirza Porat had been stoned to death by bloodthirsty Arabs. These reports were echoed in the U.S. press. A united front of the Right attended the girl's funeral—former Defense Minister and current Trade Minister Ariel Sharon; Rabbi Meir Kahane, founder of the Jewish Defense League and head of the racial supremacist Kach (Thus) party;

and Rabbi Chaim Druckman, of the National Religious Party, who declared that Beita "should be wiped off the face of the earth." "The heart of the entire nation is boiling," intoned Prime Minister Yitzhak Shamir. "God will avenge her blood."

The real story came to light very soon after. By then irreparable damage was in progress. Bowing to the settlers' pressure, the army moved in and destroyed fifteen houses, including the Da'uds'. Fifteen other houses, including Munira's mother's, were damaged accidentally because of the force of the other explosions. Some of that damage was extensive. All the demolitions took place before the inhabitants had been accused of any malfeasance. One of the houses belonged to a family that had tried to protect the settler-children. Some belonged to people who hadn't even been in Beita at the time of the incident.

In the terrible days that followed, another Beitan was shot and killed while fleeing from the army: after April 6 the military authorities dragnetted the village, arresting successive waves of villagers before they settled on a final nineteen to be brought to trial. Finally, six Beitans were deported. The other Palestinians exiled over the past twenty-one years have all been accused of being leaders of political revolts. These were the first men ever exiled for that most daily and banal of resistance activities, stone-throwing.

At the Store

Someone gave me the name of Munira's husband, Taysir Da'ud, and a phone number where he could presumably be reached in Nablus. For a futile week I kept calling Nablus, only to be told by a cautious female voice that Da'ud's whereabouts were unknown. That was when Barghuti and I went to Beita on our own initiative and found Munira's mother.

Making connections at this point in the intifada wasn't easy. The uprising had become a sort of natural condition like the weather, ever-present, ever-honored, changing the whole rhythm of life. The universal merchants' strike had collapsed the working day into a scanty three hours. At nine every morning, all stores in East Jerusalem, the West Bank and Gaza opened promptly and at noon the metal shutters slammed down over everything except designated pharmacies. If you didn't get all your business done during that time, you were stuck until the next day. There was also the constant violence. Mass arrests took place in the northern West Bank the first week of my stay, and all during my visit there was fresh weekly news of deaths and injuries—the army by now was routinely using live ammunition against the population. In the atmosphere of continual crisis tracking people down could therefore take several times as long as it would have ordinarily.

And then, the paranoia: it wasn't that people weren't wary in February, when I had made an earlier visit. It was just that they were warier now, and for good reason: by September over ten thousand Palestinians were in prison. These days, one was even more likely than during the time of my earlier visit to be imprisoned for anything the military authorities decided was an "incitement," which, of course, included being known as a press contact. The press itself had also fallen into some disrepute. This was because the Shin Bet (Israel's FBI) had posed as journalists—how often it was impossible to tell, but the result was that Palestinians were now suspicious of any journalist who didn't come personally recommended by someone they knew and trusted.

"Ahlan wa sahlan," Da'ud greeted me without surprise when I was finally brought to him. "I was busy with my case," he said. He sat in a dusty little cave of a store—one of those ubiquitous Third World places that sells everything from Royal Crown Cola to plastic sandals. On top of a battered refrigerator that stood by the door were boxes of the latter. I took note of the wares on a rickety red and green table towards the back—boxes of eggs; plastic, dusty bags of sunflower seeds; some colored boxes containing bubble gum. Outside, the sun shimmered hotly and from somewhere in the olive groves a donkey kept braying.

Da'ud has a B.A. in sociology and psychology from Najah University. "All the people are Muslims here," he said, twirling his worry beads. "More than two thousand of us have emigrated from Beita abroad. That began even before '67 but it increased greatly after." This is typical of the region, where twenty years of Israeli occupation have roadblocked development and self-sufficiency. Young Palestinian men have had to choose either menial work in Israel or emigration to ensure their families' survival. According to Da'ud, thirty Beitans with B.A.s are employed as teachers. Seventy others work as hotel cleaners and in other menial service jobs in Israel because of unemployment. The village's revenue has suffered a 30 percent cut since the beginning of the intifada. "We had 600 workers going to Israel before the intifada. Now there are only 150. Many of them were hit and beaten by Jewish persons in the cities because it was known they were from Beita, so most of them are afraid to work in Israel now. And others don't want to work in Israel because of the intifada."

Da'ud was to go to the United States for graduate work but "the Incident" brought his plans to a halt, he said. There is no other employment, so he works here in his father's store. Or rather, a poor substitute for his father's original store, which was "accidentally" demolished by the force of the explosion that destroyed the Da'uds' house adjacent to it. The earlier store dated from 1948, when, along with thousands of others, Taysir Da'ud's father was forced to flee Haifa by the invading Jewish army.

The Da'ud family is like countless others in the West Bank and Gaza, rich in stories about the disinherited past and riven with present hardship. The particular hardships attending "the Incident" included the army roundup of wave upon wave of villagers who got herded into the village schoolyard, Da'ud among them. "The first day alone they arrested maybe one hundred people. They put them in the school courtyard, they beat them with sticks, with their hands, with guns. All that night, from seven o'clock until four in the morning, they put a big projector with a searchlight on our eyes." The soldiers wouldn't let their captives move, go to the toilet, or smoke, even though they themselves demanded cigarettes from the people. The next morning Da'ud was released with many others. "This continued from April 6 to April 9, taking, freeing, taking, freeing. The settlers claimed the people used a gun or a bomb, they claimed we were terrorists. But there was much time for the villagers to kill all of them [the settler teenagers], and the villagers killed no one. It was Aldubi who killed Musa and another Taysir, who had only wanted to talk to him."

I was curious about Munira. "Just a housewife," her husband said. "She was never active. The day of the Incident she was getting clothes with her mother for a woman who had just given birth in Beita." The authorities had offered her favors in return for her cooperation; she refused.

As Da'ud spoke, a small group of men collected at the entrance of the store and swapped prison stories. "In jail," said one, "I met a person from al-'Ayn refugee camp who had been in jail before. The day he was released from jail, he got home at three-thirty and at eight the same evening they came and arrested him; they accused him of throwing stones on a day when he was in jail the first time. He is in jail still..."

Thank You For Your Cooperation

Two other men, absent from Beita during the Incident, volunteered that the army had destroyed their houses as well as Da'ud's. Muhammad 'Ali, an unemployed land surveyor with a degree in engineering, laughed after telling me he was thirty-eight. "I look older, don't I?" The ruins of his house were on the outskirts of the village, a mess of rubble and slabs of crumpled walls against a background of olive trees. 'Ali said he had nine children—five boys, four girls, ranging from fourteen and a half years to eight months—and one on the way. Sure enough, seven of the nine, playing under the trees, came running to meet us. They kissed 'Ali's hand and bowed their foreheads

to it four or five times in the traditional, strict Muslim way and then stood
wriggling their bare toes in the red earth while their father told me about the
demolition of his house.

He was in Ramallah on April 6 and the next day, when curfew hushed
the village. The day of the curfew, settlers came to the 'Ali house and banged
for a long time on the doors. 'Ali's wife hid with the children in one of the
bedrooms, covering the mouth of one crying baby with her hand. After what
seemed a very long time, the settlers left the house and the mother and
children crept out, making their way through the trees up the hillside into the
heart of the village. They had to run for awhile when the settlers spotted them
and fired some shots. When 'Ali returned from Ramallah, the couple decided
not to return to their house, but to stay the night with relatives. The next day
villagers rushed to tell them that soldiers had surrounded their house and
were probably about to demolish it. Running down the road the 'Alis
encountered an army checkpoint. 'Ali offered the soldiers his keys, pleading
that they should search the house; there was no reason for them to demolish
it. The soldiers ignored 'Ali's pleas and gave the couple five minutes to retrieve
what possessions they could from their house. Entering, they found most of
their furniture broken, food strewn on the floor, doors and windows
damaged. Then bulldozers destroyed the house and most of the family's
belongings. They also damaged the well and water cistern. 'Ali is not
permitted to rebuild on his land until the Israeli High Court issues a permit
for him to do so (this is an ordinary Israeli military proceeding and the
rebuilding permit can take years to be issued). He is also forbidden to clear
up the rubble or clean out his water cistern, which was filled with bricks and
dirt by the explosion. The family was never told why their house was
demolished.

Since 'Ali is an expert ("I have fourteen years of experience in my
profession," he told me), the villagers chose him to be their spokesman in
the unlikely event that the military authorities decided to compensate the
village for its losses. He had made blueprints of all the destroyed properties
and invited me to see them.

The 'Alis' temporary house was a moldering three-room stone affair
from the Turkish period. The pantry and makeshift privy were two small,
musty basement rooms with old-fashioned vaulted ceilings. The upstairs
room, about twelve by fifteen feet, contained a battered refrigerator, a small
double bed, a little drafting table, a metal cabinet and mattresses stacked in
the Arab fashion in shelves recessed in one wall.

I found my eyes fixing abstractedly on the purplish-gray bloom of the
drafting sheets 'Ali handed to me. An elegant tracery of black lines delineated
on this pretty paper what had once been rooms in Beita's demolished
buildings. A child brought glasses and a large container of the Palestinian-

produced, salty-sweet Royal Crown everyone was drinking at the time (the Unified National Leadership had urged a boycott of Israeli goods).

"It is nothing," 'Ali smiled and bowed slightly when I praised the quality and fastidiousness of his work. "I do it because it is my duty." It was hard to concentrate on what he was saying because of the heavy silence emanating from his wife. At the roadblock, she had told the soldiers she wanted the children to witness the demolition "so as to tell everyone about it until Doomsday." When portly 'Ali smiled and laughed, her face remained grim. In her ninth month of pregnancy, she was as small and thin as 'Ali was stout, her wrists and neck like sparrow bones at the sleeves and collar of her long dress. I got up to leave as soon as it was decently possible, saying that I would try to do what I could to publicize the village's tragedy. "Thank you," said 'Ali in his formal English, smiling and bowing again. "Thank you for your cooperation." The children lined up on the staircase for a photograph. When I flashed the camera, nine hands lifted, and nine index and third fingers all made the intifada victory sign.

Liberty or Death

Several Palestinian acquaintances said they felt Beita wasn't representative. "Too much," was one judgement. "Overdone by the press," another. According to Hafiz Barghuti, Beita was a monochrome study in suffering and victimization. Other villages were more militant. Hafiz offered to take me to fiery Qabatya where the collaborator had been killed after he had maddened a crowd of demonstrators by firing on them and killing a four-year-old with his Israeli-donated Uzi. In Qabatya, promised Hafiz, he could introduce me to a man whose hand had been permanently damaged by soldiers in a savage beating; to people whose crops had been destroyed by the army.

I took Barghuti up on his Qabatya offer several days later, but I was hardly prepared to abandon Beita. When I asked Taysir Da'ud whether Beita had been a traditionally "quiet" village before the Incident, he said with some irony, "We can say every village in Palestine was quiet. But what happens throughout Palestine influences us. There are writings on the walls, there are flags. The soldiers come every two or three weeks and order people to clean the walls." Beita was, in short, a West Bank Everyplace. In Da'ud's mind its tragedy didn't make it an exception, but a stunning example of intifada-period martyrdom. "The people here believe they are a symbol of Palestine," he said.

1936

Not far from Taysir Da'ud's mother-in-law's house is the house of an old peasant who claims his forebears established Beita 300 years ago. The *hajj*—a respectful term for a Muslim who has performed the pilgrimage to Mecca; the feminine form is *hajja*—turned out to be a thin, well-preserved old man with bright, shrewd brown eyes and a tanned face as deeply furrowed as a freshly-tilled field. He sat beside me on a mattress on the floor in a large, sunny, stone-floored room and described his experience of the thawra—the great revolt that began in 1936 and was finally crushed by the British three years later.

Beita was self-sufficient until the British Mandate, said the hajj, when young men began going to Haifa to work. They would stay away for a month or more, transport being so difficult at that time. There was only one family in Nablus with a car, and it traveled the road between Nablus and Hawwara, the village next to Beita. Everyone else before World War II used horses and donkeys to get around. That was the sort of place Beita had been at the time of the revolt.

The thawra, unlike the intifada, was an armed revolt. "We fought the British in the streets, in the mountains..." His eyes lit up with youthful fervor as he spoke, and the twenty-five men who collected in the room to hear the interview smiled with him in his enthusiasm. The tactic in those days was "hit and hide"—strike at the British, then retreat to caves in the hillsides or to hiding places in the villages. Was he willing to name people he had fought with? "That was a long time ago," said someone, laughing, "there's no danger in giving their names." As vividly as if he were recalling yesterday's events, the old man listed seven of his fallen comrades.

The general strike that began the thawra was different from the current strike: businesses were continuously closed. The people either sneaked food in or lived on stored goods like oil, bread, beans and lentils. "Generally, we are not like Westerners. We can live on very little, even on grass and wild plants." The British instituted a policy like Yitzhak Rabin's "Iron Fist," killing many leaders and crushing the revolt. Some of the old local leadership remained in 1948, but by then the thawra had long since become a memory. The next period of resistance in Beita, as in the West Bank generally, was the nationalist upsurge after Camp David. Arrests and imprisonments also ended this briefer period of militancy.

"*Inshallah* (God willing) this intifada won't be stopped," said a hefty younger man who sat next to the hajj. He was a programmer who had studied computer science in Amman and was only one course shy of his master's degree. He had worked for an American company in Dubai, but when he returned to live in Beita he could get work in Israel only as a cleaner in a hotel. "Because of such things," he said, "the intifada continues."

Return to the Land

Beita's first contribution to the uprising was the burning, at four in the morning on January 20, 1988, of the bus that had customarily taken Beita workers to their Israeli jobs. Soon after the bus was destroyed soldiers stormed into Beita, seized a group of men including Taysir Da'ud, took them to a crossroads, and beat them. After the bus-burning and before "the Incident" there were periodic confrontations with the army—the usual stone-throwing, the usual retaliatory chasings, beatings and jailings.

Like other villages I had visited since 1979, Beita was the kind of place where, after "incidents," people used to shrug and sigh, "But what can we do? This is our fate." The intifada put an end to that fatalism. Between my February and September visits to the West Bank, the character of the uprising had also changed. It had become a permanence in which history was divided into two parts: before the intifada and during. No one talked about "after." There was an in-it-for-the-long-haul, present-oriented pragmatism that precluded predictions. The intifada's continuous present had a less dramatic but more pervasive character than in February, when, for instance, I had seen barricades, or remnants of old barricades—piles of stones, rusty stove doors, anything that might stop the army's passage—everywhere. Now I didn't see very many barricades; clashes between the army and demonstrators didn't seem to be a daily occurrence, but took place mainly on the strike days called by the national leadership.

But another, invisible barricade had gone up between the people and Israel: a whole new grassroots civic government had displaced the Israeli military administration wherever possible. As far as I could tell, the "popular committees" were soviets that dealt with all areas of life, from trash disposal and public safety to health and education. By the time I arrived in September the committees had been banned by Israel and people weren't talking about them. But their existence could still be divined indirectly. During the interview with the old peasant, for instance, someone volunteered that people in Beita who had money donated it to people who didn't, adding that this was typical of the West Bank where people had been taking up collections for victims of military brutality. Popular committees had also been responsible for media work, including producing the wall posters announcing various points of the Unified National Leadership's program for any given period. The number and character of Beita's graffiti moved me to feel that their posting was organized rather than spontaneous. Whose idea, moreover, had it been to make the life-sized doll representing the guerrilla fighter? Without some organization, he wouldn't have existed. He hung against an electricity pylon near Taysir Da'ud's store, now a tattered remnant of his former self. Before Israeli soldiers had disfigured him, he had been a complete resistance fighter with kaffiya, shoes, a full outfit of clothing and a Palestinian flag.

Other signs of the organized intifada in Beita: the chickens, which scurried and pecked freely everywhere. "Free-running chickens," joked a man who had been in the crowd at the old peasant's house, and then he explained: "They're healthier that way." The Unified National Leadership had urged the population to become self-sufficient in food production, and the process seemed well underway in Beita. "Before the intifada," said the organic poultry advocate, "I used to buy eggs. But now I have my own chickens, and I even sell eggs." In a hay-strewn shed near the hajj's house was the new farmer's wealth: several victory goats, a victory cow and the omnipresent victory chickens. The organic farmer was actually a former accountant. "The shaking off" has also meant a shaking-up of Palestinian society in which members of the professional elites have been forced by necessity back to the land and into daily contact with the peasantry and manual laborers. "Photograph?" the ex-accountant volunteered, posing under the cow and pretending to pull at its udders. Then he posed next to one of the goats, both arms affectionately around its neck, his head pressed against its muzzle. Amidst general laughter and a showing of V-signs I flashed a photograph, this time not of Beita's sorrow, but of its triumph.

The Happiest Couple in the Village

Hafiz had other journalistic fish to fry besides the ones he could catch while translating for me. On his departure I found Nadia, a twenty-five-year-old British-educated Palestinian with a charming Cockney accent who was working as a part-time reporter for Agence France Presse. I had purposely looked for a woman to be my interpreter: introduced by a man, one has access only to men, since women won't talk intimately in men's presence.

Women were on my mind throughout my visits to Beita and its more militant northern neighbor, Qabatya. A friend had jubilantly announced to me before my trips to the two villages that the intifada had started women's liberation in the West Bank. Women, he said, were heading popular committees. So many thousands of men had been imprisoned that the communities now looked to women for real leadership that went far beyond the usual maternal, sororal and filial acts of courage.

Maybe this liberation was taking effect in refugee camps and towns, but as far as I could tell the great "shaking off" hadn't shaken up the situation of women in the northern Muslim villages at all. Staying with a Qabatya family of nine brothers and their wives and mother, I was, as usual, an honorary man—as was Nadia, who got asked several times if she was truly "an Arab like us." We were waited on by the brothers' mother and their wives, who retreated to the kitchen when we took our meals with the men. At night one of the wives and her sister crept in to talk with us. "How old are you?" they asked me. "Are you married? Do you have children?" There was a silence, then a chorus of "What a shame! What a shame!" when I said I had a husband but no children. And still they were fascinated by Nadia and me: how strange to travel by oneself! And how wonderful, even if frightening... "Poor thing," murmured Nadia about the sister after the women had left. "She is twenty-nine but still not married. She will stay here the rest of her life looking after her nieces and nephews."

I kept thinking about those women, and also about Munira. How would she emerge from her time in prison? "Just a housewife" before, it was certain she would come out with far more political sophistication. And then...? In February I had been in a women's demonstration in a village to Beita's south, with peasant women like Munira. In a hard, freezing rain they marched through pools of icy water chanting slogans and singing nationalist songs. With women like them in the larger town, el-Bireh, I had taken shelter in an apartment after the army closed in on their demonstration: "And if the army breaks in here what's the worst they can do to us?" shrugged one woman after hugging me to calm my fears. She lit a cigarette nonchalantly: "Perhaps they beat us, then they leave..."

In Beita I had also met Maryam, the village kindergarten teacher. She lived in a little stone house near the Beita Charitable Society, which housed the kindergarten as well as a tiny clinic and rooms for classes in literacy, maternal health and child health. There is a garden in front of Maryam's house; the privy is out back. Against the garden's front wall is the rusted-out hulk of a Volkswagen Beetle, where a small flock of victory chickens clucks and mutters. Pots of flowers cluster on the low balustrades of the little porch. On the walls of a tiny living room are the usual glories: a diploma and a photograph of the graduate, Maryam's husband, Walid. And then, posters featuring soccer players—Walid used to head a Beita sports society—and a round straw tray woven in the colors of the Palestinian flag. Inside a frame that looks like cardboard covered with tinfoil are photographs of Maryam and Walid at their wedding, with a smaller oval photograph of their four-year-old son, Bashir, when he was an infant. There is also a large colored Keane-like poster featuring a greeneyed woman with streaming, platinum-blond hair and exaggeratedly slanting blue eyes, holding a blue-eyed Persian cat.

Maryam herself has big, dark eyes: a quiet little twenty-seven-year-old woman with a round face and olive skin. Bashir looks like her. She wore the conventional long skirt, long-sleeved, high-necked blouse, high heels and wimple-like scarf, though her hair turned out to be short when she took the scarf off in the house. She cooked lunch and then she talked. "We believe, as a younger generation, that women have our role to play in the intifada. But most of the women here don't participate. There is a lot of pressure from our families." Maryam's sister-in-law, Jinan, kept getting up to chase after her own toddler and called back to me over her shoulder, "Some families prefer the women to be in the kitchen instead of getting educated, and this is wrong." When she sat down she said that with a year to go toward her high school diploma, she had married, vowing to finish her studies. But she and her husband moved into a single room in a house with fifteen people. After three days of trying to study in that chaos, Jinan gave up. Sixteen-year-old Mikhaya, Jinan's sister, sat quietly throughout most of the conversation. She was tall and dark-haired, with very pale skin, hazel eyes and a serious expression. Maryam told me proudly that Mikhaya was first in her class. So would she go on to university? "I only wish..." murmured Mikhaya. "But I don't think my family..." "They won't let you?" "You see, the high school is mixed, boys and girls, and they are against that. So I might not even finish high school. And then there are my brothers to consider. Their education comes first."

"We talk about this a lot," Maryam told me. Then she turned to Mikhaya: "It's your fault. You let them get used to governing you. Now, at your age, you have to start from zero. With me it didn't start from zero. I started refusing what they wanted when I was very young, and I succeeded. I went on hunger strike." "How long?" I asked in amazement. Maryam shrugged: "Until they saw it was serious. I would starve if they didn't give in. And they did."

At an early age, the rebel Maryam was promised in marriage to her cousin. She rejected that destiny as well. Because she didn't love the cousin, she said she would never marry him. Her father relented, knowing from her earlier revolt that she meant business. He suggested a number of alternate candidates, among them the handsome head of Beita's sport club, the serious young Walid. "I don't mind," said Maryam diffidently when her father lighted on him. The couple married a year later: Maryam took out the wedding announcements shyly and showed them to me and Nadia. One day, six months after the wedding, the men from Israeli security came for Walid. "We'll return him to you today," the security men assured Maryam, who was pregnant at the time. Instead, Walid was jailed, put on trial for membership in one of the illegal Palestinian organizations and sentenced to fourteen years in prison. The framed wedding and baby photographs are his work: the tinfoil turned out to be the insides of toothpaste tubes, some of the only art material available to Walid in Nafha prison near Beersheba. The belt woven out of the outsides of coffee bags, a present for Maryam, is also his creation. She modeled the belt for us, and then started weeping silently. "We were the happiest couple in the village," she said, tears coursing down her cheeks.

In intifada weddings, the men don't do the dabka, the line dance adopted as the hora by Jewish immigrants to Palestine. Neither do the women shimmy for hours as they do in normal times, vying with each other for sensuality and grace. There are no drums, there is no oud, no singing, no clapping. The intifada wedding is a silent affair because this is a time of mourning for the hundreds of martyrs who have died at the hands of the Israeli army.

Nadia and I were invited to the beginning of such a wedding in the village, the part where the bride sits on her dais surrounded by all the village women. The Beita bride was dressed in white tulle, a veil over her face. She clutched a corsage of red carnations and sat very still while the village women sat around in front of her on wood chairs, fanning themselves. A few little flower girls with their rouged cheeks and eyes ringed with kohl mingled with other children who came up to Nadia and me, touching our notebooks wonderingly. After a while the grandfather came in—none other than the old hajj. With other male relatives, he gave the customary pre-wedding money to the bride. Because she is to be torn from her father's family and enter her husband's, a Palestinian bride is supposed to cry before her wedding. This particular bride had been stifling yawns and embarrassed smiles, and now she dabbed dutifully at dry eyes. In a hot press of female bodies we were carried down the narrow stone stairs of the house and out into the bright sunlight where cars waited to transport the bridal party to the groom's village. An old woman with a tattooed lip grabbed my elbow and steered me to the front of the first car: "Photograph!" she commanded, so I took the bride from several angles.

Had the marriage been arranged? Had it been a love match? There was no time to ask such questions, and in any case the love-match question was a forbidden one: love before marriage is frowned on in villages like Beita. The mere knowledge that a couple has fallen in love before the wedding is enough, one village woman told me, to ruin a woman's reputation forever.

I drove one last time to the village's high point. Some boys were throwing stones across a steep drop just beyond the mosque where the fateful announcement about the settlers had issued on April 6. They were calling out something about the *jaysh,* the army. "Where is the army?" I asked playfully, the way adults do when they want to enter into a children's game. A barefoot thirteen-year-old with tawny, dusty hair and blue eyes looked at me pity:ngly. "There is no army," he replied, "we're just training. We stockpile stones. Then we throw them." I thought of a boy the same age I had seen in a hospital in February. He had been dark, with glossy crow's-wing black hair, and a big bandage around his middle. He, too, had been throwing stones in the West Bank refugee camp of Shu'fat and had been shot in the back. The bullet fragmented, spraying his small intestines with shrapnel. He had been in a demonstration, one of the barricade-builders: "We didn't want the soldiers to follow us," he told me. "When they did, we started throwing stones." Then he made a slingshot gesture and grinned. "Are you afraid?" I asked him. "No," he replied, "they are human, like me."

"Are you afraid of the soldiers?" I now asked. The Beita trainee tossed back his head dismissively. He had seen his first soldier at four; at six he had begun training. "But from the beginning of the intifada, I really began throwing stones," he explained. If schools had been open he would just be entering junior high. "All the people in this village are heroes," volunteered another, smaller boy. How long would the intifada last? "God knows! Until liberation!" answered the blond boy in a grown-up voice in which I heard both resignation and defiance.

## Part 3

Prelude to the Uprising

Children Bearing Rocks

With stones in their hands,
they defy the world
and come to us like good tidings.
They burst with anger and love, and they fall
while we remain a herd of polar bears:
a body armored against weather.

Like mussels we sit in cafes,
one hunts for a business venture
one for another billion
and a fourth wife
and breasts polished by civilization.
One stalks London for a lofty mansion
one traffics in arms
one seeks revenge in nightclubs
one plots for a throne, a private army,
and a princedom.

Ah, generation of betrayal,
of surrogate and indecent men,
generation of leftovers,
we'll be swept away—
never mind the slow pace of history—
by children bearing rocks.

—Nizar Qabbani

## Chapter 7

Palestine and the Arab-Israeli Conflict for Beginners

Lisa Hajjar, Mouin Rabbani and Joel Beinin

After World War I, the League of Nations (controlled by the leading colonial powers of the time, Britain and France) carved up the territories of the defeated Ottoman Empire. The territory now comprising Israel, the West Bank, the Gaza Strip and Jordan was granted to Great Britain as a "mandate" (a quasi-colonial form of administration). In 1922, Britain established the principality of Transjordan (east of the Jordan River), still part of its mandate but administratively distinct from Palestine.

When Britain assumed control of Palestine, over 90 percent of its population was Arab. A small indigenous Jewish population had lived there for generations, and a newer, politicized community linked to the Zionist movement had begun to immigrate to Palestine in the 1880s.

During World War I, Britain had made promises to Arab leaders for an independent Arab state that would include Palestine (the Hussein-McMahon correspondence), and to the Zionists for the establishment of a Jewish national home in Palestine (the Balfour Declaration). These commitments conflicted with each other as well as with Britain's intent to retain control over Palestine.

European Jewish immigration increased dramatically after Hitler's rise to power in 1933, leading to accelerated land purchases and new Jewish settlements. Palestinian resistance to British control and Zionist settlement climaxed with the Arab revolt of 1936-39, which was suppressed by the British army with the help of Zionist militias and the complicity of the Arab regimes.

Following World War II, Britain was unable to maintain control over Palestine and turned the problem over to the United Nations. The United Nations decided that the only means of resolving the escalating conflict between Jews and Arabs was to partition the land into two states. Although

Jews constituted only one-third of the population and owned less than 7 percent of the land, the UN partition plan assigned 55 percent of Palestine's territory to the Jewish state. The Palestinian leadership rejected partition as unjust and illegitimate, and civil war broke out between Arabs and Jews. By the time the British withdrawal had been completed, Palestinian resistance had been largely broken. British evacuation and the proclamation by Zionist leaders of the State of Israel on May 15, 1948 prompted military intervention by the neighboring Arab states, precipitating the first Arab-Israeli war.

As a result of the war, historic Palestine was divided into three parts. The 1949 armistice agreements gave Israel control over 77 percent of the territory of mandate Palestine. Jordan occupied and annexed East Jerusalem and the hill country of central Palestine, henceforth known as the "West Bank" of the Jordan River. (The Jordanian government issued a decree in 1950 which made it illegal to use the term "Palestine" to refer to this area. When Israel conquered this territory in 1967, it stopped using the term West Bank and instead refers to the area by its Biblical names, "Judea" and "Samaria.") Egypt took "temporary" control of the coastal plain around the city of Gaza, which has come to be known as the Gaza Strip. The Palestinian Arab state provided for in the UN partition plan was never established.

About 700,000 Palestinians—about one-half of the Arab inhabitants of Palestine—were displaced from their homes as a result of the 1948-49 war. During and after the fighting, Israel destroyed over 350 Arab villages inside the "Green Line" (Israel's borders from 1949 until 1967) and refused to allow Palestinian refugees to return to their homes.

Zionism

Zionism is a modern political movement based on the proposition that Jews all over the world constitute a single nationality and that the only solution to anti-Semitism is the concentration of as many Jews as possible in Palestine and the establishment of a Jewish state there. Zionism gained adherents among Jews and support from Western public opinion as a consequence of the murderous anti-Semitic pogroms of Eastern Europe and later the Nazi holocaust. Not all Jews are Zionists, although today Zionism in one form or another is embraced by a large majority of Jews. Zionism drew on traditional Jewish religious attachment to Jerusalem and parts of Palestine (traditionally referred to as Eretz Yisra'el, or the Land of Israel) but is in essence a modern political ideology, influenced by the nationalist movements of Eastern Europe and by nineteenth-century colonial attitudes.

The Land

The ongoing dispute in the Middle East between Jews and Arabs—more accurately, between Israel and the Palestinians—is not a religious conflict; it is essentially a struggle over land. For the Palestinians, this is their historic homeland, where they have lived for centuries. The Zionists base their claim to Palestine on the Biblical promise to Abraham and his descendants (Genesis 17:8), on the historic connection between the Land of Israel and the Jewish people, and/or on the desperate need for a Jewish homeland as a haven from European anti-Semitism.

Palestine is a small territory—approximately 10,000 square miles, about the size of Maryland. The competing claims to it are not reconcilable if one or the other party exercises complete sovereignty over the total territory. Partition of the land has therefore been one proposal for resolving the issue. Although few Palestinians accept the justice of the Zionist claim in principle, many now accept the existence of Israel. But they insist that an independent Palestinian state be created alongside Israel, in the West Bank and Gaza, in which they can exercise their right to self-determination. Israeli Jews are divided over the fate of the West Bank and Gaza, the Palestinian territories which Israel occupied in 1967. Some favor annexation, while others would be willing to relinquish control over some or all of those territories. At the present time, only a minority of Israeli Jews would agree to an independent Palestinian state in the West Bank and Gaza.

The June 1967 War

In June 1967 Israel decisively and quickly defeated the Egyptian, Syrian and Jordanian armies. By the end of the war, Israel had captured the remainder of mandate Palestine, as well as the Sinai Peninsula from Egypt and the Golan Heights from Syria. The newly captured parts of former mandate Palestine, known since 1948 as the West Bank and the Gaza Strip, have since 1967 often been referred to as "the occupied territories." The war established Israel as the dominant regional military power. The defeat discredited the Arab regimes, especially the radical Arab nationalism represented by Egyptian President Nasser and the Ba'th parties of Syria and Iraq. By contrast, the Palestinian national movement, which had been relatively quiescent in the post-1948 period, emerged as a major political factor after 1967 in the form of the political and guerrilla groups that make up the Palestine Liberation Organization (PLO).

The Occupied Territories

Prior to 1948, neither the West Bank nor the Gaza Strip had constituted separate geographical units. Their distinctness developed as a result of the partition of Palestine that led to the creation of a Jewish state. Since the 1967 war, Israel has continued to occupy the West Bank and the Gaza Strip. Israel withdrew from the Sinai during 1979-82, as required by its peace treaty with Egypt, but annexed the Golan Heights in 1981. In violation of international law, Israel has confiscated over 52 percent of the land in West Bank and 30 percent of the Gaza Strip for military use or for settlement by Jewish civilians.

The Israeli government and various Zionist institutions have spent more than $1.5 billion to settle Jews in the occupied territories. There are today about 65,000 Jewish settlers in some 120 settlements in the West Bank, and a similar number of Jews living in new Jewish neighborhoods in and around East Jerusalem. There are some 2,500 Jewish settlers in Gaza, 0.4 percent of the total Gaza population. These Jewish settlers consume nineteen times more water per capita than the Palestinians in Gaza. The settler-to-land ratio in Gaza averages 2.6 acres of land per capita, as compared to .006 acres per capita for Palestinians. The Gaza Strip, an area just twenty-eight miles long and five miles wide, has a population density of 3,754 people per square mile, among the highest in the world.

Israel spent $240 million on services and development projects for Palestinians in the occupied territories in 1987 but collected $393 million in taxes. In the twenty years of Israeli rule from 1967-87, residents paid Israel a net "occupation tax" of $800 million, two and a half times as much as the entire Israeli government investment directed at Palestinians in the territories over that period.

Before the intifada, some 100,000 Palestinians from the occupied territories worked in Israel, mostly in menial, low-paying jobs. Industrial production in all the occupied territories totaled some $85 million—less than that of one medium-sized Israeli firm.

Jerusalem

According to the UN partition plan, Jerusalem and its environs were to become an international zone, independent of both the proposed Jewish state and the Palestinian Arab state. In the 1948-49 war, Israel took control of the western part of Jerusalem, while Jordan held the eastern part, including the old walled city containing important Jewish, Muslim and Christian religious sites. The 1949 armistice line cut the city in two. In June 1967 Israel captured East Jerusalem and immediately annexed it. Israel reaffirmed its annexation of East Jerusalem in 1981.

Israel regards Jerusalem as its capital and rejects any negotiations over its political future. Arabs consider East Jerusalem part of occupied Palestinian territory and regard its future as an essential component of any negotiated settlement.

Palestinians

This term today refers to the Arabs, both Christian and Muslim, who have lived in Palestine for centuries. The creation of Israel entailed the destruction of Palestinian Arab society, dispersing hundreds of thousands of Palestinians to lives of exile. Today there are over five million Palestinians worldwide. About 40 percent of them—nearly 2.2 million Palestinians—still live within historic Palestine, under Israeli control. About 650,000 of them are citizens of Israel, living inside its pre-1967 borders; about 960,000 live in the West Bank (including 125,000 in East Jerusalem) and 550,000 in the Gaza Strip. The Israeli government expects the number of Palestinians in the West Bank and Gaza Strip to reach two million within fifteen years.

Only 15 percent of the West Bank Palestinians are refugees; even fewer live in refugee camps. In contrast, refugees into the Gaza Strip outnumbered inhabitants by three to one in 1948. Almost 70 percent of Gaza's inhabitants have been living in refugee camps ever since.

The largest Palestinian diaspora community, approximately 1.3 million, is in Jordan. Lebanon, Syria and Kuwait also have large Palestinian populations. Jordan is the only Arab state to have granted the Palestinians citizenship. Palestinians living in the other Arab states generally do not have the same rights as the citizens of those states.

Although many Palestinians still live in refugee camps and slums, others have become economically successful. Palestinians now have the highest per capita rate of university graduates in the Arab world. Their diaspora experience has contributed to a high level of politicization among Palestinians, from the camps to the universities.

Since 1948, Israel has consistently refused to acknowledge Palestinian national rights or to accept the Palestinians as an equal and independent party in any negotiations to end the conflict. It unequivocally rejects negotiations with the recognized leadership of the Palestinian people, the PLO, insisting instead on dealing only with Jordan and other Arab states, and rejects outright the establishment of an independent Palestinian state.

Palestine Liberation Organization

The PLO was established in 1964 by the Arab League in an effort to pre-empt the emergence of an independent Palestinian movement and control Palestinian action. The Arab defeat in the 1967 war enabled the Palestinians to take over the PLO and gain some independence from the Arab regimes.

The PLO is an umbrella organization that includes different political and guerrilla organizations with varying ideological orientations. Yasir Arafat heads Fatah, the largest group, and has been PLO chairman since 1969. The other major PLO groups are the Popular Front for the Liberation of Palestine (PFLP), the Democratic Front for the Liberation of Palestine (DFLP) and, in the occupied territories, the Palestine Communist Party (PCP). Despite continuing rifts between the various components of the PLO, the overwhelming majority of Palestinians regard the PLO as their sole legitimate representative.

Resolution 242

After the conclusion of the 1967 war, the UN Security Council adopted Resolution 242, which calls for Israeli withdrawal from the territories seized in the war and the right of all states in the area to peaceful existence within secure and recognized boundaries. There is a difference in the grammatical construction of the French and English texts of Resolution 242, both of which are official according to the United Nations. The French version calls on Israel to withdraw "from the territories" occupied in the 1967 war, whereas the English version says "from territories," which Israel (backed by the United States) interprets to mean *some* but not *all* territories. Hard-line Israelis argue that Israeli withdrawal from the Sinai has already satisfied the stipulation of withdrawal "from territories" and that no further territorial concessions are therefore necessary.

For many years the Palestinians rejected Resolution 242 because it lacks any recognition of the Palestinians' right to self-determination or of their right to return to their homeland. The only reference to the Palestinians is the call for "a just settlement of the refugee problem." Because it calls for the recognition of "every state in the area," the resolution would entail unilateral Palestinian recognition of Israel without a reciprocal recognition of Palestinian national rights.

Today the leadership of the PLO is clearly prepared to recognize Israel and negotiate with it. As the political weight of Palestinians on the "inside" has grown, especially since the intifada, Palestinian unity around this key point has correspondingly increased. This was reflected in the declaration of independence and the political statement of the November 1988 session of the Palestine National Council, which formally endorsed Resolution 242 while affirming Palestinian national rights, as well as in PLO chairman Yasir Arafat's address to the UN General Assembly in Geneva in December 1988. The PLO has thereby accepted the "two-state solution" to the Palestine question, that is, the partition of Palestine between Israel and an independent Palestinian state.

The October 1973 War

After coming to power in late 1970, President Anwar Sadat of Egypt indicated to the United States that he was willing to negotiate with Israel to resolve the conflict in exchange for Egyptian territory lost in 1967. When these overtures were ignored by Washington and Tel Aviv, Egypt and Syria launched a coordinated attack in October 1973 against Israeli forces occupying the Sinai and the Golan Heights. The crisis prompted US political intervention, along with sharply increased military aid to Israel. US Secretary of State Henry Kissinger's shuttle diplomacy brought about limited disengagement agreements in the Sinai and Golan. But by late 1975 these efforts had exhausted their potential, and no comprehensive settlement was in sight.

Due to stalled efforts to convene an international peace conference to which all parties to the dispute would be invited, Sadat decided in late 1977 that Egypt should break the stalemate by dealing separately with Israel under US auspices. His visit to Jerusalem on November 19, 1977 began what came to be known as the "Camp David process."

Camp David

In September 1978 President Jimmy Carter invited Sadat and Israeli Prime Minister Menachem Begin to the Camp David presidential retreat. They worked out two agreements: a framework for peace between Egypt and Israel, and a general framework for resolution of the Middle East conflict— i.e., the Palestinian question. This latter agreement proposed to grant autonomy to the Palestinians in the West Bank and the Gaza Strip, to install a local administration for a five-year interim period, and to decide the ultimate status of the territories after that period.

Only the Egyptian-Israeli part of the Camp David agreement was ever implemented. The Palestinians and other Arab states rejected the autonomy concept as contrary to self-determination, and Israel immediately sabotaged negotiations by continuing to confiscate Palestinian lands and build new settlements.

As a result of Camp David, Egypt became estranged from the other Arab nations. Only after Sadat's assassination did Egypt begin gradually to resume ties with the other Arab states. Egypt's separate peace enabled Israel to invade Lebanon in 1982 without fear of Egyptian intervention.

Oppression and Resistance

From 1967 to 1982, Israel's military government demolished 1,338 Palestinian homes on the West Bank. Over this period, more than 300,000 Palestinians were detained without trial for various periods by Israeli security forces. Between 1968 and 1983, according to Israeli government figures, Israeli forces killed ninety-two Palestinians in the West Bank, while West Bank Palestinians killed twenty-two Israeli soldiers and fourteen Israeli civilians. Armed attacks by West Bank Palestinians killed two Israelis between April 1986 and May 1987. During that period, Israeli forces killed twenty-two Palestinians.

In the occupied territories it is illegal to fly the Palestinian flag, publish or possess "subversive" literature, or hold a press conference without permission. One Israeli military order in the West Bank makes it illegal for Palestinians to pick and sell wild thyme, to protect an Israeli family's monopoly over the herb's production.

Although the intifada is unprecedented in scope, duration and intensity, Palestinian resistance to Israeli occupation has been a constant feature of political life in the West Bank and Gaza Strip since 1967. The number of Palestinian protests in the territories averaged 500 per year during 1977-82. Since 1982, protests have averaged between 3,000 and 4,400 a year. Among the milestones in the development of the Palestinian struggle inside the occupied territories are:

—The National Charter of the West Bank for the Current Phase, October 4, 1967. This document issued by 129 prominent West Bank residents rejected the occupation, particularly the annexation of East Jerusalem, and demanded a return to Arab sovereignty.

—General Strike of June 5, 1969. This strike was held on the second anniversary of the June 1967 war and observed throughout the West Bank; Israel deported nine strike leaders.

—Gaza, 1968-71. Armed with weapons left behind by retreating Egyptian troops in 1967, Palestinian guerrilla cells attacked Israeli forces almost daily and controlled the refugee camps by night. General Ariel Sharon's pacification campaign removed thousands of suspects' families to detention camps in the Sinai, deported additional hundreds to Jordan, imposed week-long curfews during house-to-house searches, and demolished entire sections of refugee camps to allow easy access for Israeli armored vehicles.

—Gaza, September-November 1972. Riots in Shati' (Beach) Camp spread throughout the Gaza Strip and continued sporadically throughout the fall.

—Palestine National Front, 1973-78. Formed in August 1973, this clandestine umbrella organization coordinated political activity in its role as an autonomous West Bank and Gaza affiliate of the PLO. Between the end of the 1973 October war and the 1976 West Bank municipal elections, the PNF organized a series of strikes and demonstrations, often around events such as Yasir Arafat's 1974 UN appearance. These engulfed the entire West Bank and Gaza Strip for weeks at a time, sometimes spilling across the Green Line into Israel and acquiring many characteristics of the current uprising. Then Prime Minister Rabin and Defense Minister Peres resorted to harsh repression: shootings (thirty dead and hundreds wounded in the first six months of 1976 alone), deportations, administrative detentions, house demolitions, extended curfews and other forms of collective punishment. The PNF also led the fight against Jordanian and Israeli influence in West Bank and Gaza politics during the PLO's bid for diplomatic recognition in the mid-1970s. By the time it was declared illegal in October 1978, the PNF had largely been absorbed into the National Guidance Committee (NGC).

—Land Day, March 30, 1976. Tens of thousands of Palestinian citizens of Israel took to the streets during a general strike to protest continuing land confiscations. Israeli forces shot and killed six demonstrators. Land Day has since been commemorated annually by Palestinians in Israel and the occupied territories.

—Municipal Elections, April 1976. Counting on a nationalist boycott to help install a counterweight to the PLO, Prime Minister Rabin called for municipal elections in the West Bank on April 12, 1976. The PNF fielded candidates in every locality and won a resounding victory. Despite widespread Israeli interference, including the deportation of some nationalist candidates, PNF slates captured eighteen of the twenty-four city councils, most by overwhelming margins, and won in almost all the larger cities. Over the next few years the military government deposed and/or deported the nationalist mayors one after another, put some under town arrest, and dissolved PNF-dominated city councils. On June 2, 1980, bomb attacks by

Jewish extremists maimed Nablus Mayor Bassam Shak'a and Ramallah Mayor Karim Khalaf.

—National Guidance Committee, 1978-82. This successor organization to the PNF grew out of a series of October 1978 public meetings to devise strategies for confronting the Camp David Accords. Headed by a committee of twenty-two leaders of unions and professional associations and municipal officials, the NGC spearheaded Palestinian resistance to Camp David and coordinated opposition to the Israeli-controlled "Village Leagues" and the "Civil Administration" set up during the Begin years. The NGC's role was predominantly a public one, supporting PLO participation in an eventual peace settlement. Israel responded with deportations, arrests and heavy press censorship. The expulsion of the mayors of Hebron and Halhul in May 1980, along with the bomb attacks against the other mayors one month later, dealt a severe blow to the Committee. When the NGC was outlawed in May 1982, it had already lost much of its effectiveness.

—Revolt against the Civil Administration, 1981-82. An intense round of strikes and protests broke out in November 1981 against the Begin/Sharon Civil Administration. After a brief lull, they erupted anew in the spring of 1982 with similar ferocity. Schools and university campuses were key battlegrounds; many students were killed or seriously wounded by army gunfire. This intense repression, which included large numbers of arrests, beatings and house demolitions, partly accounts for the relative quiet in the occupied territories that attended the 1982 Israeli invasion of Lebanon.

—Resistance to the "Iron Fist," 1985-87. A new round of protest in late 1984 featured spontaneous individual attacks on Israeli soldiers and settlers, especially in Gaza, Hebron and Nablus. Israeli mobs lynched several Palestinians on both sides of the Green Line. On August 4, 1985, Rabin announced the "iron fist" policy. In the next month alone, Israeli forces put sixty-two Palestinians under administrative detention (imprisonment without charges or trial), deported at least a dozen more and killed five. Several newspapers were permanently closed. Over the next two years, the military regime issued hundreds of administrative detention orders, demolished well over 100 homes, and repeatedly closed schools and universities. More than twenty Palestinians were killed and many more wounded in demonstrations, which were frequent and particularly intense during late 1986 and the spring of 1987. Once again university campuses and large towns became the focus of an escalating spiral of resistance culminating in the uprising, which began in December 1987.

Future Prospects

With the intifada, Palestinians in the occupied territories have gone beyond a situation in which political directives came from the Palestinian leadership in exile. A new leadership has emerged, aligned with the PLO but reflecting the experiences and outlook of a new generation of Palestinians who have grown up under Israeli occupation. This shift was reflected in the decisions of the November 1988 Palestine National Council meeting in Algiers, which clearly stated the Palestinian national movement's acceptance of the two-state solution. This in turn opened the way for the establishment of US contacts with the PLO and signals the opening of a new period of efforts to achieve a political settlement.

The ability of the Palestinians in the occupied territories to sustain a state of insurrection while developing new forms of mobilization and organization has demolished the status quo. While the intifada has varied in intensity and gone through different stages during its first year, it has demonstrated that the Palestinians are united, determined and capable of continuing their struggle until they achieve their national rights.

## Chapter 8

The Palestinian People: Twenty-two Years After 1967

Rashid Khalidi

However difficult the current situation of the Palestinian people may appear, it is revealing to compare it with the situation that prevailed in the wake of the June War. For while many of the problems the Palestinians face today have remained more or less constant since then, others were undreamed of in 1967. In the interim, there have been a number of fundamental changes whose significance gives us a proper perspective on these twenty-two years. It is, moreover, possible in this light to appraise both the achievements and the setbacks of the Palestinian national movement headed by the PLO.

Many basic problems the Palestinian people face today are essentially similar to those of 1967. The dominant element of the Israeli establishment still rejects the proposition that the Palestinians are a people who have the inalienable right of self-determination in their own homeland and the right to return to it. This rejection is still sustained by the support of the United States, which was limited but significant in 1967 and since then has grown lavish and unstinting. The Palestinians still have major difficulties with their Arab environment also. These difficulties involve both the unwillingness of most Arab regimes to make support for the Palestinians a central element in their relations with the United States and Israel, and bilateral issues having to do with the affairs of the Palestinian diaspora.

The new problems are legion. They include those growing from the 1967 occupation of the remainder of Palestine and the expulsion of additional thousands of Palestinians from their homeland. In a sense, once these territories had been occupied by Israel in 1967 and their former Jordanian and Egyptian administrations thereby terminated, their fate and that of their inhabitants became the responsibility of the Palestinians themselves. This new reality was formally consecrated when Jordan acquiesced in the 1974

Rabat summit's recognition of the PLO as sole legitimate representative of the Palestinian people. It was solidified in practice when the Palestinian uprising finally settled the question of Palestinian representation decisively in favor of the PLO and imposed upon King Hussein the decision to sever links between Jordan and the West Bank in July 1988.

Other new problems, particularly those with Jordan, Lebanon, Syria and Egypt, have been largely a function of the PLO's actions in the years after 1967 and the resulting contradictions with the strategies of these states. Before 1974 the PLO paid a price in inter-Arab terms for its opposition to proposals (like the Rogers Plan) which were based on UN Security Council Resolution 242 and its insistence on the total liberation of all of Palestine. After 1974 it paid for its insistence on an independent Palestinian voice in the process of negotiating a settlement and for its willingness to compromise on ultimate Palestinian goals by accepting a Palestinian state in the West Bank and Gaza Strip. Frequently opposed before 1974 by Egypt and Jordan, the PLO alienated Syria, Iraq and Libya with its new more moderate line after 1974.

Given the existence of these and other problems, what major changes have taken place over the last twenty-two years, and how do they help us to understand the PLO's record during that time? Tempting though it would be to concentrate on the important political changes which have taken place over these two decades, they have been examined elsewhere,[1] and so the main focus will instead be on less well-known structural changes which have affected the Palestinians during this period.

If we look at the core countries of the Middle East, perhaps the most important transformation to be noted is that which has affected the Palestinian people. Today that term sounds normal and natural, and the existence of the Palestinian people is contested only by a lunatic fringe. In 1967, however, it was arguably the case that the adjective Palestinian, if used at all, was utilized primarily as a modifier for "refugees," and that this was the context in which the Palestinians were best known. The importance of this semantic point, and the extent of the change since that time, can be illustrated by Golda Meir's now-infamous 1968 statement that "there are no Palestinians," which set the tone for two decades of ideological warfare against the Palestinian people.

It is not only in daily usage and in the media that the Palestinians have established themselves. In the fields of diplomacy and international law, there now exist alternate views of the core of the problem, and other prescriptions for dealing with it than those consecrated in Resolution 242. This document, which refers to the Palestinians only in terms of "a just resolution of the refugee problem," reflects the balance of power in 1967. Since that time there have been several UN General Assembly resolutions, notably GA 3236, and statements by other multilateral bodies, such as the

European Community's 1982 Venice Declaration, which treat the Palestinians as a people with a legitimate right to national self-determination.

This shift in international attitudes was positively affected by the evolution of Palestinian goals since 1967. These changed from the 1969 aim of a "secular democratic state" in all of Palestine, clearly implying the dissolution of Israel, to the 1974 provisional program's call for a "national authority" in part of Palestine, implying a Palestinian state alongside Israel, to the explicit goal of a Palestinian state alongside Israel emerging from negotiations on the basis of Security Council resolutions 242 and 338, embraced by the nineteenth Palestine National Council (PNC) meeting in Algiers in November 1988. Although the two states with the most power to affect regional outcomes, the United States and Israel, stubbornly refuse to accept the reality and the significance of such shifts, it is nevertheless noteworthy that while in the wake of the 1967 war they were able to muster widespread international support for their position, they are now almost entirely isolated on this issue.

A precondition for any achievements on the levels of international legality and world public opinion was that the Palestinians themselves change the universally held image of them as refugees. And for this image to change, it was necessary not just for the Palestinians to act but also to mobilize their people and to change their view of themselves. While in the self-contained world of the official US position—as reflected in Shultz's reasoning for his refusal to allow Yasir Arafat to address the UN General Assembly in November 1988—the Palestinians have only exchanged the pitiful image of the refugee for the sinister one of the "terrorist," there has in fact been a wholesale mobilization of Palestinians and a radical change in the Palestinian self-view over the past two decades. In the wake of the uprising which began in December 1987, it appears that this new self-image is beginning to be reflected in the US media.

This transformation of the Palestinian self-view may be the most important change in the contours of the Palestine question since 1967. The only other change in that period with the same fundamental implications for the nature of the conflict has taken place within Israel itself, where profound and sustained questioning of some of the basic ideological tenets of the Zionist enterprise has been growing in intensity, particularly since the 1982 invasion of Lebanon. This has manifested itself in a growing number of Israelis refusing to serve in the occupied territories and in Lebanon, the publication by Israelis of revisionist scholarship which has shattered some of the sanctified myths of Israeli history,[2] and the persistent criticism by respected figures of the policy of holding on to the occupied territories. The changes among the Palestinians have been more far-reaching, however, both because they have been going on for longer and because they have been rooted in a remarkable set of socioeconomic transformations.

One reason the Palestinians have stopped being identified as refugees is that in a technical sense most of them no longer are. Today less than one in five lives in refugee camps, as against more than half in the decades from 1948 to 1967. This is the case even though a large majority of Palestinians still fall into the existential category of exiles, best explored by Edward Said's *After the Last Sky*. This category applies to about two-thirds of the four to five million Palestinians: those in exile from their homeland and those in a sort of "internal exile" from their native homes and villages, living in camps and towns within their homeland. This demographic shift over the past two decades, whereby most Palestinians have ceased to live in refugee camps, has gone largely unnoticed. According to 1986 UNRWA figures, only 800,000 Palestinians, under 20 percent of the total, live in camps (nearly half in the occupied territories and the rest in the diaspora), although many others benefit from educational and other programs run by UNRWA. The rest live outside the camps, in cities, suburbs, towns and villages.

This shift is a function of many things, notably the oil-induced regional economic prosperity of the 1970s which enabled many Palestinians, particularly in Lebanon and Jordan, to move out of the camps. It is also a function of a powerful drive for upward mobility linked to a thirst for education, which has turned the Palestinians into one of the most literate and highly educated of Arab peoples, on a par with the Lebanese. This in turn has enabled them to play a key role in the vast migration of skilled labor which has transformed the Arab world in recent years.

These transformations go back in time well beyond the past two decades. They are rooted in developments of earlier years, such as the expansion of education in Mandatory Palestine: by 1946, 45 percent of the Palestinian Arab school-age population was in school. A further impetus was provided by the spread of universal compulsory education after 1949, thanks in large measure to the free schooling provided by UNRWA, resulting in near-universal literacy.

Another unnoticed process has helped to make these changes more widespread than might otherwise have been expected. This is what might be described as the melting pot effect, whereby Palestinians from the many lands of the diaspora and the different zones of occupation within Palestine, each with its highly disparate conditions, have met and worked or studied together, and often intermarried, in areas a great distance from their homeland. These include workplaces in the oil-producing, labor-importing states of the Gulf and North Africa, the educational centers of Europe, North America, Cairo, the Gulf and (before 1982) Beirut, and the scattered political, administrative, cultural, financial and military institutions of the PLO, its constituent groups, and the many private Palestinian bodies which have grown up over the past two decades.

The result has been a breakdown of many of the traditional barriers between region and region, village and village, city and countryside, and often between classes and religions. Newer distinctions, such as those which had grown up since 1948 as a result of the different conditions and experiences of Palestinians from different countries of the diaspora and regions of occupation, have been eroded as well. There has not by any means been a homogenization of the Palestinians: Jerusalem or Hebron or Gaza accents still retain their distinctiveness, and vast class differences remain and may even be growing. But it can be argued that something of a unified political culture has been made possible by these processes, which were in a certain sense organic, natural, uncontrolled and unintended. Thus while Palestinians in the diaspora were naturally drawn to one another by their shared experience of dispossession, exile and statelessness, the troubles they faced in their strange and often somewhat hostile new environments and the fact that they had many important things in common further reinforced the existing bonds between them.

These processes, already underway in the 1950s and the 1960s but greatly accelerated by the oil boom of the 1970s and the greater mobility it introduced into the whole region, made it possible for the edifice of Palestinian nationalism to be so swiftly and so successfully reconstructed over the past two decades by the Palestinian politico-military groups which in 1968 took over the PLO and have dominated the Palestinian national movement ever since.

Here we enter into a discussion of another set of underlying changes which have taken place since 1967 but which have perhaps been obscured by day-to-day developments. These are changes relating to the form and content of Palestinian nationalism. Unlike the socioeconomic and demographic transformations just described, these changes were very much subjectively determined, and were by and large the result of active organizational and mobilization efforts by Palestinian leaders and groups. The results can best be appreciated by a comparison of the current situation of the Palestinians on the ideological level with that of 1967.

It can be argued that the Palestinians have never been more at one in terms of their self-view than they are today. It is true that there exist persistent physical divisions among different groups of Palestinians, disparate conditions in each different country of the diaspora, in the West Bank, Gaza Strip and inside Israel, along with the political differences which sundered the PLO for several years after the 1982 war, some of which still persist. In spite of these facts, there exists today a strong sense of national unity, of loyalty to a unified set of symbols and concepts, and of mutual interdependence, sentiments which were lacking in 1967.

Palestinian patriotism was certainly widespread at that time; indeed, the resistance of this powerful current had already aroused the fears of the Arab regimes, provoking them into the formation of the PLO in 1964 as a means of pre-empting, channelling and ultimately controlling the destabilizing and radical force of Palestinian irredentism. But this current was not only underground but also deeply divided, with many Palestinians still involved in the transnational movements in which they had engaged themselves in the wake of the catastrophe of 1948 as the best means of reversing its results. Thus Palestinians were active in the Baʻth, Communist, and Syrian Social Nationalist parties, in the Arab Nationalist Movement and other Nasirist bodies, in the Muslim Brothers, Islamic Liberation Party and other Islamist groupings, and in other radical, anti-regime formations. All these groups had held out to the Palestinians the promise of revolutionizing the rotten Arab structure which had failed to prevent the defeat of 1948. In time, however, many Palestinians held against the Arab regimes the fact that they either had not tried, or had failed, to reverse the results of that defeat.

In 1967, although Palestinian patriotism was undoubtedly the motivating force of most Palestinian political activists, only a minority of them were involved in purely Palestinian nationalist organizations. This was already changing, as was symbolized by the success of Fatah even before 1967, a success out of all proportion to its numbers or real strength. It was to change even more radically afterwards as Palestinians flocked to small Palestinian nationalist organizations like Fatah in reaction to the devastating 1967 defeat of Arab regimes which had espoused some of the transnational ideologies many Palestinians had been counting on to achieve their national objectives of liberation and return.

But the greatest change came well after 1967. A people who had been powerless, divided and disorganized for decades, who had been the victims of forces far greater than themselves, and who before 1948 had been badly led by an autocratic and traditional elite, had to be convinced that they could affect their situation, that they could take their future into their hands, and that they could not depend on President Nasser or the Arab armies or some other *deus ex machina* to solve their problems. Moreover, they had to develop an entirely new image of themselves, discarding that of the refugee and replacing it with a more dynamic and positive one.

The first step on the long road to a new self-image was the establishment of a measure of self-rule for the Palestinian camp populations in Lebanon, Syria and Jordan after 1967. Although this process was reversed in Jordan in 1970-71 as a result of Black September and was severely limited in Syria following the November 1970 coup there, it had already had an impact, further intensified by the fact that this self-rule continued in Lebanon. There the issue of the autonomy of the camps continues to be at the core of the ongoing conflict involving the Palestinians. Moreover, the effects of this autonomy, even after it was ended or limited in some places, provided Palestinians for the first time in decades with a sometimes vicarious sense of empowerment and autonomy. Even Palestinians living at a distance from Lebanon were deeply affected as they saw the Palestinian flag, Palestinian fighters and Palestinian institutions resisting overwhelming odds in Lebanon from the early 1970s until the present.

Taking up arms against the Israeli occupation gave a further impetus to these same processes of empowerment and autonomy. In fact, from the perspective of over twenty years, armed struggle can be seen to have had far more impact on the Palestinians themselves than on its intended target, Israel, where the effect has been at best mixed. At an early stage, armed struggle turned the Palestinians nearly overnight into the vanguard of the post-1967 Arab struggle against Israel. It thus helped restore a sense of dignity to a people whose self-respect had been cruelly eroded by their expulsion by Israel and subsequent suppression by the Arab regimes. The heady impact of this change often bred a certain arrogance, for which Palestinians were to pay dearly in Jordan and Lebanon. Nevertheless, a transformation had been effected, in spite of some of its negative side-effects.

Having said this, there has undoubtedly been some exaggeration of the impact of the gun, the symbol of the resistance, and of the empowerment which it was seen as making possible. Important though it has been (and still is in the Hobbesian situation of Lebanon, where only force can hold back the encroaching jungle), the gun is less important in the complex situation of today, whether symbolically or in real terms, than it was in the years after 1967. Moreover, as the uprising has shown, for Palestinians under occupation steadfastness, organization, and ways of enabling people to remain on the land and run their own lives in their villages, towns and cities, free of the occupation, have become the priority. The various forms of resistance, from nonviolent protests to violent demonstrations, are still crucial weapons in the Palestinian arsenal against the powerful occupier and its routine daily violence and brutality. But the practice of resistance in 1967-70, when armed attacks were far more frequent, contrasts strikingly with the situation in 1987-88, where they have been virtually excluded from the arsenal of weapons used against the occupation by the leadership of the uprising.

In real terms, the gun now has primarily symbolic importance for Palestinians in exile, with the important exception of Lebanon. In practice it is only there, in spite of the fearsome restraints on them, that Palestinians can and do carry weapons freely. In the rest of the diaspora this is not possible, and it is primarily political organization and mobilization, the building and strengthening of cultural bonds, the maintenance of a social and health care safety net, and tireless diplomatic maneuvering among the treacherous shoals of the various Arab regimes which enable Palestinians in exile to maintain and increase their autonomy and the bonds between them and those under occupation. These bonds were reflected in the outcome of the nineteenth PNC, where under the impact of the new sense of self-respect resulting from the uprising, the PLO was able to downplay both the Palestine National Covenant and the old slogan of "armed struggle," neither of which is mentioned in the PNC's political statement.

However, the exception of Lebanon deserves attention, for what goes on in Lebanon has an impact far beyond its effect on the 400,000 or more Palestinians living there, important though that is. Lebanon is significant in the broader arena of Palestinian politics because the center of the modern Palestinian national movement was located there for twelve of the last twenty-two years, and because the names Sabra and Shatila, like Tal al-Za'tar before it, have acquired a powerful resonance in the Palestinian, and indeed the Arab, political vocabulary. No leadership which aspires to direct the fortunes of the Palestinian people can afford to ignore what happens to the Palestinians in Lebanon for this reason alone. The briefest perusal of the covers, editorials and lead articles of the three main Palestinian political weeklies, *Filastin al-Thawra, al-Hadaf* and *al-Hurriyya* (representing Fatah, the PFLP and the DFLP respectively), as well as others like *al-Yawm al-Sabi'* or *al-Bayadir al-Siyasi,* during the siege of the camps in Lebanon gives evidence of this. The impact of events in Lebanon on the entire Palestinian national movement is concretely reinforced by the fact that the families and relatives of so many of the leaders, cadres, office workers, bureaucrats and combatants who make up the PLO are still living in Lebanon in the camps and districts which are daily in the headlines as the scenes of continued barbarity aimed at their inhabitants.

The significance of this fact can be gauged from the rapid demise since 1982 of the political challenge posed by the small Palestinian factions controlled by Syria, such as Saiqa, the PFLP-GC and the Abu Nidal group, in spite of the collapse during the same period of the "Jordanian option" to which the PLO leadership committed itself from 1982 to 1986. That demise is arguably a function of the perception among most Palestinians that these factions' alignment with the Syrian regime has proven harmful to the Palestinian population of the camps in Lebanon, besieged as they are by Syrian allies and proxies. Even the obstacles facing the diplomatic approach followed by the PLO leadership since 1982 has not increased the popularity among Palestinians of the leadership's rivals based in Damascus. Seen in this perspective, the "war of the camps" of 1985-87 has an overarching importance, overshadowing the bitter wrangling over the leadership's "Jordanian option" and the resulting 1985 Amman accord, and the Damascus-based groups' "Syrian option." Indeed, it has had the effect of forcing the main PLO factions—Fatah, the PFLP and the DFLP—towards national unity in spite of their differences.

The impact of events in Lebanon on the entire Palestinian political arena can also be seen in the effect of the PLO's defense of the besieged camps during the winter of 1986-87. This gave a powerful boost to Palestinian nationalism in the occupied territories, which during this period witnessed intense nationalist agitation in solidarity with the Palestinians in the camps of Lebanon. Similarly, the steadfastness of the Palestinian camps in Lebanon marginally improved the PLO's situation in the Arab world. It had an impact on the successful negotiations in the spring of 1987 between the PLO and the Kuwaiti government on conditions of residence for Palestinians in Kuwait, on the United Arab Emirates agreeing to host the headquarters of the Palestine National Fund, and on the improvement of the PLO's relations with Tunisia, Libya and Algeria in 1987.

Lebanon is also important because it is the last "front" in the hot war with Israel, aside from the occupied territories themselves. However, since 1982 the war on that front has been waged primarily by Lebanese whose main aim is the final elimination of the Israeli occupation of Lebanese territory, embodied in the so-called "security zone." It is questionable whether this resistance to Israeli occupation of Lebanese soil, which so far has been remarkably successful, can be seen as more than a tactical ally of Palestinian resistance to Israeli occupation in the West Bank and Gaza Strip. This is particularly the case since many of the most active elements of the Lebanese resistance, such as Hizbullah, are committed at least rhetorically to the liberation of all Palestine and not just the West Bank and Gaza, which have been the PLO's focus since the 1974 provisional program.

The resolution of the issue of South Lebanon has exceedingly important implications, on the Lebanese and regional levels as well as for the Palestinians. In Lebanese terms, it will have an impact on the struggle for supremacy within the Shi'i community, as well as on the conflict over the future nature and orientation of Lebanon. On the regional level it will help to determine many of the actions of Syria and Israel. On the Palestinian level it will strongly influence not only the nature and course of the PLO's leadership but also the extent to which armed struggle remains central to the Palestinian national movement. It is noteworthy that in addition to omitting any reference to "armed struggle," the Political Statement of the nineteenth PNC refrained for the first time in over a decade from calling for freedom of commando action from Lebanon, instead stressing the "right of Palestinian citizens in Lebanon to practice political and informational activities and to enjoy security and protection."[3]

In any case, debate among Palestinians, whether about Lebanon or the uprising, will take place in a much different context than existed in 1967. It will be resolved in forums like the Palestine National Council, and the various unions, such as the influential General Union of Palestinian Writers and Journalists, whose February 1987 general conference in Algiers brought together writers from all the main Palestinian factions and was a prelude to the reunification of the PLO at the eighteenth PNC in Algiers two months later. It will be debated in the Palestinian press, whether that under occupation or in the diaspora, whether in PLO-run media or in newspapers published in the Gulf which carry columns written by Palestinians. It will be addressed in literature and in literary magazines, whether published in Paris or Jerusalem or the Gulf or elsewhere. And it will be discussed in research institutes, scholarly organizations and professional associations formed by Palestinians both under occupation and in the diaspora.

All these forums enable political debate to take place on the level of the entire Palestinian people, with the same themes, ideas and problems being addressed in spite of the barriers of diaspora, occupation, physical separation and great distance. Thus newspapers under occupation, student groups in Kuwaiti universities, Palestinian-American bodies in the United States and the conferences of organizations like the General Union of Palestinian Writers and Journalists all debate the same issues and are moved by the same crises, whether in the camps in Lebanon or in the occupied territories. That such a thing can take place—something which could not happen on anything like the same scale or with the same universality in 1967—in itself constitutes a remarkable change.

Moreover, the process of extending and strengthening this web of linkages tying the Palestinians together as a people suffered only a slight interruption as a result of the 1982 Israeli invasion of Lebanon, which was intended above all else to permanently disrupt those linkages. The break in the continuity of PLO institutions as a result of the defeat and expulsion of 1982, which was accentuated by the split in the movement which followed, can now be seen as no more than a hiatus in their development. In spite of their manifold failings, their inefficiency, corruption and bureaucratic nature, these institutions have survived dispersion and still function, providing services to Palestinians throughout the region, supporting both the steadfastness of those in the camps in Lebanon and the uprising against the occupation, and playing a sometimes vital coordinating role.

If these have all been achievements of the past two decades, most of them growing naturally out of the socioeconomic, demographic, professional and educational transformations of the Palestinian people and their developing national consciousness, what have been the accompanying failures? And in which direction can the Palestinian national movement be expected to go in the future?

The clearest failure is embodied in the fact that no part of Palestine has been liberated yet in spite of more than two decades of efforts and the sacrifice of tens of thousands of lives. Moreover, the Palestinian national movement has become deeply embroiled in distracting conflicts with parties other than Israel, whether Lebanese factions or Arab regimes. While these failures are easy to see, it is somewhat harder to see precisely how they could have been avoided, given the iron intransigence of Israel regarding evacuation of occupied Palestinian territory and Palestinian self-determination, the descent into decadence of the Arab world over the past decade and a half, and the relative immaturity of the modern Palestinian national movement, particularly during its Jordanian and Lebanese phases.

A less obvious but perhaps more avoidable failure has been the PLO's inability to decide on the basic strategy for changing the unfavorable balance of forces it confronts. Is this to be done by diplomatic maneuvering, by waiting or working for another war or a change in the Arab environment, or by attempting to affect the situation within Israel and the occupied territories? And if the situation inside Israel is to be changed, is this to be accomplished by conciliation, pressure or a combination of the two? While all of these have at different times been perceived as possible avenues to liberation, it is hard to see which is the primary avenue chosen by the PLO to achieve its objectives.

While diplomacy is always necessary and sometimes vital, it cannot by itself change an unfavorable balance of forces. Yet this was the means relied upon by the PLO leadership after the 1982 war when, from a relatively weak position, it entered into the now-defunct understanding with Jordan aimed at involving the PLO in the process of achieving a settlement. And while a change in the Arab world is devoutly to be wished for by Palestinians and others, their ability to accelerate such a change is limited at best. Even the Popular Front for the Liberation of Palestine, which in the 1960s used to preach Arab revolution as the means of liberating Palestine, seems grudgingly reconciled to the stability of the Arab status quo, as evidenced by George Habash's successful 1987 tour of several Gulf states, where he met with their rulers and was generally treated as an honored guest.

This question has in fact become moot since December 1987, when the uprising in effect determined that Israel and the occupied territories would be the primary arena for Palestinian action and in some measure imposed on the entire Palestinian national movement a strategy of pressure on the occupier combined with a conciliatory political stance. This was reflected in the resolutions of the nineteenth PNC.

To some extent the Palestinians have achieved a limited form of one of their objectives, self-determination, in that in some places, albeit subject to brutal restraint and often at fearful cost, they have managed to make themselves masters of their own fate. But this has either occurred outside their own homeland, creating the kind of difficulties engendered by the PLO's "state within a state" in Lebanon, or else takes place within the stifling confines of the repression, racism and hostility of the Israeli occupation. The uprising shows both the extent and the limitations of this form of auto-emancipation. Moreover, other objectives such as the return to Palestine of Palestinians in the diaspora and the establishment of an independent Palestinian state in even a fraction of Palestine still seem far off.

Given this situation, the future is likely to see a continuation of the processes of reuniting the divided segments of the Palestinian people and further efforts to strengthen the position of those living under occupation and protect them against the threat of expulsion, whether gradual and partial, or sudden and massive. These processes will continue irrespective of whatever strategy is adopted by the Palestinian national movement, or who leads it, or even whether a clear strategy is adopted or not. If such a strategy is in fact articulated, it will be determined mainly by two unpredictable factors. The first is a takeover of the leadership by a new generation, which has already begun to happen in the occupied territories. This same process can happen in the diaspora, which for the foreseeable future will continue to be the locus of leadership of the Palestinian national movement, only when a new generation is in place and can offer a new approach, and when the Arab circumstances from which the current leaders emerged and to which they are most adept at responding disappear. This in turn will be a function of the second unpredictable factor: major changes in the Arab world. This would have to be on the order of the two earthquakes which changed the Palestinian and Arab political maps in modern times. The first, that of 1948, shattered the traditional Palestinian leadership finally and irrevocably, while starting the old Arab ruling classes down the slope to their overthrow. The second, that of 1967, crippled and delegitimized the radical Arab nationalist regimes and seemed to vindicate Palestinian nationalism, providing the opportunity for the current generation of Palestinian leaders to dominate Palestinian politics. Any major change in the Arab world, even if not quite so dramatic as these, would probably stimulate similarly major shifts in Palestinian politics.

Part of any new generation of Palestinian leadership which does emerge will probably come from occupied Palestine, where new forms of organization are already appearing. It will be more sensitive to potential allies within Israeli society and to the vulnerabilities and strengths of a foe it knows at first hand, and it can thus be expected to be more subtle in its approach and strategy. Indeed, some of this subtlety has already been reflected in the tactics and strategy of the uprising. In this sense it will be unlike the current leadership, which is located entirely in exile and knows its enemy primarily from being on the receiving end of Israeli bombing raids and assassination attempts. It should be noted that Israel has the capacity to retard this process by continuing to expel prominent Palestinian figures in the occupied territories, as if trying to ensure that the entire leadership of the Palestinian national movement will remain in exile. And the difficulties of carrying on freely under occupation with some of the key political, organizational and diplomatic tasks necessary for management of this movement will ensure that most of them will continue to be done by leaders in exile. Nevertheless, the growth of the relative importance of Palestinians under occupation in the national movement as a whole, already underway, is probably inexorable and has the potential for introducing qualitative changes into Palestinian politics.

In spite of the medium- and long-term benefits to be expected from such changes, there remain grave short-term problems for the current generation of leaders and their successors. These include the prickly task of coordinating the sometimes disparate agendas of different segments of the Palestinian people, under occupation and in the diaspora, in the camps and in the cities, from the working class and the big bourgeoisie; changing the grossly unfavorable balance of forces, notably as regards the intransigence of Israel and the United States but also insofar as many of the Arab "brethren" are concerned; ensuring that the Palestinians are not dealt out of any new round of the negotiating process, and that their basic national desiderata are taken into account; and imparting a new sense of direction to a movement which has suffered from drift for many years. Even a simple enumeration such as this shows how daunting these issues are.

In any case, it is clear that the processes which have already transformed the Palestinians since 1967 will have an even greater effect in the future, in spite of the setbacks of the movement and its occasional failure to learn from some of the mistakes of the past. The reason for this is that some of these transformations have simply been the natural result of the development of Palestinian society, which has gone from being comprised mainly of poor, rural, illiterate refugees in 1949 to today's much more complex and advanced social, economic, demographic and educational profile. Other transformations which have already occurred, however, have been the fruit of the efforts of a now greying generation of Palestinian leaders, some of them prominent and others less so. Their prime is surely past, but their contributions over this period in the face of what were always daunting odds should not be forgotten after they have been superseded by the new generation.

Even now the leaders of tomorrow are waiting quietly in the wings, in the ranks of the militias in the camps of Lebanon, led by twenty-five-year-old veterans with fifteen years of combat experience; among the young intellectuals and white-collar workers in Kuwait and the Gulf who have never seen their homeland; and in the student bodies of the universities and among the inmates of the Israeli prisons in the West Bank and Gaza Strip, who have known nothing but occupation for their entire lives.

## Chapter 9

What the Uprising Means

Salim Tamari

This chapter is adapted from a talk Salim Tamari gave at the Johns Hopkins School of Advanced International Studies in Washington, DC on February 25, 1988.

1988 is the end of the second decade of Israeli occupation of the West Bank and Gaza. It's also the fortieth anniversary of the establishment of the State of Israel. This means we have two generations who grew up under Israeli control inside the Green Line and one generation which grew up under occupation in the West Bank and Gaza. Demographically, roughly 60 percent of the people of the West Bank and Gaza are today under seventeen years of age. These are the core of the people you watch every day confronting Israeli soldiers. Age is significant here: it suggests the context in which young people begin to lose fear in facing death or mutilation of their bodies.

When Israel entered the occupied territories after defeating the armies of Jordan, Syria and Egypt in June 1967, it was not very clear what it wanted to do with the territories. There was a vigorous debate between the two branches of the National Unity Government of that time, very similar to the unity government that ruled Israel from 1984 to 1988. Then it comprised the rightwing Gahal bloc made up of the Herut and Liberal Parties, the core of today's Likud, and the Labor-led Alignment. In that period the perspective of former Defense Minister Moshe Dayan determined Israeli strategy. Perhaps the best way to summarize Dayan's perspective is that Israeli rule should be felt but not seen. Arabs should be able to administer their own affairs and go through the cycle of life—birth registration, marriage, school, receiving services—without having to encounter Israeli officials. At the same time, Israel should keep a firm grip on all matters relating to security and the resources of the region.

The contesting perspective was expressed recently by Prime Minister Yitzhak Shamir: that Israel should establish a fear of the Jews in the hearts of the Arabs. It was Dayan's strategy of control through indirect means that triumphed. Dayan cleverly charted the integration of the occupied territories into the body of Israel through three institutional mechanisms—infrastructure, labor and markets. These three central control mechanisms were the foundation on which Israel constructed its political hegemony over the region, undergirded of course by Israel's monopoly of coercive force and a pervasive intelligence network.

In terms of physical infrastructure, Israel began a substantial process of restructuring the transport and communications network of the West Bank and Gaza, relinking them with Israel. It became much easier for a Jewish settlement in a place like Ariel, or Qiryat Arba in the Hebron district, to connect with Tel Aviv and Jerusalem than it was for the Jewish settlements in the West Bank to interact with the Arab villages there. There is a security function here, i.e., it allows Jewish settlers to move freely without going through Arab concentrations of population, but the original intention was to create a network that would physically integrate the occupied territories with the State of Israel.

In the same manner, the water and electricity grids and the whole system of land zoning were integrated with Israel in such a way that for water and electricity supplies the Arabs had to depend on Mekorot, the Israeli water company, and on Israeli utilities. The net result was to create forms of dependence by the Arab municipal organizations on Israel and its economy.

More important than this integration of infrastructure was the manner in which Dayan's policies opened Israeli markets for the movement of Arab labor. In the early 1970s, Israel began to absorb very large numbers of Arab workers into Israeli construction, services, agriculture and, later on, the industrial sector. These workers were absorbed at the bottom of the occupational pyramid: they did what is known as "black labor"—some Israelis call it "Arab labor." It's a phrase which replaced the idiom "Kurdish labor," because ethnically the bottom of the heap in the Jewish pecking order were the Jewish Kurds who had come from Iraq and Iran. But now the Palestinians from the villages and camps of the West Bank and Gaza began to occupy those arenas of work which were regarded as undesirable by the Jewish work force. This was especially true of the catering and service sector, and in construction as that sector evolved into a de-skilled sector of the Israeli economy.

The purpose of this integration of Arab labor was dual. On the one hand, it defused social pressures that would accrue from a high level of unemployment among the Arab population, especially given the fact that Israel now erected immense obstacles in the growth and development of local industries, both in terms of investment and in terms of markets for Palestinian products. It also allowed Israel to develop capital intensive industry to absorb the Jewish work force released from menial jobs by the influx of Arab laborers from the occupied territories. As a result, before the uprising about 100,000 workers commuted daily from camps, villages, and urban centers in the West Bank and Gaza to Israel, most of them returning to their villages in the evening. Roughly half of these workers were involved in the construction sector. This group constituted one-third of the total labor force in the West Bank and half the labor force in Gaza.

The third mechanism of integration was markets. The West Bank and Gaza became the most significant market for Israeli commodities, perhaps second only to the United States if we exclude armaments and diamonds. Nearly 90 percent of all goods imported into the occupied territories—some $780 million worth in 1986—come from Israel. This makes up more than 11 percent of Israel's total exports. The West Bank and Gaza market is tariff-free. Israel has easy access to it because of its proximity, and of course it is highly non-competitive. The Israelis do not allow Arab commodities to move into the Israeli sector, and at the same time they have thwarted the development of the local industrial manufacturing sector for the Arabs. So the Arabs are very much a captive market for Israeli processed foods which they keep in Israeli-made refrigerators and so forth.

These three mechanisms—infrastructure, labor and markets—must be seen as the institutional building blocks for Israel's political control of the territories. But they are not themselves the cement of this control. Ultimately, Israel's control over the territories is political and military, and not socio-economic. The bonding force behind the political control is the process of land confiscation and settler colonialism which began in 1968. In the first phase, the Labor Party was in control. The idea was to establish Jewish settlements acting as a human belt between Jordan and the West Bank. Israel first established a number of Jewish settlements along the Jordan valley corridor, with an outlet from Jericho to Jordan. The idea was to be able to barter the territories with Jordan against a peace treaty. This was the essence of the plan associated with the name of Yigal Allon, who was deputy prime minister in the early 1970s.

The Likud came to power in the 1977 elections and completely sabotaged the whole perspective of bartering land for peace. In order to preempt any possibility of returning the territories to any form of Arab control, the Likud began a phase of intensive settlement in the densely populated area of central Palestine, the Ramallah-Nablus-Hebron-Jerusalem area. Any attempt to negotiate a territorial deal with any Arab authority—Palestinian or an Arab state—would henceforth trigger a communal conflict within Israel. This was the period when the Likud backed the Gush Emunim, the movement of extreme religious groups associated with the settlement movement, in order to settle Arab-inhabited areas.[1] If you look at a map and you color-code the settlements—there are about 120 now in the West Bank and Gaza—you will see that Labor settlements are dotted around the western

Jordan Valley, while Likud-sponsored settlements tend to be in the central highland, in the middle of Arab-populated areas.

These settlements involved extensive land confiscation. It was necessary to take over land from private Arab owners, as well as state or public land, which now reverted to the Jewish National Fund. About 55 percent of the total land area in the West Bank and 30 percent of the total land in Gaza are now in Jewish hands. I say Jewish hands and not Israeli hands intentionally. There is an extra-territorial definition of public land in Israel so that it belongs to the Jews in totality and not to the Israeli Jews in the State of Israel. Israeli citizens who are non-Jews have no access to this land, but Jews who are not Israeli do have access. Many of the settlers in the West Bank and Gaza today are Jews who have just arrived from the Soviet Union, from North America, and to some extent from Latin America. These Soviet and US citizens have finally found peaceful coexistence in the hills of the West Bank and on the beaches of Gaza.

Before 1977 the ideological nature of the settlers and the physical location of settlements were such that they were controllable. They could be isolated in terms of future political settlements. This is exactly what happened in Sinai, when the settlers were ready to give up the land for significant amounts of compensation. The ideological commitment of the present Jewish settler movement in the West Bank is such that these people are likely to fight against any territorial deal. The Likud knows they are likely to fight, and intentionally backs up their intransigence so that in any negotiations they can say, "Look, we'd like to have peace, but we have our constituency, a large number of our citizens now who consider this to be more their land than Tel Aviv or Haifa, certainly much more than Brooklyn."

Palestinian resistance to this policy of intransigence has been well documented. It took various forms, it was persistent, it was protracted, it was occasionally violent. Here I want to contrast two different phases in Palestinian resistance to the policy of integration/annexation. One I call the phase of liberation, and the other the phase of independence. Until the mid-1970s, the Palestinian nationalist movement, in both rhetoric and program, had as its goal the establishment of a secular state in all of Palestine. The means for achieving this goal was armed struggle and protracted people's war. The Vietnamese/Chinese model was predominant, not only in the minds of the leftist segment of the movement but also in the mainstream Fatah branch.

Since the mid-1970s, and to a large extent as a consequence of the October 1973 War in which for the first time there was a stalemate between the military might of Israel and that of the Arab world, a significant shift occurred in the formulation of Palestinian nationalist objectives. Palestinians now called for Israeli withdrawal from the occupied territories and the establishment of a Palestinian state in those areas from which Israel would withdraw. In other words, the Palestine national movement signalled its willingness to establish a state coexisting with the State of Israel, given certain conditions—among which is the right of Palestinians either to return to those areas in which Israel will remain in full control or to be compensated for their losses.

One consequence of this strategy is that it distinguishes the nature of struggle for Palestinians living in Israel, whose main objective would be equality with Jews, from those living in the West Bank and Gaza, where the focus has become separation and independence. One attribute of this shift is that the language of secular politics is less used than the language of independence and sovereignty. Secularism is still the ideology of the Palestinian national movement, but the movement no longer sees the people of Palestine as belonging to confessions—Muslims, Christians, Jews. Rather, it sees the conflict as basically a national struggle between Arabs and Jews.

In this period, the PLO developed a strategy of building embryonic institutions of power in the occupied territories. First, there was the issue in 1976 of contesting municipal elections against slates of Israeli collaborators. It also meant the development of local institutions like workers' unions, professional associations, municipalities and especially universities to serve as institutional components of future power, so that when a Palestinian state arrives it will not arrive in a vacuum. It will already have an infrastructure of political and civic institutions to support it.

One aspect of this strategy of institution-building was also the notion of survival: until the Israelis withdraw, and they're going to be here for a long time, we need both the political will and the institutional fabric to help us survive these years of land confiscation, repression and deportation. This strategy of informal resistance, if you like, or institutional resistance, was actually far more successful than even its own designers envisioned. By the late 1970s, it had established the complete political hegemony of Palestinian nationalism and the PLO as the single articulator of Palestinian aspirations. And it was in response to this that the Likud introduced the "iron fist" policy in 1981 when it installed Menachem Milson, professor of Arabic literature at Hebrew University, to "administer" the West Bank.

Milson thought that Moshe Dayan had left the Arabs alone too long, and had allowed Palestinian nationalism to fester. He proposed a policy of positive interference. Israel should punish the nationalists and support the Palestinians who think "positively," meaning people who are willing to collaborate. This was part of a general policy which the Likud adopted in the early 1980s, in which the main objective was to smash the bases of PLO power both militarily and politically. The Lebanon campaign was its most violent aspect. A corollary was the political repression of nationalist institutions in the occupied territories. Israel disbanded the municipal councils which had been democratically elected in 1976. The military regime, behind the mask of a "civil administration," began a wave of arrests, detention without charges, deportations and house demolitions, and set up armed militias of collaborators known as the Village Leagues.

The accumulation of these acts of repression, coupled with the increased confiscation of land after 1981, was the prelude to the present uprising. A second phase of the "iron fist" came in 1985, after Yitzhak Rabin became defense minister. Palestinians had successfully defeated Israeli efforts to establish the Village Leagues as a counterweight to the nationalist forces. The economic downturn in the oil-producing Gulf states had closed off an important pressure release valve for young Palestinian job seekers. The PLO and Jordan had engaged in competitive funding and organizing among various sectors. Incidents of confrontation multiplied. Under Rabin, Israel qualitatively intensified its repressive measures, to which the defense minister himself applied the term "iron fist."

The acts of civil disobedience and confrontation with the military forces that we see today are not radically different from what was happening from 1981 to 1987, certainly since 1985. There were daily, weekly, monthly occurrences, but the dispersed nature of these confrontations made them containable. The Israelis were able to isolate them and, they thought, maintain a pacified population. It was a manageable insurrection.

What is new about the present uprising is both its scale and character. By scale I mean the involvement of large numbers of people who have not participated before—women, children, many workers who used to go to work in Israel, professionals and shopkeepers who are the lifeline of the economic sectors in the main urban centers.

It's interesting here to recall Rabin's remark at the beginning of the uprising, that this was a movement instigated by outside agitators. "We have good people, good Arabs," Rabin was saying in effect. "There are a few hotheads being roused by phone calls from Abu Jihad in Tunis." Two weeks later, the scale of the uprising had taken everybody by surprise—including the Palestinians, by the way. Rabin was in trouble. If indeed the PLO was instigating this, then the PLO was capable of mobilizing the whole population. And so Rabin, very embarrassed, reversed his position. Now we have intelligence reports, he said, which show that this uprising is spontaneous, the work of long years of frustration and festering wounds of unresolved Palestinian nationalism. But Rabin was still in trouble: either way it was a crisis the Israelis were not able to handle. Rabin and the Israeli defense establishment decided that it's better to deal with the spontaneity of the masses rather than the clout of the PLO.

Rabin's dilemma points to the major significance of the uprising: its scale and durability has created an unprecedented challenge to Israeli control. Israel can no longer govern "the territories."

This important point is occasionally obscured by the media's attention to questions of riot control technique: which combination of live ammunition, beatings, tear gas and rubber bullets will bring the Palestinian population to heel? The latest device, introduced in mid-March, is a "Catapulter": manifesting a creative synthesis between Palestinian ecology and Israeli know-how, the machine is composed of a large rock basket and a revolving turret which can spit hundreds of medium-sized stones with high velocity at troublemakers. The problem, of course, is that the harder the Israelis try, the more pathetic their attempts look. The image of the valiant encircled David has been shattered beyond repair. To add insult to injury, his slingshot has been appropriated—and very skillfully—by the children of Nablus and Hebron and the hundreds of villages of the West Bank and Gaza.

What it boils down to, ultimately, is that the greatest military power in the Mediterranean can no longer subdue the spontaneous defiance of a civilian population whose only armament is street stones and lack of fear.

Secondly, the uprising signifies a shift in the center of gravity of Palestinian politics, from the Palestinian diaspora communities in Lebanon, Syria and Jordan to the territories occupied by Israel in 1967. This shift began in the mid-1970s. Its landmarks were the 1974 Palestine National Council resolution calling for an independent state in the West Bank and Gaza, the contestation of the municipal election of 1976, and the institution-building strategy I described earlier. Where the external PLO leadership once led the internal movement under occupation, today the internal movement sets the tone for the formulation of Palestinian politics outside.

Thirdly, the uprising is significant also because it involved not only the West Bank and Gaza but, for the first time, full participation of Israel's Arab citizens in the Galilee and elsewhere. There have been instances of Palestinian solidarity across the Green Line before, but not on this scale and not in this manner. The general strike on December 21, 1987 was unprecedented. It was a signal to the Israelis that if they continue along this road, then they will have to deal not only with the Arabs of the territories but with "their" Arabs as well.

A fourth and very important consequence of the insurrection is that it created an instrument of political unification for all the various Palestinian factions that have so far been divided. There's something now called the Unified National Leadership of the Uprising, which has been issuing directives. The population has actually responded to and followed these directives in terms of strikes, confrontations, and civil disobedience. Furthermore, the revolutionary rhetoric of the current uprising is matched by an intensely pragmatic grasp of what the masses can and cannot do. It sets the limits of popular participation but also assumes that its scope will move in ever-widening circles. Thus one would hope that the present movement will avoid the pitfalls of the 1936 revolt which, by 1938, had fallen into brigandage.

Finally, at the political level, I think the uprising has defeated the notion that the physical, economic, infrastructural integration of the West Bank and Gaza into the body of the State of Israel creates irreversible facts. This has been the position of the school of thought associated with Meron Benvenisti, and on the Palestinian side with people like Sari Nusaibeh. Integration has proceeded too far, they said. The best we can hope for now is a fight for civic equality, for enfranchisement. It is quite remarkable that it took Palestinian children just a few days of street rage to demolish this bizarre argument of structural determinism in its entirety. I think it's clear, from both the Palestinian and Israeli perspectives, that separation is the only way, and separation along the lines of Palestinian sovereignty is becoming a very clear-cut option for the future.

Discussion

Q: You seem to agree with Rabin's second diagnosis, that the uprisings are the result of accumulated frustration and grievances.

A: I cited Rabin to give you a clue what Israeli strategists are thinking, not because I agree with his assessment. I think the word frustration is not the right one. Frustration is what you feel when your beloved has not returned your amorous overtures. What we have here is repression. It's not a psychological state of mind, but a political response to a physical state of affairs. The word frustration obfuscates the relationship between Israel and the occupied territories. One, because it obscures the hierarchical form of control. Two, because it misconstrues the nature of the response, which is not a mindless volcanic eruption but a politically motivated act, spontaneous but with clear political objectives: we want independence, we don't want you to be here, we want you to get out! The fact that it uses crude instruments of warfare, like stones, should not detract from the clarity of the political message behind it.

Q: You say it was spontaneous, not directed from outside?

A: Spontaneity and direction from outside are not necessarily exclusive categories. There is no question that in the initial phase of the uprising, the element of spontaneity was predominant, and it involved young street gangs who were not necessarily part and parcel of the national movement. It also involved a fundamentalist current in Gaza which was outside the domain of the PLO. However, by the second week, it was clear that the political currents were involved. And the manifestoes issued by the Unified Leadership made it clear that they consider themselves part and parcel of the PLO. It's not a question of PLO or not PLO, but two dimensions of the Palestinian national movement. There is a high degree of coordination between them, but they are not the same, because of physical dislocation and because of the differential weight of these components of the PLO. It's clear, for example, that the weight of the Muslim fundamentalist groups is much higher inside than outside, in Gaza than in the West Bank. In summary, I would say that the element of spontaneity took the movement unaware, but it soon gathered its momentum. Today I think there's no question that the uprising is being directed—not from the outside but from the inside. The outside has become aware of the political weight of the inside.

Ultimately your question is this: what exactly is the organic link between Fatah and the Popular Front and the Democratic Front, etc., as far as their internal cadres are concerned, with the external leadership? This is something I cannot answer.

Q: Why is the PLO directing Palestinians not to talk to Shultz?

A: Shultz's visit is in the great American tradition of refusing to deal with the Palestinian question realistically. The United States so far has been backing the most extreme interpretation of Israel's future rule over the territories, and has not considered negotiating a territorial settlement with the Palestinians themselves. It is Shultz who refuses to meet with the Palestinians. Shultz in the past has met with Palestinians, with a small "p" if you like, the kind of Palestinians who in his eyes are willing to circumvent the leadership chosen by the Palestinian people to represent them. Why don't the Palestinians meet with Shultz and tell him that? I think the problem is that Shultz knows the situation. They know that he knows that. And he knows why they would meet with him if he changes the conditions of the encounter.

It's clear that many Palestinians today are willing to contemplate interim solutions to the Palestinian problem, including forms of autonomy, provided that these interim solutions are negotiated with the Palestinian leadership, and not with Palestinian collaborators. It's now clear that the Palestinian leadership is willing to contemplate a solution which accepts a sovereign State of Israel side by side with a State of Palestine. But sovereignty must be the object of these negotiations, not "autonomy" under Israeli hegemony.

Q: How do you evaluate the role of settler intransigence in arriving at some kind of settlement?

A: This is the situation we're facing now: if Israel remains in control of the territories, by the year 2010 Arabs and Jews may achieve demographic parity in Palestine—there might be as many Arabs as there are Jews. 1987 was the first year since 1948 in which there were as many Arab babies born as Jewish babies in the Holy Land, which was Golda Meir's nightmare. What do you do about these demographics? Labor thinks that the sooner they get rid of the territories, the better. At least the dovish wing of the Labor Party. This is the preoccupation of—let's call it the left of the Israeli political establishment. The right wants to have its cake and eat it at the same time—they want the land, and they want Jewish sovereignty, and they don't want to treat the Palestinians as citizens. Now the extreme right, of course wants the land without the people, and the extreme right is gaining ground in Israel. But it's false to see Israel as a place in which only right extremism is gaining. Significant sectors of the Jewish public and the Jewish political parties are taking more courageous steps in the direction of negotiation with the Palestinians. It's unfortunate that part of the motivation for peace is racist fears of demographic parity. But this is something that works in our favor and we should thank the Lord for these small mercies. The uprising has been the latest phase in making this dent in the collective Israeli consciousness: one, you cannot continue like this; and two, the West Bank and Gaza have become ungovernable. The sooner we come to a solution, the better for everybody.

Q: What are the prospects for sustaining the uprising?

A: It's hard to tell. Already it has gone beyond the wildest expectations of most people, Israelis and Arabs. Part of it is youthful enthusiasm. But what's critical is that all people are participating with the same enthusiasm of these young people. They will have to devise mechanisms of durability in the coming months. Otherwise it's impossible to imagine how a shopkeeper economy can sustain an uprising of this sort. Already they have been very imaginative about it. For example, confrontation and sabotage is being coordinated in such a way that it does not put too much pressure on any one area or sector. The problem is going to be with the workers who work in Israel. We're talking about 100,000 people, roughly one-third of the total labor force, who live from the daily wages they receive in Israel. Unless the rest of the population can share their resources with these people, the uprising is bound to take different forms of political opposition.

Q: What can you say about the role of the Muslim fundamentalists, particularly given the unified command that's been set up?

A: Within the Palestinian national movement, the Muslim currents always were very hostile to the PLO because the PLO was a secular movement which was also colored by leftism. The whole idiom and vision of a future Palestinian society put forth by the PLO was distasteful to the Muslim currents. I see this clearly because one of the ideological bat-tlegrounds has been the university campuses. Recently, around 1983-84, the Muslim Brothers and perhaps other less radical wings began to find accommodation with the national movement. In return, the price paid by the national movement was to begin to consider the Islamist currents as legitimate strands of opposition within Palestinian society. Until then relations between these two currents were quite tense and sometimes violent. In fact, the national movement always considered the Muslim currents to be almost treasonous. There were cases where we know that the Israeli security establishment collaborated with the Muslim currents. For example, in Umm al-Fahm in the Triangle in the 1970s, Israel did supply arms to the Muslim groups. Some of these groups passed on the guns, or sold them, we're not sure, to members of Fatah. When it was exposed, the whole thing created a scandal in the defense establishment. I'm not saying that the Muslim Brothers in Umm al-Fahm were agents of the Israeli state, but certainly there was a level of manipulation.

In Gaza, the security establishment allowed the Muslim Brothers to attack the Red Crescent Society and the Communists without interference. On two occasions they burned liquor stores in Gaza, and the security establishment did nothing. So it's clear that the Israelis saw the Muslim currents as an asset in the battle against Palestinian nationalism. By 1983-84 this picture changed and two things happened. In Gaza, the Muslim currents began to gain ground, both organizationally and in terms of sympathy from the population. Also, and perhaps these two are related, they began to talk politics. For example, in the platforms of contesting university elections they don't have an ideological platform, they have what you might call a service platform: we will fight to reduce fees, we will talk with the administration about improving the food in the cafeteria, things which were always in the platform of the secular blocs. So there was, if you like, a certain degree of moderation in their politics which had a return on this investment in terms of increased adherence to their bloc.

There is also within Fatah, which is the biggest movement in the underground in the West Bank, a certain sympathy with the Muslim currents. Fatah itself is a mixture of several ideological currents. A certain wing of it is very sympathetic to the religious branch. So I think what we're seeing now is a form of symbiosis that has its positive and negative consequences. It's good because the maximum amount of unity is necessary. Its negative aspects draw from the fact that the Palestinians have always prided themselves on being a secular society and a secular movement, and today they are being infested by Khomeinism.

Q: How do you see Palestinians obtaining their political demands?

A: We can say the stones are the building blocks of the future mode of struggle. The stones will not become guns, because Palestinians in the territories do not have access to arms. The boys in the streets have proved to be more effective in using forms of civil disobedience than those with guns.

But this has to be translated into political terms, which are the following: that we are willing to negotiate, and we have the power to negotiate. We can veto any political option that does not meet our minimum. This is what they are saying. We are willing to negotiate if you come halfway in our direction. Halfway means that we will discuss interim solutions for solving the Palestinian problem, including autonomy, if we know that autonomy will evolve into sovereignty. For that to occur, two things are necessary: for Israel to disabuse itself of the notion that it can negotiate with everybody except the Palestinians—and this is very necessary—and for Washington to ally itself with this new position that Israel will have to arrive at. One would hope the US Congress would be affected by the current political mood both in Israel and in the world at large, so as to make a more realistic assessment of what the Palestinians want and therefore bring the Palestinians themselves to a more realistic formulation of their demands. I think these shifts are likely to happen dramatically—for example, new elections, a single incident, or maybe a dramatic gesture can push things very suddenly in a new direction. I think the atmosphere is very fertile for this at the moment.

## Part 4

Transforming Palestinian Society and Politics

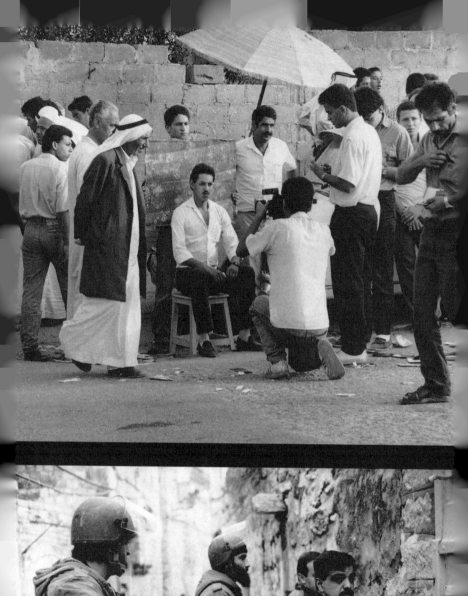

A Song for Childhood

The moon rose
over childhood
And childhood was hills
gathering sparrows and flowers
in baskets under the moon
I'll pursue it, weeping and
falling on jagged stones.

It is a confiscated childhood.
From books and oil lamps, sometimes,
to prison and release, sometimes,
sometimes my life is counterfeit
Inside a city besieged by guards.

The moon rose
over childhood
And childhood was a pine tree
leaning across the shore of a sea
and twinkling above it, in dreams,
a star with many a mystery
I'll spend a sleepless night in that tree
in the dew
and light for it
an oil lamp.

This is a confiscated childhood
From books and oil lamps, sometimes,
to prison and release, sometimes,
sometimes my life is counterfeit
Inside a city besieged...

—Hussein Barghouti

## Chapter 10

Family and Politics in Salfit

Beshara Doumani

Early December 1987

Driving to Salfit through the villages of Yasuf and Iskaka on a sunny fall day is an exhilarating experience. The asphalt road winds like a snake through hill after hill dotted by olive trees whose clusters of tiny, pastel green leaves quiver and shimmer in the light breeze. Rich brown earth, freshly turned, is strewn with stones and contoured by terraces. Closer to the road, thorny shrubs, grasses and the lazy, bleached branches of fig trees leisurely soak in the sun, anticipating the impending winter.

Salfit, a town of over 5,000 inhabitants, is tucked among the rolling hills of the West Bank about thirty kilometers southwest of Nablus. Since Ottoman times it has served as the hub of the cluster of villages in that area, but is now in the backyard of Ariel, the largest Israeli settlement in the West Bank. The old part of Salfit, where the large, meter-thick stone houses of the 'Afana and Zir hamulas (clans) still stand, lies astride a knobby protrusion on a plateau. On one side is a deep valley; larger hills surround the town and block the view to the coast.

Over the past thirty years, Salfit has spread eastward from the old square that still dominates the social life of its inhabitants, and Abu Farid's house, not yet finished, is on the very edge. From his roof, one can see the last row of Swiss chateau-type houses of Ariel, but not the long line of Israeli settlements that stretch along the trans-Samaria road all the way to Ras al-'Ayn (Rosh Ha'ayin) near the coast. On this fall day, one also can see three army lorries driving out of the center of town towards Ariel, the middle one filled with poorly clad young Palestinian men, some of them handcuffed and bent over.

Though it is almost 11 am, Abu Farid and his two younger sons, 'Aqil and Riyad, are still asleep. Only Farid, who lives with his wife and three children in the newly-built downstairs annex to the house, has been hard at work since the early morning hours. Farid's stepmother, Umm Samhan, lets me in to the family's diwan (sitting room), and is soon back with large cups of Turkish coffee. This week, it turns out, Abu Farid and Riyad, his youngest son, are working second shift, and their ride to the factory is not due until 1 pm.

'Aqil, the first to walk in, plunks on a chair, lights a cigarette and sips his coffee. He slept late for a different reason: the ordeal of a three-day detention without charge in Tulkarm prison. 'Aqil, like scores of other young people thought to be politically active by the Israeli military authorities, was detained in advance of national occasions. In this case, it was November 29, the anniversary of the United Nations partition of Palestine and now celebrated as the International Day of Solidarity with the Palestinian People.

Even if he had not been detained, 'Aqil would probably still have slept late, for that has been his habit ever since he decided to stop working about eighteen months ago, much to the consternation of his family. Unlike his father and brothers, none of whom finished high school, 'Aqil is a graduate of Birzeit University, where he majored in political science. Consequently, he has long enjoyed privileged status within the family. But with the very high rate of unemployment for college graduates in the occupied West Bank, he was forced to work for many years as a manual laborer in the construction industry in Israel, that is, until he could no longer bear the contradiction between the very high expectations held both by him and his family on the one hand, and the reality of working-class life on the other.

Abu Farid, silver-haired but vigorous, also lights a cigarette as soon as he sits down. He is a confident man, essentially at peace with himself, but with deep undercurrents of bitterness, often directed against 'Aqil. Born in 1928 to a family of landless peasants, Abu Farid has been working hard all his life just to survive, and he has little sympathy for 'Aqil's predicament.

At age thirteen, looking for work, he trekked to the Galilee, far from home. For seven years, he delivered messages on a bicycle from one English office to another. Cut off by the 1948 war, he was unemployed and "hanging around in the streets" of Salfit when Fu'ad Nassar, Fahmi 'Awad and 'Arabi 'Awad, all central committee members of the Palestinian National Liberation League (which became the Communist Party of Jordan in 1951) took refuge there. Abu Farid, along with dozens of others, joined the party, and in the 1950s Salfit became a major stronghold of Palestinian communists and a battle front against the Jordanian occupation. To this day the identification of Salfit with both communism and anti-Jordanian activities persists, at least in the minds of the older generation. A few years ago, when the assassin of a Jordanian diplomat in Turkey was identified as a resident of Salfit, the town sent a delegation to Jordan to mend fences.

"If the Ba'th had come first, perhaps we would have all been Ba'thists," Abu Farid recalls in a detached manner. "We were ready to accept any party which would deliver us from the tyranny of the Jordanian regime." Arrested, beaten and jailed in 1952, 1954 and 1956, he was finally exiled into Ma'n, Jordan, where 'Aqil was born. The charges ranged from distribution of subversive literature to participating in illegal demonstrations against the annexation of the West Bank to Jordan. "The majority really did not know what communism is, and after the 1956-57 crackdown a large number quit the party. But," he added, in reference to himself, "it is impossible for a person to forego his principles if he formed them consciously."

Until he was allowed to travel in 1962, Abu Farid and his family lived in abject poverty. "Like cats on the streets," he says. "That is how most of the people in the villages around here lived, day to day." He immediately went to Kuwait where he worked for four years as an unskilled laborer in an engineering firm. Back in his hometown for a visit, the 1967 war, like the one preceding it, cut him off from work and restricted him once again. "There was no war in Salfit," he notes, "not a single rifle was ever allowed by the Jordanians, who were long gone before the Israeli army came. The people were very afraid. Many thought that there would be massacres and they ran away. But the Israeli soldiers did not even walk about. They simply occupied the police headquarters and called on a loudspeaker for the people to deliver any weapons they might have."

The first two years after the 1967 war were ones of hard times and uncertainty for most working class Palestinians. As a son of a landless peasant, Abu Farid was a member of the social group that was hit hardest during the Jordanian occupation. King Hussein's economic policy siphoned off the West Bank's surplus for the development of the East Bank, especially its capital, Amman. Large landowners and big city merchants prospered, while most Palestinian villagers suffered high unemployment. "There was a severe economic recession until the end of 1969," Abu Farid recalls. "In Salfit the land is mountainous and all we have are olive trees. Two-thirds of the people were unemployed and, as soon as the Israeli labor market opened, many left school and began to work."

Farid, his oldest son, was one of the thousands of Palestinians who braved an alien world in order to make a living. He dropped out of school to work for an Israeli contractor as a plasterer and painter in 1970, and has branched out on his own since then. A skilled, honest and extremely hard worker, he has managed to make more money than most employees and college teachers. "I have a good name in Petah Tikva (the nearest Israeli city to Salfit). I do good work, I do it fast, and for much less than Israeli contractors charge." He has since left the Israeli labor market and is working full-time in his hometown, riding the construction boom that has overtaken many Palestinian villages since the seventies.

Farid's life goal, from the very beginning, was simple and traditional: to build his own home, marry and have children. To his great satisfaction, this goal was realized. It took him ten years to save enough money to build a large annex to the original family house. Soon after, his father married him off, and now he has three children. The house's interior, from the modern interchangeable double windows to the kitchen where the sink is made of smooth marble-like stone, were designed and installed by him. His latest acquisition is a brand new video cassette recorder, at a cost of $1,300.

Farid is a product of that early period when job opportunities in Israel, no matter how menial or degrading, represented a release from a life of extreme poverty for Palestinian villagers *cum* city workers. Consequently, Farid inherited none of his father's political commitment, and little of his profound alienation and bitterness from work in Israel. In recalling his experiences, he mentions incidents which to the listener might seem racist and humiliating, but on him they leave no visible mark whatsoever. What impresses Farid is the fact that his Israeli employers usually paid on time and in full—unlike many of his current Arab customers, as he is always quick to point out.

The youngest son, Riyad, with his modern haircut, fashionable clothes and wrist paraphernalia walks in as Umm Samhan prepares the table for a late breakfast. Born in 1967, reality for him is his job at the textile factory in Petah Tikva, his friends and Western music. The impoverished days of the Jordanian occupation, and his father's political trials and tribulations are remote abstractions. He is a sensitive, sincere young man and is embarrassed when asked why he dropped out of school. "I was just stupid, I guess," he answers looking at his feet. 'Aqil immediately interjects that the real reason was Riyad's desire to be with his friends, most of whom are fellow workers at the factory. "But," he adds reprovingly, "unlike them, he did not have to leave school in order to provide for his family. He simply couldn't wait." Riyad silently concurs, but rules out going back to school again. "Many of my friends in the factory are college graduates," he points out, "and they don't get paid any more than I do. Besides, 'Aqil has finished college and is doing absolutely nothing."

Riyad speaks earnestly about his work experiences. "I have been working in the textile factory for two years now. There are close to fifty workers from Salfit and we all know each other well. I can work all the machines, but my main job is with the 'flare' which separates the balls of cotton, polyester and acrylic into many little strings. Father has the hardest job. He works at the first stage of the assembly line moving the bales of cotton from the belt onto little carts. If he stops, everything stops."

Umm Samhan reappears with the usual breakfast items: olives, za'tar (thyme), jibna (white cheese), hummus and scrambled eggs. After a brief silence, Riyad continues in a sober voice. "Two months ago, a new management came in and they fired forty-five of the 195 workers in the factory. All the ones dismissed were Jews who, believe me, just sat around. None of us Arabs really knew what they were supposed to be doing, though they made twice as much as we did. But they lowered our wages too. Now, we get paid less for overtime, and the minimum piece-work quota was raised over 15 percent. Since then, we work harder but make less money."

Abu Farid, who has been working the same job for seven years, has a different set of complaints. "The most important difference," he points out, "is not the wages. They [Jewish workers] get twenty-two to twenty-three days a year paid vacation. For us, any vacation time is unpaid. They also receive gifts on holidays, health insurance, sick leave, pensions and trips to Eilat at the factory's expense. We get none of these things, but they deduct their cost out of our wages." Riyad continues as Abu Farid walks out of the room to get a copy of his paycheck. "Recently the Histadrut and the factory management wanted us to elect two Arabs to be our representatives. Until then, two Jews represented us, and we were not allowed to vote. Most of the workers wanted to take up this offer, but the internal regulations of the Workers' Unity Bloc state clearly that West Bank laborers who work in Israel should be represented by their own independent labor unions. After much discussion, the workers agreed not to elect representatives to the Histadrut."

Back at the table, Abu Farid's face expresses his displeasure at these comments. He has little faith in the Palestinian workers' unions, and is not enthused about Riyad's growing involvement. "They just talk. They can do nothing for those who work in Israel." 'Aqil, who has been a coordinator for the Salfit branch of the Workers' Unity Bloc for some years now, reminds him of the health insurance program, and the fact that the unions are still struggling for the right to represent the workers. But Abu Farid is not convinced. In fact, he is cynical about most sacred cows of the Palestinian national movement. "We are surrounded," Abu Farid declared during a heated exchange with 'Aqil after breakfast. "If an ant crosses the border they know about it. The future is dark. All the Arab regimes are just like Israel— they are tied to America. They are even more scared than Israel when they hear talk of an independent Palestinian state. The occupation is here to stay as long as Israel gets American support and the people here don't rise up to their responsibilities. All we can do is shout our opposition to the occupation. The old generation was better. Now there are drugs and immorality. We have been sucked into Israel and our blood is there. If Israel goes, where shall we go? Here, there are no factories. Amman helps the merchants, the contractors, the engineers and the government employees, many of whom get double salaries. But they could care less for the workers. The PLO is in Tunis, Iraq and Yemen, paralyzed. Sure they are the sole legitimate representative, but how can they get to us when Jordan and Syria are off limits to them?"

Abu Farid's cynicism does not emanate solely from the political abyss in which most Palestinians find themselves. Much of it flows from a different, more personal, source symbolized by the harsh events of 1979 when he lost his wife, his job and, in many ways, his son 'Aqil. Until then, Abu Farid held a job he enjoyed tremendously. He was steadily raising himself from the clutches of poverty. Ironically, though it locked him out from Kuwait after 1967, the Israeli occupation reunited him with the Galilee where he had previously worked. As a Jordanian citizen, he was in a position to provide an outlet to the Arab world for his Galilee friends who hired him to look up their surviving relatives in the camps of Lebanon, Jordan and Syria. For eight years he was his own boss and travelled to Baq'a, Yarmuk, Rashidiyya, Tal al-Za'atar, Sabra, Shatila and other places where Palestinians congregated, making contacts and arranging visits.

'Aqil's arrest changed all that. In the winter of that year, while a student at Birzeit University, 'Aqil was charged with membership in an "illegal organization." On the day of the trial, his mother, whom Abu Farid loved deeply, died on the way to the court when the car she was in crashed against a wall. That same day, not only was 'Aqil convicted and sent to prison but his father lost his job when the Israeli authorities, in a typical brush stroke of collective punishment, forbade him to leave the West Bank. With Farid about to get married and the downstairs annex under construction, Abu Farid, much to his chagrin, was forced to work in an Israeli orange juice factory for over two years until he found the better paying job at the textile factory. "Imagine the irony of it all," he once told me. "When I was poor and raising my family, I managed to avoid working in Israel. But when my children became educated and old enough to produce, I had to work there. After 'Aqil's arrest, I had the most difficult times of my life."

With a honk of its horn, the factory bus sweeps the men away to Petah Tikva. The family's diwan, a large bare room lined on all four sides with skinny metal chairs, is suddenly lifeless and eerie. It reminds the visitor that there is little that gives this segmented household a sense of "home." Every one seems to have a social environment of his own, and differing work schedules rarely allow them to sit together for family rituals. Each has developed a world view much different from, and often in conflict with, the others. Partly, this is due to the fact that the men were exposed to distinctly different sets of realities arising from the successive and profound changes that have overwhelmed Palestinian society over the past forty years. But in this particular household there is yet another, more fundamental, reason for the fragile family ties and the lack of a common sense of purpose. As the spartan furnishings and the dormitory atmosphere suggest, there is an absence of a strong female presence. Unlike most village households, there is no matriarch here to bond the family, and to function as a nexus around which the domestic economy, in all its cultural and social aspects, revolves.

Umm Samhan, Abu Farid's second wife, comes into the diwan for a brief rest. Married at a relatively late age to a widower with three grown sons, she never really had the opportunity to fulfill this crucial role. Energetic yet calm and collected, reserved yet always smiling and helpful, she is rarely intimidated, nor does she behave as an outsider. Yet it is clear that she is in no position to exercise any influence over Farid, 'Aqil and Riyad. They refer to her as "my father's wife" with a detached tone of respect, even though Umm Samhan takes care of their daily needs as any mother would.

After finishing her domestic chores and putting her two little children to sleep, Umm Samhan often sits in front of the television set until broadcasting ends at midnight. Aside from weekly visits to her family and occasional conversations with the neighbors, this is her favorite activity and she is quite excited at the new video. "What else is there to do?" she smiles. "In the past," she continues, referring to previous generations, "there were no water lines or electricity. Women worked day and night carrying water, gathering wood, planting tomatoes, harvesting wheat and feeding animals. Now, it is considered shameful for women to work the land. After all, Salfit is no longer a village, and city women don't work. Well, perhaps it is not shameful, but except for the olive picking season only the older women still work on the land. What is truly shameful is for women to work in Israel. Only the ones who live in the border villages do."

Late in the afternoon, Farid walks into the family diwan. He is covered with dust, plaster and paint, and his hands are even rougher than his father's, not a common phenomenon in the West Bank. Farid takes me to his old room to show me a huge oil painting he did before dropping out of school. It depicts a young courageous man crucified on a hammer and sickle with a harsh, barren landscape for background. "I wanted to portray how people are oppressed because of their ideals," he says, sincerely and without a trace of irony though the very theme of the painting contradicts Farid's own self-image. Farid is a staunchly anti-political person. "The difference between 'Aqil and I is like that between the earth and the sky," he is fond of saying. "The *mukhabarat* (Israeli intelligence) has not detained me once, while 'Aqil is always in trouble." Once, in a bitingly sarcastic mood, 'Aqil reminded Farid that he was severely beaten by soldiers several times in the past few years, yet still ignores the relevance of politics. "True, I was beaten," exclaims Farid, totally missing the point, "but it wasn't because I did anything wrong. The soldiers just did it because I was an Arab."

'Aqil can only shrug. He is alienated from his family, and is tired of being used as a measuring stick for failure. He constantly moves around from town to town because he does not feel at home anywhere. Like the overwhelming majority of young, educated but unemployed Palestinians in the occupied West Bank, he has thought seriously about leaving, but resisted joining the ranks of the hundreds that do emigrate.

'Aqil does not talk about his relationship with the family, but it is very clear that they resent his idleness, and the troubles he caused them as a result of his political activities. Umm Samhan angrily recalls the weekly raids by Israeli soldiers on the house after 'Aqil's imprisonment. "They knew that we had nothing hidden, but they wanted to harass us so that we would pressure 'Aqil to quit his political work." Abu Farid, in moments of anger, has been known to accuse his son of being responsible for his wife's death. But in more thoughtful moments, he stakes out a considered position: "I don't blame him really, but we did not have the same opportunities. There was no one to give us money. We did not have any colleges. There was no one responsible for us. One must not despair. 'Aqil cannot walk two roads at the same time. He must either face his situation or go backwards."

It seems ironic that 'Aqil, who inherited the political mantle from his father, should find himself rebelling against him and his brothers who are as working class as West Bank Palestinians can get. Then again, his father has long ago given up political activities, and his brothers, especially Farid, are concerned first and foremost with consolidating the family's rise out of poverty. Abu Farid and Riyad, compared to many other workers, have a good thing going. They work in a large, modern factory, are registered in the Israeli employment office, and receive regular paychecks. True, unlike Jewish workers they get no return from the taxes they pay, have to change shifts every week, do not receive full benefits, and work harder for less money. But their lot is much better than the 40,000 or more "illegal" Palestinian workers who flood the "slave labor" market early every morning. Such a worker has to leave his village at 4 am and hope that some Israeli contractor, when he rolls down his car window at dawn, will pick him from among the dozens vying for attention. These workers are hired on a daily basis, have to pay for transportation and are usually not back until the late evening.

For Abu Farid, the Israeli occupation, despite its ruthlessness and minute control over every aspect of his and his children's lives, has offered more than the Jordanian occupation. At least there was a rise in his standard of living, and he was able to put 'Aqil through college, a seemingly impossible dream for a man of landless peasant stock. Farid has made his twin goal of home and family come true through hard work and a healthy appreciation for humility. Riyad, faced with a choice between education and an uncertain future, or a steady job, chose the latter. He is much more politically active than Farid and his father, but at least he has made peace with the world. Only 'Aqil refuses to accept his situation. Until something drastic changes, he, like the over 12,000 unemployed college graduates in the occupied territories, has only two harsh choices: become a wage laborer in Israel, or leave the country.

Postscript: November 1988

Since the time of writing, the occupied territories, in pregnant anticipation during the previous year, have been swept by an uprising that continues unabated. The people of Salfit have given their share of blood and tears, if not more. I drove into town in January 1988, soon after the lifting of the second major curfew, which had lasted for six consecutive days. Almost every street was littered with the remains of barricades and burnt tires. Farid's old car, recently overhauled, was filled with little children rummaging through its scorched shell. During a demonstration, the young protesters needed a large object to cut off the quickly advancing soldiers. Farid offered his car which was turned over and torched.

Upstairs in the diwan, all were present except one. A week before, on January 12, two dozen Israeli soldiers stormed into the house just before midnight, grabbed 'Aqil, put him in a lorry and beat him severely in full view of family and neighbors. The cycle of resistance and repression had already galvanized the family and infused it with one mind and one spirit, an almost complete reversal of the pre-intifada period. Abu Farid broke the curfew twice in order to find out where 'Aqil was being detained, and to give his name to the Red Cross. Umm Samhan, who had screamed and pulled at the soldiers during 'Aqil's arrest, tearfully recounted how blood dripped from his face after a soldier smashed his glasses with a stick. Even apolitical Farid was filled with anger and hatred. Riyad, wanted by the mukhabarat, rarely stays home at night. As I left, three helicopters circled above. They were looking for the many young men who escaped into the surrounding hills, the same hills in which Abu Farid took refuge thirty years ago while being pursued by the Jordanian intelligence services.

Of my many subsequent visits, the two during the last week of March are unforgettable. On Sunday, March 27, I escorted a bus load of academics from the United States and Europe on a day trip to the northern region of the West Bank. On a brilliant sunny day we made our way to Salfit along the winding Yasuf-Iskaka road. This time, it was punctuated by stone barricades every half mile or so. After negotiating with the young men in these two villages, the bus proceeded slowly as rocks were moved and then put back into place.

In Salfit, we were warmly welcomed and taken on a tour of the old part of the city. The town, like the road, was full of Palestinian flags. Portrayed in the Israeli press as a prime example of a community in which an effective alternative structure of local control had emerged, Salfit had been "liberated" since February 1, 1988. On that winter day, the Leadership Committee of the Intifada in Salfit (LCIS), comprising the various underground political factions, released its first communique, and staffed local guard outposts that effectively kept the army out of town. The official municipal structure had long since collapsed, and the LCIS established new procedures regulating daily life.

High spirits and obvious pride glowed in the faces of the men, women and children who gathered around. Soon many little groups formed, and Riyad approached me and recounted the events of the past few weeks. He and his father no longer work at the factory. They made that decision soon after 'Aqil's arrest. What excited Riyad, however, was not the act of leaving, but the collective action taken by the Arab workers before quitting. "First," he said, "we refused to go beyond the minimum production quota assigned to each person. Then, we began a slowdown strike and only produced about 60 percent of the piece-work required. Finally, we began sabotaging machines. You know, no one understands the machine better than the worker who labors on it all day. We found ways of causing them to malfunction so often that the factory was finally forced to close."

Most likely, there were other reasons for the shut-down. The textile sector, and others such as construction, tourism and furniture making, have been hit hard by the double blow of the intifada and the increasing financial difficulties of the industrial enterprises operating under the Histadrut umbrella. Nevertheless, whatever their actual effectiveness, Riyad and his fellow workers believe they were responsible, an attitude typical of the feeling of empowerment which the intifada has engendered in people's minds.

The conversation with Riyad came to an abrupt end when shouts of "army," "army," rang out from rooftops. Within seconds, the town square stood hauntingly empty. We quickly boarded the bus and made our way towards Ariel and the main road, but our bus was soon stopped by an army command jeep and lorry. After half an hour of questioning—during which the soldiers established our identity, where we came from and were going, and the fact that this was a Birzeit University bus—we were escorted to the trans-Samaria road. During this half hour one of our passengers, a Hebrew speaker, listened to the commander relay this information to his superior.

On our way to Bidya, where three houses had been demolished the week before as punishment for an attack on the village mukhtar, a notorious collaborator and land dealer, we saw a long convoy of cars, vans, pickups and jeeps with their headlights on racing the opposite way. A few hours later, when we stopped in Nablus, we heard a rumor that a young man in Salfit had been shot dead. Our shock only deepened that evening when we heard the Israeli television and radio broadcasts announce that the army had shot dead two young men in Salfit while "rescuing a bus of tourists that was hijacked by an Arab mob and attacked with stones, glass bottles and iron bars." That same evening, the bus passengers quickly drafted a statement denying this version of events and contacted the media, but the next morning the Israeli newspapers carried the official story on the front page. In response the passengers held a press conference, and by the following day the army was forced to change its story.

On Land Day, March 30, the West Bank was in state of siege, and traffic between towns and villages was choked to a trickle. Nevertheless, five of us carrying a personal letter signed by the bus passengers and addressed to the people of Salfit went in a taxi to visit the families of the deceased. We were stopped and turned back often, but four hours and many dirt roads later we finally arrived. Our letter was copied and posted on trees and the father of one of the martyrs recounted how his son was shot by a sniper wearing a white T-shirt and kneeling down among budding stalks of wheat. The boy's body was carried by his comrades to a nearby hill, laid down under an olive tree and covered with grass. It has become an intifada tradition to claim the dead before the army does. Otherwise, the body is sent to an Israeli morgue at Abu Kabir, autopsied and then returned to the family under the condition that no one but immediate relatives be allowed at the burial, usually a midnight affair.

The young men who carried his bleeding body to the thick olive groves, leaving only his mother at its side, explained to us that this was necessary because the army's method goes against Islamic law, costs the family hundreds of dinars in fees and, most importantly, deprives the martyr of a proper nationalist funeral. In this case they were successful. An army helicopter gave up the search after an hour and then the entire town turned out for a mass march to the cemetery.

Despite the high cost, the quick defensive action was successful and the army withdrew beyond Salfit's borders. The town remained "liberated" until, on the moonless night of April 14, the army re-established its presence on a daily basis by executing a massive military operation: eighty youths who played a leading role in the town's struggle against the occupation were detained. Luckily, Riyad made it out safely. But the mukhabarat had a long list of wanted youths already prepared, and the parents of those not found were served with written orders demanding that they bring in their sons the next day. Abu Farid sent messages out to Riyad that same night, and the next day escorted him to the Tulkarm military headquarters. "What else can I do?" he exclaimed, "The military commander made it clear that if I don't show up with Riyad, they were going to come the next day and smash everything in the house." Riyad was one of the fortunate few released eighteen days later.

'Aqil, who some believe was instrumental in founding the LCIS, is still under administrative detention (imprisonment without charge or trial) at the notorious Ansar III prison in the Negev. He and his family, indeed the entire town of Salfit, have been rejuvenated and marked, once again, by the long and bloody struggle for national liberation.

## Chapter 11

Palestinian Women: Building Barricades and Breaking Barriers

Rita Giacaman and Penny Johnson

Umm 'Uthman (the mother of 'Uthman) is forty-six years old. A member of the black community of the Jericho area, she is tall, fine-boned, almost Ethiopian in appearance. She lives in 'Ayn Duyuk, a small community of about 1,000 persons, where the race divide of black and white still dominates economic and social relations, a rarity in Palestinian society. Umm 'Uthman is to us Umm Ruqayya, because we came to know her through her radical and activist daughter.

Ruqayya, twenty-six years old, is a worker at one of the sewing sweatshops in nearby Jericho. She is reputed to be one of the main figures fuelling the activism of the local chapter of the Seamstresses' Union. As her friends and family put it: "She has driven the owner and administration of the workshop mad with her clever strategies and plans for improving work conditions." Ruqayya is also well-educated, modern and "cultured" (*muthaqqafa*). She reads regularly, writes well, argues points beautifully and, in sum, represents the best characteristics of a new generation of progressive women political activists.

With innate characteristics not so unlike her daughter's, but without having had the chance to grow up in an era where these characteristics could develop, Umm 'Uthman is haggard, very tall and very thin, except for that pouch of a belly, the nagging evidence of many pregnancies, twenty-two in all. About half were lost before birth or early in childhood. Twelve children remain, with the oldest aged twenty-eight and the youngest a mere six months old. She has no regrets about having had so many children because children, she says, "are needed, especially in these days of strife, when every Palestinian counts." Umm 'Uthman's sense of responsibility toward family and community is embodied in her awareness of her important role as a mother, a role enhanced in her mind and the community's by the current uprising.

We went to visit her on November 6, 1988, when we heard that the family house had been demolished by the Israeli army. Hers was one of more than 100 houses destroyed in the northern Jordan valley, leaving about 1,000 persons homeless and devastated. The army's rationale was collective punishment of these remote communities for allegedly having hidden in their midst someone who had thrown a molotov cocktail at an Israeli bus, resulting in the deaths of an Israeli mother and her three young children. In fact, the Israeli army had apparently been intending to empty that particular area, a sensitive security zone, of its inhabitants.

We found Umm 'Uthman seated on the floor, clutching her breastfeeding infant with one hand and a cigarette that she puffed deliberately and systematically with the other. Chairs were quickly brought to seat the guests and Umm 'Uthman began to recount her story :

> It was on the night of October 30 that our lives were pulled upside down. That evening, just a day or two after the bus incident, we heard helicopters flying in the sky. They came down towards our village at the same time as soldiers began to move in. We immediately closed our door, put out the lights and went to bed, wondering to whose neighbor's house they were heading. So you can imagine our shock when they began to ferociously bang at our door. They came in and began to break everything they had in front of them. They took away my five sons and informed me that I had ten minutes to pack my belongings because they were going to demolish the house. But there was no one to help me pack because they had kept away all the villagers and had succeeded in isolating us and our house. I was alone with my youngest child. I was hardly able to carry some clothes for my baby with me when I was pushed, shoved and forced out of the house, and the house with everything in it and all our belongings were dynamited.

Of all the members of this community, it was Ruqayya who mobilized immediately in response to the destruction of her house, three more in the village and many others in the valley, as well as the arrest of her five brothers. When we arrived Ruqayya had already left for Jerusalem to talk to lawyers, the Red Cross and any other institution or agency capable of assisting the family and the community in these hard times. Within a day, she had singlehandedly "moved mountains," utilizing her skills and contacts developed through her activism in the local women's committee and her Seamstresses' union.

Ruqayya's activism and her education thus gave her a considerable amount of power not only within the world of women, but at the level of her entire village. Although a woman, Ruqayya was indispensable to her community during this crisis. She could serve her community in areas where no one else could, so why bother about the fact of her womanhood? To the community, what mattered most was survival in these times when the formal networks of support were breaking down and when conditions were creating new and pressing needs. Survival dictated a changing attitude towards the activism of women in general and to Ruqayya's full participation in political life in particular.

Ruqayya is one of many women forging a new chapter in the history of the Palestinian women's movement. She is the antithesis to the image of obedient wife and mother, of the silent woman who executes the wishes of husband and kin without a word uttered. *Tum bila lisan* (a mouth without a tongue) is how traditional society usually characterizes "good" women. Ruqayya exemplifies an emerging new consciousness regarding the status of women in Palestinian society and their participation in political life. Ruqayya is the daughter of the uprising, having risen to the status of a community leader of both men and women just during the past several months.

Observers of the intifada have tended to focus on its impact on the Palestinian political agenda, as exemplified in the decisions of the November 1988 meeting of the Palestine National Council in Algiers. But equally important for the lives of the Palestinian people, and in particular women, are the transformations the uprising has wrought in the forms of struggle. Mass insurgency and collective defiance in the context of a popular revolt have become the new cornerstones of political action, a change from the previous emphasis on armed struggle, shuttle diplomacy and limited mass action. The development of the popular and neighborhood committees, and a partial shift in the locus of authority and action from formal institutions and networks of political action to the streets, have also had far-reaching social ramifications. In the framework of the new informal and popular networks of community support and action, important shifts in women's participation in political life have taken place.

On the basis of interviews with women activists, particularly leaders and activists in the women's committees, as well as the authors' own observations and conversations with women in camps, towns and villages during the course of the uprising, we have tried to explore how the dramatic political changes outlined above have affected the position of Palestinian women in the world of politics, both formal and informal. We wanted to delineate the various roles women have played in the uprising: in confrontations, in political organizations and political decisionmaking, in community survival and in community organization. We have only tentative answers for some of our questions, including the all-important question of whether women's political role in the uprising will lead to permanent changes in women's participation and status in the society of the future. That question remains to be asked—and ultimately answered—by Palestinian women themselves.

The Palestinian Women's Movement

From its inception in the 1920s, the women's movement in Palestine was the product of the economic and social changes set into motion by the opposing forces of colonialism and nationalism. Women as a group began to be involved in political action in the context of the national struggle.[1] In other words, women were propelled by their nationalist sentiments—and in many instances encouraged by society—to deviate from their traditional roles by protesting and even establishing their own organizations. This development was not, however, necessarily accompanied by autonomy for the new women's organizations.[2]

After 1967 Palestinian women responded to the nationalist movement and to the new conditions generated by occupation. Structural economic changes, particularly the employment of Palestinians inside Israel, also affected women, whether directly as women workers or as the wives, mothers or sisters of male workers. Another important development, not directly related to the occupation, was a dramatic increase in the education of women, including higher education.

Women were politically active from the very beginning of the occupation. As early as February 1968, for example, several hundred women demonstrated in Jerusalem against land confiscation and deportation. A few even joined the armed groups that formed in that period. However, the major framework for women's organization and activity were the over one hundred traditional charitable societies located in the towns. Among the most successful of these were In'ash al-Usra (Family Rehabilitation Society),[3] which grew from two rooms in 1965 to a large modern building with over 100 employees, an orphanage and a wide variety of programs, and the Arab Women's Union in Nablus, which runs a hospital. These societies were motivated by nationalist as well as charitable sentiments and were led largely by urban middle-class women, although in some cases these women were actually major-domos for male leaders. While these societies were very active in serving the rural and refugee poor, they did so largely without their participation.

In the late 1970s, a new generation of young activists launched a number of grassroots committees and movements in the West Bank, and to a lesser extent Gaza, including the volunteer work committees (begun as a voluntary work movement in 1971-72), trade and student unions, youth movements and a grassroots health movement. A new generation of women, many of whom had been politicized in the student movements at Palestinian universities, founded grassroots women's committees that, in contrast to the charitable society network of women's organizations, sought to involve the majority of women in the West Bank who lived in villages, along with women in camps, the urban poor and women workers as well as intellectuals and urban middle-class women, in a united women's movement. Reflecting the leftist ideas current in student circles and political organizations, the first two committees—the Women's Work Committee and the Working Women's Committee—began by focusing on the conditions of women factory workers. The first project of the nascent Women's Work Committee, for example, was a 1978 survey of women textile workers in the Ramallah area. These committees, joined in 1982 by the Palestinian Women's Committee and in 1984 by the Women's Committee for Social Work, launched a series of projects serving women: literacy, small-scale production training, nurseries and kindergartens, and health education. These projects were animated by the desire to mobilize women and raise their nationalist consciousness. Three of the committees articulated a program of improving women's status in society, although national liberation remained the overriding concern. The four committees reflected the four main political streams in the nationalist movement, a factionalism which created competition and occasionally hampered their attempts to respond to local conditions and women's needs.

By the eve of the uprising, the women's committees had developed to include seasoned women leaders and a base with firm roots in towns, villages and camps. While not the generators of women's mass participation in the uprising, the committees played a major role in shaping that participation.

From Home to Community: Women's Expanded Role During the Uprising

"We told the shabab (young men), stay home and sleep, today we're in charge."

These words were spoken by a smiling young woman from the Ramallah-area village of Kafr Na'ma as she described a march by several hundred women from the village in celebration of International Women's Day, March 8, almost three months into the uprising. It was Kafr Na'ma's first local celebration of International Women's Day. In previous years women activists from the village might have travelled to celebrations held by the women's committees in Jerusalem, but this year women from the village actually demonstrated twice, going in the morning to Ramallah to join ranks with urban women teachers, grandmothers in peasant dress, and blue-jeaned teenagers for an impressive march through the center of town.

By March 8, a qualitative change had taken place in women's participation in public and political life, although whether this change was (or is) obvious to the largely male leadership of the uprising remains a question. Images of daily life in this period attested to this change: a middle-aged woman in Ramallah helps young men build a barricade, a woman in Aida camp fights and even bites a soldier who is trying to take her son, women in Gaza carry trays full of rocks on their heads to supply demonstrators, women in camps under extended curfew defy the military to smuggle food and fuel into the camp. Even women's language, as one activist noted, had begun to change:

> Women now sit together and talk about the uprising, about politics: who was detained, what the latest communique says, strike days, curfews. They no longer chat about petty concerns.

Urban women organized their own protest activities, for example sit-ins at the International Red Cross to protest mass detentions and prison conditions. However, many of the political actions that engaged masses of women—particularly informal actions—were not the province of the urban women who have traditionally been the most active in women's organizations, or even necessarily of students, who have often carried the banner of political mobilization in the occupied territories. Women in refugee camps and villages have in fact been more active than women in towns, reflecting the uprising's focus on the central role of these communities. This constitutes a historic reversal in the orientation of the women's movement in Palestine, although it is not yet reflected in women's leadership since decision making still remains largely in the hands of urban middle-class women.

In the widespread participation of women some have discerned an emerging new role for women in society. For example, Birzeit University Dean of Arts Dr. Hanan Mikhail-Ashrawi argues that women's activity in the uprising "has removed the basis of authority of the male. Traditional hierarchies are challenged by new hierarchies." Some have gone even further. Israeli journalist Ehud Ya'ari, for example, has described the uprising as a gender rebellion, "an internal revolution of children against fathers, women against husbands, poor against rich, refugees against the propertied classes."[4]

Careful scrutiny of the kinds of actions women have most frequently taken during the course of the uprising suggests another hypothesis, though Ashrawi's point about new hierarchies is provocative and important. Although it is often asserted that women's traditional domestic role in the family is an obstacle to public political action, that the world of the home and the world of the polity are sealed off from one another,[5] these barriers seem to have become permeable for Palestinian women during the uprising. Women, and particularly those not already organizationally identified with a political movement or group, have enlarged or extended their traditional role rather than adopting a completely new role. Many of their forms of political participation are based on aspects of this role, particularly defense of family, nurturing and assisting family members, and mutual aid between kin. These aspects of women's role have become a source of resistance because women have transformed their family responsibilities to encompass the entire community. In a real sense, particularly in villages and refugee camps where the community is closely bound together, the community has become the family in this time of sustained crisis.

A clear example is offered by the myriad accounts of women struggling with soldiers to reclaim young men whom soldiers have seized to beat or detain. The common refrain, echoed by a multitude of women as they attempt to snatch a youth from the clutches of the army, has been, "He's my son!" Initially a spontaneous response, some women have made it a "profession," in the sense that they are on the streets ready to confront the army. In Ramallah, Akram, the son of Jamila, was detained near the mosque on January 29 after Friday prayers. Jamila, a youthful middle-class woman and a US citizen, struggled in vain to free her son who was surrounded by a group of soldiers who were kicking him with their boots and pounding him with their rifle butts. Then, one elderly woman in peasant dress got hold of Akram and smothered him in a huge embrace while soldiers try to beat him back.

"He's my son!" she cries, "don't you touch him!"

"Liar," says a soldier, barely out of his teens, "how can you be his mother?"

"They are all my children, not like you motherless lot!"

Another women's activity that clearly derives from their traditional role is visiting the sick and wounded, which is now not restricted to relatives or immediate neighbors and can even become an organized activity of a women's organization, such as a visit to a village that has been attacked by the army. Attending funerals of martyrs—the equivalent of a demonstration—is the most politicized version of this activity.

Confronting soldiers during army raids (usually at night) when they come to detain youths is yet another activity of women that has been extended from the family to the community, to the extent that women call each other to confront the army as it enters a camp or village. Women have also been involved in smuggling food and other provisions into refugee camps under curfew, a major contribution to sustaining the uprising.

The courage of women confronting soldiers in the most difficult of conditions—unprotected, late at night, in remote villages and curfewed refugee camps—is uncontestable. Three different women in the northern West Bank village of Ya'bad told us of an older woman, Umm Kamal, who during a massive army raid against the village in February tried to block the soldiers' entrance into her house and was clubbed and teargassed. A younger married woman, Umm Mahmud, alone with her children and her elderly father, gave a lively account of soldiers invading her house in the same dawn raid: they smashed her solar heater and the concrete steps leading to her house, dumped her household possessions outside, and pushed her with clubs. Her answer was simply: "I am not afraid." A teenager, her hand bandaged, described with some relish an irritated soldier, stick poised to beat her because of her defiant behavior (she had thrown a brick from the roof), angrily saying: "What's this? You are trying to defeat the occupation all by yourself?"

This kind of women's activism is not reflected in the gloomy statistics of deaths, woundings and detentions. Of 204 Palestinians killed in the West Bank (excluding Gaza) by soldiers or settlers and documented by al-Haq, the Ramallah-based affiliate of the International Commission of Jurists, fifteen were women or girls. An estimated 300 women have been detained for longer than a day or so in the course of the uprising, compared to about 20,000 males. Al-Haq recently reported that thirteen Palestinian women were placed under administrative detention (imprisonment without trial, usually for six months), in contrast to 3-4,000 men.[6] Since these indicators are also used by Palestinian society to measure activism, it is unclear how visible or valued women's activities are in the collective assessment of society.

The assessment of the family, of course, is often the individual woman's most important measure. Women's movement from family to community has broken one major barrier for many women: the barrier of shame, of family restrictions on the movement of women. This critical transformation is evidenced by the participation (and even leadership) of unmarried women in mixed settings, whether demonstrations or neighborhood committees. Such participation is made easier when the community is close-knit, as in villages. Still, although some women find that their families (and especially their fathers) are proud of their new political activism, others still face conflict with their parents over political participation.

Demonstrations are perhaps the clearest of political actions, and the least tied to traditional women's roles. Demonstrations of women in towns reached their peak in February and March when marches from mosques on Fridays and especially churches on Sundays drew the widespread participation of women not necessarily bound by religion. In Ramallah, for example, many women attended both Friday and Sunday marches. Other protests, particularly at the village and camp level, drew strength from communal and family roots. During a visit in late October to the Nablus-area village of Kafr Thuluth, 'Aziza, a youthful married woman, barefoot in a bright blue dress accented in red and black, confidently discussed the complicated political situation of her village while her husband served cola and occasionally chimed in. She is a new activist in the Women's Work Committee and has apparently developed by leaps and bounds in the course of the uprising. When she calls women to demonstrate against soldiers, she begins with her sister, aunt and cousin—a sort of family demonstration unit. As a Birzeit University faculty member put it, "The extended family has been put to use."

For Palestinian women under occupation, the conditions of the past twenty-one years have consistently thrust them into politicized situations, and their roles, and perhaps the functions of the family itself, have stretched accordingly.[7] In the absence of a state and in the presence of an implacably hostile authority, the family's role as protector, arbiter and social authority has undoubtedly been important, and this has made it more resistant to other social forces undermining its authority. Women's role has "stretched" to include numerous encounters with the army, military courts, prisons and police as women have, for example, taken on the responsibility of caring for imprisoned family members. As attorney Lea Tsemel notes in a recent book:

> I often see women because during the years of occupation they have become the most active ones over the everyday problems of detention. They go to the police, they ask for permits—it's not traditional, but they have become very active. They're more stubborn than the men.[8]

The politicization of women has resulted from both the repression of males and the new consciousness engendered mainly by the new generation of educated women, which includes young women in camps and villages since under occupation higher education expanded far beyond the middle class. It has led to women taking on greater political responsibilities. With so many men under detention, women have been propelled into new political roles and have often replaced the lost cadre. The case of Ruqayya cited in our introduction is one example of female community leadership in a situation of crisis. To what extent this leadership exists at formal rather than informal levels is another question.

Women as Political Leaders

In the town of Ramallah last April, a middle-class music teacher, joined by other women in the neighborhood, worked tirelessly to set up a full alternative curriculum for children and high school students in her neighborhood, because all schools in the West Bank were closed by military order on February 2, 1988. Her tasks ranged from calling and chairing meetings of the newly- founded neighborhood committee to hauling blackboards and finding school supplies. A neighborhood away, an older women summoned the other women nearby to a sex-segregated neighborhood committee to plan classes and plant a community garden. In the next street, a Birzeit University student became the acknowledged dynamo of her "coed" neighborhood committee and was appointed to the committee that guards the neighborhood at night, a previously unheard-of role for a single woman.

Women have been prominent, and sometimes leaders, in the neighborhood committees which sprang up in many locations in the occupied territories in March 1988, parallelling the establishment of the more political popular committees.[9] The community-service functions of the neighborhood committees and their all-inclusive and democratic form encouraged the participation of women. While many of the activities of these committees, for example teaching and home gardening, are not explicitly political, the self-organization of the community and the philosophy behind it—to disengage from existing Israeli structures and to build Palestinian alternatives—make the neighborhood committees political instruments in a broad sense, as their banning by the military authorities on August 18, 1988 attests.

It is not only the extension of the family role to the community that explains women's heightened activity in these committees and other forms of public action. Paradoxically, it is precisely women's inferior social status which gives them greater flexibility to respond swiftly to new situations and new needs, even when the action is foreign or "beneath" them. For example, women seem to have done the bulk of the alternative teaching, although professional teaching in Palestinian society is the domain of both women and men. On the other hand, the rigidity of men's role in society clearly made it harder for adult men—as opposed to the youth confronting the army—to adapt to new roles, for example community service functions.

Neighborhood committees are the clearest example of how the new forms of authority born of the uprising include a greater role for women than do the more traditional structures of power, including the nationalist institutions. It is difficult, however, to gauge the real extent of women's empowerment or how this new empowerment affects the older structures of inequality and domination. Palestinian women in the occupied territories are after all clearly not in possession of instruments of power, such as wealth, control of institutions, or legal authority. To a lesser extent, despite the dramatic rise in education among women, many of the necessary political and professional skills remain in the male domain.[10] Thus, women are still many steps behind men: even their institutions are in part miniature versions of those of men, and they are still struggling to formulate an alternative agenda that defines gender (and class) as legitimate issues along with the national cause.

Despite these handicaps, women have taken on political tasks that require a substantial amount of authority—usually associated with males— such as distributing clandestine leaflets or telling shopkeepers to close their shops during a strike, although single women are more active in these more organized roles than married women. Whether even highly politicized women in political organizations have leadership roles or remain implementors of male decisions is less clear. Some activists assert that women should play a greater role in decision making, while others point out that, as one put it, "in any case men in the West Bank and Gaza Strip do not make decisions either. The decisions are made outside and we inside... we execute." This comment underlines how the understanding of political dynamics, in this case what is called in Palestinian politics the relationship between "inside and outside," has a direct bearing on women.

Neighborhood committees are the only semivisible new structures of organization where women's role can be gauged, because the popular committees and the other local middle-level formations that guide the uprising are clandestine. At this level, and in the more flexible grassroots formations like student and union groups and the health movement, women seem to be playing increasingly important roles. But there is no evidence that women have an increasingly important role in established nationalist institutions like the universities and the press. Nor (with significant exceptions) do activists from the women's committees believe that women are represented in the Unified Leadership of the Uprising. Indeed, women have been barely mentioned in the almost thirty clandestine communiques from the Unified Leadership, despite repeated appeals and commendations to other sectors of society—merchants, prisoners, workers, students. An exception is Communique no. 29, the "Call of Celebration of the Independent State," which offers

> congratulations to the mother of the martyr, for she has celebrated only twice: when she gave her son and when the state was declared.

The "mother of the martyr," a heroic role enshrined in Palestinian history and the Palestinian present, has the qualities of stoical courage but not necessarily of active resistance. In the Declaration of Independence,

which affirms equality between men and women, women are praised but
nonetheless portrayed in a static role:

> We render special tribute to that brave Palestinian woman, guardian
> of sustenance and life, keeper of our people's perennial flame.

The prevalence of these two images in nationalist consciousness
suggests that women's current role has not been adequately assessed and
may not be sufficient to improve her status in the future.

The pattern of women's mobilization during national liberation and
backsliding after liberation is well-known: Algeria is the example best known
among Palestinian women. The form of mobilization itself may well inhibit
further development. Examining the role of Palestinian women in Lebanon,
Rosemary Sayigh noted "how crisis continually recommits women to struggle, how its form prevents them from consolidating or 'feminizing' their
struggle, with national priorities forcing it to remain spontaneous, auxiliary."[11]

Many women activists in the occupied territories are well aware that
the role of women in a Palestinian state will be determined before, not after,
liberation. As one remarked:

> I feel that if we do not raise the issues relevant to women now we
> will never raise them, for now is the time. I am afraid that if we do
> not raise the social issues now during national liberation, women's
> position will regress after liberation.

Toward a Women's Liberation
Strategy for the Nascent State

The conditions and consequences of the uprising have already had a
considerable influence on the women's committees' short- and long-term
strategies for women's and national liberation. Women's political action has
passed through roughly three phases, parallel with the stages of the uprising
itself. From January through March/April, women's political action was
primarily, although not solely, characterized by direct and immediate confrontations with the Israeli army at the level of the street. Women were at the
barricades, organizing sit-ins at the doorsteps of humanitarian and human
rights organizations, and staging demonstrations which grew in size and
impact, reaching a peak on March 8, 1988, when demonstrations were held
in most of the major towns and localities of the West Bank and Gaza Strip.

The second phase lasted until around September and was dominated
by the building and consolidation of the network of neighborhood and

popular committees. Slogans such as "Expanding and Strengthening the Popular Committees in All Areas" and "Neighborhood Committees: Organizing for Self-Reliance" reflected the core strategy of the women's committees in the arena of politics. As a result, by August 1988, women probably formed the organizational core of the neighborhood committees. On August 18, 1988, the popular and neighborhood committees were declared illegal by the Israeli military, and membership in, assistance to or even contact with them could bring a sentence of up to ten years in prison.[12] This considerably curtailed the visible activities of neighborhood committees and, consequently, dampened women's committees' efforts to continue building and consolidating them.

By November 1988, a new phase began, in which political and social action was being evaluated in terms of future state structures. Some leaders of the women's committees now began a serious examination of the ways in which the women's movement could consolidate the gains of the uprising to achieve permanent changes in the social and political status of women. As one leader of the women's movement put it, "What is needed now is to unite all women to keep the gains once statehood is achieved."

The Palestinian women's movement today faces at least two strategic problems that might make unity difficult to achieve and could therefore not only hold the whole women's movement back but also limit the possibilities of radical change in the position of women in all spheres of life. First, there is the divergence of perceptions and therefore strategy and tasks among the different women's organizations. While the three committees on the left clearly stress the need for action to achieve social change and call for an agenda for women's liberation that is separate from national aspirations, the fourth committee is characterized by "mainstream" views and equates national liberation with female liberation in a mechanistic way. As one Women's Committee for Social Work activist asserted, "with liberation we should be able to attain all of our rights as women as well, so there is no need for feminism."

The other problem is structural: the fact that the women's movement was conceived and born as part of a nationalist struggle may make it difficult for it to develop a balanced feminist agenda. This dilemma surfaced in the first few months of the uprising, when service provision to women—up to that point the main focus of the women's committees' activities—declined considerably because of the avalanche of national political work that women activists had to take on. As one committee activist noted:

> We even closed down some of our kindergartens and nursery schools, temporarily of course, because we could not succeed in combining the new political work that fell on our shoulders and

our previous activities. Now we are beginning to be aware of the
need to work on both types of work together, but this is very
difficult.

It is of course understandable that the women's committees opted for
national-political over feminist work when they were no longer able to cope
with everything at once. Women could not have easily forsaken the new
political role that they were suddenly able to play for the more ordinary work
of providing services. Indeed, such service work was not at the center of most
women's concerns during this period, especially in view of the increasing
awareness that effective long term change in the status of women must be
preceded by women's taking over important political positions. On the other
hand, nursery schools and kindergartens form the framework for mobilizing
the potential constituencies of the women's committees in the villages,
refugee camps and towns to participate in political and social action. To
suggest that both types of activities are needed is obvious. Less obvious is
how to reconcile the two when resources are limited.

A purely radical feminist agenda for the women's movement is also
problematic in the Palestinian context, as it in other settings. As Michele Barret
notes:

> In posing women's oppression simply as the effect of male domina-
> tion, it refuses to take into account the widely differing structures
> and experiences of that oppression in different societies, periods
> of history and social classes.[13]

A brand of feminism that reduces everything to equality between men
and women, without taking sufficient note of the fact of power relations and
structures, not only fails to serve the national political struggle which
dominates the lives of Palestinian women but is bound to fail because it does
not take into consideration what can realistically be achieved. This leaves us,
once again, with the problem of reconciling national, class and gender issues
in a new synthesis that could guide the women's movement and inform its
strategy. The task ahead is a difficult one.

In the Palestinian setting, a radical change in economic relationships
may be difficult to achieve in the immediate future. However, the basis of
authority of men over women can nonetheless be challenged by demanding
transformations in law and education, through the struggle for civil law and
equality as sanctioned by law, the right of equal inheritance, the right to own,
the right to travel and the right to vote, to name only a few pressing demands.
This is why activists and leaders from three of the four women's committees
cite the legal status of women and the replacement of the *shari'a* (Islamic
law) with civil legislation as a critical area. The problem of the gender-based

division of labor in the home, in childcare and housework, can also be addressed by calling on the new state to provide state-subsidized nurseries, bakeries, restaurants, and laundries. Equal opportunity in work is another demand voiced by some women activists.

Guided by the Declaration of Independence, which proclaims the new Palestinian state to be based on the principles of "equality and non-discrimination" between men and women, the women's movement could now embark on the path of providing the mainstream and progressive nationalist camps with a critique of the flaws in their conceptions of the status of women, making it clear that the removal of national oppression alone will not solve the problems of women. Radical change in the status of women in Palestinian society is also linked to broader changes in society, especially at the level of the economy. A strategy must therefore be formulated to foster the building of autonomous women's organizations that participate in the national and class struggles.

In this respect the story of Ruqayya is telling. Ruqayya, the daughter of the uprising, develops and struggles in the contexts of home, community and workplace. Both the national battle against occupation and the desire for economic and personal rights mobilize her, while the grassroots organization she belongs to—her women's committee and her trade union—provide a forum for action. She and the many other women like her, the breakers of barriers and the builders of barricades, have emerged as political actors. Their rights in the future will rest on their ability to consolidate this new position in the form of permanent and far-reaching changes in the position of women in Palestinian society.

## Chapter 12

The Islamic Resistance Movement in the Palestinian Uprising

Lisa Taraki

By the beginning of the first week of October 1988, as the Palestinian uprising moved into its eleventh month, the Islamic Resistance Movement (*Harakat al-Muqawama al-Islamiyya,* known by its Arabic acronym Hamas) had issued its thirtieth communique. Hamas appears to be engaged in a competitive race with the Unified National Leadership of the Uprising for direction of the daily struggle of the people of the occupied territories. Yet despite the fact that Hamas is six communiques ahead of the Unified Leadership, it is another matter altogether whether it can command the kind of legitimacy and influence required to direct the Palestinian struggle against occupation.

Israeli and foreign journalists reporting from the territories have been preoccupied of late with this new political force on the Palestinian political scene, devoting much copy to those occasions on which Hamas managed to call a general strike in the West Bank and Gaza. The media are rife with predictions about Hamas' ability to make inroads into the Palestinian body politic. Israel Television's Arabic service has studiously avoided interviewing or giving prominence to Palestinian nationalist figures since the beginning of the uprising. Yet in early September 1988, it broadcast a wide-ranging interview with Shaykh Ahmad Yasin, the head of the Islamic Center in Gaza, describing him as the "spiritual leader" of the Islamic movement in the occupied territories. A week later followed another interview with Shaykh Bassam Jarrar, a charismatic young teacher and Muslim intellectual associated for the past few years with the Islamic movement, mainly in the West Bank. Neither interview revealed anything of note concerning the aims of Hamas, nor did these personalities acknowledge that they were in fact associated with it. The only message, and indeed the aim of the exercise, was to herald the emergence of a serious rival to the Palestinian national movement in the occupied territories.

At about the same time, Israeli and foreign media took the lead in publicizing the distribution of the Charter of the Islamic Resistance Movement, a forty-page booklet setting forth in thirty-six articles Hamas' program and views on resolving the Palestine conflict. This document, and the increasingly aggressive policy of Hamas in declaring and enforcing general strikes, provided yet another opportunity for the Israeli pundits to warn of the consolidation of a real alternative to the Palestinian Liberation Organization and the impending fragmentation of the collective national effort represented by the uprising.

A more sober consideration of the fortunes of Hamas would raise some questions here. What is the recent history of the organization? What does it offer Palestinians who have suffered under the yoke of Israeli occupation for twenty-one years? How seriously should we take it?

Chain of Jihad

Hamas emerged on the scene during the early months of the uprising, first in Gaza and then in the West Bank. Its traces its origins back to the 1930s, when the influence of the Society of the Muslim Brothers—the earliest and largest Islamist movement in the Arab East—began to spread from its birthplace in Egypt to surrounding areas in the Middle East. Hamas considers itself a "wing" of the Muslim Brothers in Palestine, the most recent link in the "chain of *jihad*" ("struggle") beginning with the revolt of Shaykh 'Izz al-Din al-Qassam and his comrades in the 1930s through the jihad of the Palestinians in 1948 and the operations of the Muslim Brothers since 1968.

Hamas' claim of direct descent from and identity with the Brothers draws our attention to the recent history of the Brothers in the occupied territories. After a period of relative inactivity during the first decade of the occupation, they renewed their political and educational work in the late 1970s.[1] This effort was centered around mosques, schools and universities, and aimed at inculcating youth with a religious education as well as forming the basis for a political alternative to the secular mainstream of the Palestinian national movement and what the Brothers viewed as the "bankrupt" ideologies of PLO's component groups.

The most successful effort of the Muslim Brothers was the mobilization of hundreds, perhaps thousands of youths to join Islamist student and youth groups. This drive coincided with the rise and proliferation of mass organizations affiliated with the national movement, particularly student blocs at schools, two-year colleges and universities. The Muslim Brothers, along with other Islamist groups, established "Islamic blocs" at educational institutions in the West Bank and Gaza, and joined the student movement with great zeal and energy.

Relations with the nationalist student blocs were fraught with tension and conflict throughout this period, especially in the mid-1980s. Several violent conflicts between nationalist and Islamist students erupted on campuses, sometimes spilling over into the community and requiring great conciliation efforts. Editorials in newspapers associated with the national movement, and public statements issued by nationalist figures and institutions, denounced the violent methods of the Islamic blocs, particularly at Birzeit and Najah universities, and at the Islamic University in Gaza.

The consolidation of a large and organized social base for the Palestinian national movement represented by the PLO during the 1980s increasingly marginalized the Muslim Brothers, who chose to remain outside the nationalist consensus by rejecting the PLO as the embodiment of the Palestinian national will. Any legitimacy they had in the early years was rapidly dissipating. This was exacerbated by the fact that their political program was never clearly spelled out, aside from references to the necessity of establishing an Islamic state in Palestine.

Social Movement, Moral Order

In fact, the Muslim Brothers' work among the youth and the community prioritized creating the preconditions for an Islamic moral order rather than active struggle for an Islamic state. Their publications and teaching emphasized the importance of remolding the Muslim individual and the necessity of combatting the corrupting influences of the secular and godless society in which Muslims were forced to live. On university campuses they jealously guarded their reputation as hardworking, disciplined, serious individuals, and rarely participated in political activities organized by the nationalist groups. They also eschewed "frivolous" student activities such as folk dancing, theater and excursions, and concentrated instead on organizing study circles and communal prayers, and commemorating religious occasions in public events and rallies.

On the community level, the mosque and a number of charitable societies founded by the Brothers served as foci for their educational and social efforts. They were particularly successful in bringing a significant number of young refugee camp and urban women out of their homes and into the mosque and other groupings, largely under the influence of a number of charismatic women leaders in the main towns in the West Bank and Gaza. Increasing numbers of young women and even girls adopted the "uniform" of the Islamist movement—the distinctive head covering and coat. Such manifestations attested to the Islamists' success in fashioning a religious consciousness and identity different from the religious consciousness of most Palestinian Muslims.

Still, the success of any social movement depends on its ability to put forth a political and social agenda responsive to the real needs and aspirations of its constituency. This agenda must also appear to be capable of implementation, and must take into account the configuration of prevailing social and political forces. What do the Muslim Brothers—and by extension Hamas—have to offer the people of the occupied territories?

It is not difficult to understand why the Muslim Brothers chose to adopt a new name when they entered the political arena during the uprising. Their history of conflict with the national forces, coupled with their absence from anti-occupation activities throughout the preceding two decades, had seriously compromised their standing as a credible political force. The new name, denoting a more militant stance, was meant to rehabilitate the Brothers in the charged atmosphere of the uprising.

Hamas Communique no. 30 invites the public to read the Charter of the Islamic Resistance Movement to learn the truth about Hamas and to "know what it is, and what its aims are." A central tenet, as spelled out in the charter, is that the land of Palestine is an Islamic trust (*waqf*), to be held as such for generations of Muslims until the Day of Judgment. No one has the authority to give up any part of Palestine. Nationalism is a function of religious belief, and the defense of Muslim land is the duty of every Muslim. This view is equivalent to that of religious Zionism, which sees the Land of Israel as a divine trust granted to the Jewish people in perpetuity.

This premise means that negotiations with the enemy over the land of Palestine are tantamount to treason. In response to one of the main slogans of the uprising, calling for the convening of an international conference to decide the future of Palestine, Hamas says this in its charter: "Such conferences are nothing but a form of judgment passed by infidels on the land of the Muslims. Since when have unbelievers been fair to the people of faith? ...There is no solution to the Palestine question other than sacred struggle. Initiatives, proposals, international conferences—they are all a waste of time and an exercise in futility. The Palestinian people are too precious to have their future, their rights and their destiny thrown away."

Hamas admits that the path of jihad is not an easy one. Here is how the charter places the struggle for Palestine within the context of a pan-Islamic liberation movement: "The issue of liberating Palestine is connected to three circles—the Palestinian, the Arab and the Muslim. Each circle has its role and its obligations in the struggle against Zionism. It is the height of folly and ignorance to neglect any one of these circles, for Palestine is an Islamic land...Once the matter is dealt with on this basis and the potentials of the three circles are mobilized, present circumstances will change, and the day of liberation will come nearer." Hastening that day requires "the dissemination of Islamic consciousness among the masses on the local, Arab and Muslim levels. The spirit of jihad must be spread among the *umma* ("the Islamic polity"), the enemy must be engaged, and the ranks of the *mujahidin* ("strugglers") must be joined."

Competing Vision

This then is what Hamas has to offer the people of the occupied territories: a vision of an all-Islamic Palestine, to be realized only through tireless work in spreading Islamic consciousness all over the Arab and Islamic worlds and through mobilizing Muslims everywhere to join the ranks of the fighters for Palestine. Based on this vision, Hamas is unlikely to become a significant political force in the occupied territories. Quite simply, it is very difficult to imagine how Hamas can mobilize Palestinians in the occupied territories around a strategy that calls for the total liberation of all of Palestine, this being conditional upon the mobilization of the Arab and the Islamic peoples. Hamas' prospects appear to be even more remote if the political process gains momentum and continues to move forward, and if the current level of mobilization around the agenda of the Unified National Leadership of the Uprising is maintained or intensified.

The Unified Leadership in the occupied territories has far outstripped Hamas in the clarity of its political vision and in the concreteness of its aims. For the first time since the occupation, the Palestinian national movement has been able not only to sustain a popular rebellion but to formulate a political agenda capable of enlisting widespread international support. Hamas considers itself part of the uprising *without* subscribing to its slogans and objectives: it does not recognize the PLO as the sole legitimate representative of the Palestinian people, it is against the convening of an international conference and it does not support the establishment of a Palestinian state.

On the face of it, it is difficult to understand Hamas' zeal in furthering the uprising while at the same time rejecting its main slogans. This enigma can be understood on two different levels. The most simple explanation, and one which has some currency in the occupied territories, is that the Israeli intelligence services have incited or at least encouraged Hamas to sow discord and disunity among Palestinians. The history of the relationship between the Muslim Brothers and the national movement, and the long-held suspicion on the part of the movement that the Brothers were encouraged by occupation authorities, help give credence to this interpretation.[2] Army patrols on the streets have generally not interfered with their attempts to impose general strikes on days other than the ones designated by the Unified National Leadership of the Uprising. Fairly or unfairly, people see these facts as evidence casting doubt on Hamas' purity of intent.

This view is further strengthened by the growing distinction in the public's mind between Hamas and the militant Islamic Jihad Organization, generally believed to have been founded in the early 1980s. Several months before the outbreak of the uprising, in May 1987, Jihad caught the public's attention by the sensational jailbreak of several of its members from Gaza Prison. In August, Jihad was back in the news when an Israeli officer was shot at close range in a crowded Gaza intersection by a man identified as a member of the organization. In early October, three of the prison escapees and four other men, all believed to be associated with Jihad, were killed in ambushes set by Israeli security forces in Gaza.

The widespread demonstrations which gripped the Gaza Strip and West Bank following these killings highlighted Jihad's growing weight in the struggle against the occupation, especially in the Gaza Strip. The deportation in April 1988 of Shaykh 'Abd al-'Aziz 'Awda, a teacher at the Islamic University in Gaza and considered to be a prominent Jihad leader, was followed by a wave of arrests, still continuing, of members and associates of the organiza-tion. The Islamic Jihad Organization, unlike Hamas which has been spared this type of persecution, has earned itself important nationalist credentials. Throughout the uprising, Jihad has adhered to the national consensus and is reported to be in close contact with the Unified Leadership.

To return to the question of Hamas' motives in joining the uprising, the more likely interpretation has to do with Hamas' long-term objectives. Though Hamas does not support the uprising's specific aims, it wants to shore up its image in preparation for carving itself a niche in the very state for whose establishment it is not prepared to struggle. Hamas is employing here the strategy for which the Society of Muslim Brothers has become known in Egypt during certain periods, where it promotes a degree of coexistence with the prevailing authority in order not to risk a total loss.[3] Hamas knows that it cannot block a political settlement once the process is initiated. Given this, it aims to guarantee a presence "on the streets," so to speak, during the process leading up to and beyond such a settlement.

Once the uprising has borne fruit and Palestinians begin to take hold of their own political future, Hamas will be there to influence that process. The efforts of Hamas will most likely be concentrated in the areas of political and social legislation. One can expect that it will press for freedom of political organizing, the application of the shariʻa to as many spheres of life as possible, and changes in the character of the educational system, particularly at the university level.

Hamas' active participation in the uprising, then, should best be seen as part of the campaign of a prospective opposition Islamist party in the future Palestinian state. As such, there is no doubt that Hamas should be taken seriously.

## Part 5

Israel and the Intifada

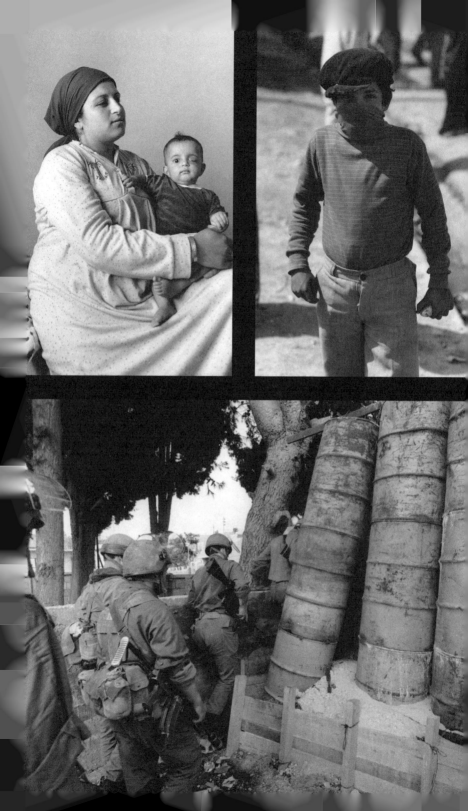

In My Shoes

For some people a Palestinian is Yasir Arafat,
A youth throwing a Molotov cocktail at a bus,
A boy hurling taunts at soldiers and cursing their mothers.
When you say "Palestinian" to me, I think of Walid.
The only Palestinian I know and who knows me,
And with whom I converse (in my language, of course).
He is thirty or so, married with children,
Has a pleasant smile and speaks passable Hebrew.
An intelligent fellow, with a degree in accounting
Who reads for pleasure classical Arab poetry,
Philosophy and religious works.
He has a good sense of humor and he's an optimist.
I wish I had more friends like him.
He uses his education in our local supermarket,
Weighing vegetables and making home deliveries.
In his spare time he washes cars or cleans apartments
In our neighborhood, as many hours as possible.
He has a family to keep
And he may not be able to come tommorow.
There might be a curfew
Or he might find himself "inside" like his brother
Six months administrative detention without trial.
Every day he has a story to tell.
Minor incedents, not what you would call atrocities.
His identity card was torn up by a reserve soldier
For no particular reason.
Trucks turned up suddenly with soldiers without uniforms
And loaded a few of his cousins—(our cousins).

Some people think of Yasir Arafat or Abu Nidal
When you mention Palestinians.
I think of Walid.
When we tactfully offered Walid parcels of secondhand clothes for
His relatives in the village
He accepted gratefully without taking offense.
How strange to think that someone, somewhere
In Walid's village near Nablus,
Is wearing my shoes now.
Once, not so very long ago,
I was in *his* shoes.

—Dan Almagor

## Chapter 13

Original Sin

Zachary Lockman

The officials responsible for organizing the celebration of Israel's fortieth anniversary must have been rather depressed. They had planned a collective submersion in the warm bath of national mythology, a triumphal tribute to Israel's birth, survival and achievements that might—at least for a while—allow its Jewish citizens to forget their troubles. But reality intruded, in the form of the Palestinian uprising in the occupied West Bank and Gaza. It was bad enough that the Palestinians ruined Israel's party; even worse, the brutal repression with which the Israeli government responded severely damaged Israel's image in the United States and the world.

So this fortieth anniversary project had to become a celebration with a purpose: to purge US and European minds of those awful images of Israeli soldiers shooting and beating Palestinians. Officials hoped that primetime broadcasts of *Exodus,* choruses of "Hava Nagela," stories about hardy pioneers making the desert bloom, and countless op-ed articles extolling Israel as the only democracy in the Middle East would do the trick. And no hard questions to mar the festivities, please.

But the questions did not—and will not—go away. Significantly, since 1982 Israeli Jews themselves have been posing them with increasing force. Some have begun to wonder if Israel's present predicament does not stem, at least in part, from the traumatic events of its first year of existence, and they have undertaken a politically important reappraisal of some of the myths surrounding Israel's foundation. The most central of these myths concerns the origins of the Palestinian refugee problem.

With a Wave of His Hand

On July 9, 1948, the month-long truce that had temporarily halted the war between the newly-created state of Israel and the Arab states bordering

Palestine came to an end. The Israel Defense Forces (IDF) had taken full advantage of the truce to reorganize, train new Jewish immigrants and equip itself with the weapons flowing in from Czechoslovakia and elsewhere.

Now it took the offensive. Its main objective during the ten days of fighting that ensued before the United Nations again imposed a truce was to relieve pressure on the Jewish sector of Jerusalem, besieged by the Arab Legion. Operation Dani was to secure Israeli control of the corridor to Jerusalem by conquering Lydda and Ramle, the largest Arab towns on the central coastal plain, as well as Latrun, where a police fort controlled the Jerusalem road. Ramallah, in the hill country north of the road, would be conquered in a later phase of the operation.

At that time Lydda and Ramle had a combined population of some 50-70,000, about 15,000 of whom were refugees from Arab towns and villages that had already fallen under Israeli control. The IDF quickly conquered the two towns, only lightly garrisoned by the Arab Legion. In Ramle there was no civilian resistance to the conquest, but in Lydda there was an outbreak of sniping and Israeli soldiers were ordered to open fire on anything that moved. At least 250 Palestinian civilians were killed in the massacre that ensued, as compared to four Israeli soldiers.

The Israelis wanted the region cleared of its large Arab population and hoped that the inhabitants of the two towns would flee as a result of the fighting. When this did not happen, Israeli commanders confronted the question of what to do with them. Their fate was sealed at a meeting attended by Israeli Prime Minister David Ben-Gurion and top IDF commanders on July 12. "According to the best account of that meeting," Israeli journalist and historian Benny Morris tells us, in *The Birth of the Palestinian Refugee Problem,*

> someone, possibly [Operation Dani commander Yigal] Allon, after hearing of the start of the shooting in Lydda, proposed expelling the inhabitants of the two towns. Ben-Gurion said nothing, and no decision was taken. Then Ben-Gurion, Allon and [Allon's deputy Yitzhak] Rabin left the room. Allon asked: "What shall we do with the Arabs?" Ben-Gurion made a dismissive, energetic gesture with his hand and said "expel them" *(garesh otam)*.[1]

Over the next several days, tens of thousands of Palestinian men, women and children were forced out of Lydda and Ramle with the few possessions they could carry, most of them walking miles to the Arab Legion's lines without food or water under a hot summer sun. Many had their money and valuables stolen as they passed through IDF checkpoints; some died along the way. The towns they left behind were thoroughly looted by Israeli soldiers and civilians.

This is not the official Israeli version, of course. For forty years Israeli propagandists have stubbornly insisted that there were no deliberate expulsions of Palestinians in 1948. Rather, they argue, the Palestinians themselves must bear responsibility for their own dispossession and exile, along with the Arab regimes. The Palestinians, the official version claims, ignored repeated Jewish pleas that they remain and become equal citizens of the new state; instead, they obeyed orders from their leaders and the Arab governments to evacuate their homes in order to allow the invading Arab armies freedom of action.

The specious character of this official version of history has been clear for many years. The 700,000 Palestinian refugees themselves certainly knew what had actually happened to them, even if they could only rarely find a Western audience willing to listen. Many Israelis have also known for a long time that this was not the way things actually happened. In his book *1949: The First Israelis*,[2] Israeli journalist Tom Segev reproduces an excerpt of a Knesset debate from August 1949. A member of Menachem Begin's Herut party had boasted that "thanks to Deir Yassin we won the war, sir!"[3] When Knesset members from the Labor-Zionist Mapai party headed by Ben-Gurion protested, the Herut member told them, "If you don't know [about the Deir Yassin-type massacres that you yourselves performed], you can ask the Minister of Defense [Ben-Gurion]."[4]

Living With Oneself

While Israeli rightists boasted about the expulsions and massacres that accompanied Israel's creation, liberal and leftwing Zionists in Israel and abroad have tenaciously defended and propagated the official version. There is some irony in this, since the Israeli officials and army officers who actually oversaw the dispossession of the Palestinians in 1948 were overwhelmingly drawn from the ranks of the Zionist left—from Mapai and (especially in the case of the IDF) from Mapam (the United Workers' Party), at the left end of the Zionist spectrum. Believing themselves to be good socialists, democrats and humanitarians, they could not acknowledge their complicity in deeds that contravened the moral and political principles they professed.

There was and still is a powerful need among many liberal Israelis to deny responsibility for Palestinian suffering. This denial, manifested throughout the official histories of Zionism and Israel, served as an effective mechanism for avoiding guilt or political responsibility for the catastrophe that befell the Palestinian people. Labor Zionism's long record of denying the very existence of a distinct Palestinian Arab people whose interests might be damaged by the Zionist project facilitated this process. Yet the suffering of the Palestinians was incontrovertible, and so responsibility for it had to be assigned. To whom better than the Palestinians themselves?

The official version of what happened in 1948 also fit in nicely with the political need to protect Israel's wholesome image abroad. It has been the historic task of the left and liberal wings of the Zionist movement to explain and win support for the Zionist project as not only necessary to Jewish survival but also as entirely consonant with the highest ideals of "Western civilization." Thus Zionism's victims must be made to disappear or, if that fails, to bear the blame for their situation.

The myths surrounding Israel's establishment and the simultaneous dispossession of the Palestinian Arab people have proven remarkably tenacious. In Israel itself, the educational system and a well-developed propaganda apparatus constantly reinforce them and, as a consequence, most Jewish Israelis have assimilated an official discourse that all but excludes thinking of Palestinians as real human beings. This discourse, fixated on a manipulated conception of Israeli security and given tremendous emotional force by a narrow interpretation of the Holocaust, indeed of all Jewish history, contains little room for any empathetic understanding of Palestinian pain or aspirations. It hardly seems able even to acknowledge that Zionism may not have been an unmitigated blessing for the Palestinians.

The myths have also been pervasive among US Jews. Debate over the Israeli-Palestinian conflict in the United States is usually so much cruder than in Israel because most US Jews are ignorant about things that are common knowledge in Israel and regularly discussed in the Israeli media. The role of such organs of misinformation as the *New York Times* in abetting this ignorance requires no elaboration.

Israeli liberals sometimes aid this conspiracy of silence with a self-censorship intended to "protect" US Jews, and US citizens in general, from the seamier aspects of Israeli reality. They understand Israel's total dependence on US good will and, when addressing foreign audiences, take on the role of unofficial ambassadors by toning down the criticism of official policies they are only too happy to voice at home. Ze'ev Schiff, for instance, military correspondent of the liberal daily *Ha'aretz* and a critic of the invasion of Lebanon, wrote a history of the Israeli army intended for an US audience in which he concludes his discussion of Operation Dani with this masterly euphemism: "Some 50,000 Arab inhabitants of Lydda, Ramle, and neighboring towns fled the region, this time without the Israelis preventing them or suggesting that they remain."[5] Sometimes dangerous information is withheld from both Israelis and foreigners. When Yitzhak Rabin published his memoirs, Israeli censors forced him to excise passages describing the expulsion of Palestinians from Lydda and Ramle from both the Hebrew and English editions.[6]

It must also be said, though, that most US Jews have displayed little desire to know too much. Denial plays its part here too, reinforced by the guardians of ideological purity who are ever vigilant for signs of slackening fervor. The initial weakness of US Jewish protest against Israel's attempts to crush the intifada again demonstrated the effectiveness of the mechanisms of denial and rationalization that have evolved over the years.

Historical Demolition

Alternative perspectives on 1948 have long been available to those who were interested. In May 1961, for example, Irish journalist Erskine Childers conclusively demonstrated the falsity of Israeli claims that Arab leaders had ordered the Palestinians to leave. He showed that while there was no record of Arab radio broadcasts calling on the Palestinians to leave, there were numerous appeals from Palestinian and Arab officials telling the Palestinians to stay put.[7] Childers later published additional evidence refuting Israel's version of events and documenting Zionist complicity in the flight and expulsion of the Palestinians.[8] Other research on the events of 1948 has been published by Palestinians, Europeans and (occasionally) US historians.[9]

Except for some short articles produced by members of the tiny anti-Zionist left, however, Israelis did little new research. From time to time, as memoirs appeared or as political parties jockeyed for advantage, the question of 1948 would briefly surface, generally when the Zionist right would argue that it was only advocating the policies that Ben-Gurion and the Zionist left had implemented in 1948: aggressive expansionism, a hard line against the Arabs, the confiscation of Arab land for Jewish settlement and annexation of occupied territories. But for three and a half decades the subject was virtually ignored by Israeli scholars and journalists interested in serious and objective research.

Suddenly, in the last three or four years, Israelis have published a number of books and articles explicitly and self-consciously challenging many of Israel's foundation myths. These include the study of the refugee problem by Benny Morris, mentioned above; Tom Segev's book *1949*; veteran peace activist Simha Flapan's *The Birth of Israel: Myths and Realities,* published in 1987 just after Flapan's death; and Avi Shlaim, *Collusion Across the Jordan: King Abdullah, the Zionist Movement, and the Partition of Palestine.* All four authors see themselves as breaking free of Israeli consensus history. All four books help to undermine the "heroic" version of the foundation of the state and constitute part of a broader "revisionist" tendency among Israeli historians and social scientists.

What accounts for this upsurge of Israeli revisionism? In part it is because many important government and IDF documents and private papers on the events of 1948-49 were declassified and released in the early 1980s, giving researchers access to a wealth of new information. But this project of historical demolition and revision has much more to do with a shift in the outlook of a small but significant segment of the Israeli left and liberal intelligentsia in the wake of the Lebanon war. Before discussing this shift and its significance, however, let us take a look at what these books and articles have to say.

The Transfer

Benny Morris analyzes material from a variety of state, Zionist and military archives, as well as private papers, in order to explain the Palestinian exodus of 1948 and, more broadly, to outline the process by which a relatively homogenous Jewish state was erected on the ruins of Palestinian Arab society. His findings are important not so much because they tell us something radically new but because they furnish a wealth of detail, drawn from unimpeachable Israeli sources, that shows us more clearly than ever before how the job was done.

Among the key documents which Morris unearthed is an IDF Intelligence Branch report of June 1948 analyzing the causes of Palestinian flight. This report, which Morris finds to be generally accurate, determined that as of June 1, 1948, some 240,000 Arabs had fled from towns and villages located within the area assigned to the Jewish state by the United Nations; another 150,000 had fled their homes in areas earmarked for the Palestinian state or from the Jerusalem region, which was to be internationalized. The report attributed some 70 percent of this Arab exodus to "direct, hostile Jewish operations against Arab settlements" by the Hagana/IDF and the right-wing Jewish militias (Begin's Etzel and Shamir's Lehi), or to the "effect of our hostile operations on nearby [Arab] settlements"—for example, the fall of nearby towns. Another 2 percent is attributed to Jewish psychological warfare aimed at frightening Arabs into fleeing, and 2 percent more to "ultimative expulsion orders." Morris suggests that this last figure is an underestimate, with several instances of deliberate expulsions being counted under the rubric of military operations. By contrast, evacuation orders by Arab leaders and military commanders account for no more than 5 percent of the total, and these were issued for local military reasons. The remainder of the exodus is attributed to "general fear" (10 percent) and "local factors" (8-9 percent).

Morris points out that if this report demolishes the Israeli claim that the Palestinians fled their homes on Arab orders, it also refutes the claim put forward by some Palestinians that this first phase of the exodus was the result of a deliberate Zionist plan of systematic expulsion. He argues that most of the exodus of some 400,000 Palestinians from their homes in the period from December 1947 through May 1948—the period covered by the IDF report— can best be explained as the natural response of unarmed civilians to war: as their towns and villages were attacked or threatened, Palestinians sought refuge in safer places. From the standpoint of the Zionist civil and military authorities, the depopulation of Arab villages and towns was largely an incidental, if favorably regarded, side-effect of Jewish military operations.

After May 1948, however, things were different, and for this crucial and chaotic period in particular Morris' study helps us determine much more precisely than ever before the degree of Zionist/Israeli complicity in the radical demographic transformation of Palestine and the creation of the Palestinian refugee problem. From June onward and into 1949, deliberate expulsions multiplied, helping to create an additional 300,000 refugees as Lydda and Ramle were followed by many other, less well-known, incidents of expulsion by IDF commanders. At the same time, it became Israeli policy not to allow Palestinian refugees to return to their homes behind Israeli lines, transforming temporary wartime displacement into permanent exile.

Was there an explicit Israeli policy to expel Palestinians from the territory of the new state? A motive certainly existed. As of November 1947, Arabs constituted some 45 percent of the 1.1 million people living within the territory assigned by the UN to the Jewish state, while there were very few Jews in the proposed Arab state. Many Arabs had already fled or been expelled from their homes by May, but large pockets of Arabs still remained and Israel was moving to conquer more of Palestine. Unless the number of Arabs living within what would become Israel's borders could be drastically reduced, its viability as a Jewish state would be in serious doubt. Furthermore, the idea of "transfer"—the removal of Palestine's Arab majority outside the country to facilitate the establishment of a homogeneous Jewish state—had long enjoyed an important place in Zionist thinking, going back to Herzl. It became more prominent from the late 1930s, when the creation of a Jewish state in Palestine began to seem a realistic prospect. In effect, liberal and left Zionists like Ben-Gurion and Chaim Weizmann adopted the principles if not the rhetoric of Jabotinsky and his right-wing Revisionist Zionists. Never having accepted that the Arabs of Palestine constituted a distinct people entitled to self-determination, they naturally saw no great injustice in moving the Palestinians—against their will, if necessary—outside of Palestine.

A Smoking Gun?

Although historians have been able to point to numerous specific cases of expulsion, particularly from June 1948 onward, no one has come up with the "smoking gun"—evidence of an explicit decision taken at the highest levels of the government and the army to render the new state more homogeneously Jewish by expelling Palestinians and barring their return.

Morris brings us as close to finding the "smoking gun" as we are likely to get. His work suggests that there was in fact no explicit and general Israeli decision to expel. Instead, a number of individuals and agencies, with the tacit but nonetheless clear support of Ben-Gurion and other top leaders, worked throughout 1948 to take advantage of what began as the limited and spontaneous flight of segments of the Palestinian urban middle and upper classes by helping to transform it into the "miracle" of permanent mass depopulation, clearing the way for the settlement of abandoned towns and villages by new Jewish immigrants. In a chaotic situation, various officials and IDF commanders, acting with the unspoken approval of their superiors, took the initiative and made decisions designed to rid the new state of Arabs and make their return impossible.

Morris shows that Jewish leaders were at first surprised when well-to-do Palestinians began to move to safer places at the end of 1947 and the beginning of 1948, and they did not foresee that larger numbers of Palestinians would flee their towns and villages as they were threatened or conquered in the Jewish military operations of the winter and spring of 1948. Gradually, however, some began to realize that it was to their advantage to transform this still limited exodus into a deluge. Plan Dalet, adopted in March by the Hagana as its blueprint for seizing the offensive and gaining control of areas assigned by the UN to the Arab state, already provided for the "expulsion over the borders of the local Arab population in the event of opposition to our attacks" and the destruction of villages. When Plan Dalet was actually implemented in a series of military operations beginning in April, it opened the floodgates. Largely unarmed and without leadership, unable to mount effective military resistance, still demoralized by the brutal suppression of their revolt a decade earlier and frightened by Zionist "whispering campaigns" and terrorist actions, the Arab populations of Haifa, Jaffa and scores of smaller towns and villages fled when attacked by Jewish forces. News of the massacre at Deir Yassin on April 9-10 accelerated this mass flight. This massacre, perpetrated by Etzel and Lehi forces, was condemned by the Jewish authorities, but the attack on Deir Yassin had been approved by the Hagana as part of its strategic plan to gain control of the Jerusalem corridor.

Ben-Gurion, head of the Jewish Agency executive and after May 15 prime minister and defense minister of Israel, was quick to grasp that a demographic transformation was underway from which the new Jewish state could benefit if it could be made permanent. He also understood, however, that an explicit expulsion policy would not go over well with those on whose goodwill the new state was still dependent: the United Nations, the United States and the Soviet Union. Such a decision would also be unacceptable to Mapam, a member of the coalition government, and would trigger a political crisis the new state could ill afford in wartime, especially as so many of the IDF's best officers belonged to that party.

Ben-Gurion therefore sought less public and direct ways to implement a transfer policy, without any formal cabinet or IDF command decision and without leaving a paper trail which might someday prove embarrassing. This indirect approach—conveying approval of controversial policies in private conversations or obliquely through hints or silences—was very much in keeping with Ben-Gurion's personal style and had served him well throughout his long career in Zionist politics and diplomacy.

Perhaps the key figure lobbying for and actually implementing a coherent transfer policy in 1948 was Yosef Weitz, and Morris has made an important contribution by bringing his role to light. In 1948 Weitz was the director of the Lands Division of the Jewish National Fund (JNF), the Zionist movement's land-acquisition agency, as well as the JNF's representative to the committee which coordinated the activities of the various Zionist agencies and also chairman of the committee responsible for governing the Jewish settlements in the Negev. Weitz had ready access to top government officials, friends in many Jewish settlements and close links with the IDF, and he was widely respected as an expert on land affairs and on Arabs. From early in 1948, Weitz began pushing the Jewish authorities to take advantage of the anarchy and violence that were engulfing Palestine to gain control of more land and evict Arabs from their villages in regions he considered vital for future Jewish settlement. Working with local Hagana commanders and kibbutzim, he succeeded in getting Arabs expelled in the Haifa and Beisan regions and establishing new kibbutzim on their lands.

But these partial and local successes were clearly inadequate, and in March Weitz began lobbying for a coordinated national policy of expulsion. Frustrated that the leaders of the Yishuv (the Jewish community in Palestine) were apparently too preoccupied with other matters to make the decisions he deemed necessary, and fearful that this historic opportunity to resolve the "Arab problem" once and for all would slip away, he took the initiative, for example by drawing up lists of Arab villages to be evacuated and destroyed. By June he had set up an informal "transfer committee" that sought official recognition as the body that would coordinate "retroactive transfer"—the systematic destruction of abandoned Arab villages and the establishment of Jewish settlements in their place. He never obtained written authorization from Ben-Gurion to carry out his plans, but Morris demonstrates that there is no doubt Ben-Gurion knew and approved of what was being done.

Weitz worked tirelessly, travelling around the country to press for the expulsion of Arabs, oversee the destruction of villages and plan new settlements. He got the government to order the IDF to prevent displaced Palestinians from returning to their villages, even to harvest their crops or retrieve their possessions. Even after his semi-official Transfer Committee ceased to function at the end of June for lack of funds, manpower and explicit government authorization, the work went on unabated through 1948 and into 1949.[10] IDF officers and local officials expelled Arabs who had surrendered to Israeli forces and destroyed their villages. Their orders were usually couched in terms of security considerations, but in fact these were secondary. By the summer of 1948, the unofficial policy was unmistakable: the residual Arab population within Israel's borders was to be made as small as possible.

Morris also shows that a powerful lobby quickly developed which opposed the return of Palestinian refugees, even those from "friendly" villages. Older kibbutzim which took over Arab lands, new immigrants settled on the sites of destroyed Arab villages or housed in former Arab neighborhoods, settlement officials with big plans for the future—these and others pressured the government to take a hard line against any return of refugees to their homes. Even as the Israeli government was solemnly stating its willingness to be flexible on the refugee question once the war was over, the bulldozers were at work erasing all traces of some 350 Palestinian villages and setting up Jewish settlements in their place. As early as June, in fact, the cabinet had reached a consensus against allowing the refugees to return to their homes.

There is more information in Morris' book than can be summarized here. But one further issue is worth raising: who invented the official Israeli version of the Palestinian exodus? It seems that it was none other than Weitz and his colleagues, the very people who had spent the previous nine months working to rid that part of Palestine which became Israel of as many Arabs as possible. They were apparently the first to claim, in an October 1948 report to the government, that the flight was "deliberately organized" by the Arab leaders to arouse feelings of revenge, to create a refugee problem artificially and to prepare the way for the Arab invasion. The Arab villages which they themselves had ordered bulldozed were, they now claimed, damaged in the course of the fighting. These cynical lies quickly became a mainstay of Israeli propaganda, and remain so to this day.

Morris' book is not without its flaws. He makes little use of Arab sources and rejects altogether the use of oral history. These choices have the effect of implying that only official Israeli documents can be trusted to yield valid and reliable knowledge. One can also take issue with the way Morris has explained the depopulation of certain towns and villages, although it is true that it is often difficult to distinguish the effect of Jewish military assaults from deliberate expulsions. At times Morris seems reluctant, or even unable, to draw the harsh conclusions that his own evidence would seem to warrant. He seems to be afraid of straying too far from the official Israeli consensus, a limitation that has also manifested itself in much of his journalistic work for the *Jerusalem Post* where, despite what one might expect from reading his book, he has generally remained within the boundaries of Zionist discourse. Nonetheless, *The Birth of the Palestinian Refugee Problem* constitutes an important new starting-point for discussion of this crucial historical episode.

From Ben-Gurion to Begin?

Despite—or perhaps because of—the political dynamite they represent, Benny Morris presents his findings in rigorous scholarly fashion, without extraneous comment or moralizing. Simha Flapan has a much more explicit political and personal agenda in *The Birth of Israel*. He covers much of the same ground as Morris and uses many of the same sources; but unlike Morris he rejected the advice of his friends and colleagues to present his findings in a "noncommittal, academic manner...leaving the conclusions to the reader (pp. 3-4)." Instead, he is intent on destroying the "long-held and highly potent" myths surrounding Israel's foundation, on undermining "the propaganda structures that have so long obstructed the growth of the peace forces in my country."[11]

Flapan was a leader of Mapam, founder of *New Outlook* magazine and for many years active in the Israeli peace movement. Writing this book must have involved a painful process of self-examination for him:

> There is also a personal issue—for me as for tens of thousands of Israelis, ardent Zionists and socialists, whose public and private lives have been built on a belief in those myths, along with a belief in Zionism and the state of Israel as embodying not only the national liberation of the Jewish people but the great humanitarian principles of Judaism and enlightened mankind. True, we did not always agree with many official policies and even opposed them publicly.... But we still believed that Israel was born out of the agony of a just and inevitable war, guided by the principles of human dignity, justice, and equality. Perhaps it was naivete. Perhaps it was

the effect of the Holocaust that made us unable, unwilling to be fundamentally critical of our country and ourselves. Whatever its sources, the truth cannot be shunned. It must be used even now in the service of the same universal principles that inspired us in our younger days.[12]

Flapan was shocked when Menachem Begin claimed, during the Lebanon war, that the only difference between his policies and those of Ben-Gurion was that the latter had resorted to subterfuge. Now Flapan admits that Begin was basically right and contrasts the Israeli/Zionist myths about 1948 with the truths his diligent research has uncovered. In a less detailed and scholarly but more lively manner than Morris, Flapan argues the following:

—Zionist acceptance of the UN partition plan was only a tactic, part of a larger strategy aimed at thwarting the creation of the proposed Palestinian Arab state through a secret alliance with 'Abdullah of Transjordan and the conquest of territory beyond the borders proposed by the UN.

—While many Palestinians were willing to accept partition, it was Ben-Gurion's adamant opposition to the creation of a Palestinian Arab state that destroyed hope for a peaceful partition.

—Israel's political and military leaders prompted the flight of Palestinians.

—The Arab states intervened in Palestine not to destroy Israel but to prevent 'Abdullah from implementing his schemes for a Hashemite-ruled Greater Syria with Israeli collusion.

—The Arab invasion became inevitable because the Jewish leadership was unwilling to postpone declaring Israel's independence while exploring a political solution.

—Israel was on the defensive for only the first four weeks of the war, after which the IDF had the upper hand.

—Israel rejected many peace proposals made by Arab governments and neutral mediators in the belief that its military superiority would allow it to dictate terms.

As with Morris, most of Flapan's work will not greatly surprise anyone outside the Zionist mental orbit. But the book is in general well-argued and based on careful use of the documentary record, and it is worthwhile reading for students and activists alike.

Wishful Thinking

On two related issues, however, Flapan's analysis is open to criticism. It is true, as he argues, that the Palestinians were divided, demoralized and relatively passive in 1948. But it is wishful thinking to claim that many would have rejected the Arab Higher Committee's call for resistance to partition and accepted the loss of half their country had not the Yishuv taken a hard-line stance and colluded with 'Abdullah to abort the unborn Arab state. Flapan acknowledges that acceptance of partition was regarded as tantamount to treason in the Arab community. He nevertheless suggests that the communist-led League for National Liberation—which followed the Soviet lead and endorsed partition—might have been the Arab partner with whom a more enlightened Zionist leadership could have cooperated to achieve peaceful partition. This greatly overestimates the League's strength. More importantly, it assumes that there was some real possibility of the Zionist movement making a different choice in 1948. In fact, with the exception of Flapan's own faction and a few isolated liberals, the Zionist movement had for some time been operating from the premise that it was strong enough to achieve its goals without far-reaching concessions and that if it needed a local ally, it should be not the Palestinian Arabs but the Hashemite dynasty in Amman.

Flapan must also come to terms with his own party's behavior in 1948. As information about expulsions, looting of Arab property and the destruction of villages began to circulate, some of Mapam's leaders did protest in party forums and in the cabinet. But others, drawn from the party's right wing which later split off and ultimately rejoined Mapai to form the Labor Party, defended the IDF's actions. Many of the IDF officers who oversaw expulsions were Mapam members. On the whole, Mapam's protests were weak and ineffectual. To people like Weitz, they also appeared hypocritical: even as Mapam's leaders were protesting the transfer under way, he noted, kibbutzim affiliated to the party were taking over Arab lands, stealing abandoned Arab property and lobbying against any return of refugees. By the end of 1948, Mapam had come to accept the *fait accompli*.

Flapan is honest enough to admit that "Hashomer Hatzair [Mapam's leftwing component] was unable to wage an uncompromising struggle because its fight for the rights of the Palestinians conflicted with the reality that the members were building their lives on the property of an expelled population."[13] He is still sometimes a little too easy on Mapam, however, perhaps because, as he notes in the Introduction, "I have never believed that Zionism inherently obviates the rights of the Palestinians, and I do not believe so today." Flapan is willing to criticize Israel's foundation myths, to acknow-

ledge the culpability of former heroes like Moshe Sharett and Chaim Weizmann, to admit his own party's failings in 1948 and even to assert that "the
line from Ben-Gurion to Begin is direct."[14] But he cannot quite bring himself
to take the next step and see that most of what happened in Palestine in 1948
was inherent in the Zionist project of creating a Jewish state in an Arab land.
The entirely predictable rejection of that project by Palestine's Arabs made
Ben-Gurion's path all but inevitable if Zionism was to achieve its goals. Flapan
clings to the notion that things might have been different had the more
enlightened and humane Zionists somehow triumphed over the "hard-
liners." He does not explain, however, why the hard-liners won out so
consistently. To do so might undermine his vision of "another Zionism,"
benign but also outside of history.

That caveat notwithstanding, Flapan's book marks a significant departure from the left-Zionist historical consensus. He quite explicitly rejects the
Labor Party's attempt to present Ben-Gurion's idea of a democratic Jewish
state as the alternative to the Likud's Greater Israel. He insists that the Zionist
left must thoroughly re-examine and criticize its past record, acknowledge
that the establishment of Israel resulted in the dispossession of the Palestinians and recognize their right to self-determination. Only then will the
forces of peace and progress within Israel have any hope of winning. *The
Birth of Israel* is a fitting testament to this veteran activist, and despite its flaws
one must hope that it will have the impact Flapan wished.

Zionists and Hashemites

In *Collusion Across the Jordan,* Avi Shlaim analyzes in much greater
depth the first of Flapan's demythologized "realities" and shows how the
Zionist leadership secretly colluded with 'Abdullah, then the *amir* of
Transjordan, to prevent the establishment of a Palestinian Arab state and
instead partition Palestine between them. This too is not a new story, but
until Shlaim no one has told it with such wealth of detail, scholarly rigor and
subtlety of analysis. In a series of secret meetings between 'Abdullah and
Zionist leaders (especially Golda Meir), a deal was struck whereby 'Abdullah
would occupy and annex central Palestine—known today as the West
Bank—and leave the rest to Israel. This deal allowed 'Abdullah to transform
Transjordan into Jordan and make himself into a full-fledged king, while
giving the Zionists a free hand to defeat the military forces of the other Arab
countries and conquer most of the rest of Palestine.

The Hashemite-Zionist alliance was of course not entirely free of
conflict: in 1948 the IDF and the Arab Legion battled for control of Jerusalem,

and in 1967 King Hussein lost the Palestinian territory that his grandfather had conquered two decades earlier. But despite these clashes the Israeli-Hashemite "special relationship" endured for decades, rooted in a common rejection of Palestinian rights and independence. It was, in the end, the intifada that finally induced Hussein to despair of reasserting Jordanian influence in the West Bank and formally renounce his dynasty's claim to Palestine, opening the way for the November 1988 proclamation of an independent Palestinian state led by the PLO.

The Year After

Tom Segev's *1949* covers some of the same ground as Morris, Flapan and Shlaim, but he adopts neither Morris' scholarly distance, Flapan's explicit political agenda, nor Shlaim's narrow focus on the Hashemite connection. Rather, his book draws a portrait of Israeli society in the first full year of the new state's existence by using government documents, the press, personal diaries and interviews. *1949* aroused controversy when it was published in Israel because it "shattered a firmly established self-image and exposed as mere myths a large number of long accepted truisms."[15] The book's rather offhand iconoclasm and its lively and engaging style make it fascinating and important reading, differentiating it from much of the popular literature about Israel, so steeped in forced nostalgia.

Segev deals with three aspects of Israeli history: relations with the Arabs inside and outside the new state; the social, political and cultural impact of the massive wave of immigration that by the end of 1949 had increased Israel's Jewish population by 50 percent; and conflicts between religious and secular Jews. In the chapters on the Arabs are scattered numerous tidbits of information which, though not analyzed in depth or used to construct a coherent critique of Israeli policy, nonetheless add up to a rather damning indictment. For example, Segev shows that expulsions of Palestinians continued well into 1949 and beyond, long after the fighting between Israel and the Arab states was over, and that it was official policy to shoot Palestinians trying to cross the armistice lines and return to their homes. Effectively undermining the IDF's claim to "purity of arms," he also notes that many Israelis were disturbed by reports of widespread atrocities, rape and looting committed by soldiers.

Like Flapan, Segev argues that Israel's short-lived offer to accept the return of 100,000 refugees was never intended seriously, and he describes how Israel spurned repeated Arab peace proposals. Israel's leaders, convinced that time was on their side, had lost interest in trying to achieve a final peace settlement, especially one that might require the return of the refugees and perhaps the cession of some territory. In one of the book's most poignant passages, Segev describes how, by the summer of 1949, new Jewish immigrants had already settled on the site of Deir Yassin.

In other chapters Segev details the manipulative methods used by Zionist agents to induce Jewish immigration, mainly in order to enhance the state's military might and permit the rapid settlement of conquered Arab lands. His descriptions of the terrible conditions that prevailed in the camps that housed the new immigrants are chilling. Perhaps most importantly, he shows how the Ashkenazi elite which ran Israel—good socialists all—immediately stereotyped the immigrants from the Arab countries as ignorant, lazy savages and thieves. Immigrants from Poland received preferential treatment in housing and jobs, while the Moroccans and Yemenis were dumped in remote border settlements. The section on the conflicts over issues of religion and state reminds us that not much has changed in the last forty years.

There is a great deal more to *1949*, despite its reluctance to draw explicit conclusions. The book shows the Israelis of that year, elevated in the official mythology to the status of selfless and flawless Zionist heroes, to have been more or less normal people displaying the entire range of human behavior. "The everyday routine of the first Israelis was thus less pioneering and heroic than they had dreamed it would be," Segev concludes, "and the society they shaped was less enlightened, less idealistic, less altruistic and less Ashkenazi than they had hoped." And yet, he insists, "They argued, they struggled with themselves, hesitated, and sometimes changed their minds, but the road they took was the road they believed to be right, and they followed it with wholehearted confidence and belief in their cause. For that, they are to be envied."[16]

Lost Innocence

Envied by whom? Clearly by today's liberal intellectuals, who have come to feel that they have lost their way, their self-confidence, their faith in the righteousness of their cause. Indeed, many feel that they have just about lost "their" country, that Israel has been taken over by a strange new breed of hysterical nationalists, religious fanatics, avowed racists, feuding and bumbling politicians unable to chart a clear course, and an illiberal Oriental Jewish majority.

The invasion of Lebanon in 1982 marked a watershed for many liberal Israelis. The national consensus that had prevailed during Israel's previous wars began to crumble, although most liberals and left-Zionists criticized not so much the use of military force against the Palestinians as the duration and visible brutality of a war directed largely against civilians. The era of the quick clean kill was over and many Israelis were unhappy about the price.

The antiwar movement faded away when Israeli soldiers stopped coming home from south Lebanon in coffins. But Lebanon had left an indelible imprint on the consciousness of many Israelis. In the 1984 elections the Labor Party promoted itself as the party of "sane Zionism," heir to what it claimed were Ben-Gurion's policies of military self-restraint, democracy and tolerance, which it contrasted with the Likud's belligerence and extremism. This did succeed in restoring to the fold many Israelis who harkened back to the days when Israel won its wars quickly and cheaply, was not a pariah in the world community and allowed its liberals to live with their consciences. More reflective and honest Israelis, however, were induced by the traumatic events of 1982 to ask themselves some hard questions about what was happening to their country. Was Begin right when he claimed to be the heir of Ben-Gurion? Why were the secularists always on the defensive? Why had the problem of the Palestinians not gone away?

The erosion of the national consensus created some new political space. Grappling with the realities of an Israel which had turned out to be something from which they were profoundly alienated, a Frankenstein monster, some Israeli liberals and leftists were receptive as never before to a critical re-examination of their country's history. They began to sense, however inchoately, that a Labor Party victory would not solve Israel's problems, that the rot had set in long before the Likud's victory in 1977 and even before 1967, that there was some original sin in Israel's very birth that had to be confronted: the dispossession of the Palestinians which had accompanied and made possible the creation of Israel. The release of rich new sources of information allowed this work of historical revisionism on 1948 and its aftermath to take place, but liberal Israelis were motivated to undertake this project by the post-1982 mood of confusion and self-doubt.

Initially, it was not mainly the persistence of the Palestinian question, the continuing resistance of the million and a half Palestinians in the occupied territories, that compelled Israeli liberals to push toward the margins of the national consensus and sometimes beyond. "Quality of life" issues, such as the growing religious coercion which threatened secularists' way of life (witness the battles over showing films on Friday nights) usually had a more direct and palpable impact on people's daily lives than the Palestinian question. One could argue about the fate of the occupied territories, but in the meantime the army seemed to have things well under control. Nonetheless, it gradually became clearer to those willing to think it through that such things as the spread of racism, the growing strength of the right, the country's economic difficulties, the erosion of democratic norms, the decline of Israel's image abroad and other symptoms were in large measure the consequence of the occupation and could not be effectively fought unless one was willing to end the occupation. In the final analysis, it was the fact that the Palestinians not only refused to acquiesce in Israeli occupation or in some deal with Jordan—that apparently ineradicable fantasy of the Labor Party—but were continuing to demand their rights which ultimately fused together disparate issues and focused attention on the question of the territories and Israel's conflict with the Palestinians. And then the intifada exploded, accelerating this process and driving home the need to confront the past as a way of making sense of the present and of finding some guidepost toward an acceptable future.

While the emergence of this revisionist tendency is certainly a positive development, one must be cautious about predicting its ultimate political impact in Israel. The fate of another recent book, Yehoshafat Harkabi's *Fateful Decisions*,[17] may be instructive. Harkabi, former head of IDF intelligence and once the chief propagator of the doctrine that the PLO's "National Covenant" of 1964 proved for all time the impossibility of Israel's negotiating with the Palestinians, now argues forcefully that Israel must, out of self-interest, seize the opportunity to make a deal with the PLO and accept a Palestinian state in the West Bank and Gaza.

The defection from the official consensus of an establishment figure like Harkabi did allow other Israelis to voice their dissidence more safely, but neither his book nor those of the other revisionists have altered the terms of political debate in Israel. Most Jewish Israelis initially responded to the intifada by backing the government's hard-line stance, apparently unfazed by the unprecedented brutal methods used to crush resistance. Even as Shimon Peres droned on about the "peace process," his Labor Party colleague Yitzhak Rabin (with the support of most party members) was busy orchestrating the killings, beatings, detentions, curfews and torture in the territories, while the right waited in the wings for its chance to implement an even more brutal line.

The response of the left-liberal opposition was at first weak and fitful: the usual suspects published statements of protest in the newspapers, the small left parties submitted motions of no-confidence in the Knesset, and Peace Now organized some demonstrations, although it still would not allow groups like Yesh Gvul, which advocates refusal of military service in the territories, to share its platforms. As the months passed and the casualties mounted, however, growing numbers of Israelis were driven to speak out against the occupation, and some went even further. Benny Morris is a case in point: although he certainly still regards himself as a liberal Zionist, he went to prison in the summer of 1988 rather than perform his reserve military service in the occupied territories. Even Peace Now has come out in favor of talks with the PLO. Yet, although there are today more Israelis than ever before who agree with this stance, those who would accept a Palestinian state alongside Israel remain a minority among the Jewish population. In the November 1988 Knesset elections they more or less held their ground, while openly fascist, racist and/or clericalist parties made significant gains.

The US Jewish community was also slow to respond to the challenge of the intifada. Many Israeli liberals have seen Jews abroad as their country's last hope, which perhaps explains why some of the revisionists first published their research in English and why Harkabi has spent so much time lecturing in the United States and Europe. The monolithic character of US Jewish attitudes toward Israel has in fact eroded considerably since 1982, and more Jews than ever before have spoken out against the policies of the Israeli government. But despite growing unease, too many US Jews still take their cues from Israel, and a sizeable and vocal dissident bloc capable of influencing US and Israeli policy has not yet coalesced. Sadly, the daily killings in the occupied territories and the Shamir-Peres team's rejectionist stance toward the Palestinians still seem to disturb US Jews less than the prospect that Israel's Law of Return might be revised under pressure from the religious parties. In Israel, too, many liberals seem a lot more worried about the growing power of the orthodox and the threat that they will not be able to see movies or go to the beach on Shabbat than about what the IDF is doing in their name a few miles away.

Still, the uprising has created important new political space in Israel and undermined key arguments used to justify and rationalize the occupation. In the year since the intifada began, the Palestinians have forced their way onto the Israeli political agenda, destroying long-held illusions, dispelling the pessimism and inactivity into which opponents of the occupation had sunk and compelling Israelis to face facts. By their ability to withstand massive repression and their manifest willingness to make peace with Israel, the Palestinians have also won the political and moral high ground.

As Israeli Jews come to grips with the new situation, they will become more polarized. For some time to come, most will probably cling to the illusion that domination and repression can provide security. But some will make the choice to finally come to terms with Palestinian nationalism and Palestinian rights, if only because continuing occupation will increasingly turn Israel into a place in which they do not want to live. The publication of these books may help provide Israelis (and Jews abroad) with the new historical understanding that they will need in order to accept their share of responsibility for what has happened to the Palestinians and go on to develop a new discourse of peace, justice and equality.

## Chapter 14

From Land Day to Peace Day...
And Beyond

Joel Beinin

On December 21, 1987 the Palestinian Arab citizens of Israel observed a country-wide general "strike for peace" in solidarity with the two-week-old uprising in the West Bank and the Gaza Strip. Such general strikes by the Palestinian Arab community have become regular events since the Land Day strike of 1976, but Peace Day was more comprehensive and raised more explicit nationalist demands than any of its predecessors. It was nearly universally observed by the 650,000 Palestinian Arabs, who comprise over 16 percent of the citizens within Israel's pre-1967 borders, in coordination with a general strike in the West Bank and the Gaza Strip the same day.[1] Nearly every one of Israel's Arab population centers witnessed some form of strike activity. Some 250,000 Arab workers stayed away from their jobs. As many as 50,000 demonstrated in Israel's largest Arab city, Nazareth (pop. 50,000); 10,000 in the Galilee village of Kafr Yasif and 5,000 in the city of Umm al-Fahm in the heavily Arab Triangle region.[2]

The strike leaders chose the designation "Peace Day" to emphasize their nonviolent intentions, and observance of the strike was generally nonviolent and disciplined. The strikers called for: peaceful resolution of the Arab-Israeli conflict by convening a UN-sponsored international conference with the participation of all parties, including the PLO; Israeli withdrawal from the West Bank and the Gaza Strip; and establishment of an independent Arab state in those territories.

A small number of violent incidents during the strike received widespread publicity, especially because some occurred in communities long known for their political quiescence, like the Bedouin settlements of the northern Negev, Jaffa (where only 10,000 Arabs remain in what was the largest Arab city in mandate Palestine, overwhelmed by the Jewish majority in the combined municipality of Tel Aviv-Jaffa) and the village of Abu Ghosh in the Jerusalem corridor (where Tehiya party leader Ge'ula Cohen was sheltered when she was an Irgun terrorist evading capture by British mandate authorities). In the villages of Tayyiba and Kafr Qasim tires were burned, and the Afula-Hadera road which passes through the heart of the northern Triangle was blocked for two hours by demonstrators from Umm al-Fahm led by the Sons of the Village, a militant nationalist organization that rejects the existence of the State of Israel.

Peace Day was initiated by the National Committee of Arab Local Councils (NCALC), which has firmly established itself as the representative of Israel's Arab community. All five Arab members of Knesset (MKs), all the Arab members of the Executive Committee of the Histadrut (trade union federation), the unions of high school and university students, teachers and parents unions and the National Committee to Defend the Land endorsed the strike call. There was, therefore, no doubt that the strike and its demands reflected the consensus of opinion among Israel's Arab citizens.

Jewish officials responded to the strike with panic, threats and a show of force, using tear gas and water canons to disperse demonstrations. On the morning of Peace Day, the Likud proposed reimposing military rule, in effect from 1948 to 1966, on Israel's Arab citizens. The most ominous aspects of Peace Day for the Israeli political establishment were not the relatively few violent clashes, but its comprehensive character, political program and coordinated general strikes by Palestinian Arab citizens and those living under military occupation in the West Bank and the Gaza Strip. Peace Day was an unequivocal assertion of collective Palestinian national identity by those who are officially termed Israel's "non-Jewish minorities" in unity with those living over the Green Line.

Equality Day

Peace Day's success was partly due to experience gained in two previous general strikes called by the NCALC earlier in 1987 which enhanced its stature and consolidated its position in the Arab community. The first of these, the Equality Day strike of June 24, demanded equal rights for Israel's Arab citizens in the areas of municipal services, job opportunities and education. A second strike on September 1, the first day of the school year, focused on educational demands.

As Israeli officials never tire of pointing out, Arab citizens' standard of living has improved dramatically since 1948. However, they lag far behind Jews in every indicator of social welfare. The Israeli National Insurance Institute's annual survey for 1987 revealed that while 8.3 percent of Israeli

Jewish families live below the poverty line, 46.1 percent of Israel's "non-Jewish" families have incomes below this minimum.[3] In 1988 the International Center for Peace in the Middle East published the results of a comprehensive research project directed by Henry Rosenfeld, professor of anthropology at Haifa University, surveying the conditions of Israel's Arab citizens.[4] According to this study the life expectancy of Arab citizens is two years less than that of Jews; infant mortality for Arabs is twice the Jewish rate; 26.4 percent of Arab families live in highly crowded conditions, as opposed to 1.1 percent of Jewish families.

Institutionalized discrimination against the Arab population is facilitated by segregated living patterns. Most of Israel's Arab population lives in purely Arab settlements: three cities (Nazareth, Umm al-Fahm and Shafa 'Amr) and some 100 villages. A small minority lives in six "mixed cities" (Tel Aviv-Jaffa, Haifa, Jerusalem, Acre, Lydda and Ramle) which are preponderantly Jewish.

The main issue in the Equality Day strike was the unequal allocation of budgets for local councils and municipalities. Budgets for Arab local authorities, which are allocated by the Ministry of Interior, are 25-33 percent of the per capita rate of their Jewish counterparts.[5] According to Mayor Hashim Mahamid, the annual development budget for Umm al-Fahm (pop. 25,000) is about $100,000.[6] By contrast, Meron Benvenisti's West Bank Data Base Project has calculated that the development budget for the West Bank provided $80,000 for each family in a Jewish settlement through 1985. Because of their inadequate budgets, Arab local authorities face large deficits which leave them unable to meet payrolls or provide adequate services. Roads, water supply and sewage disposal are far below the standards maintained in Jewish communities. Municipal cultural, recreational, sports and youth programs are minimal. To compensate for the lack of funds and draw attention to their needs, Nazareth, Jaffa and Umm al-Fahm have organized annual volunteer work camps with international participation to carry out municipal improvement projects.

A second major demand of the Equality Day strike was for jobs. In mid-1987 Israel's national unemployment rate was 5.6 percent. Unemployment among Arabs has always been several percentage points higher than the national rate because of the historic policy of preferential hiring of Jews (the "conquest of labor") and the virtual exclusion of Arabs from many jobs in the leading sector of Israel's economy, the military-industrial complex, on security grounds. When the mainly peasant population that remained in Israel after 1948 began to enter the urban wage labor force in large numbers in the 1960s they filled positions at the bottom of the wage scale as Jews moved into higher paying jobs. With some notable exceptions they have remained on the lower rungs of the wage ladder. New job opportunities have been limited in recent years because there has been virtually no economic growth in Israel since mid-1985, when soaring inflation forced the government to cut its budget and reduce investment in the public sector.

Government budget cuts have also created a crisis for the Israeli educational system, but the impact on the Arab community has been more severe than on the Jewish community because of previously existing inequalities. Allotments for educational services in Arab communities are as low as 25 percent of the per capita level in Jewish localities.[7] The compulsory education law has never been enforced in the Arab community, and the drop-out rate of Arab pupils is 15-30 percent, depending on the locality. Consequently, according to Aziz Haidar's review of social welfare services for Israel's Arab citizens in the International Center for Peace in the Middle East study, 46 percent of Arab children aged thirteen to seventeen do not attend school, as opposed to 6.3 percent of Jewish children. The Ministry of Education admitted several years ago that there was a shortage of 1,200 classrooms in Arab localities. After building 200 new classrooms in 1987, the ministry proposed adding only sixty additional classrooms. The Equality Day strike demanded more new school construction, especially technical schools. Only two of Israel's forty-five vocational-technical schools are in Arab localities (Nazareth and Umm al-Fahm). The Arab school system, already suffering from understaffing, was disproportionately affected by the budget cuts. Though they comprise 10 percent of all teachers nationwide, Arab teachers make up as much as 20 percent of those dismissed due to the lack of funds to pay salaries.[8]

In an effort to raise new funds for hard-pressed universities, in the spring of 1987 the Ministry of Education proposed to institute higher tuition fees for those who are not veterans of the Israeli armed forces, a frequently employed euphemism for Arabs since only a small minority of the Arab community, primarily Druze and Bedouins, serves in the military. All the university administrations rejected this proposal as discriminatory, but the rancor it aroused was part of the context for both the Equality Day strike and the September 1 strike around educational issues.

The National Committee of Arab Local Councils

The most significant achievement of Equality Day was the consolidation of the NCALC as an effective country-wide Arab leadership. The NCALC has demonstrated an impressive capacity to sustain organization, discipline and unity. All three 1987 strikes were supported throughout the Palestinian

Arab community by partisans of all political tendencies from Labor to the Communists. After Equality Day the government announced that it would direct additional funds to Arab localities, a *de facto* recognition of the stature and representative character of the NCALC.

The NCALC was established in 1974 by fifteen Arab local council chairpersons with the encouragement of the Israeli authorities.[9] The Rabin government tried to use the body as a counterweight to the increasing Communist strength in the Arab community. Communist local council chairpersons were at first excluded from the organization.

In 1975 Arab municipal politics was transformed by the victory of the Communist Party (Rakah) in the Nazareth municipal elections.[10] The Communists won an absolute majority of the vote, and Tawfiq Zayyad became the first Communist mayor, Arab or Jew, in Israel (or anywhere else in the Middle East). The Communists had commanded 35 to 45 percent of the vote in Nazareth since Israel's first Knesset elections in 1949. Their breakthrough to majority status in Israel's largest Arab city inspired an upsurge in political mobilization, a new sense of militancy and improved political organization.

The Communists built on their Nazareth electoral success by initiating the National Committee to Defend the Land, which organized the Land Day general strike of March 30, 1976 to protest the continuing expropriation of Palestinian lands. Six Palestinians were killed by Israeli troops during demonstrations that day. Land Day captured the enthusiasm of the entire Arab community and has been commemorated ever since as a national day of protest by Palestinians everywhere. There was public outrage against several of the non-Communist local council chairpersons who had not supported Land Day. Some were ousted by their councils; in other cases government authorities intervened to prevent this.[11] The mass support for Land Day, and the government's refusal to address Arab demands made following the strike, radicalized the NCALC. The Communists were invited to join. The committee was reborn and adopted a more militant perspective.

With the momentum created by its Nazareth municipal election victory, its leadership of the Land Day protest and its participation in the NCALC, the Communist Party established the Democratic Front for Peace and Equality (DFPE), a Jewish-Arab electoral front to contest the 1977 Knesset elections. The DFPE received a majority of the Arab vote, and the new NCALC chairperson, Hanna Muways, joined the Front and won a seat in the Knesset on its list.[12] The DFPE, in which the Communist Party is the dominant element, thus emerged as the strongest political force in the Arab community.The current head of the NCALC is Ibrahim Nimr Husayn, a non-party political independent who has been mayor of Shafa 'Amr for eighteen years. Shafa 'Amr's population is 49 percent Muslim, 35 percent Christian and 16 percent Druze. This gives the mayor legitimacy among all sectors of the Arab community, and his political effectiveness is widely respected. The Communists, though they comprise the largest single bloc in the NCALC, have accepted Husayn's leadership. In contrast to their historic tendency to dominate coalitions in an exclusionary and undemocratic manner, the Communists have functioned responsibly and cooperated with their partners and rivals. The policy of taking all decisions by consensus has kept political differences under control.

The NCALC has established a permanent committee including all the Arab MKs, Arab members of the Histadrut Executive Committee, representatives of the National Committee to Defend the Land and the national federations of Arab secondary and university students. This body, composed of all elected Arab leaders with a national constituency, is consulted before major political decisions are adopted, and it approved both the Equality Day and Peace Day general strikes. The NCALC has also convened subcommittees to address specific problems in health, education and economic development. It has drawn on the talents of the Arab intelligentsia to prepare proposals and present the government with independent statistical analyses. Thus, the NCALC has begun to function as a quasi-parliamentary body for Israel's Palestinian Arab citizens.

Workers and Intelligentsia

Underlying the continuity of the leading role of the Communists from Land Day to Peace Day and beyond is the transformation of the social structure of the Arab community. The historic process of the proletarianization of the Arab peasantry has accelerated since the 1970s. There is still a fairly rigid ethnic and national division of labor in the Israeli economy in which the most privileged positions are generally occupied by Ashkenazi Jews. Nonetheless, Arab citizens have become a more permanent and stable part of the wage labor force. Their labor power is critical in agriculture, construction and many services. The food processing and textile industries also have high concentrations of Arab workers, including a growing number of women (See Table 1). The temporary, casual and lowest paid work which Palestinian citizens performed in the 1950s and 1960s is now done by residents of the occupied territories.

The growth and stabilization of the Palestinian working class in Israel has increased its self-confidence and capacity for political struggle. Many workers have long supported the Communists who, in addition to their consistent struggle against national oppression, championed Arab workers' right to join the Histadrut (formally achieved in 1959, but implemented only in 1965 when Arabs were permitted to vote in Histadrut elections for the first time) and for equal wages and working conditions. Other Arab workers, especially those dependent on Histadrut-owned enterprises and the kibbutzim for their employment, have tended to support Labor or Mapam, though Labor's influence has been declining for many years.

Along with the growth of the Palestinian working class, there has been a significant expansion of the ranks of the intelligentsia. University education is no longer a rarity in the Arab community. In Umm al-Fahm, 200 residents now attend university each year. The neighboring village of Kafr Qara' (pop. 6,000) has about 200 university graduates. University graduates have assumed important political roles in many villages, challenging both the traditional leadership of the clan chiefs and the status of the Communist Party as the preeminent fighter for Arab rights. Organizations like Sons of the Village and the Progressive Movement (the Arab component of the Jewish-Arab Progressive List for Peace), as well as several smaller local organizations draw their support largely from the young, university-educated middle strata of the community.

Proletarianization and education have been the motor forces behind the political mobilization of Israel's Palestinian Arab community. During the 1950s and 1960s Mapai (precursor of Labor) and its affiliated Arab lists received a majority of the Arab votes in Knesset elections by relying on traditional leaders like the landed magnate Sayf al-Din al-Zu'bi, who delivered the votes of his clients in Nazareth and the surrounding villages in exchange for personal political influence and prestige. Until it was abolished in 1966, the military government also helped to maintain Mapai preeminence in the Arab community by making clear that only cooperative Arabs would be given travel permits and be permitted to conduct their daily business without harassment. The military government was kept in place when challenged by opposition parties in the Knesset with the help of the votes of Arab MKs from Mapai's Arab lists and Mapam.

Al-Zu'bi and others of his generation and class background did not dream of demanding equal rights for Israel's Arab citizens. Today, even the most moderate Arab political leaders are far more assertive. In the 1984 Knesset elections the Labor Party abandoned the practice of forming affiliated Arab lists because the clan heads upon whom this system depended had lost much of their power to deliver the vote. Instead, 'Abd al-Wahhab Darawsha was given a position as a Labor candidate on the Alignment list (composed of Labor and Mapam) that guaranteed he would enter the Knesset. Soon after the elections he made headlines by calling for negotiations between Israel and the PLO and attempting to attend a meeting of the Palestine National Council in Amman. In February 1988 Darawsha resigned from the Labor Party, protesting Defense Minister Yitzhak Rabin's policy of deploying "force, might and beatings" to suppress the Palestinian uprising in the occupied territories. Darawsha then formed the Arab Democratic Party. He now occupies the single seat his party won in the 1988 Knesset elections.

Many young members of the intelligentsia have adopted a more radical nationalist orientation than that of both Darawsha and the Communist Party. The Sons of the Village, for example, call on Arabs to boycott Knesset (but not local) elections as an expression of their nonrecognition of the state. Their call apparently received little response in 1988, as 75.6 percent of the Arab community voted, a higher proportion than in the two previous elections.[13] The Progressive Movement, unencumbered by the class content of the Communist Party's line and its uncritical support for the Soviet Union, sharply challenged the Communists in the 1984 and 1988 elections, forcing them to compete for nationalist legitimacy. As a result, the Communist Party, though still by far the largest party in the Arab community, has not been able to retain the majority status it won in 1977.

The response to the series of general strikes since 1976 is a further indicator of the extent of Arab political mobilization in Israel. In contrast to the reticent attitude of many non-Communist Arab local council chairpersons toward Land Day, all of them, including those associated with the Labor Party, supported Equality Day and Peace Day, as did 'Abd al-Wahhab Darawsha, Mapam's Arab MK, Muhammad Watad (who has since resigned from Mapam and joined the DFPE), and Progressive List for Peace MK Muhammad Mi'ari. This reflects the broad-based mobilization of the entire Arab community beyond the ranks of the supporters of the DFPE or the Communist Party.

Jewish political leaders have gradually adjusted to the new realities without fully accepting them. After it became radicalized in 1976, then-Prime Minister Rabin refused to accept the NCALC as the representative of the Arab community. But when Ezer Weizmann became the minister responsible for Arab affairs in the national unity government from 1984 to 1986 he did unofficially recognize the representative character of the NCALC. Weizmann instituted some significant reforms in government policy during his tenure, closing the unpopular government Arabic daily *al-Anba'*, restoring sequestered land in the infamous "Area Nine" in the Galilee to its owners and granting municipal status to Umm al-Fahm. Weizmann's successor, Moshe Arens, dismissed Equality Day as "Communist incitement," but the government's response to the strike indicated that no one actually believed this explanation of the event. In 1980 the Likud government banned a congress scheduled to be held in Nazareth to found an Arab political party and forbade meetings to protest the ban, while in 1988 the national unity government headed by Shamir quietly accepted the formation of the Arab Democratic Party—the first all-Arab party to be legally established in Israel.

Civil Rights and National Rights

Equality Day and Peace Day represent the two poles of Arab political action in Israel: the struggle for civil rights and the struggle for national rights. For most of the period since 1948, the focus has been on the demand for civil rights and equal treatment under the law, even by those forces like the Communist Party who have consistently defended the national rights of the Palestinian people to self-determination and an independent state.

The Palestinian Arab intelligentsia has often been the most articulate advocate for the civil rights and equality of the Arab community. This is not because the intelligentsia suffers more from discrimination than the working class; the opposite is probably the case. But the intelligentsia is more likely to feel entitled to equality and more able to express its demands articulately to an Israeli Jewish audience. College graduates feel particularly aggrieved because they are frequently unable to find work appropriate to their qualifications, and if they do it is likely to be outside their villages in the mainly Jewish cities where they are subjected to all forms of discrimination, abuse and even physical danger.

A more far reaching demand for full integration of Arabs into Israeli society has recently been raised as a result of the activity of a small number of extraordinary individuals who have achieved success in the world of arts and letters: novelist Anton Shammas, television journalist Rafik Halaby (author of *West Bank Story*) and actor Muhammad Baqri (co-star of the film *Beyond the Walls*). There are also dozens of other less well-known authors, journalists, academics, artists and professionals who have graduated from Israeli universities, speak and write fluent Hebrew and socialize easily in Jewish society.

Shammas has written an autobiographical novel, *Arabesques,* published in finely crafted Hebrew and he presents it as his identity card in what he hopes will become a binational Israeli state. This vision may ultimately pose an even more radical challenge to Israeli society than the nationalist political movement of the Palestinian masses, because it requires reconceptualizing the content of the term "Israeli" and its transformation into a territorial identity which could be shared equally by both Jewish and Palestinian Arab citizens of the state.[14] Such a prospect is frightening, even to many liberal Zionists, because this might mean that ordinary Palestinian Arabs might live in a kibbutz or a moshav, own a factory employing Jews or establish an Arab university in Nazareth, all developments which have been blocked in recent years. Perhaps an Arab could even become minister of defense! Moreover, as has been evident by their response to the uprising, if the Arab citizens of Israel advance toward full civil rights and equality, this is bound to intensify the demand for national rights both within and beyond the borders of pre-1967 Israel.

Backlash

The citizenship status of Israel's Palestinian Arabs does impose some restraints on how they are treated, especially in comparison with residents of the West Bank and the Gaza Strip. However, these restraints are sometimes frail, as was the case in the attack on two Arab residents of the Ramat Amidar neighborhood of Ramat Gan, a suburb of Tel Aviv, on June 22, 1987. About 100 Arabs, both workers and students at nearby Bar Ilan University, had been living in Ramat Amidar for years. Following a quarrel in the street, about twenty Jews broke into an apartment shared by two Arab workers and threw one of them out the second story window. The next night the Jews returned and set the apartment ablaze. All the Arab residents of Ramat Amidar abandoned their apartments, fearing for their lives. In a bizarre twist underscoring the mythological character of the politics of national identity, evidence presented at the trial of the Jewish assailants two years later revealed that according to Jewish religious law the two Arab victims are actually "Jews" because their mother is a Jew and their father is an Arab. A week after the Ramat Amidar assault, Arab workers in nearby Ganei Tikva were beaten in the street.

The liberal Israeli press termed these incidents "pogroms," and there were two small protest demonstrations near Ramat Amidar. The Oriental Jewish residents of Ramat Amidar insisted that this was yet another example of the Ashkenazi Jewish intelligentsia maligning their community. But the more they protested that the affair was simply a neighbors' quarrel and that they were not racists, the more apparent it became that this was yet another episode marking the increasing acceptability of unvarnished racism and racially inspired violence in broader sectors of Israeli society ("But the Arabs have to know their place and not try to date Jewish women").

Ramat Amidar and Ganei Tikva symbolize the dilemma Arab citizens pose for Israeli society. The Arab working class and intelligentsia, despite considerable obstacles, in fact now participate more fully in the Israeli economy and society. Legally, they are fully entitled to do so; in practice, they have historically been confined to their village ghettos, and there has been fierce opposition to their efforts to break out of them. Arab achievements have led to stronger demands for equality and greater opportunity. If these demands are granted, much of what is popularly considered to be a manifestation of Israel's Jewish character will have to change. If Arab demands are not met, Israelis may have to admit that there may be a contradiction between being a Jewish state and a democratic state, a troubling idea for liberal Zionists.

In response to increasing Arab political assertiveness, a Jewish backlash has developed, intensified by fear of the significance of the uprising in the occupied territories. The Equality Day strike received at least verbal support from many leading Jewish government and Histadrut leaders from the center and left of the political spectrum. But the nationalist demands of Peace Day were supported by many fewer Jews. The national unity of the Palestinians of the occupied territories and those inside the Green Line was met with hysterical denunciations by Jewish leaders from Labor to Rabbi Kahane's Kach.

Throughout 1988, Palestinian Arab citizens of Israel manifested their support for the uprising and its objectives—by demonstrating, striking and organizing supplies of food, medicine and other material assistance. On September 11, 2,000 mourners in the Triangle village of 'Ar'ara marked the fortieth day after the death of the first martyr of the uprising from inside the Green Line, Muhammad Ahmad Sayf.

In response, repression against Arab citizens has intensified. Prime Minister Shamir, acting as minister of interior, closed the Communist Party's Arabic daily, *al-Ittihad,* for a full week before Land Day in order to impede the call for an Arab general strike. The popular Nazareth weekly, *al-Sinara,* has been subjected to heavy censorship since the start of the uprising. The Central Electoral Commission tried and failed for a second time to prohibit the Progressive List for Peace from participating in the Knesset elections (widely regarded as a compensatory measure to offset the banning of Kach because of its racist program; Israel can't have only Jewish racists). As these actions were being taken, public opinion polls indicated that 55 percent of Israelis opposed granting equal rights to Arab citizens; 45 percent believed Israel is "too democratic;" and 41 percent favored "transferring" the Palestinian Arabs of the West Bank and the Gaza Strip out of the country.[15]

The harsh reaction of Israeli officials to Arab citizens exercising their democratic rights to free expression and dissent had a chilling effect on the political activity of the Arab community after the first several months of the uprising. This was reflected in the election results, which did not exhibit as significant a radicalization of the electorate as many had predicted. At a symposium convened to discuss the election results in the Arab community, representatives of Labor, Mapam, the Citizens' Rights Movement, the Progressive List for Peace and the Arab Democratic Party agreed that the election had been a defeat for the left and for the Arab community.[16] The failure was attributed to the fierce competition between the three non-Zionist parties within the Arab community. Their refusal to cooperate resulted in the loss of two additional Arab seats (one would have gone to the DFPE and one to the Progressive List for Peace). In addition, if the 24 percent of the Arabs who abstained had voted, another one or two Arab MKs could have been elected. Finally, the Arab community remains divided by religious, family and geographic rivalries which, though they are far less significant than most Israeli analysts believe, still allow the Zionist parties to divide and coopt a significant proportion of the Arab vote. Some sectors of the Arab community still have little political consciousness, as demonstrated by the Arab votes for the Likud and other parties of the right.

Despite the overall failure to crystallize the political mobilization and consciousness developed during the intifada, the electoral results still produced some notable gains. A record 58.3 percent of the Arab community voted for non-Zionist parties, a continuation of a trend that is likely to persist. Labor suffered a substantial loss of influence in the Arab community, while the Citizens' Rights Movement established a respectable toehold for the first time ever. Mapam's weak showing was very likely due to its having been part of the Alignment from 1968 to 1984, and hence its identification as a party of the regime. Continued opposition and separation from Labor will likely strengthen Mapam's presence in the Arab sector. After the elections, Arab political leaders from all the parties of the center and left realized the cost of their disunity and began to make conciliatory statements expressing willingness to cooperate. In contrast to the moderate electoral results, a week after election day hundreds of youths in Tayyiba (pop. 14,000) confronted Israeli police for three days, burning tires and hurling stones in a failed attempt to prevent the demolition of fifteen houses built without construction permits (routinely denied in Arab villages). In the course of their struggle the villagers declared a general strike. A week later, on November 15, Israel's Arab citizens held a nationwide general strike of solidarity protesting the destruction of the houses the same day Palestinians in the occupied territories observed a general strike to mark the declaration of Palestinian independence by the Palestine National Council. Once again Israeli officials reacted with hysteria at the prospect of coordinated general strikes on both sides of the Green Line, despite the assurances of strike leaders that the coincidence of the strikes was unintentional. The tactics and the political self-confidence developed during the uprising are being shared across the Green Line. This has made Israeli resistance to all Palestinian demands more obstinate at the same time that it underscores the essential unity of the problem: Israel's Arab citizens cannot gain full equality unless the national rights of the Palestinian people are recognized as well.

## Chapter 15

The Uprising's Impact on Israel

Azmy Bishara

The Palestinian uprising has stripped away the credibility of Israel's external propaganda and its internal ideological defense mechanisms, as political rationality has steadily retreated before the state's frantic response to the anticolonial revolt in the occupied territories. This has led to a polarization which has penetrated all of Israel's political parties, burst the existing boundaries of the national political consensus and raised the real questions facing Israeli society. As the uprising continues, the cleavage in Israeli society becomes deeper over two basic issues: negotiations with the PLO and recognition of the Palestinian right to self-determination, including the establishment of a state. This has already made the Palestine question the primary agenda item for the first time ever in an Israeli electoral campaign.

Israel's existing political formations have so far been unable to pose a coherent response. Over this past year some groups in the Likud moved closer to Tehiya and others to the right wing of Labor. Similarly, some groups in Labor moved closer to Mapam (the United Workers' Party, formerly Labor's junior partner in the Alignment) and the Citizens' Rights Movement (CRM), others towards the Likud. This polarization within each bloc has created a new center in the Israeli political structure comprising groups from both the Likud and Labor who oppose negotiations with the PLO and a Palestinian state but also refuse to annex the occupied territories. This is the political foundation of the "national unity" government.

Convergence

Ariel Sharon articulated the program of this new center in March 1988, when the Labor Party began to speak of "American pressure" in the form of the Shultz initiative. Sharon drew a line which, he said, no amount of US government pressure could breach. According to Sharon, the Likud and

Labor agreed on the most important points concerning the future of the occupied territories: 1) United Jerusalem is the eternal capital of Israel; 2) The Jordan River will remain forever Israel's eastern border; 3) No non-Israeli military force will be allowed to enter the West Bank of the Jordan River; 4) Israel is responsible for the internal and external security of the land to the west of the Jordan; 5) There will be no foreign sovereignty in "Judea, Samaria and the Gaza Strip"; 6) There will be no Palestinian state west of Jordan; 7) Settling the refugee question should be part of any solution; 8) The Golan Heights are an integral part of Israel; 9) The Arabs of the occupied territories should maintain their present nationality and should be given relatively broad authority to administer their internal affairs without interference.[1]

The election campaign saw some convergence of Likud elements and Labor Party hawks. Thus, during discussions between Labor and Likud branches in Jerusalem, Labor supported annexing the satellite settlements around Jerusalem, while the Likud rejected this on the grounds that the time was not ripe. At the start of the electoral campaign, Sharon, who appears to be the most hostile toward Labor, proposed annexing parts of the West Bank and the Gaza Strip in accord with the Allon Plan, using the demographic threat argument favored by Labor.[2] Rabin responded that Sharon's distinction between important and unimportant occupied areas brought him very close to Labor's thinking.[3]

The recomposition that has drawn together fractions from Likud and Labor to form this new center has driven others from Labor to the Zionist left and from the Likud to the extreme right. The new right consists of groups from the Likud, the National Religious Party (NRP), Tzomet (Crossroads), Moledet (Homeland) and, finally, Tehiya (Renaissance)—the classic Greater Israel party with both religious and secular elements. They demand annexing the occupied territories and regard Jordan as the Palestinian state. They reject autonomy for the territories and call for increasing the suffering of the Palestinians in the territories until total "transfer" is achieved. These parties also represent the settlers' lobby.

The new Zionist left includes groups from Labor, Mapam and the CRM. They are ready to negotiate with the PLO under certain conditions, accept Israeli withdrawal from most of the territories and recognize the principle of partition.

A fourth political bloc, the non-Zionist ultra-orthodox parties (Agudat Yisra'el, Shas and Degel Hatorah), puts political issues as a third or fourth priority. This results in a flexible position on the territories which currently reflects the prevailing right-wing atmosphere.

The fifth bloc in Israeli politics is composed of the non-Zionist left parties—the Communist Party, the Progressive List for Peace and the Arab

Democratic Party. They have consistently supported a Palestinian state in the territories occupied in 1967.

"Peace for Nothing"

Before 1977, the Likud had advocated annexing the occupied territories to Israel. Yet once it attained power, it realized that enforcing Israeli sovereignty on the territories was no rhetorical matter, and shifted to maintaining the status quo. Menachem Begin's autonomy plan at Camp David was an attempt to reconcile the Likud with its ideology by giving a de jure status to a de facto situation.

The Likud has relied on one basic propaganda line: calling for direct negotiations with the Arabs and simultaneously anticipating their results—"peace for peace" as Shamir likes to declare, or "peace for nothing." Despite the uprising, the Likud introduced no change in its political program. But it would be wrong to assume that the Likud has not been affected by the uprising simply because it has not changed its political program. During the last year, Moshe Arens, Dan Meridor and others proposed "unilateral autonomy"—i.e., without a peace treaty—after elections in the territories.[4] They reject annexation and propose to leave open the question of sovereignty. Other Likud factions, which opposed forming the national unity government, called for immediate annexation of the territories.

During the campaign, the Likud's position was clearer than that of Labor. It rejected all peace proposals and did not offer a plan of its own. Shamir declared repeatedly that the conflict is not a question of borders, but of existence: either all of Israel or no Israel at all.[5] No negotiations with the PLO—not now, not in the future and not under any circumstances.[6]

Likud's forty Knesset seats (30.8 percent of the votes) were not a direct consequence of its political positions. Likud supporters are the least ideological group in Israeli society. In order to market itself, the Likud purveys a hostile attitude to the Ashkenazi, defeatist Labor Party which has treated Oriental Jews with contempt and discrimination and exploited the state's economic resources for its failing projects (the Histadrut's Kupat Holim health insurance plan, the Koor industrial complex, the kibbutzim). For the Likud, making peace means putting an end to the uprising. As in any business deal, one starts by demanding the maximum. This language of the market finds receptive ears among Likud voters.[7]

The nonideological stance of Likud voters does not mean that they are ready to change their political allegiance. Nor does the lack of ideology at the base diminish the ideological commitment of the leadership. The Likud constituency would not present an obstacle if the leadership changed its position, but the absence of ideology among its voters is insufficient to change the party's political positions. More likely, it will be exploited by the demagoguery of the leadership.

The Labor Party seemed to be the most confused during the uprising. The right accused Foreign Minister Peres of being defeatist and of dragging Israel into an international conference adventure more dangerous than the status quo; the left accused Defense Minister Rabin of carrying out the Likud's policy in the territories. Labor's political line was based on the "demographic threat"— the fear that the Arabs might become a majority if Israel insisted on keeping all the occupied territories. But the Israeli Jewish public's comprehension of this racist notion does not necessarily favor territorial compromise. People are more likely to conclude instead that the Arabs must be expelled, or that they should not be counted as citizens—in other words, apartheid.

The "Generals' Plan," introduced by some senior officers close to the Labor Party before the elections, called for withdrawal from the populated Arab areas in the West Bank, positioning the Israeli army along the Jordan River, demilitarizing the area, setting up early warning stations and keeping the Jordan Valley and Jerusalem under Israeli sovereignty. This plan complements a political proposal by Peres and Rabin to negotiate with a joint Jordanian-Palestinian delegation in the framework of a nominal international conference, hold elections in the occupied territories six months after suppressing the uprising, and thereby reach a temporary settlement of the "problem of the territories."[8] The Peres-Rabin plan also includes a pledge not to withdraw to the 1967 borders or remove the settlements.

Abba Eban polarized the party when he proposed amending the Labor program so that it did not specify with whom Israel refuses to negotiate, but instead set out the conditions for negotiations with any Palestinian party (the three US conditions—recognition of Israel, acceptance of 242 and 338 and renunciation of terrorism). Yossi Beilin, Haim Ramon, Avraham Burg and Ezer Weizmann supported Eban in terms that resembled the stand of Mapam or the CRM. These elements within Labor also generally opposed establishing a national unity government. Labor's hawks viewed Eban's conditions as a means to prevent the PLO from participating in negotiations; their prevailing interpretation ended up making Labor's platform very similar to Likud's. Rabin reiterated that he would never accept withdrawal to the 1967 borders, even if this position would prevent peace.[9]

Right and Left

The programs of the extreme rightwing parties, religious and secular, presented the clearest response to the uprising: 1) suppress the uprising with all necessary force; 2) increase settlements; 3) annex the territories; 4) "persuade" the Palestinians to emigrate. Two new rightwing parties have emerged: Tzomet, led by Rafael Eitan (chief of staff during the Lebanon war) and Moledet, led by General (reserves) Rehavam Ze'evi. Both come from the Palmach, the elite military organization of Labor Zionism during the 1940s. Their political-ideological message is not justified by religious mysticism, but is posed as a pragmatic answer to practical necessities. Eitan believes that the main challenge is educating youth and imbuing it with "the spirit of the first pioneers." If achieved, this will be sufficient to end the conflict with the Arabs (Eitan refrains from using the word Palestinians).[10] As for the uprising, Eitan's solution is very simple: "a bullet in the head of every stone thrower."

Moledet openly calls for transferring the Arabs out of the country. Its supporters, unlike Kahane's, represent a broad ethnic and geographic spectrum of Israeli society. It is true that its electoral support in the settlements is higher than its national average, but its highest rate of support (45 percent) came from Kibbutz Beit Guvrin, within the Green Line.[11]

Both parties are the product of the rightwing forces which have always existed in Israeli society, yet the atmosphere of the uprising contributed to their crystallization. Together they attained four seats in the Knesset, while Tehiya lost two, and Kach was disqualified from participating in the elections. In other words, the extreme right (without the ultra-orthodox parties) won seven Knesset seats (one more than in 1984) and 6.5 percent of the vote; together with the NRP they received twelve seats and 10.5 percent of the vote—the same as in the previous Knesset.

The uprising precipitated an important change in Mapam and the CRM. Mapam had left the Alignment in 1984 when the previous national unity government was formed and ran independently of the Labor Party for the first time since 1965. Mapam received three seats and 2.5 percent of the votes. Its April 1988 congress amended the party program to include willingness to negotiate with the PLO if the PLO recognized Israel and renounced terrorism, and recognition of the Palestinians' right to self-determination in the framework of an Israeli peace initiative.[12] The CRM also amended its political program during the uprising to include recognition of the Palestinian right to self-determination and negotiations with the PLO provided that the latter recognized Israel's right to exist and ceased hostile actions.[13]

Until the uprising, the Communist Party of Israel (and the electoral list it leads, the Democratic Front for Peace and Equality) and the Progressive

List for Peace were the only parties which called for a two-state solution and for recognition of the PLO. Endorsements of these positions by writers, artists and university professors did not represent the official programs of the Zionist parties with which, for the most part, they identified. Only in 1988, as a direct result of the uprising, has a relatively large left-Zionist camp emerged calling for negotiations with the PLO and for establishment of a Palestinian state. Mapam and the CRM together won eight seats in the Knesset, as opposed to the three won by the CRM alone in 1984. (In the previous Knesset, two more MKs joined the CRM after they were originally elected on other lists, while Mapam received seven Knesset seats—far more than its real strength—because it ran as part of the Alignment.)

Security and Anxiety

The uprising has sparked an unprecedented debate over the strategic importance of the occupied territories for Israel. Hundreds of high-ranking officers have contributed to this discussion through dozens of interviews and symposia. Military arguments were widely used in the election campaign by the two major parties. One group of senior officers believes the occupied territories are the most important strategic defense factor for Israel in a coming war and should be kept under Israeli control even if this prevents peace. In any case, peace with the Arab world is not on the agenda, and Israel should adopt Henry Kissinger's notion that no-war arrangements are better for Israel than peace agreements. This doctrine is best articulated by Yehoshu'a Sagi, former head of military intelligence.

A second group would give up most of the territories with certain security arrangements (observation points, disarmament, etc.). Proponents of this view advocate a wide range of political positions, from autonomy to confederation with Jordan. It is best represented by former chief of staff Mota Gur, Uri Or, former commander of the central region, and Avraham Ben Gal, former commander of the northern region. All are supporters of Labor, as are most high-ranking officers.

A third group of officers regards the territories as a burden which threatens internal security and increases the likelihood of a future war. They call for negotiations with the PLO and do not object to the establishment of a Palestinian state if that is the only solution. They are best represented by Yehoshafat Harkabi.[14] Organizations like the Labor-leaning Committee for Peace and Security, which includes more than 130 senior officers, are careful not to cross the line from the second to the third positions.

The prevalence of national security discourse in Israeli political culture confuses the analytical categories of the protest movement and those of the military establishment. This hinders the development of the protest movement because peace groups expend great energy trying to prove their patriotism at the expense of effective opposition to atrocities in the occupied territories. Peace Now wasted a lot of time contributing to the security discussion within the Labor Party. Only on November 23, 1988, after a year of the uprising and much criticism from its supporters, did Peace Now call for negotiations with the PLO. Militant organizations like End the Occupation, Yesh Gvul, Women in Black, Women for Political Prisoners and other movements in solidarity with the Palestinian struggle do not employ the security discourse.

The uprising has highlighted the failure of Israeli democracy when it clashes with the national question. This is evident in the closure of the newspaper *Derech Hanitzotz/Tariq al-Sharara*, imprisonment of those who refuse to serve in the occupied territories for reasons of conscience, confiscation of foreign reporters' press credentials, restrictions on radio and television reports and politicization of the judicial system. Anti-democratic norms common in the occupied territories have been transposed to Israel.

Wide media coverage of extreme instances of oppression has played some part in removing Israel's internal masks: the village of Salim, where soldiers buried alive several inhabitants; Beita, which suffered a pogrom when the army believed the lies of the settlers; the trial of Givati brigade soldiers accused of beating an injured prisoner to death; three Arab workers burned alive in Or Yehuda; atrocities of the army in the raid on Qalqilya (publicized by the participants);[15] a prison guard training a schoolboy to beat up Arab prisoners. Since reality is what is represented in the media, these events have shaken the Israeli collective consciousness by forcing Israelis to watch themselves in the mirror. Some blame the media; others learn to live with it—because atrocities may be normalized through repeated public exposure. Others are shocked and anxious.

But anxiety is not enough to provoke action. It can be treated; defense mechanisms are available. The chief education officer of the army demonstrated one of these mechanisms in a lecture to his troops:

> The 18-year-old Israeli soldier who grabs the club considers the Arab the source of all his problems. The Arab takes a stone and throws it at the face of the soldier, and suddenly 2,000 years of diaspora, the destruction of the first and second temple, and his girlfriend, lying on a Tel Aviv beach—all this enters his hand [which holds the club].[16]

That the 2,000 years of diaspora and the destruction of the first and second temple will smash the head of the Palestinian in another instant does not seem to bother the officer. But does the 18-year-old soldier really think about all these things before the education officer puts them in his head?

Such cynical use of historical Jewish suffering is an extreme expression of the psychological approach to the uprising, which typically tries to understand the oppressors, not the oppressed (who in any case lack a psychology). Palestinians cannot become agents for assuaging Israeli fears. They cannot be expected to presuppose such fears among their oppressors. Moreover, they do not see this as their task when they are suffering from occupation. If the Palestinian issue is a psychological problem for the Israelis, the cure might be group therapy, or it might be eliminating the problem—i.e., "transfer." This psychological approach is another obstacle to the expansion of the Israeli protest movement.

In any case, the psyche of the mythical "average" Israeli is home to many conflicting ideas: We should teach the Arabs a lesson so that they won't be able to raise their heads again; but we are tired of these problematic settlers. We should make peace with the Arabs; but they are liars from birth. We should negotiate with the PLO if it is ready for peace; but who believes the PLO; we should eliminate it. We should negotiate with Hussein; but he wants the West Bank and East Jerusalem; we won't give them to him. Anyway the people of the West Bank and Gaza want the PLO, not Hussein. All the world is against us; but our international relations have never been so good. The United States supports us; but it talks to the PLO. Sharon is a provocateur. Why did he move to East Jerusalem? But he is the only one who can smash their heads; we should kill them all....

Opinion polls find considerable (even majority) support for all these ideas. One indicated that 51 percent (including 39 percent of Likud voters) favor negotiating with the PLO if the latter recognizes Israel and renounces terrorism. Another poll showed that 41 percent of Israelis supported the idea of "transfer," and 45 percent regard Israel as too democratic.[17] These contradictory ideas can coexist simultaneously because none of the political leaders of the new Likud/Labor center has been willing to speak honestly and explain in unequivocal terms the real options Israeli society faces. Instead, demagoguery and outright lies have been deployed to exacerbate people's fears and insecurities and encourage political fantasies and delusions.

The Uprising and the Economy

While Israel has minimized the economic impact of the uprising, there was a certain Palestinian illusion in its early stage that it would be possible to deliver a heavy blow to the Israeli economy by achieving total civil disobedience. This notion derives from an abstract understanding of civil disobedience, divorced from the actual situation. The struggle against the occupation has essentially been a political conflict with important economic, social and cultural aspects. It is not an economic struggle with political aspects. Strikes, boycotts, refusal to pay taxes—these are primarily political tactics to mobilize as many people as possible into the struggle against the occupation. But the results have indeed transformed the occupation into an economic burden for Israel.

Shlomo Gazit, writing in 1985, summarized Israeli economic policy in the West Bank at the beginning of the occupation: 1) "Political and security" considerations should be placed above economic considerations; 2) While planning for economic activity in the territories, priority should be given to the needs of the Israeli economy; 3) There should be no Israeli investments in the economy of the occupied territories; 4) The Palestinian economy should have safety valves (open bridges, work in Israel, etc.). But economic forces have constantly created new realities, randomly and without prior planning.[18] Today the economy of the occupied territories is subordinate to the Israeli economy and bound to it in a periphery-center relationship.[19] The "national" income in the occupied territories amounts to $1.5 billion, of which two-thirds comes from local resources and one-third from elsewhere, mainly work in Israel. Production per capita in the West Bank is only one-third of that in Israel and in Gaza only one-sixth. Comparing consumption per capita results in about the same ratio.[20]

Agricultural products constitute about one-third of the West Bank's production, less in Gaza. The proportion of the West Bank labor force engaged in agriculture has declined from 46 percent in 1968 to 27 percent in 1985, and in Gaza from 32 percent to 18 percent. West Bank exports constitute only 2-4 percent of Israel's agricultural exports.[21] In the West Bank, 54 percent of the wage labor force is employed in Israel; in Gaza, 67 percent.

In 1986 Israel's exports to the occupied territories were valued at $780.3 million, about 10 percent of its total exports and 1.5 percent of the Israeli GNP. The same year, the occupied territories' exports to Israel amounted to $289.1 million.[22] Israel collects $383 million in taxes from the occupied territories and allocates $240 million for expenditures in the territories. The residents of the occupied territories (like all Israeli residents) also pay a value added tax on all purchases and services from Israel. Palestinian workers in

Israel save about $500 million for Israeli employers in lower labor costs, not to mention the amounts they save the Israeli treasury in social security benefits that they do not receive despite deductions from their paychecks. All this totals more than $1 billion in net revenue for Israel.[23]

This balance of economic power means that the uprising cannot defeat Israel economically. But it has made the occupation a losing economic proposition for Israel. In March 1988 the Governor of the Bank of Israel, Michael Bruno, gave a press conference in which he minimized Israel's economic losses due to the uprising.[24] Today the situation looks dramatically different.

Military expenditures are the most important because they also reflect the escalating level of the uprising. In March 1988, Finance Minister Moshe Nissim claimed that the ministry of defense had not asked for a budgetary supplement and that the construction of 600 new police and border police posts in the territories had been decided on before the uprising. Three months later, the army requested an additional $450 million to cover the expenses of its activities in the territories. Reserve service was increased from forty-five to sixty days per year, at an estimated cost of $100-200 million.[25] This loss may become permanent, as large numbers of Israeli troops will have to remain in the territories. Four months after the uprising began, the army had increased the number of troops in the territories by up to five times.[26] It is likely that the number of troops has doubled since then.

In early March, the government-operated labor exchanges began to hire workers from south Lebanon and Portugal to work in hotels and agricultural harvesting. The Likud's former Minister of Labor (now Transport) Moshe Katsav, who opposed the idea of importing new workers, announced that he had given 3,576 work permits to foreigners as of March.[27]

The labor shortage was more serious than this number would indicate. In July the head of the contractors' association called for importing 10,000 workers from abroad "to rescue the construction sector" from collapse.[28] On November 28, 1988, the director of the agricultural association declared that there was a shortage of 4,000 workers for the citrus harvest. Labor contracting companies and land owners asked the government to import an additional 2,000 workers from Portugal and Turkey.[29] According to the ministry of industry, in the first three months of 1988, industrial production dropped by 3.5 percent, and over 70 percent of the decrease (2.5 percent) was related to the "disturbances" in the territories—work absences and loss of sales.[30]

There are two Israeli views about the absence of Arab workers. Moshe Katsav claimed that things would return to normal and that work in Israel should be seen as a means to normalize relations with the territories. He rejected the idea of importing workers, arguing that there is no alternative to the labor force from the territories. Others claimed that, for security reasons, strikes and work absences should be used to punish the residents of the territories and disrupt the plans of the organizers of the uprising. Workers from active villages should not be allowed to work in Israel. In May, Rabin declared that he supported "importing 3-6,000 workers from abroad, even 8,000, for the construction sector, because this is of security value." He wanted the Palestinians "to understand that work in Israel is an advantage that we provide, not a favor that they extend to us."[31]

From Asset to Liability

Strikes have been one of the most important weapons of the uprising. For the Palestinians, as for Israel, political considerations (strikes as an expression of rejecting the occupation) remain more important than economic losses. The uprising has maintained a balance between these two considerations: workers are allowed to work in Israel; incidents of burning buses which transport workers have stopped. The continuation of the uprising and the ability of the people to live with it are two sides of the same coin—resistance and steadfastness.

Palestinians have boycotted Israeli products whenever an alternative local product is available and have tended to buy only necessities. Demand for fresh beef has dropped by 70 percent, creating a crisis for Israeli ranchers, because Arabs are the main consumers of fresh (as opposed to imported, frozen) meat. In response, the army considered providing troops with fresh meat instead of the frozen meat they usually consume.[32] Dubek cigarette company sales decreased by 16 percent.[33] By May 1988, the purchasing power of Arab residents of the territories had decreased by 35 percent due to diminished income and the boycott of Israeli products.[34]

On December 15, 1988, Finance Minister Nissim estimated that total production losses during the first year of the intifada were equivalent to 2.5 percent of the total production of the business sector. Three sectors were especially hard hit: textiles, construction and tourism. Textiles and shoemaking depend considerably on subcontractors with small and medium-size workshops in the territories, especially in Hebron and Nablus. Losing contact with these workshops led to the closure of dozens of medium-sized workshops in Israel.[35] The existence of some textile enterprises in the territories contributed to the success of the boycott on Israeli textile products. Before the uprising certain Israeli textile products used to find their way to Arab countries through the West Bank, but this has now stopped.[36]

The loss of production in the construction sector—caused mainly by the absence of Palestinian workers—is estimated at $16 million monthly, equivalent to 8 percent of the economic activity in this sector.[37]

Through March 1988, tourist reservations registered a drop of only 4 percent because reservations had been booked before the uprising. In April, Jerusalem hotel reservations were down 40 percent compared with the previous year.[38] The ministries of finance and tourism in August 1988 set up a special team which allocated $2.2 million for publicity and marketing and postponed all payments due to the government from hotel owners.[39] For all of 1988 the decline in reservations compared to 1987 was expected to total 15 percent—a direct loss of $110-150 million to the hotel industry alone.[40] The comprehensive loss to the tourist industry in 1988 may have been as high as $500 million.[41]

There is no official or semi-official estimate of the impact of the uprising on tax collection. Tax payments dropped in response to the political call to refrain from paying taxes and because diminished income reduced people's capacity to pay them. The civil administration announced it would reduce its services—paid for by the Palestinian taxpayer—because of the decrease in tax collection.[42]

Certain economic losses do not fit the categories of Israeli reports. For example, Egged bus company reported damages to 1,260 buses since the beginning of the uprising, of which forty-one were totally burned.[43]

Former Economy Minister Gad Ya'acobi estimated that the total cost of the intifada to the Israeli economy in 1988 exceeded $900 million.[44] But the economic aspects of the intifada must be set in their political context. As Israelis refrain from residing in the territories and others even leave, the ministry of housing has decided to increase the construction of apartments in the territories by 33 percent, from 1,500 in 1987 to 2,000 in 1988. The ministry also raised its share of the investment in contractors' projects. The financial support to every family wishing to buy an apartment in the territories is higher by 20,000 shekels.[45] These figures represent an economic loss, but indicate that the government is committed to maintaining the status quo which the uprising is challenging and, to a considerable extent, is still able to do so.

The uprising has not yet accomplished anything significant in the area of foreign economic pressure on Israel. The refusal of the European parliament to approve the EEC agreement with Israel in March 1988 was not based on political convictions. The parliament later approved the agreement by a vote of 314 to 25 with 19 abstentions. And the uprising had no impact on the $3 billion of US aid Israel received in 1988.

True, the uprising has transformed the occupation from an economic asset into a liability. But this pressure on the Israeli economy is insufficient in and of itself to force a change in Israeli policy; this cannot be achieved unless the gains on the level of the world public opinion are translated into foreign economic pressure on Israel. The Western countries will only threaten to apply such pressure when they come to realize that the continuing uprising may endanger their interests in the Middle East.

A Losing Project?

The new Israeli government has so far pursued the same policies toward the uprising as the previous one. Shamir continues to assert, at least in public, that he is prepared to crush the uprising by any means necessary. Rabin and Peres continue to hope that the uprising will give birth to a new Palestinian leadership that will "qualify" for "negotiations" with Israel. While recent public opinion polls indicate that a majority of Israelis favor negotiating with the PLO, this sentiment has as yet had no impact on government policy.[46] Israel's campaign to portray the uprising as "terrorism" has largely failed. But long before Washington agreed to talk with the PLO, the Israeli government had decided that the issue was not one of recognition, acceptance of Resolution 242 or renouncing "terrorism." Members of the Israeli establishment from both the Likud and Labor have stressed that their refusal to negotiate with the PLO is a consequence of their belief that such negotiations will eventually lead to a Palestinian state. The questions facing Israel today are those which face any colonial power: Has the occupation become a losing project or not—politically and socially as well as economically? Are there enough forces in the colonial state to sustain it even if it is losing?

Self-determination and a Palestinian state are the objectives of the uprising. Israel's ability to block these goals is still substantial, but the intifada has overturned the post-Lebanon war balance of power and become the basic strategic asset for future Palestinian action.

## Chapter 16

The Protest Movement in Israel

Reuven Kaminer

Jewish opposition to Israeli government policy in the Palestinian-Israeli conflict reached unprecedented proportions during the 1982 Lebanon War with the emergence of a massive popular protest movement. Before the outbreak of the war, the Committee for Solidarity with Birzeit University (CSBZU) had achieved prominence after a series of demonstrations in the occupied territories (November 1981-February 1982) against the closure of the university. The CSBZU also supported the Palestinian struggle against the attempt of the newly-created Civil Administration (in fact, a special branch of the army) to take over all Palestinian municipal functions.

When Israel invaded Lebanon, the CSBZU was quickly converted into the Committee Against the War in Lebanon (CAWL). The broad coalition of forces in the CAWL gained significant support from independent Peace Now sympathizers who were deeply disturbed that Peace Now hesitated about taking action in the streets against the war. The Peace Now leadership, despite its reservations about the invasion, was influenced by the message that officer-activists sent home to the movement from the front: sit tight and wait to see what happens.

As Peace Now agonized over how far to go in opposing the war while the fighting was in progress, the CAWL began to organize. After a series of local actions, it called for a national anti-war demonstration in Tel Aviv on June 26, 1982. Over 20,000 rallied to the call, far more than the usual response to CSBZU demonstrations and a substantial increase over the previously assumed potential of CAWL forces. The message was clear; the waters had been tested. Peace Now issued a call for a similar rally one week later. The Peace Now rally was even more successful, an indication that something new and important was happening in Israeli politics. For the first time in its history, the country was witnessing a broad-based militant movement against a war in progress.

Peace Now worked in tandem with the CAWL and other organizations that emerged in the heady anti-war atmosphere. While Peace Now and the CAWL never concluded a permanent alliance, despite occasional overtures from the latter, they rarely operated at cross-purposes, and their simultaneous but separate campaigns crystallized all opposition to the war.

With the retreat of Israeli forces from most of Lebanon, the protest movement lost its momentum. The radical left redirected its attention to the occupied territories, but was unable to inspire any kind of broad action.

On the Eve of the Intifada

On the eve of the intifada, Peace Now had been languishing in a state of limbo for quite a while. It occasionally issued statements against atrocities by the settlers in the occupied territories or particularly hawkish speeches by Sharon or Shamir. Though it has been the most widely recognized peace group both in Israel and abroad, Peace Now did not move beyond the Israeli national consensus on the Palestinian question. It has generally supported the Labor Party's vague formulation of "territorial compromise" for peace and endorsed Peres' efforts to implement the Jordanian option. Peace Now did not call for Israeli negotiations with the PLO until nearly a year after the beginning of the intifada (see below). While recognizing in principle the Palestinian people's right to self-determination, Peace Now has not demanded the establishment of an independent Palestinian state; it has never advocated Israeli withdrawal from all the territories occupied in 1967; and it has supported the annexation of Jerusalem, echoing the official line about the "unified" character of the city.

The more consistent elements in the peace movement were also less active after the Israeli retreat from Lebanon, though the forces that supported the Palestinian people's right to statehood kept the fight against the occupation alive. For example, the ad hoc committee created to mark the twentieth anniversary of the occupation brought nearly 6,000 to Tel Aviv to demonstrate for an end to the occupation and establishment of a Palestinian state alongside Israel through recognition of the PLO as the representative of the Palestinian people and participation in an international peace conference.

Despite other differences, Peace Now and the more radical committees shared in common a negation of the occupation and a recognition of its inherent instability.

Meeting the Challenge of the Intifada

The intifada reactivated the peace movement and the forces of the left, gave new life to the various groups which had previously participated in the movement and inspired the creation of new formations. The upsurge of activity created new and qualitatively different forms of protest and political activity and attracted a new generation of activists.

The main achievements of this many-faceted response have been the scope and depth of the protest and the higher level of interaction between Israelis organized through the peace movement and Palestinians from the occupied territories. These achievements are due to the efforts of many groups and organizations. This survey focuses on those who, based on their view that the occupation is the common enemy of both peoples, raised the perspective of saying "yes" to the intifada. It is far from exhaustive, and lack of space has prevented discussion of specialized groups like the Beita Committee and New Immigrants Against the Occupation. For the same reason, the more traditional activity of the peace movement, its role in the universities and among the intelligentsia, is not treated extensively here.

Dai Lakibush (End the Occupation)

Dai Lakibush, especially its Jerusalem branch, was a leading component of the peace movement in the early stages of the intifada when many were seeking an appropriate response to the brutal attempts to suppress the intifada. The political composition and militancy of Dai Lakibush have been the keys to its relative success. Its main slogans have been, in addition to ending the occupation, negotiations with the PLO as the sole representative of the Palestinian people, establishment of an independent Palestinian state alongside Israel and the negotiation of peace in the framework of an international conference.

The activists of Dai Lakibush come from three main sources: 1) members of left-wing organizations who participate as an expression of their broader political vision; 2) unaffiliated veterans of previous campaigns for peace; 3) a wave of new activists. For most of the latter this was the first time they felt a sense of responsibility and dedication to the success of a political project.

Dai Lakibush has created an organizational form that has profited from the support and experience of the organized left while simultaneously allowing unlimited scope for the initiative and leadership qualities of new and unaffiliated individuals. All participants in Dai Lakibush act as individuals, though the relations between the previously organized elements have affected the life of the organization. It has adopted a loose, spontaneous style of operation. There is no formal membership, and anyone attending the weekly meetings (up to forty or fifty people) can have a say in discussions. During periods of intensive mobilization, dedicated but previously unaffiliated individuals have comprised the majority of Dai Lakibush activists. It concentrates the largest number of new adherents to the peace movement in a militant formation, encouraging non-sectarian unity.

The political groups represented in Dai Lakibush are: 1) The Democratic Front for Peace and Equality, dominated by the Communist Party (Maki, formerly known as Rakah), which has great influence among the Palestinian Arab citizens of Israel but is a small and relatively isolated force in the Jewish sector; 2) Shasi (Israeli Socialist Left); 3) The Revolutionary Communist League (RCL); and to a lesser degree 4) former members of the Progressive List for Peace who have acted more as a "tendency" than an organized force. These groups are also active in other protest movements. The Citizens' Rights Movement (CRM) and the left-Zionist Mapam party have boycotted Dai Lakibush as a matter of principle, refusing to cooperate with non-Zionists.

Dai Lakibush has given Maki an opportunity to participate as a respected partner in a relatively broad-based public organization in the Jewish sector. However, Maki's presence has entailed serious difficulties. Despite the lack of evidence, opponents of Dai Lakibush have tried to dismiss the group as a sophisticated front organization. But there have been complaints within Dai Lakibush that Maki is not always sensitive to the group's need for autonomy. Maki has made an invaluable contribution to Dai Lakibush through the active participation of a small but capable and devoted contingent of Arab members who inspire the entire organization with a justified sense of pride in the spirit of Jewish-Arab unity.

Shasi is an independent Marxist organization that grew out of the New Left phase in Israeli politics (1968-1973). Shasi numbers dozens of activists throughout the country and aspires to be the kernel of a new radical party on the left while devoting its main efforts to broad peace coalitions. Shasi's two-state position on the Israeli-Arab conflict is similar to that of Maki, but it has been critical of Maki's sectarian tendencies and lack of openness. Shasi has urged moderation on Dai Lakibush and other radical formations, stressing the ultimate importance of building a strategic bridge to supporters of Peace Now and the left-Zionist parties.

The RCL is the Israeli section of the Trotskyist Fourth International. Its role in Dai Lakibush has been complex because its own political program rejects the two-state solution and favors a secular democratic state in all of historic Palestine. The RCL has worked, often devotedly, in Dai Lakibush because it sees it as the best catalyzer of mass activity against the occupation. At the same time, RCL is also associated with a smaller coalition of anti-Zionist and Trotskyist groups and individuals called Hala Hakibush (Down With the Occupation) which supports the demands of the intifada without taking any stand on the resolution of the conflict.

Dai Lakibush's main contribution to the peace movement has been its readiness to go into the streets to vent its outrage over the rising tide of cruelty and repression. Dai Lakibush has demonstrated more than any other group, repeatedly launching timely rallies and vigils against fresh acts of brutality. It has also sought to develop new forms of activity to express solidarity with the Palestinians, such as weekly educational visits to villages and refugee camps in the territories which allowed many Israelis (some of them quite incredulous) to hear first-hand reports of the courageous popular resistance against an occupying army composed of their own relatives and neighbors. Dai Lakibush has also brought Palestinians to house meetings in Israel to talk about the impact of the intifada on their towns, villages and camps. Recently released internees from Ansar III were honored guests at Dai Lakibush forums and public meetings. Lastly, Dai Lakibush built coalitions bringing other militant groups into an alliance for several major demonstrations and actions.

There Is a Limit

Yesh Gvul (There is a Limit) achieved prominence after 2,500 reserve soldiers signed its petition to the government asking that they not be sent to serve in Lebanon. During the three years of the Lebanon war, more than 160 Israelis were jailed for refusal to serve in Lebanon. Thus, Yesh Gvul was prepared for its role during the intifada. As early as March 1986, the group initiated a petition campaign extending its refusal to serve in Lebanon to the occupied territories and issued a position paper stating:

> The war in Lebanon, the settlements, and the acts of oppression in the occupied territories show a disregard for human life and a loss of values and sense of reality. They block the option for peace with the Palestinian people and our other neighbors, isolate Israel in the world arena and prove that the government prefers territories to peace.... We have taken an oath to defend the welfare and the security of the State of Israel, and we are faithful to that oath. Therefore, we request that you permit us not to participate in the operations of repression and occupation in the territories.[1]

In the first days of the intifada Yesh Gvul decided to sharpen its tone and circulated an updated version of the same petition. It also published a "declaration of refusal" to serve in the territories or to "take part in the suppression of the uprising." Close to 500 reservists, including two majors, had signed it as of early June 1988. "We were surprised that so many signed it, as it is not a request but a declaration of intent, a commitment," said Yesh Gvul spokesperson Yishai Menuhin.[2]

When the recurring rumors about officially-inspired IDF torture and brutality were confirmed by thinly disguised policy statements of the chief of staff and the minister of defense, Yesh Gvul published a small booklet, similar in format to the official soldier's handbook, and distributed it widely to soldiers passing through urban centers. It featured selections from the Geneva Conventions, court judgments and statements by eminent jurists arguing that soldiers who carried out orders to beat and victimize defenseless prisoners were not legally protected by the claim that they were merely obeying orders. An illegal order, the booklet argued, is no defense for war crimes. As a result of this publication the General Security Service (Shin Bet), whose policy of torturing detainees under interrogation was previously exposed in an official report, initiated an investigation of Yesh Gvul.[3] The Israel Broadcasting Authority decided that it would no longer permit television news reports of Yesh Gvul demonstrations.[4] IDF Chief of Staff Dan Shomron convened a meeting in his office to discuss what to do about Yesh Gvul.[5] After a tremendous wave of criticism, the television ban on reporting Yesh Gvul events was lifted and so far the attorney general has not indicted Yesh Gvul members for the crime of reminding soldiers of their legal obligation to refuse to execute illegal orders.

Over fifty reservists have been sent to military prison for refusing to serve in the occupied territories during the first year of the intifada. It is impossible to estimate how many others have avoided prison sentences by making arrangements with their commanding officers allowing them to perform their reserve duty in places where they would not come into contact with Palestinian civilians.

Refusal to serve in the military is highly controversial in those sections of the peace movement that have sought to avoid isolating themselves from the national consensus. The leaderships of Peace Now, Mapam and the CRM have all strongly opposed this tactic. They argue, first, that the liberal and progressive forces have an interest in upholding the rule of law and respect for civic obligations because the right, especially the settlers, has repeatedly threatened to rebel against the authority of a democratically elected government that might order an Israeli withdrawal from the occupied territories. Second, they argue that the presence of liberals and humanists in the army can positively influence what happens "on the ground" and make a difference in the battle for influence over the direction of the military.

In an emotionally charged newspaper column, MK Yossi Sarid (CRM) tried to explain to Defense Minister Rabin that the number and the stature of the "refuseniks" is such that were he in Rabin's place he would call in the General Staff to discuss an intelligence report that the army faced a potentially grave danger. Nonetheless, Sarid has worked to persuade youngsters to "do their duty:"

> I continue to roam the country to explain our old line, trying to convince hundreds of young people before mobilization and before reserve duty...I am invited to schools, to youth movements, to kibbutzim—the number of concerned invitations is on the increase—and I do the work of Yitzhak Shamir and Yitzhak Rabin and ask myself why I have to do this kind of work, and I reply and convince myself...I want Rabin to take notice: service in the territories is not a simple matter for many people, and it is getting less and less simple for more and more people.[6]

Sarid's own words reveal that the strategic caution of the moderate doves may be mistaken, as some of their own followers have reached a point where they feel that the only way that they can remain true to their values and sense of integrity is by embracing Yesh Gvul. Yesh Gvul's appeal has in many cases transcended divisions within the peace movement. When thousands of mobilization orders are issued every month, many who oppose government policy must make a moral choice. Many if not most of those who have refused have had little prior contact with the militant left. Refusal may be the first political act of their lives that places them beyond the boundaries of the national consensus. Until now, only a small minority have been ready to accept the consequences of refusing a military order. But Yesh Gvul's example has set the terms for much of the sincere soul-searching in broad sections of the intelligentsia. Many who have so far hesitated to refuse speak openly about it as a genuine possibility in the future if things continue as they are.

The Twenty-First Year

During the first weeks of the intifada, thousands of Israelis signed an extraordinary document entitled "The Twenty-First Year Covenant for the Struggle Against the Occupation." Many of the signers' names were printed in three full-page ads in the press. Though the idea of the Covenant predates the intifada, the widespread support it won among circles who had hitherto marched under the flag of Peace Now is directly attributable to the impact of the intifada.

The Covenant was premised on the analysis that the occupation has permeated all aspects of Israeli society, economy, education, the judicial system and culture, and caused the debasement of the Hebrew language and political thought:

> For more than half of its years of statehood, Israel has been an occupying power; the State of Israel is losing its democratic character. The continued existence of a parliamentary system of government within the Green Line cannot disguise the fact that Israel rules over a population, the Palestinian Arabs, which is deprived of all democratic rights. The occupation, thus, is not only a deplorable situation affecting the lives of the Palestinians; it has an equally pernicious effect on the very political and spiritual substance of Israeli society. The occupation has become an insidious fact of our lives. Its presence has not been confined to the occupied territories. It is, alas, among us and with us.

The Covenant indirectly criticized Peace Now's approach, arguing that, "Expressions of protest against the occupation are circumscribed by the national consensus; protests do not transgress the boundaries deemed permissible by the occupation regime." It concluded: "The presence of the occupation is total. Our struggles against the occupation must therefore be total." It outlined a new approach to struggle against the occupation, speaking in terms of "refusal to collaborate," "resistance" and willingness "to pay a personal price," and offered some suggestions for possible actions: boycotting goods produced by Israeli settlements in the territories and non-compliance with orders to participate in acts of repression.

Translating the Covenant into viable day-to-day tactics has been only partially successful and the Twenty-First Year has mainly operated well within acceptable boundaries. The movement's main achievement has been to organize the intelligentsia and young academicians in a radical framework which has broken from the national consensus. The group made a seminal contribution to the fight for freedom of the press when it strongly opposed a government ban on the publication of *Derech Hanitzotz/Tariq al-Sharara* (The Way of the Spark). It defiantly issued a new publication (*Shomer Hanitzotz*) which echoed the name of the banned journal and exposed the government's motives:

> For the past several years a journal entitled *Derech Hanitzotz*...was a reliable source...used by a broad spectrum of the Israeli and

foreign press. It assumed even greater importance with the outbreak of the Palestinian uprising.

Three months ago, the journal was ordered shut by the Israeli authorities...two months later most of the editorial staff was detained. Charges have been brought against four members of the staff. The government has announced that there is no connection between the crimes of which the journalists are accused and the closing of the journal.

The Twenty-First Year believes that the closing of the journal, regardless of the guilt or innocence of its editors, is a dangerous precedent.[7]

The Twenty-First Year has also organized a sub-committee which sends Israelis to serve as witnesses of the occupation, in the hope that the physical presence of Israeli protesters may prevent some excesses by the military. At the least, this presence has provided reliable information that can be relayed to the media. Other committees have organized seminars for high school students on the problem of military service during the occupation. The organization also led timely demonstrations against deportations and conditions in Ansar III and other prison camps.

There is a similarity between the approach of the Twenty-First Year and Yesh Gvul: an appeal to personal moral responsibility and a striving for a new politics of refusal to cross certain "red lines." Two of the three drafters of the Covenant, university lecturers Adi Ofir and Hanan Hever, also belong to Yesh Gvul, and Ofir has already been jailed for refusing military service in the occupied territories.

The Twenty-First Year, Yesh Gvul and Dai Lakibush have provided the mass base for the militant peace movement. The three organizations were the active core of one of the most successful actions of this sector of the movement: a demonstration of nearly 10,000 people in Tel Aviv on June 4, 1988, to mark the twenty-first anniversary of the occupation. Nonetheless, the Twenty-First Year is hesitant about identifying with the more traditional left. The group does not want to restrict itself to conventional forms of struggle and fears that it will lose its drawing power if it becomes just another factor in a broader coalition.

Professional Responses

One indication of the breadth of opposition to the occupation among the intelligentsia has been the expression of political dissent in professional organizations. Professors and students have always played a decisive role in the protest movement. But the variety of professional groups that have raised their voices against the massive repression in the territories is unprecedented.

The activity of mental health workers has been particularly outstanding. In June 1988 a conference of 600 psychologists and mental health workers, including Jews and Arabs, convened, bypassing the previously existing professional organization, and called on members of their profession to become more involved in the events in the territories. The conference grew out of a successful campaign to gather signatures on a statement which said in part:

> We are a group of mental health workers. Usually, we do not express our political positions in public. However, if we continue to be silent now, we will be supporting the destructive influences of continuing occupation. For twenty years Arabs have been living under our rule, without rights, in fear and in degradation. Arabs are thrown out of their homes, separated from their families, subjected to mass arrest, to torture and recently, shot to death with horrendous frequency. There are women and children among the killed. There is no doubt in our hearts that this situation must be stopped.
>
> This situation also has terrible influences on the Jewish population. It will also cause mental victims among Jews. Many of our children are employed daily in carrying out repressive measures. We have all learned, over the years, to stop up our ears, to deaden our feelings, as if these things were not happening amongst us, to us and with our responsibility. We are all being drawn into a life of fear, violence and racism. We are losing our sensitivity for human suffering. Our children are growing up on values of discrimination and racism, and IDF soldiers are thrown into morally impossible situations. We hope that more and more people will join our protest against the destructive occupation.[8]

The mental health workers' conference was marked by a high level of cooperation between Israeli psychologists, both Jews and Arabs, and psychologists from the occupied territories. At the conclusion of the meeting the participants formed Mental Health Workers for Social Responsibility.[9] Since many had just overcome their qualms about taking a public political stand, they compromised by deciding to act as professionals independently of existing political groups.

Other professional groups who have organized against the occupation include medical school teachers and students, painters and sculptors, musicians, performing artists, ceramicists, lawyers, writers, architects and physicians. The strength and level of activity of the professional groups has varied widely. Many cooperate closely with their Palestinian counterparts and there has been much solidarity work that has gone unnoticed by the media. These are new constituencies in the peace movement that tend to be independent and move into action only if and when they can find issues to which they can relate as professionals. Yet these organizations indicate the extent to which opposition to the occupation has sunk deeper roots in certain sectors of Israeli society.

Women in Black and Other Women

The message is as simple and stark as can be. A hundred or so women gather in Paris Square, a five minute walk from the center of Jerusalem and a stone's throw from the prime minister's residence in the staid Rehavia neighborhood. They are all dressed in black and they are mourning. Each carries a small sign in the form of a palm containing one simple and short message: End the Occupation. They come once a week, every Friday at 1p.m., and stand silently for one hour. No banners. No speeches. But they do have one other sign which says, Honk Twice If You Support Us. Smaller groups hold similar weekly vigils in Tel Aviv and Haifa. There have also been symbolic demonstrations by women in black in Paris, New York, Berkeley and elsewhere abroad.

Less a coalition, more a "coming together" of women with different views and affiliations, Women in Black has been a stunning way for many women to make a statement that they were unable or unwilling to make in any other framework. Organized women from all shades of the left have participated, but there have also been many women who want to act as women and nothing else. Some who are far from the left or even from other active sections of the peace movement come to Women in Black to express clear, personal and direct opposition.

No other demonstrations have rivaled Women in Black in the invective-received department. Paris Square is a busy intersection and many male drivers spew out a constant stream of offensive comments and curses augmented by sexual innuendos. These silent women are apparently quite threatening. But there are also many double honks of support during the hour.

The Women in Black vigils have been a favorite spot for counter-demonstrations by the youth groups of Kahane and the Tehiya Party. So far, the women have successfully used non-violent tactics to counter attempts to disturb them. When the hooligans tried to disrupt the vigil by occupying the square before the women arrived, Women in Black simply moved to another spot on the main thoroughfare. When the rowdies waved flags in their faces, Women in Black moved away. Since the women have been more persistent and numerous, this approach has worked, but there is always tension in the air. Yet the women return to Paris Square again and again.

Other women's organizations have also emerged in response to the intifada. The Jerusalem-based Shani (Israeli Women Against the Occupation) centers its activity around bi-weekly discussions. Meetings have often featured Palestinian speakers. Discussions have focused on both general political questions and specific aspects of the occupation such as children, education, health and the role of women in the intifada. Many of the Shani women have little or no prior political experience, and the meetings are conducted in a supportive educational atmosphere. The success of the Jerusalem Shani group, the activity of feminist groups in Tel Aviv and Haifa and the appearance of other women's organizations (like Women for Political Prisoners) have enlarged the autonomous role of women in the peace movement.

When it became clear that the occupation and the intifada were not important enough subjects to get on the agenda of the First International Jewish Feminist Conference in Jerusalem in late November 1988, activists from Shani and other women's groups organized a highly successful post-conference meeting entitled "Occupation or Peace: A Feminist Perspective." Over 300 women, Jewish and Arab, Israeli and North American, attended (including some who had also participated in the Feminist Conference) and agreed on the need for a clearly articulated feminist response to the occupation.

Peace Now in the Shadow of the Intifada

When the intifada broke out, Peace Now felt vindicated by the new and convincing evidence that the status quo was untenable and that the policy of "creeping annexation" was running into real trouble. It felt and expressed outrage over the victimization of the Palestinians in the territories and was no less upset over the degradation of the IDF and its soldiers. It openly expressed anxiety that this kind of dirty work might actually impair the fighting capacity of the army. However, the intifada demanded greater clarity on the critical questions like negotiations with the PLO and the Palestinian Arabs' right to establish an independent state.

Towards the end of December 1987, Peace Now returned to the streets to protest government policy. Though the demonstrations attacked the "government of national paralysis" for blocking any compromise or political solution to the Palestinian-Israeli conflict, they said nothing about Peace Now's formula for a solution. This silence was tantamount to supporting Labor Party leader Peres' policy of pursuing the Jordanian option through convening an international conference without the PLO. Peace Now sympathized with the plight of the IDF: "The security forces can only hold their fire temporarily; the only answer is negotiations, talks and a compromise."[10] In the same vein, a week later Peace Now demanded a political solution to stop the violence, without mentioning the political solution it sought. But the intifada did push Peace Now into taking an important step forward. On December 19, 1987, for the first time, the movement hosted a speaker from the occupied territories, Dr. Zakaria al-Agha, chair of the Gaza Medical Association.

By January Peace Now was able to mobilize tens of thousands of Israelis to demonstrate against government policy in the occupied territories, but it remained very cautious. Its call for a demonstration on January 23, 1988 advocated "returning the territories to Jordanian-Palestinian rule on the basis of demilitarization and security arrangements."[11] Peace Now reaffirmed its commitment to the Jordanian option by calling for elections in the occupied territories after "cessation of violence on the West Bank and Gaza, and terror from outside." The elections would choose representatives who would join "the Palestinian-Jordanian delegation to negotiate peace with Israel."[12]

However, Peace Now, which previously avoided joint appearances with Palestinian Arab citizens of Israel, invited a representative of the National Committee of Arab Local Councils to speak at the January 23 demonstration and sent a delegate to Nazareth to address a mass rally against the occupation. In February *al-Fajr* editor Hanna Siniora spoke at a Peace Now rally. The increased interaction between Israelis and Palestinians and the broader opportunities for Jewish-Arab cooperation in opposition to the occupation gradually eroded Peace Now's allegiance to the Jordanian option. Nonetheless, Peace Now believed that US Secretary of State Shultz's abortive initiative offered a real chance for progress. It threw itself into a campaign to "say yes" to the United States. Just as it demonstrated on the eve of Begin's departure for Egypt in 1978, it called for a demonstration on the eve of Shamir's March 1988 visit to the United States. Of course, the Shultz mission was a train that never left the station, while Peace Now waited somewhere down the tracks, flowers in hand, like a dejected lover. The failure of the Shultz initiative left Peace Now without a political program. Its way out of the intifada was blocked when King Hussein relinquished any role in speaking and acting for the Palestinians. While the sections of the peace movement that acted in a spirit of solidarity with the Palestinians were having an increasing impact on the public, Peace Now went into a period of quiescence, reexamination and reevaluation.

A particularly ugly action by the Israeli government provided the impetus for Peace Now to reassess its position, though typically it was a Palestinian who paid the price. On July 27, 1988, Faysal al-Husseini addressed a Peace Now meeting in Jerusalem called to discuss the implications of Bassam Abu Sharif's declaration that the PLO's aim was to establish a Palestinian state alongside Israel. Al-Husseini, considered close to the PLO leadership, declared, "The solution is two states, one alongside the other." Three days later he was put in administrative detention for six months. Peace Now called a militant demonstration in front of Defence Minister Rabin's home. The government's clear rejection of a Palestinian peace initiative was an important factor in transforming Peace Now's attitude toward the PLO. While September and October were an interlude dominated by the Israeli and US elections, the Palestine National Council (PNC) meeting in November transformed the political situation and accelerated the pace of Peace Now's development.

Give Peace Some Clout

The Knesset election campaign was a bitter period for the protest movement. After September, the peace movement lost much of its momentum as the political parties mobilized for the November 1 balloting. Many of the rank and file activists in the peace movement were divided by party loyalties and unable to act as a single force in the electoral arena. Others were alienated from the entire process. The media focus on the campaign directed public attention away from events in the occupied territories.

The election campaign slump reflected one of the peace movement's basic weaknesses. Both the militant and moderate wings of the movement eschew parliamentary ambitions and deny any desire to compete with existing propeace parties, stressing instead their spontaneous and extraparliamentary approach. They do not endorse any one electoral list for fear that this would divide the movement. The peace movement has refused to undertake the careful long-range organizational efforts needed to ensure survival as a unified and coherent force during the electoral process, preferring instead the advantages of informal structures and a political ideology restricted to the level of slogans. The price has been an inability to maneuver through the forests of party politics as a viable independent force. Too often the protest movement has embraced the naive belief that there is a way to do politics without articulating positions, disseminating information and educating the public.

This weakness may be linked to the relatively narrow social base of the protest movement. As currently constituted, it has almost no support in the working class, in low-income strata or in the housing projects of the poorer neighborhoods. It is composed almost exclusively of well-educated Ashkenazi Jews, a great proportion of whom are employed in the service sector. It is concentrated in the major urban centers, is almost nonexistent in the medium-sized and smaller towns, and has no presence in the newer (and largely Oriental Jewish) "development towns." A movement operating within these narrow social parameters has little need to develop a permanent organizational structure or political outlook, but failure to do so will also tend to keep the movement within these limits. As individuals, members of the peace movement are painfully aware of this weakness and the danger of leaving the streets to the purveyors of racism and chauvinism. But the movement as a whole devotes little attention to this question as efforts are directed toward achieving immediate goals.

Because of its narrow social base and the limitations of Peace Now's perspective during most of the first year of the intifada, the protest movement can only serve as a moral force for peace and solidarity with Palestinians fighting to end the occupation. Despite the great symbolic importance of the peace forces and the restraining influence of their militancy on the government and the army, it must be clearly stated that this is not enough. The peace movement must aspire to have more practical influence on the course of events and to become a force that the political establishment must reckon with.

If the elections tended to dissipate the energy and effectiveness of the peace movement, nothing in the results changed the basic political realities. As everyone in Israel was sitting back waiting to see what kind of government coalition would emerge from the shameless post-election bartering, the PLO added a dynamic political and diplomatic dimension to the intifada.

The resolutions of the PNC in Algeria transformed the political outlook and infused new energy into the peace movement. Within days of the PNC decisions, Peace Now, in a major policy shift, came out clearly and without reservations for negotiations with the PLO.[13]

Now that one of the major differences between the militant and moderate wings of the peace movement has been overcome, there is reason to hope that Peace Now will, in the foreseeable future, openly support the establishment of an independent Palestinian state alongside Israel and the voices of sanity and reason will become much stronger in Israel.

## Part 6

The United States and the Intifada

A Bullet, A Lie
(to Sami and his family)

ahmad had those
wildly intense
eyes that
would stare through you
as he spoke and
would light up
every now and then
as he listened and
would drive me crazy
what
does he want from me?

i remember ahmad
when
he returned from prison
to ya'bad
and his grandmother
ululated in jubilation
danced in happiness
served coffee to share
her happiness

and it was ahmad
who took me around the village
when i came on
mundane visits
to see all houses
demolished or sealed
in town
recording a history
of occupation

human rights work
is nice
when you have time to spare

and now
ahmad's eyes speak no more
nor listen
their words were far too strong
the message uncompromising:
freedom for Palestine
now

on october 8 of 1988
the army came to ya'bad
and took
a single shot

at ahmad

—Joost Hiltermann

## Chapter 17

Israel's Role in US Foreign Policy

Noam Chomsky

This chapter is based on a talk given at Tel Aviv University, April 13, 1988.

I will focus these remarks on US foreign policy with regard to the Middle East region and the role that Israel has played within it. Any such analysis is, of course, based on certain assumptions and implicit values, which influence the selection of historical facts and even the choice of terminology. To avoid misunderstanding, let me try to clarify the general assumptions I will adopt with regard to the Arab-Israeli conflict, perhaps the most contentious issue.

Two national groups claim the right of self-determination within the former Palestine: the indigenous population and the Jewish settlers who established the State of Israel. By the term "Palestine," I refer to the Palestine of the British mandate, putting aside more expansive claims that are still prominently voiced.[1] I take both claims to be valid without further discussion.

I will, accordingly, refer to those who deny the rights of one or the other of these contending groups as "rejectionists." Qaddafi, Khomeini, Syrian-backed Palestinian organizations and a few others refuse to accept the existence of Israel, and therefore fall under this category. Both major political groupings in Israel have always been rejectionist, adopting slightly different ways of expressing their denial of Palestinian national rights, with Likud calling for some form of extension of Israeli sovereignty over the occupied territories and the Labor Alignment advocating the "territorial compromise" or "functional compromise." The same is true of many of those regarded as doves, Abba Eban, for example, who advocates Labor Party rejectionism, and, with more ambiguity, Peace Now, which has been unwilling to separate itself clearly from this position.

Within the United States, articulate opinion in the mainstream ranges from the hawks, who support the Likud variety of rejectionism, to the doves, who advocate the Labor version. Within the US Jewish community, and in some other circles, there is also quite substantial support, both ideological and financial, for elements more extreme than Likud; and, particularly in recent months, some growing support for an authentic political settlement. The prevailing rejectionism is so dominant within the United States that Shimon Peres and the Labor Party are regularly described as "the peace camp," and US efforts to implement a rejectionist political settlement are invariably described as "the peace process," even in the scholarly literature. The term "rejectionism" is restricted to the denial of rights to Jews, not to Palestinians, who are implicitly regarded as lacking any such rights.

The rejectionist stance in Israel and the United States is so extreme that Palestinians have not even been granted the right to select their own representatives for eventual negotiations; as it is beyond serious question that these representatives would be the PLO leadership. In Jordan in April 1988, Secretary of State George Shultz, pursuing his "peace mission," announced again that the PLO or others "who have committed acts of terrorism" must be excluded from peace talks, which would leave the bargaining table quite empty. He also "explained his understanding of the aspirations of Palestinians," *New York Times* reporter Elaine Sciolino wrote, by citing the example of the United States, where he, Shultz, is a Californian, and George Bush is a Texan, but they have no problem living in harmony, so the Palestinian aspirations into which he shows such profound insight can be handled the same way.[2]

Departures from this extreme form of rejectionism have been very rare within the mainstream media and journals in the United States, and within the political system close to nonexistent although, as polls have shown for many years, the general population supports a nonrejectionist two-state settlement with security guarantees by about two to one.[3] But until the intifada, there had been virtually no articulate expression of that view within the mainstream, a reflection of the extraordinary extent to which the educated classes in the United States, and the media and political system, have backed Israeli policies.

Most of the world has backed a nonrejectionist political settlement since the mid-1970s, including the major Arab states and the PLO. The terms of the prevailing international consensus for many years with regard to this issue have been essentially these:

> The inalienable rights of the Arab people of Palestine must be secured up to, and including, the establishment of their own state. It is essential to ensure the security and sovereignty of all states of the region including those of Israel. These are the basic principles.

This formulation was presented in a speech by Leonid Brezhnev at the Communist Party presidium in February 1981, expressing what has been the consistent Soviet position with regard to Israel and its rights. His statement was unanimously endorsed by the Palestinian National Council at its April 1981 meeting. All of this was excluded from the US media, and still is; the *New York Times* published excerpts from Brezhnev's speech, excluding these passages and the PLO endorsement.[4]

In summary, it is quite fair and appropriate to say that the United States and Israel lead the rejectionist camp. Since US-Israeli power is decisive in the region, they have been able to block a meaningful political settlement. Recognition of these facts is a precondition for a serious consideration of the issues, in my view.

From shortly after the June 1967 war, it has been clear enough that the occupation would lead to an escalating cycle of repression, resistance, harsher repression, more resistance, punctuated by regional wars, possibly engaging the superpowers and leading to terminal global war. There is nothing obscure about the dynamics of ethnic conflict under a harsh military occupation—and there is no other kind of military occupation. As long as the United States and Israel persist in their rejectionist stance, the process will continue along this course, leading to the probable eventual destruction of Israel, the Palestinian community, much of the region and perhaps well beyond.

With regard to US policy towards the region, two views have been counterpoised in Israel. The first has been developed in several publications by former military intelligence chief Yehoshafat Harkabi, who sharply criticizes the common belief in Israel "that our services to the United States are so vital that the United States will continue to support us, whatever we do," so that US criticisms of Israel are not to be taken seriously but are merely "performance of a duty and throwing sand in the eyes of the Arabs" in the course of a "family quarrel, tactical and not strategic, and we will soon have our way."[5]

The second position is expressed clearly in a headline in *Yediot Ahronot* shortly after the US presidential elections of 1984: "Jewish money buys the vote"—the pun ("...buys everything"), I presume, is intended—summarizing a speech by Tom Dine, director of AIPAC, the official Israeli lobby, extolling the "great victory" won by "Jewish power," a victory not of Jewish votes, but of "Jewish money": "the consequences of this success will be evident until the end of the twentieth century," he added triumphantly.[6] Such a headline, and the accompanying article, could not appear in the United States, where the sentiments would be regarded as vulgar anti-Semitism in the style of the Protocols of the Elders of Zion.

Dine's speech at the convention of Jewish Federations of North America is a clear expression of what Harkabi describes as "the error that is widespread in the community." Of these two contrasting views, Harkabi's is accurate, in my view. Israel in fact plays a small role in US global strategy, however expedient it may be for US planners to exploit the relationship at certain moments and for certain specific goals. Tactical decisions could quickly change that role, at which point the power of the Israeli lobby will decline or disappear.

To mention some relevant history, Jewish political pressures surely influenced President Truman's decision to recognize Israel in May 1948, overruling State Department objections. Similarly, political pressures induced Truman to refrain from insisting that Israel repatriate or compensate Palestinian refugees in accord with UN General Assembly Resolution 194 of December 1948, which stated that "the refugees wishing to return to their homes and live at peace with their neighbors should be permitted to do so at the earliest practicable date."[7] In 1956, however, these pressures were unavailing when Israel, together with England and France, invaded Egypt. The United States strongly opposed this military operation, which it interpreted as a threat to US interests. On the eve of a presidential election, when domestic political pressures are at their height, President Eisenhower and Secretary of State Dulles compelled Britain and France to withdraw, demanding that Israel follow suit and threatening severe reprisals if it failed to do so. It was not that the United States had an objection in principle to Israeli conquest of the Sinai; in 1967, Israel conquered the Sinai with full US backing. But in 1956, Israel chose the wrong allies: France and Britain, traditional rivals of the United States, which it had effectively expelled from the region in the preceding years. In 1967, Israel made a wiser choice of allies, performing a service for the United States itself, so the Israeli lobby was influential, lining up with US power. In 1956, in contrast, its influence was slight. It would be a serious misunderstanding of the US sociopolitical system to believe that this might not happen again.

For a realistic assessment of Israel's role within US global planning, we must consider how US notions of world order have evolved since World War II, which brought about major changes in the structure of the international system. The United States emerged from the war with about 50 percent of the world's wealth and an incomparable position of security. It was in a position of global power with few if any parallels in history.

US elites were well aware of these facts and gave considerable thought to the contours of the postwar world. From 1939 through 1945, State Department planners and the Council on Foreign Relations, representing the major components of the corporate system with international interests, conducted the War and Peace Studies Project to deal with what they called the "requirements of the United States in a world in which it proposes to hold unquestioned power." They developed the concept of the "Grand Area," a region understood to be "strategically necessary for world control," subordinated to the needs of the US economy.

In the early stages of the war, the Grand Area was conceived as a US-led non-German bloc, which was to incorporate the Western hemisphere, the Far East, and the former British empire, to be dismantled along with other regional systems and incorporated under US control. By the early 1940s, it was becoming clear that Germany would be defeated and the Grand Area concept was extended to include the Eurasian land mass as well, insofar as possible.[8]

One basic principle laid down in internal documents is that the United States must prevent what is called "ultranationalism." It must act to bar "nationalistic regimes" that are responsive to popular demands for "improvement in the low living standards of the masses" and production for domestic needs, and that seek to control their own resources. Rather, the United States must encourage "a political and economic climate conducive to private investment of both foreign and domestic capital," including "opportunity to earn and in the case of foreign capital to repatriate a reasonable return" (NSC 5432, 1954, and many others). In the Third World, it is necessary to "protect our resources" (as George Kennan put it) and to encourage export-oriented production, within a framework of liberal internationalism that guarantees the needs of US investors, who were expected to prevail in any competition, a plausible expectation in the light of the economic realities of the time, and one that was amply fulfilled for many years. For similar reasons, Great Britain had been a passionate advocate of free trade during the period of its hegemony, abandoning this stand and the elevated rhetoric that accompanied it in the interwar period, when Britain could not withstand competition from Japan and others. The United States is pursuing much the same course today in the face of similar challenges, which were quite unexpected forty years ago, indeed until the Vietnam war. The unanticipated costs of US aggression in Indochina seriously weakened the US economy while strengthening its industrial rivals, who enriched themselves through their participation in the destruction of Indochina, particularly Japan and South Korea, which owe their economic take-off to these opportunities (for Japan, primarily the Korean war, which gave the first major impetus to the Japanese economy).

These were the essential principles of planning, worldwide, clearly articulated in the documentary record and executed in practice.[9] Unless these principles are understood, one will have only a limited comprehension of postwar history, including the role assigned to Israel in US global planning.

The first task faced in the postwar period was to destroy the anti-fascist resistance, often in favor of Nazi and fascist collaborators, and to restore traditional conservative business-based elites to power, weakening unions and other popular organizations and blocking the threat of radical democracy and social reform for domestic needs. These operations were conducted worldwide.

In the Middle East region, hundreds of thousands were killed or expelled in the course of a counterinsurgency operation in Greece, organized and directed by the United States, which restored traditional elites to power, including Nazi collaborators, and suppressed the peasant- and worker-based Communist-led forces that had fought the Nazis. A major concern in this case was Middle East oil, Greece being regarded as an outpost of US power "protecting" these resources for the United States and its clients. A February 1948 CIA study warned that if the rebels were victorious, the United States would face "the possible loss of the petroleum resources of the Middle East." A Soviet threat was fabricated in the usual manner. The real danger was the familiar one: indigenous nationalism, with its feared demonstration effects elsewhere.

At the rhetorical level, the threat was always the Soviet Union. In reality it was independent nationalism, described characteristically as a "virus" that might "infect" other countries, a "rotten apple" that might cause the "rot to spread," contaminating the region and beyond, a "domino" that might topple others through the demonstration effect of successful independent development. Much the same reasoning holds throughout the postwar period, including current US organization of a terrorist attack against Nicaragua.

The Grand Area was intended to have a definite structure. The industrial countries were to be reconstituted, but in a specific way, restoring something like the traditional order, but now under US control. The industrial world was to be organized under its "natural leaders," Germany and Japan, which had demonstrated their prowess during the war years.

It was understood that the reconstituted industrial powers required a hinterland. Southeast Asia was to "fulfill its major function as a source of raw materials and a market for Japan and Western Europe," in the words of George Kennan's State Department Policy Planning Staff in 1949. This reasoning led directly to US intervention in Indochina, at first in support of French colonialism, later alone. In Latin America, the same principles were developed and successfully applied. The region largely fell under the control of the United States, displacing Britain from traditional areas of influence. Africa was regarded as a natural hinterland for Europe, to be "exploited" for the reconstruction of Europe after the war, as George Kennan explained (PPS 23, February 1948). History might have suggested a different project: that Africa should "exploit" Europe to enable it to reconstruct from centuries of devastation at the hands of European conquerors. Needless to say, nothing of the sort was remotely thinkable.

Turning finally to the Middle East, the primary US concern was, of course, the incomparable energy reserves of the region, primarily in the Arabian peninsula. These were to be incorporated within the Grand Area, under US control. The State Department regarded Saudi Arabian oil as "probably the richest economic prize in the world in the field of foreign investment" (1948), and three years later President Eisenhower described the Middle East as the most "strategically important area in the world."[10]

President Truman's Palestine policy was highly unpopular in the Arab world, but—crucially—it did not threaten US oil concessions. In those years, the United States largely displaced Britain and France from the areas of their traditional influence, coming to dominate Middle East oil production, which remained the major world source until 1968, while retaining its control over the Western hemisphere.

A critical task was, as always, to prevent the growth of indigenous nationalist forces that might try to control their own resources, independent of US control. As noted, the counterinsurgency operation in Greece was partially motivated by the concern that the "rot" of independent nationalism there might "infect" the Middle East, as Dean Acheson warned. The same factors led to the CIA coup restoring the Shah in Iran in 1953, overthrowing a conservative nationalist regime and partially displacing Britain from its monopoly over Iranian oil production. Later, Nasser became an enemy for similar reasons, and Khomeini was perceived as posing another such threat. In the case of both Nasser and Khomeini, the prime concern has been that the virus of "radical nationalism"—meaning, nationalist forces not under US influence and control—might spread to the major oil-producing regions of the Arabian peninsula.

The United States did not need Middle East oil for itself. Rather, the problem was to control the world system, in particular, to ensure that Europe and Japan, heavily reliant on these supplies of energy, would remain docile clients within the US-dominated Grand Area. At the time, Japan was not considered a potential competitor; until the Vietnam war, the United States was concerned to maintain the viability of the Japanese economy. Some, however, foresaw potential problems, among them George Kennan, one of the major architects of the postwar world. In internal discussion in the Policy Planning Staff in 1949, he observed that US control over Japanese oil imports would help to ensure "veto power on what she does need in the military and industrial field." His advice was followed. Japan was helped to industrialize, but the United States maintained control over its energy supplies and oil-refining facilities.[11] US interest in the military bases in the Philippines also derives in part from concerns over the Middle East; they form part of the US military system surrounding the region from Turkey to the Indian Ocean and beyond, designed to ensure that there will be no threat to control over its resources by the United States and local elites linked closely to it. The United States is a global power, and plans accordingly.

When Nasser gained power in Egypt, the United States was undecided for a time as to whether to regard him as a potential client or as a nationalist threat. The Israeli terrorist operations in Egypt aimed at US installations and other civilian targets were, it appears, in part designed to ward off the danger of closer relations between Nasser and the United States. By the mid-1950s, it had become clear that Nasser would not be a willing client, and US policy adopted its normal course in the face of the threat of "ultranationalism." At the same time, Israel developed its "periphery policy," attempting to form alliances with Turkey, Iran and Ethiopia, with the support of the United States, according to Israeli sources.[12]

In 1958, the National Security Council noted that a "logical corollary" of opposition to radical Arab nationalism "would be to support Israel as the only strong pro-Western power left in the Near East." In the 1960s, US intelligence regarded Israel as a barrier to Nasserite influences in the Arabian peninsula, and Israel's successes in the 1967 war, eliminating the nationalist threat, reinforced the conception of Israel as a "strategic asset" that could serve US interests. This thesis received further support as Israel acted to prevent possible Syrian intervention in support of the Palestinians at the time of Black September in 1970, regarded in the United States as a potential threat to the Hashemite kingdom and the US clients beyond. The "strategic asset" thesis was framed within the Nixon Doctrine, formulated in the light of the recognition that the United States could "no longer play policeman to the world" and would now "expect other nations to provide more cops on the beat in their own neighborhood" (Defense Secretary Melvin Laird)—though police headquarters, it was understood, remained in Washington. In Henry Kissinger's phraseology, other states must pursue their "regional interests" within the "overall framework of order" managed by the United States.

In the early 1970s, a tripartite alliance developed among Israel, Iran, and Saudi Arabia—the first two serving as the "cops on the beat." The matter was explained with particular lucidity by Senator Henry Jackson, the Senate's ranking expert on Middle East oil affairs and a leading proponent of the idea that Israeli power might serve US interests. The relationship became closer still as Iran was lost to the cause in 1979. It hardly comes as a surprise that in the years that followed, Israel and Saudi Arabia collaborated to provide US weapons to Iran, in the hope of establishing links with the military and instigating a military coup that might restore the former arrangements, as explained by Uri Lubrani, David Kimche, Ya'akov Nimrodi, and others.[13]

Meanwhile, Israel began to provide secondary services for the United States. In the 1960s, Israel helped penetrate Black Africa with a large CIA subsidy, helping to establish and maintain the rule of Mobutu in Zaire, Idi

Amin in Uganda and others, and also offering the United States a way to evade the UN embargo against oil shipments to Rhodesia. Israeli relations with South Africa probably fall within the same framework, at least in part. Israel also served US interests in Asia, for example by sending US jet fighters to Indonesia in the course of the murderous aggression in Timor, when the Carter administration was unable to do so directly. The major services, however, were in Latin America, particularly after congressional human rights legislation prevented the US executive from providing direct assistance to the most savage tyrants. Israel maintained close contacts with the neo-Nazi regimes of the southern cone, undeterred by the vicious anti-Semitism of the ruling generals. Israel supported Somoza until almost the last days of his bloody rule, through the period when his forces had slaughtered some 40-50,000 Nicaraguans. Israel also lent valued support to the terrorist rulers of El Salvador in the 1970s, until the United States took over the task of organizing and directing the massacre directly. Perhaps the most significant services were in Guatemala, where Israeli assistance was instrumental in near-genocidal slaughters and repression at a time when the US government was inhibited by popular pressures, reflected in congressional legislation, from direct participation. More recently, Israel has helped in the training and support of the terrorist forces attacking Nicaragua. As one Israeli analyst put the matter when the Iran-contra affair erupted: "It's like Israel has become just another federal agency, one that's convenient to use when you want something done quietly."[14]

All of this constitutes the substantive meaning of the concept "strategic cooperation." As B. Michael explained the doctrine, with characteristic insight: "My master gives me food to eat and I bite those whom he tells me to bite. It is called strategic cooperation."[15]

At the same time, Israel forged close links with US intelligence and the Pentagon, both in the production of weapons and the testing of advanced weapons under battlefield conditions or against defenseless targets, again providing valuable services for US power.

The strategic asset thesis gained domestic support after the 1967 war. Elite groups, including US liberals, were deeply impressed with Israel's success in demonstrating how Third World upstarts should be handled at a time when the United States was unable to crush Vietnamese resistance. Israel's successful use of force to impose order gained further symbolic significance among US elites in the context of the rise of the student movement, the ethnic movements, the women's movement, resistance to the war and other worrisome challenges to authority. Israeli power also attracted other sectors, among them, the rising Christian fundamentalist movements. Another striking example is the leadership of the labor movement. Israeli propagandists exult over the fact that many unions purchase Israel Bonds with pension and welfare funds despite their "very low rate of interest". The *New York Times* observes that "pension fund administrators say that the Israel Bonds do not offer a return as good as other investments," but they buy them nonetheless "to show support for Israel."[16] Apart from the fact that such decisions on the part of administrators are probably illegal, there is little doubt that they would arouse considerable anger, and possibly even a wave of anti-Semitism on the part of the workforce (largely black and Hispanic), if they were to discover that they are sacrificing pension and welfare benefits to subsidize Israel.

It must be stressed, however, that while these domestic pressures have been extremely influential, effectively limiting open discussion and instituting the doctrines of Israeli *hasbara* ("explanation," i.e, propaganda), nevertheless this position of influence was reached and maintained only because "support for Israel" conformed to the perceived needs of important segments of US power.

One should take careful note of the logic that lies behind the reasoning of the Israeli lobby and its associates in the intellectual community. Israel is useful as a strategic asset if it is highly militarized, a pariah state lacking an independent economy, dependent on the United States for survival and therefore dependable, available for services on demand. To function as a useful "federal agency," Israel must remain in a situation of permanent military confrontation, its very survival constantly threatened. If there were a peaceful political settlement, Israel would be slowly integrated into the region as its most technologically and industrially advanced sector. It would become a Switzerland or Luxembourg, not a mercenary state available to bite those whom the master tells it to bite, not a strategic asset.

The logic is clear enough. Those who call themselves "supporters of Israel" are, in fact, the supporters of Israel's moral degeneration and ultimate destruction, the likely consequence of an unending military confrontation.

Within the United States, a serious split developed among US elites over these issues. The doves, among them powerful domestic elements, advocated a political settlement, while the hawks, preferring an Israeli Sparta, favor continued occupation and military confrontation. The split was evident by 1970. It was symbolized by the confrontation between Secretary of State William Rogers, who formulated the official policy in the Rogers plan of December 1969 calling for a general political settlement in the terms of the prevailing international consensus, and National Security Adviser Henry Kissinger, who advocated what he called "stalemate." In part, Kissinger's position derived from the strategic thinking that lay behind the Nixon doctrine; in part, so his memoirs and other evidence indicate, he was motivated by the desire to overcome his major antagonist on the world scene,

William Rogers and the State Department (the Soviet Union was a distant second).

Matters came to a head in February 1971, when President Sadat of Egypt offered a full peace treaty to Israel in the terms of the international consensus. Israel's Labor government rejected the offer, while recognizing that it was a genuine peace proposal. Haim Bar-Lev explained the reasoning: "I think that we could obtain a peace settlement on the basis of the earlier [pre-June 1967] borders. If I were persuaded that this is the maximum that we might obtain, I would say: agreed. But I think that it is not the maximum. I think that if we continue to hold out, we will obtain more."[17] A similar offer by Jordan a few weeks later apparently elicited no response.

By 1971, Kissinger had succeeded in taking control of Middle East policy, and in accordance with his preference for "stalemate," supported Israel's refusal to reach a peaceful diplomatic settlement. His position has dominated US policy making since, with a few fluctuations, though the split among elites remains evident today and policy choices might tilt in the other direction, as assessments and tactical decisions change.

Dismissing warnings from the oil companies and US ambassadors, and relying on the illusions of US and Israeli intelligence, Kissinger rejected Sadat's efforts to achieve a peaceful settlement and convert Egypt to a US client state, which, his memoirs indicate, he did not understand; in fact, his misunderstanding of Middle Eastern affairs and simple ignorance were stupendous.[18] This blindness, which was mirrored in Israel, led directly to the 1973 war, particularly after Israel began settling the northeast Sinai and establishing the city of Yamit after driving out the local population.

Egypt made good its threats in October 1973 when Egypt and Syria attacked the Sinai and Golan Heights with a degree of success that astonished Israel and the United States. Knowledgeable Israeli analysts agree that Sadat's goal was to obtain "a partial military success by seizing the Suez Canal from the Israelis" and thus to "prompt the superpowers [in fact, the United States] to pressure Israel" to accept a political settlement.[19] Kissinger has always been able to understand violence, and these successes led to a shift in US tactics.

Let us take a brief look at Israeli politics during the crucial 1967-73 period, which Abba Eban describes as "the most unattractive period in Israel's national memory,"[20] a period of ecstatic triumphalism and harsh military repression in the occupied territories. A detailed record is provided by Yossi Beilin in his illuminating study *Mehiro shel Ihud* (see note 1). The basic principle was expressed clearly by current Israeli President Haim Herzog, regarded as a dove, who explained in internal discussion, with regard to the Palestinians, that "I am certainly not prepared to accept them as participants in any way in a land that has been consecrated to our people for thousands of years. To the Jews of this land there cannot be any partner." On these assumptions, even pro-Jordanian political activities were blocked, as when Golda Meir, in 1972, ordered Minister of Police Shlomo Hillel to forbid a pro-Jordanian political conference in the West Bank, overriding Moshe Dayan, who raised no objections.[21]

Dayan's view was that the occupation was permanent.[22] As for the Palestinians in the territories, his advice was to tell them: "You shall continue to live like dogs, and whoever wishes, may leave, and we shall see where this process will lead." We see today very clearly "where this process will lead." To Shimon Peres's protest that "it is necessary to consider the moral stand of Israel," Dayan responded: "Ben-Gurion said that whoever approaches the Zionist problem from a moral aspect is not a Zionist."[23]

This attitude of contempt for the native population has deep roots in Zionist history. Yitzhak Shamir has a respectable tradition behind him when he speaks of crushing them like grasshoppers. Chaim Weizmann, after the Balfour declaration, told Arthur Ruppin that "with regard to the Arab question, the British told us that there are several hundred thousand negroes there but this is a matter of no consequence."[24] One can find even more shameful statements—not to speak of actions—on the part of the founders of the United States, for example, George Washington, who described the native population decimated by the terror of the colonists as "beasts of prey, tho' they differ in shape," who must be treated accordingly. But facts remain facts, and they help understand what is happening today, and will be still more terrible tomorrow.

Beilin reports a secret offer transmitted via the United States after a divided (11-10) cabinet decision of June 19, 1967, calling for a settlement at the international borders with Syria and Egypt (with Israel keeping Gaza), but no mention of Jordan and the West Bank. This proposal, which Eban described as "the most dramatic initiative that the government of Israel ever took before or since,"[25] was cancelled a year later, when Israel proposed a settlement in terms of the Allon Plan ("territorial compromise"). There appear to be no subsequent Israeli initiatives, and Israel has forcefully rejected other proposals apart from the Camp David arrangements, which the government interpreted as granting it effective control over the occupied territories. The record leaves little doubt, as Beilin observes, that Israel could have had a peace settlement in terms of the prevailing international consensus, offering nothing to the Palestinians, by 1971. Beilin holds that Israel's "security problems with regard to terror," including katyusha rockets, became serious from mid-1971, that is, after the rejection of the Egyptian and Jordanian peace proposals.

Nevertheless, Beilin observes, security arguments were secondary throughout. Far more significant was the "demographic problem," and the question of the water resources of the West Bank is frequently raised. Israel now depends on these heavily, and as a recent study of the Washington Center for Strategic and International Studies concludes, the entire region is facing an "alarming" and imminent problem of water shortages, one particularly severe for Israel and the occupied territories.[26] Under the best of circumstances, this problem would pose a serious barrier to political settlement.

After 1973, the United States recognized that Egypt could not simply be disregarded, as had been assumed. A tactical shift was therefore required to preserve Israel's status as a "strategic asset." To maintain Israel's regional dominance while evading a long-term political settlement, it became necessary to remove Egypt from the conflict, a task undertaken in Kissinger's shuttle diplomacy and finally, the Camp David agreements, with their predictable consequences. With the major Arab deterrent force removed, and a huge increase in US aid, Israel was free to expand its control of the occupied territories and to attack Lebanon—exactly what happened.[27]

The international consensus on a political settlement has passed through two phases. In its first phase, until the mid-1970s, the consensus was completely rejectionist, offering nothing to the Palestinians. It was based on UN Resolution 242 as understood throughout most of the world, calling for a settlement on the internationally recognized (pre-June 1967) borders, with perhaps minor modifications and various security guarantees, as outlined in the Rogers Plan and Sadat's very similar 1971 proposal. After the mid-1970s, the terms had changed to include a Palestinian state in the West Bank and Gaza, at which point the PLO and the major Arab states joined, sometimes with a degree of ambiguity, sometimes with much clarity. Israel and the United States, meanwhile, vehemently opposed such a settlement, and still do.

In January 1976, the "confrontation states" (Egypt, Syria, Jordan) proposed a settlement in these terms at the United Nations, with the support of most of the world, including the USSR and the PLO; according to Haim Herzog, then UN ambassador, the PLO not only supported the resolution but actually "prepared" it.[28] The proposed Security Council resolution, which incorporated the crucial wording of Resolution 242, called for a settlement on the pre-June 1967 borders, with "appropriate arrangements...to guarantee...the sovereignty, territorial integrity and political independence of all states in the area and their right to live in peace within secure and recognized boundaries," including Israel and the new Palestinian state.

Israel strongly opposed this proposal and refused to attend the session. The Rabin government announced that it would not negotiate with any Palestinians on any political issue and would not negotiate with the PLO under any circumstances. Apart from these pronouncements, Israel's reaction to the calling of the Security Council session was the usual reflex: bomb

Lebanon. On December 2, in apparent retaliation against the United Nations, Israeli jets bombed and strafed Palestinian refugee camps and nearby villages, killing fifty-seven people according to Lebanese and Palestinian sources: "Israeli officials stressed that the purpose of the action had been preventive, not punitive."[29] In accord with the regular pattern, large-scale Israeli terrorism passed without notice in the United States. The United States vetoed the Security Council resolution.

These events, like Sadat's 1971 proposal, have disappeared from history as far as US intellectual culture is concerned. In the media, they do not exist, and are unmentionable. According to the standard version, to which no challenge is tolerated, the first departure from unremitting rejectionism in the Arab camp was in 1977, when Sadat broke ranks and joined "the peace process" by travelling to Jerusalem, an act of courage that led to his assassination, proving that Arabs fear and hate peace. The media consistently maintain that prior to this visit, Sadat (like all Arabs) refused to consider any political settlement with Israel. Scholarship downplays these events or ignores them completely, defining the "peace process" as whatever course the United States happens to be pursuing, a convenient doctrine, since it then follows, as a matter of logic, that the United States is the leader of the peace-loving nations and that those who do not follow its orders reject peace and are therefore to be scorned, reviled, repressed or simply murdered.[30]

The record of the following years follows the same pattern. A few examples will illustrate.

The Carter administration initially moved towards the international consensus, including an October 1977 Soviet-US statement which called for "termination of the state of war and establishment of normal peaceful relations" between Israel and its neighbors, as well as for internationally guaranteed borders and demilitarized zones. This statement was endorsed by the PLO, but Carter backed away under protest by Israel and the domestic lobby.

In the following years, there were numerous opportunities to move towards, perhaps realize, the general terms of a nonrejectionist two-state settlement, but Israel and the United States rebuffed or ignored them. In March 1977, the Palestinian National Council called for the establishment of "an independent national state" *in* Palestine—rather than a secular democratic state *of* Palestine, as before—and authorized Palestinian attendance at an Arab-Israeli peace conference; the response of Prime Minister Rabin was that "the only place the Israelis could meet the Palestinian guerrillas was on the field of battle."[31] A few months later, the PLO leaked a "peace plan" in Beirut stating that the Palestinian National Covenant would not serve as the basis for interstate relations, just as the principles of the World Zionist Organization do not, and that any evolution beyond a two-state settlement "would be achieved by peaceful means."[32] Then followed the Camp David agreements with their predictable consequences in the occupied territories and Lebanon.

Moving on to the 1980s, I have already mentioned Brezhnev's February 1981 proposal and the PLO endorsement of it in April. The Israeli literature gives an interesting picture of what came next. On May 28, strategic analyst Avner Yaniv wrote, "Israel launched a massive air attack on the PLO in Lebanon," an attack that "resembled the last stages of the Canal War more than a decade earlier," lasting until June 3 and "causing a great deal of material damage as well as approximately 100 casualties."[33] The attack was un-provoked and the PLO did not respond. Israel renewed the attack on July 10, again violating the cease-fire without provocation, this time eliciting a PLO response and an exchange in which 6 Israelis and hundreds of Pales-tinians and Lebanese were killed in IDF bombing of densely-populated civilian targets. Of these incidents, all that remains in the collective memory of the US media is the tragedy of the Israeli inhabitants of the northern Galilee, subjected to the terror of katyusha rockets.

When the cease-fire was reestablished under US auspices, the editors of the *Washington Post* wrote that it might "provide a bit more time for opening up a political alternative to the PLO" or the United States might "consider addressing the PLO in order to persuade it to make a true peace with Israel. Everyone knows the PLO is ready for more war. The current calm provides an interval in which to probe whether, as some elements in it claim, the PLO is also ready for an honorable settlement"—meaning, presumably, a settlement on US terms.[34] Against the background of what had just occurred, the editors write further that "It was no surprise to find the PLO raining terror on civilians" (in response to Israeli bombing of Palestinian targets, they fail to note), but this time "the Israelis shed all pretense of avoiding civilians too," as they had been doing in Lebanon on a scale that dwarfs PLO terror since the early 1970s, evoking little notice or interest in the United States.

In his review of the strategic thinking that led to—and in his view justified—the invasion of Lebanon, Yaniv observes that "several develop-ments in the summer and fall of 1981 may have heightened Israel's anxieties concerning the PLO," most ominously, the threat that the PLO would observe the cease-fire agreement, and PLO efforts "to convince the Saudi government to promote" a diplomatic two-state settlement.[35] In the following year, Israel attempted with increasing desperation to evoke some PLO response that could be used as a pretext for the planned invasion of Lebanon, designed to destroy the PLO as a political force, establish Israeli control over the occupied territories, and—in its broadest outlines—to establish Sharon's "new order" in Lebanon and perhaps beyond. These efforts, including bombing of civilian targets in Lebanon, failed to achieve their objective. Israel then used the

pretext of the attempted assassination of Ambassador Argov by Abu Nidal—
who had been at war with the PLO for a decade and did not so much as have
an office in Lebanon—to launch Operation Peace for Galilee. It was clear
enough at the time, and is now widely conceded, that the perceived threat
of the PLO was its commitment to a peaceful settlement and renunciation of
terror, a point first made, to my knowledge, by Yehoshua Porath,[36] and
developed in detail by Yaniv. The primary goal of the invasion of Lebanon,
he writes, was "to halt [the PLO's] rise to political respectability"; "dealing a
major blow to the PLO as a political force was the raison d'être of the entire
operation."[37] It may be noted that this fear of "Arab moderation" also has deep
roots in Zionist history, for reasons that are evident.

The facts are unacceptable and are therefore ignored—or more accurately, denied—in public discourse on these matters among the educated
classes in the United States, who are, for the most part, either well-disciplined,
or misled by the elaborate disinformation system, or simply intimidated by
the defamation apparatus organized by the Anti-Defamation League and
others. This last factor should not be discounted. Defamation and vilification
have become a highly developed art, and its agents have learned that with
their easy access to the media, they can construct the most outlandish array
of lies and deceit and establish them by mere repetition. Few are willing to
expose themselves to such slander operations, against which there is essentially no defense, as the practitioners of these Stalinist-style practices understand very well. In the political system particularly the tactics are highly
effective.

Despite the partial success of the Lebanese war in provoking a new
wave of terrorism on the part of its desperate victims, the PLO persisted in its
dangerous and intolerable moves towards a political settlement. In April-May
1984, Yasir Arafat made a series of statements in Europe and Asia calling for
negotiations with Israel leading to mutual recognition. The offer was immediately rejected by Israel and ignored by the US government.[38] The *New York
Times* refused to publish the facts or even brief letters referring to them.

As the semi-official Newspaper of Record, the *New York Times* must
be more careful than most to safeguard the preferred version of history. When
its Jerusalem correspondent Thomas Friedman reviews "Two Decades of
Seeking Peace in the Middle East," as he did a few months later, the major
Arab (including PLO) initiatives of these two decades are excluded, and
attention is focused on the various rejectionist US proposals: the official
"peace process." Four days later, the *Times* editors explained that "the most
important reality is that the Arabs will finally have to negotiate with Israel,"
but Yasir Arafat stands in the way "and still talks of an unattainable independent state" instead of adopting a "genuine approach to Israel" to "reinforce the healthy pragmatism of Israel's Prime Minister Peres" by agreeing to

accept King Hussein as the spokesman "for West Bank Palestinians"—regardless of their overwhelming opposition to this choice, irrelevant in the case of people who have no claim to human rights. Shortly after, in yet another review of the "peace process" under the heading, "Are the Palestinians Ready to Seek Peace?" diplomatic correspondent Bernard Gwertzman asserts that the PLO has always rejected "any talk of negotiated peace with Israel." Note that Gwertzman need not ask whether Israel or the United States is "ready for peace." For the United States, this is true by definition, since "peace" is defined as whatever the United States is ready to accept. And since the Labor Party, with its "healthy pragmatism," is basically in accord with US rejectionism, it too is automatically "ready for peace."[39]

On December 10, 1986, Friedman wrote that Peace Now has "never been more distressed" because of "the absence of any Arab negotiating partner." A few months later, he quoted Shimon Peres as deploring the lack of a "peace movement among the Arab people" such as "we have among the Jewish people," and saying that there can be no PLO participation in negotiations "as long as it is remaining a shooting organization and refuses to negotiate" (March 27, 1987). Six days before Friedman's article on "the absence of any Arab negotiating partner" for Peace Now, a headline in Ma'ariv read: "Arafat indicates to Israel that he is ready to enter into direct negotiations." The offer had been made during the tenure of Shimon Peres as prime minister. His press advisor, Uri Savir, confirmed the report, commenting that "there is a principled objection to any contact with the PLO, which flows from the doctrine that the PLO cannot be a partner to negotiations." Yossi Beilin observed that "the proposal...was dismissed because it appeared to be a tricky attempt to establish direct contacts when we are not prepared for any negotiations with any PLO factor." Yossi Ben-Aharon, head of the prime minister's office and Shamir's political adviser, explained that

> There is no place for any division in the Israeli camp between Likud and Ma'arach (Labor). There is in fact cooperation and general understanding, certainly with regard to the fact that the PLO cannot be a participant in discussions or in anything... No one associated with the PLO can represent the issue of the Palestinians. If there is any hope for arrangements that will solve this problem, then the prior condition must be to destroy the PLO from its roots in this region. Politically, psychologically, socially, economically, ideologically. It must not retain a shred of influence... The Israeli opposition to any dealings with the PLO will lead to the consequence that it will weaken and ultimately disappear... This depends to a considerable extent upon us. For example, no journalist may ask questions about the PLO or its influence. The idea that the PLO is a topic for discussion in the Israeli press—that is already im-

proper. There must be a consensus here, and no debate, that the PLO may not be a factor with which Israel can develop any contact.[40]

None of this was reported in the mainstream US media, though Friedman was alone in using the occasion to issue one of his periodic laments over the bitter fate of the only peace forces in the Middle East.

Friedman's services are much appreciated. In April 1988, he received the Pulitzer Prize, the highest journalistic award, for "balanced and informed coverage" of the Middle East, of which these are a few typical samples.

A year after Peres' rejection of "direct negotiations," just reviewed, the Hebrew press in Israel headlined Arafat's statement that "I am ready for direct negotiations with Israel, but only as an equal among equals," and Shimon Peres' report that "the PLO is ready for direct negotiations with Israel without an international conference."[41] Israel again rejected the offer. A few days later, Arafat reiterated the PLO call for "an independent Palestinian state in any part of the territory of Palestine evacuated by the Israelis or liberated by us," adding that this state should then form "a confederation with the Jordanians, the Egyptians, the Syrians, and why not, the Israelis."[42] Again, the US reader was spared knowledge of these facts.

On January 14, 1988, Arafat reiterated his position that the PLO would "recognize Israel's right to exist if it and the United States accept PLO participation in an international Middle East Peace conference" based on all UN resolutions, including 242.[43] Once again, however, the *New York Times* refused to publish Arafat's statement, or even to permit letters referring to it—though the facts were buried in an article on another topic nine days later. Arafat had expressed similar positions many times, for example, a few months earlier in an interview in the *New York Review of Books,* and in a September speech at the UN Non-Governmental Organizations meeting in which he called for an "international conference under the auspices of the United Nations and on the basis of international legality as well as of the international resolutions approved by the United Nations relevant to the Palestinian cause and the Middle East Crisis, and the resolutions of the Security Council, including Resolutions 242 and 338,"[44] also unreported in the Newspaper of Record.

In March 1988, the *New York Times* at last permitted readers a glimpse of the facts, but in an interesting manner. A front-page headline read: "Shamir and Arafat Both Scornful of US Moves for Mideast Peace." Two stories follow on the villains who scorn the "peace process." One deals with Yitzhak Shamir, who says that "The only word in the Shultz plan I accept is his signature"; the other, with Yasir Arafat, who repeats his endorsement of all UN resolutions including 242 and 338, once again accepting Israel's existence in return for withdrawal from occupied territories, and calls for Palestinians to be represented in negotiations through their chosen representatives—the two forms of "extremism."[45]

In April 1988, Arafat again endorsed partition, referring explicitly to the *principle* of a two-state political settlement, not the borders of the original 1947 UN Resolution 181. The next day, Rabin announced that Palestinians must be excluded from any political settlement, and that diplomacy can proceed only "on a state-to-state level"; a few days earlier, Yitzhak Shamir had informed George Shultz that "UN Resolution 242 does not contain territorial provisions with regard to Jordan," meaning that it excludes the West Bank. At the end of April, the Labor Party once again adopted a campaign platform rejecting Israeli withdrawal from the occupied territories, and Rabin clarified that the plan was to allow 60 percent of the West Bank and Gaza Strip to be part of a Jordanian-Palestinian state, with its capital in Amman.[46] All of this appears to have passed without notice in the US press, though it did report that both Rabin and Peres now insist that there are no "basic differences between us."[47]

A few weeks later, at the Algiers meeting of the Arab League, the PLO circulated a document written by Arafat's personal spokesman Bassam Abu Sharif, submitted to the major US media and reported in a cable to the State Department of June 8. The document once again explicitly accepted UN Resolutions 242 and 338, explaining why the PLO will not accept them in isolation. The reason, of course, is that "neither Resolution says anything about the national rights of the Palestinian people, including their democratic right to self-expression and their national right to self-determination." "For that reason and that reason alone," Abu Sharif continued, "we have repeatedly said that we accept Resolutions 242 and 338 in the context of the U.N. resolutions which do recognize the national rights of the Palestinian people." The same considerations are what underlie the insistence of the United States and Israel that the PLO accept 242 and 338 in isolation, thus agreeing to abandon their right to self-determination and self-expression. The Abu Sharif statement was published in the small left-wing weekly *In These Times*. The *Washington Post* refused publication. The *New York Times* published excerpts as an opinion column, accompanied by a front-page news story headlined "An Aide to Arafat Comes Under Fire: Hard-Line Palestinian Groups Criticize the Adviser's Call for Talks With Israelis." The article focuses on the condemnation of Abu Sharif by the Popular Front for the Liberation of Palestine and groups that oppose the PLO, barely mentioning the contents of the proposal.[48]

In the United States, the roots and nature of rejectionism are off the agenda. The editors of the *New York Times* lament that "tragically, no one has an answer" to the problems of Gaza. "Neither Egypt nor Jordan wants these Palestinians," so they "have become solely the problem of Israel." The idea that "these Palestinians" might themselves "have an answer" is not denied; it is irrelevant. In the *Washington Post,* the editors write that the war goes on "in part because of a continuing Arab refusal to sit down and make peace"; make peace, that is, in the rejectionist terms acceptable to the United States and Israel. In a January 26 letter to the *Times* considered so important as to merit notice in the news columns, Irving Howe, Arthur Hertzberg, Henry Rosovsky, and Michael Walzer write that Israel's "strong-arm methods...strengthen the hand" of the Arab and Jewish "extremists" who "reject negotiations" and refuse a political settlement, neglecting to mention that the Arab extremists include Qaddafi, Abu Nidal and Syrian-based breakaway elements from the PLO, while the extremists on the other side include both major political groupings in Israel, both US political parties, the major US media—and, for many years, the writers of this letter. Helena Cobban and Yagil Weinberg write in the *New York Times* on January 17 of "recent signs that a moderated negotiating position may now be acceptable to the PLO," but unfortunately "the peace camp" in Israel "seems virtually paralyzed," in particular Foreign Minister Shimon Peres. As they know full well, these "signs" are not "recent" and go far beyond "signs," while Peres, the leader of the "peace camp," had only a few days earlier reiterated his unwavering stand that Israel "will not negotiate with the PLO because such negotiations would lead to the establishment of 'a Palestinian state with a Palestinian army'." His position remains: "I object completely to any dealings with the PLO."[49]

As this survey indicates, from December 1987 there has been a slight increase in the willingness to concede bits and pieces of the truth about PLO positions. The reason is the intifada and Israel's failure to repress it by force. As long as repression was successful, it was unnecessary to face the question of Palestinian rights or to take notice of PLO offers for a political settlement. But with the apparent failure of violent means, positions are naturally reassessed. Much the same was true with regard to Sadat's proposals before and after Egyptian successes in 1973.

Within the general framework of the international consensus, there are variants of the two-state formula that have been acceptable to its advocates, including some form of federation between the Palestinian state and Jordan, perhaps even a broader arrangement including Israel. There are various specific proposals as to how to attain security goals. Such measures might include demilitarization of the Palestinian state and international supervision of it, though in reality, the most severe threat to security will be faced by the Palestinian state, contained within a hostile Jordanian-Israeli alliance, at least tacit. In the Abu Sharif document of June 1988, the PLO stressed that the Palestinians "accept—indeed, insist on—international guarantees for the security of all states in the region, including Palestine and Israel," and would agree to "the deployment of a UN buffer force on the Palestinian side of the Israeli-Palestinian border." Other modalities could be investigated if negotiations within this general framework were undertaken.

If we want to advance beyond slogans, it will be necessary to face hard questions. A peace treaty with Syria will require a settlement of the issue of the Golan Heights. The status of Jerusalem also raises serious problems. Like almost all other countries, the United States has not accepted Israel's annexation of occupied East Jerusalem. Few would look forward to a restoration of the barriers dividing East and West Jerusalem. One possibility that might be achieved in the course of negotiations is the internationalization of a unified Jerusalem as the joint capital of Israel and Palestine, in accordance with the basic principles of the original UN partition resolution. Access to resources, including water, is another serious issue. Furthermore, the problem is regional, a fact that has been recognized by the United States since the Eisenhower administration, which initiated efforts to develop a constructive regional water management policy. This problem alone—and it is severe—provides a reason to work towards some kind of federal arrangement in the region in accord with the concepts of the original partition resolution.

Other problems also arise; they are not simple ones, and they can be addressed only in meaningful negotiations, based on nonrejectionist principles. The alternative is very grim. Apart from the two-state proposals, there is no feasible basis for settlement on the horizon, and this one, with all its difficulties, has the merit of recognizing the legitimate claims of the contesting parties, of according with world opinion generally and the positions of most of the regional actors, and of offering a way to reduce the level of conflict and the threat, never remote, of a destructive war that might even expand well beyond the region, with incalculable consequences.

## Chapter 18

The Israeli-Palestinian Conflict and the US Peace Movement

Todd Jailer and Melani McAlister

On June 12, 1982, six days after Israel's invasion of Lebanon, nearly one million people jammed the streets of New York City in one of the largest peace demonstrations the world had ever seen. Hundreds of thousands chanted slogans calling for nuclear disarmament. From the main stage in Central Park and an auxiliary stage at the United Nations, dozens of speakers addressed the need to redirect our national priorities away from preparation for war and nuclear death, and toward social justice.

Only one movement leader, Norma Becker, used the occasion to denounce the invasion of Lebanon. No one else on the seemingly endless roll of speakers sought to rouse opposition to Israeli militarism or call for recognition of Palestinian self-determination as necessary to achieving a lasting peace in the Middle East. This was not an oversight on the part of the demonstration's organizers: it was the result of bitter disagreement among the various organizations that made up the US peace movement. It was also a shameful abdication of responsibility.

Five and a half years later, the world's attention was once more riveted on the Middle East as the uprising initiated by the Palestinians in December 1987 brought the struggle against Israeli occupation to a new level of intensity. In a dramatic reversal of images, the media brought home the deadly realities of the occupation. But once again, most of the larger organizations in the US peace movement were distressingly quiet, a testament to their continuing failure to address the Israeli-Palestinian conflict.

It is essential that Middle East peace activists try to understand why much of the movement has such a blind spot—the most generous characterization possible—that it refuses to oppose US Middle East policy and repressive Israeli behavior. The reasons for the silence are multifaceted: anti-Arab racism, confusion of opposition to Israeli policies with anti-Semitism, government-sponsored anti-Iranian and anti-Libyan crusades taken up by the media and an unwillingness to challenge US strategic objectives and policy in the region. Movement activists have also feared jeopardizing funding from Jewish donors and from funding sources unwilling to deal with the issue.

The task of disentangling the motivations and challenging the silence is an urgent one. It is not, however, a task we can take up in detail here. Rather, our focus is on the development of US peace movement responses to Israel's attempts to crush the Palestinian uprising. We will look at some of the organized responses to the uprising, examine their successes and failures, and pose some possible directions for the future. In order to better understand developments since the intifada began, however, we must examine the context in which Middle East peace activists have organized since 1982. And for that, we have to go back to the streets of New York and the silence around the invasion of Lebanon that made one of the peace movement's greatest achievements also one of its greatest failures.

June 12: The Missed Opportunity

The coalition that came together to organize the June 12 March for Peace and Justice, planned to coincide with the UN Second Special Session on Disarmament, was one of the broadest and most diverse to date. At the height of the Nuclear Freeze campaign's popularity, some of the organizers from the Freeze, SANE and other larger peace and justice organizations believed that a single-issue focus on disarmament was the most appropriate rallying cry for the fledgling movement. After months of struggle with other organizations—including Mobilization for Survival (MfS), the War Resisters League, the US Peace Council, the Women's International League for Peace and Freedom and a number of Third World groups—over whether it was possible to talk about peace and disarmament without also raising a call against US intervention in the Third World, the debate was settled in favor of the larger, better-financed groups and their narrow focus on nuclear weapons.[1]

In the evaluations that followed the demonstration, the organizers focused more on whether the coalition should continue than on the efficacy of a program for peace that ignored US non-nuclear intervention. The blindness to the invasion of Lebanon didn't even come up.

"I had two deep and distinct feelings about June 12," remembers Joseph Gerson of the American Friends Service Committee (AFSC). "The first was an absolute sense of pain at the silence regarding the invasion. The second was a more distant observation of how silent the demonstration was. There was no anger, and that concerned me..."

In response, Gerson joined with Boston activists George Sommaripa of the Freeze and Tony Palomba of Mobilization for Survival to plan a December 1982 conference and educational campaign that would place the nuclear threat in the context of US foreign policy. The idea of a "Deadly Connection" between intervention and nuclear policy provided a theoretical construct that allowed activists to synthesize the experience of Vietnam with the horrors of Hiroshima into a larger understanding of the "Pax Americana" of nuclear imperialism. In conjunction with similar work by Michael Klare of the Institute for Policy Studies, over thirty Deadly Connection conferences were held around the country over the next few years.[2]

These conferences and other activities were designed, Gerson says, to "light a fire under the movement heavies who knew this stuff but hadn't felt safe to say anything earlier." The concept took off because people were ready for it. As Leslie Cagan, former program coordinator of Mobilization for Survival, put it, "Perhaps around the Middle East more than anywhere else, the Deadly Connection gave a handle to activists to talk about intervention and foreign policy issues."

In response to the general neglect of Middle East issues by the June 12 organizing committee and the space opened by the Deadly Connections concept, Mobilization for Survival (MfS), a broad grouping of local chapters and affiliated organizations, began to address this failing in its work. MfS embarked on a national education campaign consisting of dialogue with its autonomous local chapters, production of an educational packet and leadership in the Breaking the Silence conference held in 1983. Because of the decentralized nature of the organization, the effect of these activities varied among the constituent groups. Middle East work was taken up most strongly in Boston, New York and Milwaukee.

Leslie Cagan recalls: "Mobilization for Survival took on the responsibility of raising the issue of the Middle East in our broader coalition work, whether it flew or not. It almost always met with an acknowledgement that it was an important issue and related to other issues, a situation around which something needs to be done and around which the peace movement needs a position. But, they would say, it's not appropriate here."

The invasion of Lebanon also galvanized many progressive Jews, active around a variety of issues, to come together to develop a specifically Jewish opposition to Israeli policies. Encouraged by the emergence of an active antiwar movement in Israel itself, especially the Peace Now and Yesh Gvul movements, many Jews overcame their feelings of ambivalence about criticizing Israel and were able to speak out against the brutal character of the invasion. The formation of New Jewish Agenda in 1980 both supported this new Jewish activism around Middle East peace and benefitted from it, since many ad hoc committees later became Agenda chapters. Again, the success of organizing work varied from city to city. In some places, groups focused their work solely on the Jewish community; elsewhere Jewish groups worked with the broader progressive community. Probably the most successful group in the second category was the Washington (D.C.) Area Jews for Israeli-Palestinian Peace. The Jewish groups sometimes worked in coalition with Palestinians and Arab-Americans, often a new experience for all concerned, though not always a successful one.

The upsurge in Middle East organizing tapered off by 1985 as the war in Lebanon faded from the front pages and people's memories, as developments in Central America and South Africa began to claim larger portions of activists' agendas, and as the Israeli peace movement demobilized. On other anti-intervention issues activists had done their jobs well: both SANE and the Freeze were talking about South Africa and Central America by 1985-86. Neither, however, would even touch the Israeli-Palestinian conflict.

The stalwarts of the Middle East peace movement in the United States—the American Friends Service Committee, Mobilization for Survival, Palestine Human Rights Campaign, November 29/Palestine Solidarity Committee, New Jewish Agenda, the American-Arab Anti-Discrimination Committee (ADC) and various other organizations—continued to educate and organize during the next two or three years. But the Middle East peace movement still remained in an embryonic state, even as the occupation neared its twentieth anniversary. Its main components spent the years between the post-Lebanon War demobilization and the uprising developing the movement's *political* resources: the deadly connection between regional conflict and nuclear war; the links between Central America, South Africa and the Middle East; an analysis of US political/economic interests in the region; and an anti-interventionist focus intended to give work on this issue a broader base than the ethnic identity and solidarity groups who dominated it. Unfortunately, these forces were less successful at developing the movement's *institutional* resources, in large part because the larger, more mainstream peace organizations and—crucially—peace movement funders kept away from the issue.

These failures became even more disturbing as the PLO's position regarding a two-state solution to the Israeli-Palestinian conflict became increasingly clear. The PLO declared its support for an international peace conference; denounced the use of terrorism against civilians (though it insisted on its right to engage in armed actions inside Israel and the occupied territories); and participated in meetings with Israeli peace activists, some of whom faced criminal prosecution in Israel as a consequence. Despite these unmistakable PLO moves toward conciliation and a negotiated settlement, the attitude of the large US peace organizations continued to hover some-where between blatant avoidance of the whole issue and firm rejection of the Palestinian initiatives.

Some activists have argued that the changes in the PLO position before the uprising, important as they were, simply did not go far enough to affect the difficulties of organizing around this issue in the United States. Until as late as December 1988, the PLO's positions on the two-state solution and armed action against Israeli targets were inconsistent, reflecting divisions within the PLO itself. Of course, a truly "evenhanded" evaluation would not hinge support for Palestinian self-determination on the PLO's stance on these issues. After all, support for Israeli self-determination does not, and should not, depend on Israel accepting a two-state solution or an end to all violence against Palestinians. Self-determination is a basic right, not a reward for good behavior—a point lost on much of the peace movement.

In order to broaden our base significantly, or just to encourage some movement *within* the broader peace movement, Middle East activists had to overcome significant emotional opposition. The limiting factors included pervasive anti-Arab and anti-Palestinian racism, the hegemonic myth of Israel as a beleaguered underdog facing the threat of annihilation, and the complex ways in which support for Israel has become a way to avoid confronting anti-Semitism in our society. Without unambiguous PLO statements in favor of a two-state solution in hand, some activists felt there were real limits on how far a movement for Middle East peace could go. In this context, Middle East activists often felt we needed the PLO to perform the "strip-tease" Arafat offered in December 1988.[3] We may, however, have underestimated what would be needed to convince the peace movement to address the primary conflict in the world's most militarized region. Sadly, to judge from the results in the first months of 1989, the PLO's extraordinary peace initiative seems to have brought about more movement in the Reagan and Bush administrations than it has within the major funding and political organizations of the peace movement.

The consignment of the Israeli-Palestinian conflict to the categories of "too divisive" and "too difficult" in the period before the uprising was a major factor in the inability of the Middle East movement to create viable national campaigns. Middle East activists and organizations were isolated, under-funded and marginalized. Middle East activists also often felt besieged, under attack even by individuals and organizations "on our side." Given this situation, it is perhaps no surprise that the organizing sometimes turned inward. Instead of building a broad, independent base of support, the movement focused on developing statements and organizing relatively comfortable "solidarity events."

But Middle East activists must also take some responsibility for these failures. By focusing so intensely on developing a common agenda among the Arab-American, Jewish, religious and peace groups engaged with the issue, we often failed to move beyond statements to action. While this desire to consolidate our small numbers is certainly understandable, our focus on developing coalitions among groups that did not necessarily share a common politics (a common *concern,* perhaps, but not a common politics) turned us away from the basic work of organizing in the broader community. Sheila Ryan, of New York's Middle East Peace Network, voiced the dilemma this way: "Our work must involve both Arabs and Jews. That creates a context that invites other people in, that makes it clear that this is a peace/policy question, that you aren't lined up for one people and against another. But the solution doesn't lie with either the Jewish or the Arab communities; it lies with the other 95 or 96 percent of the population. In the past, our particular obsession with coalitions between Jewish and Arab groups has caused extraordinary introspection: we think a broad coalition is ADC and New Jewish Agenda. Maybe it's time to form 'Others for Middle East Peace.' "

That obsession with "perfect" coalitions led to the failure to develop any nationally coordinated response to the twentieth anniversary of the Israeli occupation in June 1987. Representatives from a dozen national organizations began meeting in the spring of that year and spent hours in meetings discussing the wording of a common statement. The attempted coalition fell apart over wording calling for an international conference. The crucial question was whether to support "an" international conference or "the" international conference called for by the United Nations. This apparently minor distance between wordings did in fact represent real political differences, but by seeing the crack as a chasm, the group failed to take any common action. And, because most organizations had focused their energy on the expectation of coalition work, the twentieth anniversary passed in silence, with virtually no significant national work by any active Middle East organizations.

Since December 1987, these struggling but committed organizations have suddenly found their ranks growing as the uprising put the injustice of occupation and statelessness in the headlines all over the world. In general, though, the Middle East peace organizations have proven unable to transform the newfound public interest in the Israeli-Palestinian conflict into a coherent, sustained campaign of political action. Despite this lack of an overall strategy, however, activists in diverse communities have fashioned responses that offer valuable lessons and may point to directions for future organizing.

The Uprising: Short Term Responses

The uprising that began in December 1987 affected organizing work in the United States in immediate and dramatic ways. The change in how Palestinians were presented in the US media set the stage: suddenly the nightly news was filled with images of Palestinian children being attacked by a brutal and ruthless Israeli army. The old image of Israel as the valiant but outgunned David facing an Arab Goliath was turned on its head—and this time the message reached nearly every home in the country.

During the first three to four months of the uprising, the media was the single most important influence in moving Middle East peace work forward. While the activist organizations did respond in some creative ways to the new situation presented by the uprising, the US media was clearly (if unwittingly) leading the way. "One thing had to be done: sensitize people to the issue. And that, the media did," says Denis Doyon of AFSC. And in that dramatically different context, activists found that our demonstrations and statements reached new audiences through the media.

In December, January and February, Arab-American and Palestinian solidarity groups took the lead in organizing protests against the rising tide of Israeli violence. Emergency coalitions of Arab organizations, solidarity groups and some peace groups sprang up in several cities, including Chicago, Boston and Washington, D.C. The demonstrations in those months often had a human rights focus, although, as time went on, cutting aid to the occupation became a more prominent demand.

Viki Tamoush was working with the Palestine Human Rights Campaign (PHRC) at the time. She believes that the uprising, and the new images it provided, changed the way Arab solidarity organizations worked. "Everything began with the kids; those children with stones became our image, our focus. And we learned to take a very different approach to statistics. Before, we counted bodies. Then we learned to make it much more human: it isn't just 'three were killed,' but a mother and two children, their names were this, and they were this old, from this village. We talked about *how* they were killed. We forced the press to acknowledge that these were real people, real deaths. The Arab community learned how to use statistics; we discovered what we could achieve with them: sympathy, press coverage, opinions."

Indeed, the public responded powerfully to detail and activists brought an impressive energy to the work of humanizing Palestinians' lives. For example, Palestinian women's groups in the United States, spearheaded a "From the Homeless to the Homeless" meal. Activists also delivered miniature paper "coffins," each bearing the name of a Palestinian who had been killed and facsimiles of US dollars, to the offices of US elected officials. On Christmas

Eve, a few groups leafletted services at major churches in several cities, calling for worshippers to "remember the victims of violence in the Holy Land." In Chicago, activists organized well-attended protests outside the Israeli consulate every ten days or so from mid-December until the end of February. On January 7, six leaders of local Arab-American associations were arrested when they attempted to stage a visit to the Israeli consulate and refused to leave the building until they were allowed to see a consulate representative.

On February 27, Chicago was one of the half-dozen US cities to stage a symbolic funeral and memorial for Palestinians killed during the uprising. More than 180 cars, each draped with a Palestinian flag and marked with the name of one of the dead, wound solemnly through the streets of the city. "In Black and Latino neighborhoods, the support was significant. People came out to watch and applaud," recalled Dick Reilly, Midwest Palestine Solidarity Committee coordinator. At the memorial gathering at the end of the procession, protesters were addressed by two city alderpeople, the leader of Operation Push, and the head of the Black Press Institute.

These demonstrations, often hastily organized out of a sense of emergency, mobilized many Arabs and Arab-Americans, some Jews, and others who had not been previously active. They were also concrete responses that could pull together diverse peace and solidarity groups. However, they did not, for the most part, bring in people who had not already been "convinced" before the uprising. It is in the nature of "emergency response" to draw on networks already in place and on activists who are ready to move to relatively militant action on short notice. (And it is important to remember that, for most North Americans, any demonstration that includes shouting or chanting controversial slogans while marching in a circle in some public place counts as militant action.) The fact that most of the activist organizations (quite understandably) did not expect the uprising to go on indefinitely kept them in an "emergency" mindset for nearly six months, organizing quick demonstration after quick demonstration. It meant also that little effort was made to capitalize on the shift in public opinion to recruit new activists. People who were concerned and who wanted more information or were willing to take some action found little in the way of "entry level" activities (mailgram campaigns, teach-ins, boycotts, etc.) to bring them into the movement.

In addition to the demonstrations and protests, the Arab-American community responded to the uprising with material aid campaigns. Roots, a Palestinian foundation, raised money for ambulances; other groups solicited funds for medical supplies, assistance to the families of those who had been killed and support for the alternative structures that Palestinians created during the uprising, such as schools and cooperatives. The Palestine Solidarity Committee sponsored concerts in three cities on the first anniversary of the uprising to raise money for material aid. In Chicago, the popular black composer Gil Scott Heron performed for thousands of people at a concert also notable for the presence of Jesse Jackson and other leaders of the Rainbow Coalition. Local musicians in San Francisco and Washington, D.C. proved to be successful fundraisers, but didn't generate a high level of visibility.

For the most part, the main Jewish organizations doing Middle East work—the International Jewish Peace Union (IJPU) and New Jewish Agenda (NJA)—were not members of these coalitions. Jonathan Boyarin of the IJPU in New York, which has a history of work in coalition with Palestinian solidarity organizations, felt that the uprising made it harder to do joint Arab-Jewish demonstrations. "Palestinians were, rightfully, very angry about what was happening in the occupied territories. A lot of new people came to the demonstrations, which is of course a strength. But it meant that it was nearly impossible to have the kind of discipline [about chants and slogans] that is necessary for these coalitions. For the time being, we felt we didn't belong there."

There is another side to this, of course. Many Palestinians feel that their deep sense of grievance and their principled opposition to Zionism often have to be suppressed in order to make Arab-Jewish coalitions work, that concern for Jewish sensitivities and Israel's welfare and security often get priority. Given the daily toll of dead and wounded in the occupied territories, it is not surprising that some feel this puts an unfair burden on the Palestinian side.

NJA, IJPU and other groups organized specifically Jewish actions to protest the Israeli repression. In New York, IJPU spearheaded a diverse coalition of Jewish organizations that organized a Passover Peace Action in April 1988. The coalition ranged from IJPU to the Jewish Peace Fellowship to Friends of Peace Now and the Labor Zionist Alliance. More than 3,000 people showed up to call for an end to the occupation, mutual recognition and an end to violence on both sides. "It was not a militant demonstration," recalls Boyarin. "In tone, it was a Peace Now demonstration. *But*—it was the first one in America."

The same coalition planned a second Passover Peace Action for April 1989, with demands including a call for Israeli negotiations with the PLO. The organizers also prepared a set of inserts for a Passover Hagadah to focus on the occupation. Along the model of the earlier "Freedom Seder," this Hagadah asked "four questions about the occupation." The Hagadah was used during the Peace Action, and was distributed widely to participants and Jewish groups.

According to Ezra Goldstein, co-chair of NJA's national Middle East task force, many of the organization's forty chapters organized some sort of response during the first year of the uprising: a demonstration, vigil or educational event. But neither Jewish group has been able to develop a coordinated national response to the uprising.

The Jewish groups have clearly seen their role primarily as organizing within the Jewish community. At a time when there is a sea change in Jewish opinion on the Israeli-Palestinian question, this is a crucial role. It does, however, raise some questions about the visibility of organized Jewish support for Middle East work in the broader community. Without Jewish-identified organizations as members, many Middle East coalitions face real handicaps in their work, both in the peace movement and in the broader Jewish community. This problem surfaced, for example, in the 1988 referenda campaigns on Middle East peace proposals. And there is some evidence—from work in the Democratic party in Seattle, for example—that without joint work among the general public, organizing within the Jewish community will be far less effective. Thus the importance of a consistent, visible and principled Jewish presence in the Middle East peace movement should not be underestimated.

One way Jews organized to register dissent within the larger community was through a series of advertisements placed in national and local newspapers by ad hoc groups. For several weeks in December and January, peace/protest statements signed by Jews appeared in the *New York Times* and to a lesser extent the *Washington Post,* the *Nation* and elsewhere. (Arab-American groups also placed ads, as did supporters of Israeli policies.) The newly-formed Jewish Committee on the Middle East went so far as to call on the United States to disassociate itself from Israel and reduce or terminate military aid; other groups stressed the need for a two-state solution, US recognition of the PLO, an international peace conference, etc. New Jewish Agenda chapters placed ads in about fifteen local Jewish papers, and the issue was also fought out in numerous opinion columns and letters to editors.

Goldstein says that Jews placed ads because of "a genuine desire for a very public, very visible response to the uprising. We were tired of reading statements by people who claim they are speaking for the Jewish community. Morris Abrams [past president of the Conference of Presidents of Major American Jewish Organizations] says in public that Jews must support Israel right or wrong, even though behind the scenes he is speaking critically to the Israelis. Individual Jews begin to hear that stupidity, and they say, 'This guy can't speak for me.' We wanted to make it clear that there is far more than one Jewish voice."

In addition, some Jews have protested by redirecting contributions from mainstream groups like the United Jewish Appeal (UJA) to alternatives like the New Israel Fund. The figures are hard to come by, but anecdotal evidence suggests that the UJA and other establishment groups are alarmed. Meanwhile, the New Israel Fund, which supports projects in Israel for Arab-Jewish coexistence and the empowerment of low-income people (but has not endorsed a two-state solution), and the Jewish Fund for Justice, which supports both Jewish and non-Jewish social justice projects all over the world, have both reported increases in donations since the uprising.

As media interest in the intifada began to wane in the spring of 1988 and stories on the killings began moving from page one to page six, then back to their old spot on page sixty-four, some groups tried "keep it in the public eye" campaigns. Perhaps the most visible of these was a transit system advertisement placed in Boston by the Campaign for Peace with Justice in the Middle East (CPJME). The ad, which ran in three hundred subway cars for a month, featured a photo of Israeli soldiers dragging a young boy and the heading, "Your tax dollars pay for the violence in the Israeli-occupied territories." Although an earlier ad to commemorate twenty years of occupation had been ignored by the media, this ad created an immediate stir. The "controversy" around the ad, fueled by reporters hungry for new angles, received extensive coverage in the Boston area and beyond. But once again, lacking a coherent plan of action, the CPJME was unable to capitalize on the media attention in a way that involved significantly more people in political action.

The Long Haul

By spring it had become apparent that the uprising had developed from a spasm of protest into a long-term campaign of political action. The response of US organizers would need to mirror that development. From March/April 1988 until the first anniversary of the uprising in December, several new campaigns developed which reflected a sense among organizers that we needed to move beyond the traditional demonstrations and educational activities to more coordinated and strategic campaigns.

These longer-term strategies generally fell into three categories: 1) work to influence the position of other political groupings, primarily the Democratic Party; 2) citizen diplomacy initiatives, including Israel/Palestine tours, local referenda on the November ballot and sister city campaigns; and 3) coalition work and demonstrations (both national and local), including the work of UN-affiliated groups, like the various non-governmental organizations (NGOs). It is interesting to note how many of the new campaigns had an electoral focus: both the Democratic Party activism and the referenda were longer-term campaigns that were nonetheless rather time-limited.

Looking at several of these campaigns—the Eyewitness Israel program of the ADC; work within the Democratic Party, with a closer look at Seattle; the referenda in Berkeley, San Francisco, Cambridge and Newton; and the human rights-oriented work of the North American non-governmental organizations affiliated with the United Nations—raises some serious questions. We need to look at the strategies, tactics and participants in the campaigns; raise some questions about what worked, what didn't, and why; and take a look at how the campaigns might fit into a broader movement. The purpose is not to attempt any final summations, nor to divorce the tactics of the campaigns from the diverse politics of their organizers. Instead, the goal is to open a serious dialogue among Middle East and peace activists about political strategy for the coming years.

Eyewitness Israel

The American-Arab Anti-Discrimination Committee's "Eyewitness Israel" program was developed in the spring of 1988, after Israel had moved to suppress news and information coming out of the territories. "The idea was to send in Americans just to see for themselves what was going on," says ADC staffer Chris Abbasse.

Eyewitness Israel has sent more than 110 people to the area for three week trips. Roots, a Palestinian foundation in Washington, D.C., has also sent fact-finding delegations of activists for low-cost one- to two-week trips to the occupied territories. Roots delegations have involved about 200 people.

Participants in the ADC-sponsored trips stay with Palestinian families, spending half their time in the West Bank and half in Gaza. The program primarily focuses on allowing participants to get a sense of the day-to-day lives of Palestinians and of the patterns of human rights violations, rather than on formal meetings or extensive travel in the territories. The trips are heavily subsidized: until January 1989, the package cost participants only $500. (The current price is $1000.) In return, participants agree to go back into their communities and talk about what they've seen.

"We've been very fortunate," says Abbasse. "People have been very active, especially with slide shows and lectures. Some folks have been really going out into their communities—to the churches and to their Central America groups...We're very pleased with the program."

Recently, however, applications for Eyewitness Israel are down from the very high level of spring and summer 1988. The higher price has almost certainly had an effect, as has the time of year. But it may also be that as the uprising is featured less prominently in the news, fewer people are motivated to seek out the story for themselves. While a program like Eyewitness Israel can play a valuable role in building a movement, it also needs a movement to sustain it when the media loses interest.

The Democratic Party

Jesse Jackson's Rainbow Coalition arrived at the 1988 Democratic National Convention with an agenda that included a reevaluation of the US role in the Israeli-Palestinian conflict. This was, not surprisingly, an extremely controversial position. Rainbow organizers reported threats that funding would be lost, fistfights would break out on the floor, etc., should the convention take up the issue. Although tensions ran high, the debate remained peaceful. Unfortunately, the only television coverage was carried by C-Span, a cable station with limited distribution.

Rainbow representatives agreed in the platform committee not to push the Israeli-Palestinian peace plank, and the convention did not ultimately vote on the issue. Still, the debate on the convention floor was a first in national electoral politics. It was a testament to the hard work of both Arab-American and Jewish Rainbow members. Arab-Americans were an active constituency for the Rainbow, which—unlike other political formations—welcomes their participation *as* Arabs and addressed Arab-American concerns. But the platform debate also indicated a fairly broad sentiment in favor of a change in policy: a poll of delegates to the convention showed that the majority would have supported a two-state position had they been voting their consciences rather than their candidate's platform. The unusual openness in Atlanta helped to reinforce the sense of local organizers that by bringing the issue to previously closed forums, the intifada was changing everything.

A comprehensive overview of the nationwide Rainbow/Democratic Party organizing that led up to the convention debate isn't possible here. Instead, we will focus on the case of Seattle, Washington, as an illustrative example for organizers.

In both 1984 and 1986, the Democratic Party in Seattle had adopted platform planks in favor of Israeli-Palestinian mutual recognition. The battles had been bitter. One side was led by representatives of the Rainbow and Kadima, the local NJA chapter, the other by the Jewish Community Relations Council (JCRC), a coalition of almost all the Jewish organizations in Seattle.

Early in 1988, just after the uprising began, organizers began discussing how to approach the platform plank at the state convention. Kadima member Dan Petegorsky recalls: "We had two options: we could up the ante and call for US recognition of the PLO, or we could go with the old resolution and try to gain broader support." The group decided to go with the old resolution. A series of meetings were held with the JCRC to discuss compromise language for the resolution; ultimately, a letter in favor of the platform plank was sent out on JCRC letterhead to every Jewish group in the city. At the convention, a Dukakis delegate (a Jew) and a Jackson delegate (an Arab-American) worked out a final resolution that further strengthened the plank; the final version called for an "independent state" and made reference to the "representative chosen by the Palestinian people." The plank was passed by acclamation.

"It was an extraordinary breakthrough," says Petegorsky. "Two years earlier we had a bitter, furious debate. At that time, the JCRC wouldn't even consider negotiating language with us. The Dukakis delegate who worked out the stronger language this year had, two years ago, been bitterly opposed to the resolution and had told supporters that she would 'see us at the bottom of the Mediterranean.' Now she's coming out in favor, and—more importantly—you have major Jewish organizations supporting the need for Palestinian self-determination and a Palestinian state."

Petegorsky believes that the shift in public opinion caused by the uprising was a major factor in the JCRC's turnaround. The major Jewish groups, after evaluating previous battles, were aware they couldn't win or stonewall so they decided to negotiate. Yet, within the organized Jewish community, Kadima and other two-state supporters are still officially pariahs: members of the JCRC are not allowed to have Kadima members speak at their events; no JCRC member can participate on a panel with anyone from Kadima. "If the playing field is just the Jewish community, they won't even let us show our faces," says Petegorsky. "But when the playing field is broader, we have a lot more power and they have to recognize that."

Clearly, movement within the mainstream Jewish community is to some degree dependent on the political climate of that broader "playing field." Again, the interdependence of work within the Jewish community and organizing among the broader public is apparent. Without a Jewish presence, Middle East organizing aimed at the general public is guaranteed to be labeled both "fringe" and anti-Semitic (though these labels will probably be applied by some people in any case). And without a movement that has influence beyond the Jewish and Arab-American communities, organizing within the Jewish community is more difficult and more easily isolated.

The Referenda

Four initiatives relating to the Israeli-Palestinian crisis appeared on local ballots in the November 1988 elections. Measure J in Berkeley, California, sought to adopt the occupied Gaza town and refugee camp of Jabalya as a sister city. In San Francisco, Proposition W called for a two-state solution. The only winning campaign was waged in Cambridge, Massachusetts, where Question 5 called for an end to United States support of Israel's occupation of the West Bank and Gaza and the establishment of a Palestinian state. In Newton, Massachusetts, a mild proposition calling on the United States to *consider* a two-state solution was defeated. The campaigns each had their unique features and are worth investigating in some detail.

Berkeley's Measure J

Berkeley's Campaign to Adopt Jabaliya grew out of the Emergency Coalition for Palestinian Rights (ECPR), a group formed in the early days of the uprising by Middle East activists in the East Bay. In 1984, another ballot initiative, Measure E, calling for cuts in aid to Israel proportional to its spending on illegal settlements in the occupied territories, was defeated. The sister city proposal was chosen as a focus in 1988 because of the potential it offered for concrete material aid, political support and education. It was also seen as an important people-to-people campaign that didn't propose a comprehensive solution to the conflict but did clearly criticize the denial of Palestinian rights under the occupation.

The focus on Palestinian rights as a human rights issue of concern to all citizens—not just Jews and Arabs—was central to the campaign. As activist Marianne Torres explained, "Two-thirds of our group was Jewish and we faced the constant struggle between making that fact known and trying to keep the focus on human rights, not the Israeli/Palestinian conflict."

In January 1988, Berkeley City Councilmember Maudelle Shirek introduced a statement of concern about the violence in the occupied territories. Her resolution was defeated and sent to the city's Peace and Justice Commission, which eventually recommended acceptance of the ECPR proposal to adopt Jabalya. In four days, over 1,200 signatures were collected to place the measure on the ballot.

The group that carried out the organizing itself was rather small, consisting of a core of some twenty members and another twenty people who did a lot of the footwork. There was not much participation from Arab-Americans—most community activists focused on the San Francisco campaign—although some Palestinians from San Francisco pitched in toward the end. Important endorsements were won from members of the black religious community, the Berkeley Black Caucus, the Oakland-Berkeley Rainbow Coalition and the United Muslims of America, who raised some of the funds.

New Jewish Agenda didn't endorse the measure because it didn't contain explicit recognition of a two-state solution, a necessary precondition for their participation in coalitions. NJA members from the East Bay were instead active on the Proposition W campaign in San Francisco. Measure J was however endorsed by the International Jewish Peace Union.

The measure encountered stiff opposition from Berkeley's Mayor Loni Hancock, a strong supporter of Berkeley's other sister cities in Nicaragua, El Salvador and South Africa. Her opposition limited the support which other solidarity groups in Berkeley gave to the Campaign to Adopt Jabaliya.

On the University of California campus, the Committee for Academic Freedom in the Occupied Territories tabled daily from mid-September until the election. They also sponsored events, including two debates, to educate and mobilize the university community.

Just as the Palestinians confront one of the world's most sophisticated armies with only stones, the two West Coast referenda were vastly outgunned by their opposition. Unable to afford an office or paid staff, Friends of Jabaliya raised a total of $10,000 to run their campaign. With these funds they developed one main piece of literature and a few subsidiary pieces and placed a few quarter- and eighth-page ads in local newspapers. The opposition to the campaign, organized as the Coalition for Middle East Peace and Justice, raised over $120,000 for the most heavily funded campaign in the Berkeley election. They mailed six different pieces in the last two weeks of the campaign and placed full-page ads in local papers. One of their most controversial mailings, designed by the same firm that directed the "No on W" campaign in San Francisco, featured a glossy photo of the Vietnam War Memorial; inside it read: "If we learned anything from the tragedy in Vietnam, it's the futility of taking sides in a dispute between warring parties. Whether it's Vietnam, Nicaragua, the Persian Gulf or El Salvador...America can't impose solutions on people who should be deciding their own destinies for themselves. Defeat Measure J."

Berkeley activists cite lack of resources as chief among the reasons Measure J was defeated, by a margin of 29-71 percent. Most of the money they were able to raise came in too late to be spent most effectively. Personality and "turf" conflicts also hindered outreach, as did the perception that the campaign was "too radical" because it did not contain explicit support of a two-state solution.

One goal of the campaign was achieved, however: Friends of Jabaliya will continue as an ongoing committee providing material aid and keeping the people of Berkeley informed of developments in the occupied territories.

San Francisco's Proposition W

The Middle East has been a "back burner" issue in the broader San Francisco peace movement since 1984. For years, activists have tried to get their slogans—"No US Intervention in the Middle East," and later "End US Support for the Occupation"—taken up by the annual Spring Mobilization for Peace, Jobs and Justice, but each year the broad coalition sponsoring the event refused. So the opportunity to build a coalition around Middle East issues presented by Proposition W was an important step for the Bay Area.

Proposition W, which called for a two-state solution to the Israeli-Palestinian conflict, was initiated by National Association of Arab Americans (NAAA). It was the first major foray by San Francisco's Arab-American community into city politics; the American-Arab Anti-Discrimination Committee and the Ramallah Young Adults Club joined in as well. An important aspect of the coalition-building experience was the involvement of New Jewish Agenda and the endorsement of the International Jewish Peace Union.

These and other groups collected 19,000 signatures to get the question on the ballot. They also lined up several important endorsers, including the Harvey Milk Lesbian and Gay Democratic Club and several church leaders. In the weeks prior to the election, a poll showed them leading 33-25 percent, with 38 percent undecided. Why then was the final vote so negative: 32 percent in favor, 68 percent opposed?

Activist Jeffry Blankfort gives three reasons: the opposition's seemingly unlimited supply of money; the almost complete support of the city's liberal establishment for the "No on W" position; and the Proposition W campaign's refusal to criticize Israeli repression of Palestinian rights while focusing solely on the two-state solution.

While the Proposition W coalition was able to raise $84,000, the opposition raised over $400,000, which was spent primarily on a number of well-targeted pieces of literature produced by the city's prime political public relations firm, Campaign Performance Group. These slick mailings included separate pieces targeted on different constituencies. A piece directed at the black community featured photos of Martin Luther King and California Speaker of the Assembly Willie Brown and bore the legend, "The Dream hasn't been completed yet...—Vote No on W." A flyer aimed at the gay community showed Harry Britt in front of the monument to Harvey Milk and read, "In the spirit of Harvey Milk, vote no on W." A similar piece targeting the Central America peace activist community sported a photo of Costa Rican President Oscar Arias. As in 1982, Middle East peace work suffered because of other peace and solidarity groups' failure to develop even a basic position on the Israeli-Palestinian conflict.

The $400,000 raised by the opposition came from a half-dozen political action committees (PACs) around the country, as well as wealthy San Francisco and Southern California donors. Many of these donors are important sources of campaign funds for city and state politicians, and it was clear to many politicians that support for Proposition W could mean no donations to their own upcoming campaigns. Activist Matthew Hallinan recognized that Proposition W was "too hot for a lot of people to support, so we didn't go to them."

San Francisco Mayor Art Agnos stayed neutral through much of the campaign, despite tremendous pressure from the San Francisco Jewish community. He finally buckled and came out against W, reportedly after a phone call from Senator Paul Sarbanes of Maryland. This put the ADC in an embarrassing situation, since it had earlier asked the mayor to co-host its annual banquet. While he was not "disinvited," he decided not to attend and sent a representative instead.

Jeffry Blankfort also believes that "Proposition W didn't raise the real issues of the occupation" and, with its focus on not offending Jewish sensibilities and making clear its support for Israel at every turn, it in fact acted as a buffer against criticism of Israeli policies. "The coverage in the daily papers and TV news of the intifada was more compelling than anything coming out of our campaign; and that's no way to win an election. The other side played hardball. Proposition W played softball." Other activists disagree with Blankfort's assessment of the campaign's focus and attribute its defeat more to lack of resources, the resulting inability to reach the voters and the intrinsic difficulty of this issue.

Question 5 in Cambridge

The nonbinding referendum question in Cambridge and a small part of neighboring Somerville called on the US government to "demand that Israel end its violations of Palestinian human rights and its occupation of the West Bank and Gaza; stop all expenditure of US taxpayers' money for Israel's occupation of the West Bank and Gaza; and favor the establishment of an independent Palestinian state in the West Bank and Gaza, with peace for all the states in the region including Israel." Initiated by the Coalition for Palestinian Rights, which included a number of Palestinian and Arab-American groups, the Boston Peace Council, Boston Mobilization for Survival and others, the campaign began in earnest in June 1988 by gathering the signatures needed to get on the November ballot. New Jewish Agenda did not endorse Question 5, but many members did work on the rather different referendum question on the ballot in Newton.

The campaign did not devote much of its limited energies and resources to seeking endorsements from local elected officials; their opposition was more or less taken for granted, and organizers hoped that, at best, otherwise progressive local politicians would stay neutral. Members of the local religious community and activists in the Central America solidarity community did endorse Question 5, and some participated in the campaign.

The Coalition raised around $34,000, most of which was spent on a brochure which was mass-mailed to all registered voters and also distributed by hand to almost every mailbox in the city; there was also leafletting and literature tables at subway stops and shopping areas. On election day, volunteers distributed "For Peace in the Middle East, Vote Yes on 5" cards at every polling place. The Coalition was able to rent an office and pay a full-time staff person who, along with a ten-person steering committee, coordinated the outreach work of the thirty or so core members of the Coalition and about thirty other volunteers. The campaign also featured a well-attended debate at Harvard University between Alan Dershowitz and James Zogby.

The opposition forces seemed to be better organized on the Harvard University campus than anywhere else in the community. Harvard Hillel was able to organize 200-300 students to change their voter registration from their hometowns to Cambridge so they could vote against Question 5, and rabbis sermonized against the measure during High Holiday services at Harvard. As it turned out, the Harvard area was one of only two precincts in which Question 5 didn't win a majority.

The Coalition's strategy, dictated in large part by the resources available to it, was to run a grassroots campaign that could mobilize the concern that people in Cambridge felt about Israel's repressive tactics and transform it into a strong, progressive political statement. The opposition in Cambridge, unlike its counterparts on the West Coast, did not mount a very slick, well-financed or effective campaign. It sent out two rather poorly produced mailings featuring local Congresspersons Joe Kennedy and Barney Frank and placed a few ads in local newspapers, despite a war chest of about $60,000. About 75 percent of these funds apparently came from the Combined Jewish Philanthropies, although defending the occupation is not exactly the "widows and orphans" image that charity organizations like to evoke.

Question 5 organizers were surprised by the lack of coverage the issue received in the generally liberal *Boston Globe,* whose reporting on the intifada and the Israeli-Palestinian conflict has been far superior to that of the *New York Times.* The *Globe* editorialized against Question 5 on the grounds that nonbinding questions relating to foreign policy should not be on the ballot, then buried Question 5's victory (by a 53-47 percent margin) in a hard-todecipher list of vote totals. The next day the *Globe* actually reported that Question 5 had lost! It seems unlikely that many readers ever saw the correction; the only other mention of Question 5 was in a story which focused on the losing ballot question in Newton.

Amy Engel believes that the initiative was successful because "the wording of the question spoke directly to people's concerns—the misuse of their tax dollars and a two-state solution, as opposed to an abstract notion of 'peace in the Middle East.' The weakness of the opposition was a big factor. Also, the education and outreach that was done addressed the current developments in the occupied territories, which were on people's minds." Other Question 5 activists echoed Engel, stressing the importance of the linkage between repression in the occupied territories and the US funding that makes it possible.

The campaign marks a real victory for Middle East organizing in Boston/Cambridge, not only because of the victory at the polls, but because of the experience and trust built up among the Middle East and Central America solidarity communities and the traditional peace movement.

The Newton Referendum

The ad hoc committee that organized the ballot question in Newton, Massachusetts, aimed to prove that, even in that bastion of the Jewish community, the Israeli-Palestinian conflict could be critically discussed. The committee was composed largely of individual Jews from the Newton area, many of them members of New Jewish Agenda.

Committee activist Roger Hurwitz traces the initiative's 69-31 defeat to several sources. First, he points out, the campaign had a very difficult time with media coverage. The *Boston Globe* didn't report on the issue until after the election, while the *Newton Tab* was openly hostile. It published tirades against the question by Representatives Barney Frank and Joe Kennedy but refused to run the Newton committee's response.

At the same time, Hurwitz believes, the Newton referendum was negatively affected by the question in nearby Cambridge. Although the language of the Newton resolution was much more "moderate" than in Cambridge and Newton organizers sought to disassociate their campaign from its more "radical" counterpart, the opposition lumped the two together and attacked both indiscriminately. This was easy to do, since they were both designated "Question 5." In Newton, as elsewhere, organizers faced an opposition that didn't hesitate to lie or to misrepresent the contents of the resolutions.

Demographics also made a difference. A comparison of voting patterns in Cambridge and Newton showed that in both cities working class,

Democratic and non-Jewish districts were more likely to vote for the two versions of Question 5. "The Jewish establishment likes to say that Cambridge voted for the referendum because of all those weirdo intellectuals over there," Hurwitz points out. "But in fact, Harvard faculty and students were much more likely to vote against the question. Clearly this is a class issue, an ideological issue, an ethnic issue."

In the end, however, the major problem of the Newton campaign was organization: it had few activists and little money. Although the committee was able to send out a leaflet to every Newton resident, place paid ads on the radio and in the press and hold a "lightly attended" public event, there were simply not enough activists or enough money to get the word out in the face of the overwhelming opposition of the liberal establishment.

Non-Governmental Organizations

In June 1988, the North American committee of Non-Governmental Organizations at the UN sponsored the biennial meeting on the Question of Palestine. The NGOs represent a loose coalition of national organizations from the United States and Canada concerned about the Israeli-Palestinian conflict, including the American Friends Service Committee, American Arab Anti-Discrimination Committee, New Jewish Agenda, Palestine Human Rights Campaign, Palestine Solidarity Committee and others.

As a result of that meeting, the NGO coordinating committee (with strong leadership from the Palestine Solidarity Committee and the Palestine Human Rights Campaign) established an Action Alert network to respond to human rights violations during the uprising. According to Jeanne Butterfield, national chair of the Palestine Solidarity Committee and chair of the NGO coordinating committee, the network's main focus was response to specific human rights violations: mistreatment at the infamous Ansar III prison, the repression of social service organizations in the occupied territories, and the censorship or closing of newspapers and magazines (including two published within Israel). Although only a few groups were involved in these activities, they did at least represent a systematic attempt to try to work together.

Several organizations under the NGO umbrella plan to lobby at the annual Congressional hearings on human rights violations. Using the State Department's Country Conditions report as an opening, activists will try to present testimony and to demand that the issue of human rights violations should at least *inform* the debate over US aid to Israel.

In addition, the NGOs are considering a coordinated "statement campaign" that would attempt to gather petition signatures and generate advertisements in support of a single statement in favor of an independent Palestinian state and an international peace conference with the PLO and Israel. This campaign would be modeled along the lines of a local campaign by the Middle East Peace Network in New York. There, organizers have already begun to collect signatures, aiming for both "big names" and large numbers of "ordinary people."

The Issue of Aid

More than a year after the uprising began, US activists are still searching for a strategy that will build on the changes in US public opinion and the glimmers of change in US policy to create a real movement for peace and justice in the region. For many, organizing against US aid to the occupation is the obvious approach. Others believe that raising the issue of US aid could be the wedge that divides and splinters a fragile movement. The issue of aid goes to the heart of questions about how to build a mass movement and change US policy in the Middle East.

Some organizers argue that reaching out successfully to that vast majority of Americans who are neither Jewish nor Arab means discussing US aid. "That's the hook, that's the visceral issue," argues Roger Hurwitz. "Most people think 'two states, blue states—who cares?' But when you say '*your* money is hurting people'—that's the issue on which a lot of contact is made."

Viki Tamoush agrees: "Whenever somebody thinks I'm talking about a foreign issue that doesn't concern them, I bring up taxes. 'You may not know who's shooting who,' I tell them. 'But you bought the guns.' There are many, many tragedies and human rights violations in the world; unless Americans understand—in a direct and immediate way—why they have a particular role to play in the Israeli-Palestinian conflict, they will have no reason to take political action."

Other activists, while agreeing that it is important to point out the US role, argue that challenging US aid to Israel is one sure way to alienate the Jewish community and divide the movement. Many Jews who are now willing to recognize Palestinian rights and are beginning to accept a Palestinian state would be strongly against any move to reduce aid to Israel. For example, the intifada touched off a major debate on the aid issue within New Jewish Agenda. Dan Petegorsky, for one, has argued strongly that New Jewish Agenda should not take a position on aid. "It might be appropriate for some groups. But we're in a position where the Jewish community is *finally* debating the central issue—a Palestinian state and recognition of the PLO. We are seeing doors open. So why fight that battle [over aid], which is really a question of tactics and is much, much more difficult, when people are moving on the central issue?" The issue is sure to be discussed heatedly at NJA's national convention in July 1989.

The discussion in NJA has real implications for the larger movement: should NJA (the largest of the Jewish activist groups) decide against addressing the aid issue, peace coalitions that did take up aid would risk losing a significant, organized and necessary Jewish presence. However, if US aid to Israel is seen as the key to broadening the movement, the battle to hold together the coalition could result in losing the war to change US policy.

Some Middle East peace activists feel that while aid is an essential issue to educate people about, it shouldn't be *the* organizing focus. Sheila Ryan argues that "you need to say that US aid is involved; it really gets people's attention. But nothing can be done about it at this point. It's just too far out of the realm of possibility. For a political campaign or a lobbying effort, we need to focus on the state issue. That's an area where there is room for some movement." It is worth noting, however, that in other struggles—Central America and southern Africa—the question of US aid has been central. The victory of Question 5 in Cambridge provides some evidence that a challenge to aid can be successfully incorporated into our work.

To build upon the dramatic changes of the past year, we must set about building a movement. That means continuing our efforts at education, but it also means action—action that is clear-cut, direct and meaningful. In order to broaden our movement to include people who don't already feel a direct (ethnic, religious, ideological, etc.) connection to the issue, we need an organizing tool that makes clear the appropriateness and necessity of their participation. And if we want to reach people in an empowering way, we need to propose political action based on more than asking them to write letters to some guy in Washington asking him to ask some other guys to talk to some other guys in Geneva.

A campaign to cut aid to the occupation could provide such a vehicle. It could also allow for a variety of related campaigns: "alternative aid" campaigns that focus on material aid as a counter to US government aid to the occupation; sister city campaigns that offer locally-based, people-to-people alternatives of diplomacy and friendship; more referendum campaigns to raise the issue and build public support for a new US policy; and of course petitions, sit-ins, demonstrations, advertisements, etc.

The Challenges Ahead

As we write, in the spring of 1989, the US movement for Middle East peace has seen no big wave of activity, no effective, nationally-coordinated response to the most significant event in the twenty years of occupation of the West Bank and Gaza. The stalwart organizations with the strongest links to the broader peace movement, such as AFSC and Mobilization for Survival, were for internal reasons unable to take sustained leadership in broader efforts. Some attempts at larger coalitions have been made. Roots and some other organizations have recently formed the Middle East Justice Network. Yet, most have not developed into vibrant and growing organizations. The Network for Israeli-Palestinian Peace grew out of a series of meetings in spring 1988, but it has not yet developed beyond a common political statement. The NGO umbrella was, for many months, simply a network for sharing information.

There are some real possibilities, however, for developing a common campaign. Jeanne Butterfield notes that "There are some disagreements [among groups doing Middle East work]. People are cautious. But nobody at this point has any illusions of going it alone. We are searching for common ground."

That common ground may not be as elusive as it was in the past. The new leadership coming from people living in the territories and the subsequent clarifications of the PLO position has had a significant impact on organizing here. Most of the Palestinian solidarity groups have become much more willing to accept two-state language. Butterfield explains: "When national coalition efforts were being made that included 'alongside Israel' language, or when referenda were coming up in various parts of the country that called for explicit two-state language, the Palestine Solidarity Committee had a series of discussions. We decided that OK, this isn't our traditional language, but it's not in conflict with our statement of unity [which calls for self-determination for the Palestinians in whatever form they choose]. So this language should not be an obstacle to us at this point to working in coalition if we think the work that is being done is important." And some Jewish and church groups previously insistent on "balancing" language that often blurred the very real differences in power between Israelis and Palestinians have also become more flexible.

While the question of whether or not—much less *how*—to take up the issue of cutting aid remains unresolved, the possibilities for successfully coordinated national campaigns seem more likely at present than they did just two years ago. However, the resources to engage in work on a national scale remain elusive. We need more than good intentions and good politics.

We need money. We need staff. We need to be able to support and help channel the incredible outburst of creativity, energy and hope that has been generated by the intifada. Until progressive and peace movement publications, organizations and foundations begin to face the Israeli-Palestinian conflict squarely—they are currently trailing behind not only the general public but even the Bush administration—we will be unable to take advantage of the unprecedented openings for resolving the Israeli-Palestinian conflict and defusing the explosive tension in this most militarized area of the world.

Authors' Note: We would like to thank the following people who generously gave us interviews for or comments on this article: Chris Abbasse, Greg Bates, Joel Beinin, Jeffry Blankfort, Jonathan Boyarin, Jeanne Butterfield, Leslie Cagan, Louise Cainkar, Steve Chase, Carl Conetta, Denis Doyon, Amy Engel, Sara Freedman, Joseph Gerson, Ezra Goldstein, Roger Hurwitz, Zachary Lockman, Dan Petegorsky, Cynthia Peters, Michael Poulin, Dick Reilly, Sheila Ryan, Viki Tamoush, Marianne Torres and Corinne Whitlatch. Of course, responsibility for the views expressed remains solely with the authors.

## Part 7

Beyond the Intifada

O Negev (Ansar III prison song)

O Negev
O Negev
You must be desire
You must be honor and exploration
You must be a sword
You must be a lesson
One of the lessons of the intifada

O Negev
O Negev
They want you as a grave for us
But we turned the grave into a flower
And carried the sun as a dawn
No, no to the forms of oppression

O Negev
O Negev
You must be desire
You must be honor and exploration
We sipped warmth as a glass of elixir
And we loved the sand as a whisper
We bore the night as a wedding
A sovereign state

O Negev
O Negev
We have built a fortress now
Evidence of how great is our wound
How many martyrs proclaimed: All hail...
All hail to martyrdom

O Negev
O Negev
The children of the stones
Set fire to the land
Their voice brought a decision
Its own leadership

O Negev
O Negev
We are the voice of the people
The sharpened sword of revolution
We say no, no voice will sound
Over the voice of the intifada

O Negev
O Negev
You must be desire
You must be honor and exploration
You must be a sword
You must be a lesson
One of the lessons of the intifada

—Ibn al-Jabal

## Chapter 19

The Road Ahead

the editors of *Middle East Report*

In 1988, in the land of Palestine/Israel, the "generation of occupation" rewrote the equations that describe the political dynamics of the Middle East. Ordinary children, women and men, a million and a half of them, have confounded the State of Israel, Washington's closest ally in the Middle East, with their incredible courage and resourcefulness. Their resounding demand for political independence then prompted the Palestine Liberation Organization to declare unequivocally for a Palestinian state alongside Israel—a resolution based on "possible rather than absolute justice," as Yasir Arafat told the UN General Assembly in Geneva on December 13, 1988. More than one hundred governments have officially recognized the new state while others, including the major Western European states, have upgraded their relations with the PLO.

On December 8, as the uprising ended its first year, Defense Minister Yitzhak Rabin called his campaign to smash it "one of the toughest ordeals I have experienced.... It is far more simple, convenient and easy to tackle an external armed enemy than civilians under your rule."

It was not only Israel's rulers who were forced to acknowledge the new agenda inscribed by the uprising. In late July, King Hussein, whose grandfather had occupied and annexed the West Bank, felt compelled to renounce his dynasty's claim on the political future of the territories. In October, Algerian demonstrators invoked the example of the Palestinians as they fought their own police and army in the streets; six months later Jordanians followed suit. At their 1987 summit, the Arab states scarcely mentioned the Palestine conflict. By the end of 1988 the uprising had become a major new component of the political balance in the Arab world.

By far the most significant impact of the uprising has been on the Palestinians making it. They have transformed themselves, discovering new dimensions of cohesion and resourcefulness. The slings and stones, the leaflets and demonstrations are only the most visible signs of this. The invisible aspects—underground communal networks that sustain the revolt, neighborhood committees organized to meet social and material needs from childcare to fresh vegetables, a newfound pride and determination tested under fire—are likely to prove to be its most enduring features, for they point the way toward the construction of an independent political authority. The courage and daring of the youngsters in the streets have been all the more remarkable for the sober matching of demands, needs and capabilities embodied in the directives of the Unified National Leadership.

As in most situations where people rise up to demand their rights, the Israeli response so far has been to send in more troops, to seek more effective tactics of repression and to refuse accommodation. The November 1988 election produced a stalemate enshrined in yet another "national unity government," although the strong electoral showing of the Jewish religious parties obscured the fact that over 58 percent of Israeli voters cast ballots for parties which are at least on record as open to some degree of territorial and political compromise. Polls since the election suggest that three out of five Israelis (and over half of Jewish Israelis) would not rule out direct negotiations with the PLO. Even Peace Now, which until recently has functioned as an adjunct to the Labor Party, has explicitly called for Israeli negotiations with the PLO. It is particularly striking that many of the Israelis who oppose negotiations with the PLO and the establishment of a Palestinian state nonetheless seem to feel that these things will probably come to pass within the next few years.

However, Israeli policy is not determined by opinion polls or the number of signatures on protest ads in the newspapers. The composition of the new government, with Shimon Peres delegated as finance minister to bail out Labor's failing kibbutz and Histadrut enterprises, suggests that opposition to any compromise will be as resolute as ever. April 1989, the seventeenth month of the uprising, was one of the bloodiest yet. The prospect is for even greater repression and violence against Palestinians, with the threat of "transfer"—mass expulsion—discussed and openly promoted by some Knesset members and plotted by settler groups. Between the alternative scenarios of political negotiations and forced removal of the Palestinians lies the prospect of continued revolt and repression, though the pace and intensity will vary.

The combined force of the developments of the first year of the uprising finally led the United States to open formal talks with the Palestine Liberation Organization. Washington's "major recognition of reality," as the *Boston Globe* termed it, marks a new stage in the struggle for Palestinian rights. It has removed a gag from public discourse in this country which will be difficult to reimpose. Already it has profoundly altered the demonized image of the

PLO long purveyed by the US government, the Israel lobby and most of the media.

It is important, though, now that the enforced silence on this issue has been broken, to guard against any sense of complacency that Palestinian national rights can be achieved without our active engagement. The policy of talking with the PLO is designed to achieve what the policy of boycotting failed to accomplish: to end the uprising through a combination of Israeli repression and vague promises to address "legitimate Palestinian rights." Only if the Bush administration can be persuaded that the uprising cannot be crushed and will not be bargained away, and that the present situation is more threatening to its regional interests than a negotiated settlement, will Washington seriously press Israel to negotiate with the PLO and withdraw from Gaza and the West Bank.

Clearly this is not yet the case. The year of the uprising was also the year when the United States and Israel signed a five-year agreement codifying the extensive joint military, economic, political and intelligence ventures developed over the course of the Reagan administration. There is, as Deputy Assistant Secretary of Defense Edward Gnehm told a House Foreign Affairs subcommittee in March, "a formalized and highly efficient military relationship" between the two countries, one that almost trivializes tactical differences between the Bush and Shamir governments.[1] The Bush foreign policy team, moreover, is largely comprised of men deeply committed to the conception of Israel as a "strategic asset" and responsible for constructing the "strategic relationship" of the Reagan years. Some—Lawrence Eagleburger, Brent Scowcroft, Peter Rodman—are on loan from Kissinger Associates. Dennis Ross, the new director of State Department policy planning, most recently was a Senior Fellow at the pro-Israel Washington Institute for Near East Policy.

This institute, founded in 1985 by former deputy director of research for the American-Israel Public Affairs Committee Martin Indyk, has provided what appears to be the policy script for the new administration. A report of the Institute's Presidential Study Group, co-chaired by Eagleburger, cautioned against any US peace plan or involvement in an international conference. What is needed, said Eagleburger, Ross *et al.,* is "a different kind of initiative—one designed to reshape the political environment, stabilize the military balance and provide [the] administration with the means to resist pressures to pursue a procedural breakthrough...."[2]

It is not difficult to read the Bush administration's initial moves and statements in precisely these terms. Talk with the PLO in Tunis, but not in Washington. Produce an unusually candid human rights report on the occupied territories, but veto UN resolutions critical of Israeli practices. Suggest that the Palestinians wind down the uprising in return for Israeli relaxation of repressive measures—in effect restoring the status quo ante. Dissuade the European states from undertaking any initiatives toward convening an international conference.

The administration's problem, and our opportunity, is that the situation is far from static. The Eagleburger-Indyk-Ross script, drawn up before the US decision to talk with the PLO, was out-of-date the day it was published. It presumes a situation of deadlock, when in fact the political field is very much in motion. It dismisses the Palestinian leadership as "inchoate and radical" while characterizing Israel as "divided between those who seek peace through territorial compromise and those who seek peace through negotiating autonomy."[3]

The contrast between the Washington Institute report and one issued in March 1989 by Tel Aviv University's Jaffee Center for Strategic Studies is instructive. The Israeli team concludes, first, that a Palestinian state in the West Bank and Gaza "would not necessarily threaten Israel" and, second, that no settlement "is possible without direct negotiations with authoritative representatives of the Palestinians," noting elsewhere that "only the PLO...meets this criterion."[4] By contrast, Secretary of State James Baker's statement that "meaningful negotiations" between Israelis and Palestinians "may" require PLO participation hardly qualifies as visionary.[5]

Sharp differences within the Israeli political elite have been transposed to their counterparts among US Jews. When Prime Minister Shamir convened an international solidarity rally of Jewish leaders in Jerusalem in late March, some from the United States decided not to attend, and a few even talked of organizing an "alternative" event in New York. Among them was Theodore Mann, a former chairperson of the Conference of Presidents of Major American Jewish Organizations. "The problem is that right now the American Jewish community is running faster than the Israeli government or the US government," says Seymour Reich, head of B'nai Brith and present chair of the Conference of Presidents.[6]

What is true for Jewish communities in the United States is also true for the broader public. Developments in 1988—Jesse Jackson's presidential campaign, the ballot referenda in various cities and the successful campaigns led by the American-Arab Anti-Discrimination Committee (ADC) to halt tear gas shipments to Israel and to get the Federal Trade Commission to investigate Israeli treatment of Palestinian trade unionists—all represent the kinds of concrete steps that are possible in the new environment created by the intifada.

Just as the uprising has eroded the political base in Israel for that state's rejectionist policies, so has it fostered splits in both popular and elite opinion in the United States concerning Washington's support for this intransigence. The time is therefore right for a coherent effort to build on the achievements of the uprising by working to change US policy toward the Palestinian people. There is an urgent need for a more vocal and organized network in this country demanding that the US stop facilitating continued Israeli occupation of Palestinian territories and support Palestinian self-determination.

As we see it, this means challenging the level of US aid to Israel. This should be done in the context of a campaign for a moratorium on military aid and sales throughout the region. Even a public discussion of aid cuts would increase the constraints on Israel's use of violence against the Palestinians. We should also support Israeli opponents of the occupation and increase political and material aid to the Palestinians in order to help them endure Israeli repression and continue their struggle until they have attained their rights.

The intifada is more than an uprising against an intolerable status quo or a movement of defiance. It is also a movement of construction, the harbinger of the formation of an independent Palestinian state. That state already exists in the hearts and minds of those who have taken to the streets and, by their fierce and irrepressible resistance and determination, taken their destiny into their own hands. In the months and years ahead there will be many twists and turns along the road to Palestinian self-determination. The realization of that goal—an essential component of any future in which Palestinians and Israeli Jews might co-exist in peace, justice and security—is still out of sight beyond the horizon. But through the intifada the Palestinians in the occupied territories have ended the long years of political stalemate and opened up new possibilities for a just peace in the Middle East. Our active engagement in the ongoing struggle can help transform those possibilities into reality.

April 1989

## Part 8

Appendices

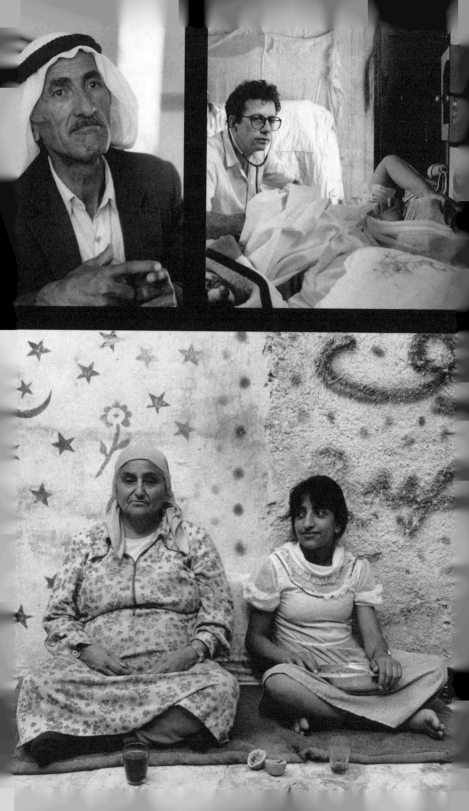

Demonstration

The tire burns in an empty square.
One child, pockets filled with
Carefully collected stones,
Stares at the army patrol.

At his funeral we chanted
"Mother of the martyr rejoice,
All youths are your children."

—Hanan Mikha'il-Ashrawi

The Martyrs of the First Year

This list records the names of the 390 Palestinian men, women and children in the West Bank and Gaza who died as the direct or indirect result of Israeli repression during the first year of the uprising—popularly referred to as the "martyrs" of the intifada. This total includes 287 civilians shot dead by Israeli soldiers, police, security agents and settlers in the period December 8, 1987 through December 8, 1988; 37 other individuals who died as the result of beatings and other forms of physical abuse; and an additional 66 people who died after tear-gassing induced asphyxiation or heart attacks. Several dozen other cases are still under investigation.

These figures were compiled by the Database Project on Palestinian Human Rights, based in Chicago and Jerusalem (1 Quincy Court, Suite 1308, Chicago IL 60604; c/o Arab Studies Society, P.O. Box 20479, Jerusalem). They show a much higher toll of human life than the Israeli military authorities have acknowledged because the latter refuse to admit responsibility for (and count) most deaths caused by teargas, beatings or settler gunfire, purported cases of "suicide" among prisoners, or cases in which the bodies of shooting victims are taken by their families and buried without official autopsy. Despite the superior accuracy of Palestinian sources, most of the US media continue to cite the Israeli army's statistics.

Palestinians Killed By Shooting

#	Name, Age	Residence	Date
287.	Yusef Moh'd Yusef Sbeih, 17	Kfur Rai/JENIN	Dec 8
286.	Asmaa Suleiman Abu Abadi, 15	Shati RC/GAZA	Dec 5
285.	Hamed Moh'd Ahmed alHaj, 14	Beit Furiq/NABLUS	Dec 3
284.	Hani Sami Hersha, 16	Qafin/TULKARM	Dec 1
283.	Farid Rajab M'ghari, 14	Nuseirat RC/GAZA	Nov 26
282.	Muhib Halayem, 12	Beita/NABLUS	Nov 22
281.	Yusef Moh'd Ahmad Shibbli, 22	Bakat al-Hatab/TULK	Nov 20
280.	Tareq Ataya Abu Samhadaneh, 25	Rafah/GAZA	Nov 15

#	Name, Age	Residence	Date
279.	Sabri Abdallah Arandas, 25	Khan Yunis RC/GAZA	Nov 14
278.	Alam Moh'd Hantuli, 27	JENIN	Nov 13
277.	Osama Ahmad Abu Ghanima, 3	Shuja'iyeh/GAZA	Nov 9
276.	Ahmad Hussein Besharat, 21	Tamoun/JENIN	Nov 7
275.	Ismat Jamil Mahmud, 21	Salem/NABLUS	Nov 7
274.	M'jahid Moh'd Ahmad Abdul Karim, 18	Yasid/JENIN	Nov 6
273.	Jalal AbdulQader Fayoumi, 21	Qalqilya/TULKARM	Nov 2
272.	Iyad Bishara Abu Saada, 19	Beit Sahour/BETH	Oct 30
271.	Basel Mustafa Halabi Dweikat,17	Rujeeb/NABLUS	Oct 29
270.	Ziad Thabet, 15	Nuseirat RC/GAZA	Oct 27
269.	Manal Ahmad Samour, 14	Shati RC/GAZA	Oct 25
268.	Moh'd Yusef alShahin, 17	Fara' RC/NABLUS	Oct 24
267.	Diya' Jihad Fayez Moh'd, 5	NABLUS	Oct 18
266.	Khaled AbdulWahab Tabeileh, 15	NABLUS	Oct 18
265.	Osama Wasfi Shalabi, 18	Atil/TULKARM	Oct 16
264.	Omar Abd Yusef Assi, 18	Kfur Malek/RAMALLAH	Oct 14
263.	Ahmad Yaacob Mustafa Ajrab, 19	Qibya/RAMALLAH	Oct 14
262.	Mahmud Abu Khader, 18	Judeideh/JENIN	Oct 13
261.	Nazim Jum'a Abu Judeh, 18	Dheishe RC/BETH	Oct 11
260.	Osama Subhi Ahmed Abu Dahi, 19	Rafah/GAZA	Oct 9
259.	Kamal Moh'd Hassan alSaria, 23	Yatta/KHALIL	Oct 9
258.	Fadel Ibrahim Shehadeh Najjar,24	Yatta/KHALIL	Oct 9
257.	Ahmed Moh'd Haj Salim Zeid Kilani, 28	Yaabad/JENIN	Oct 8
256.	Moh'd Fawzi AbdulQader Ahmed,24	Ein BeitalMa'RC/NABLUS	Oct 8
255.	Ali Izzadin Sa'eh, 20	NABLUS	Oct 7
254.	Ahmed Mahmud Said Mashharawi, 21	NABLUS	Oct 7
253.	Nidal Ali Najjar, 18	NABLUS	Oct 7
252.	Samir Bahlul, 26	NABLUS	Oct 7
251.	Adnan Ahmed Khanfa, 31	NABLUS	Oct 6
250.	Nitham Abu Hawaila, 24	Balatta RC/NABLUS	Oct 5
249.	Zein Moh'd Ghazi Karaki, 18	KHALIL	Sep 30
248.	Kayed Hassan Salah, 42	KHALIL	Sep 30
247.	Ayman Abu Sharar, 17	Nuseirat RC/GAZA	Sep 27
246.	Hussam Mukhtar Gharbawi, 19	Daraj/GAZA	Sep 27
245.	Osama Ahmad Mahmud Breika, 18	Khan Yunis/GAZA	Sep 27
244.	Nabil Moh'd Yusef Jamal, 21	Beit Surik/RAMALLAH	Sep 26
243.	Naser Ahmad Jundi, 22	Nur Shams RC/TULK	Sep 26
242.	Jamal Ibrahim Matar Shqeirat,23	Jebal Maqaber/QUDS	Sep 26
241.	Jihad Moh'd Zaino, 20	Daraj/GAZA	Sep 26
240.	Nahil Tukhi, 12	Amari RC/RAMALLAH	Sep 23
239.	Hanni Odeh Abu Median, 15	Breij RC/GAZA	Sep 21
238.	Imad Isma'il Abu Thuriya, 17	Rimal/GAZA	Sep 19
237.	Munjed Ismail Sarhan, 26	Luban Sharqiya/NAB	Sep 17
236.	Imad Ahmed Qeisi (Arqawi), 17	JENIN	Sep 17
235.	Rami Khalil Abu Samra, 10	Zaitun/GAZA	Sep 14
234.	Ahmad Ali Dababseh, 26	Nuba/KHALIL	Sep 10
233.	Moh'd Abdullah Abu Salah, 39	Silat al-Harthieh/J	Sep 8
232.	Abdel Karim Baruud, 18	Rafah/GAZA	Sep 6
231.	Minawi Munir Araysha, 17	Rimal/GAZA	Aug 31
230.	Louai Fakri Barghouthi, 22	Deir Ghassaneh/RAM	Aug 31
229.	Ayman Izzat Abdel Aziz Yamin,16	Tel/NABLUS	Aug 26

#	Name, Age	Residence	Date
228.	Moh'd Ghaleb Shqeir, 31	Zawiya/TULKARM	Aug 24
227.	Khaled Hashhash, 22	Balata RC/NABLUS	Aug 23
226.	Ahmad Hussein Shaghnubi, 23	Askar RC/NABLUS	Aug 22
225.	Na'el Moh'd Musleh Hamad, 18	Breij RC/GAZA	Aug 21
224.	Rajah Moh'd Suwafneh, 17	Toubas/JENIN	Aug 21
223.	Rasha Hazem Arqawi, 9	JENIN	Aug 17
222.	Asad Jabri Shawwa, 19	Sheja'iya/GAZA	Aug 16
221.	Ibrahim Samoudi, 27	Yamoun/JENIN	Aug 16
220.	Jamal Odeh, 19	TULKARM	Aug 15
219.	Mahmud Abu Rizq, 20	Shaboura/GAZA	Aug 14
218.	Moh'd Abu Rizak, 52	Shaboura/GAZA	Aug 13
217.	Yusef Damaj, 12	Jenin RC/JENIN	Aug 13
216.	Riad Salman Abu Mandil, 26	Mghazi RC/GAZA	Aug 11
215.	Ahmad Faleh Ali Abu Salah, 17	Toubas/JENIN	Aug 10
214.	Hussein Hassan Asway, 14	KALKILYA	Aug 9
213.	Nidal AbdulKarim Bouzieh, 16	Kufl Haress/TULKARM	Aug 5
212.	Ala'addin al-Aghbar, 18	NABLUS	Aug 2
211.	Hani Adel a-Turk, 37	Gaza City/GAZA	Jul 28
210.	Abdel Fattah Yusef Alayan, 17	Deir Abu Daif/JENIN	Jul 27
209.	Suheir Fouad Afani, 13	Shatti RC/GAZA	Jul 26
208.	Yasser Hanun Sabaana, 25	Qabatya/JENIN	Jul 24
207.	Jiryis Yuseis Qunqar, 43	Beit Jala/BETHLEHEM	Jul 24
206.	Hussam Abdul Aziz, 23	Old City/NABLUS	Jul 21
205.	Maher Abu Ghazaleh, 24	Old City/NABLUS	Jul 21
204.	Muhanid Ahmad Taher Saif, 17	Arara/TRIANGLE	Jul 21
203.	Fuad Bassam Urrabi, 16	JENIN	Jul 20
202.	Hisham Khaled Zeid, 26	Qiferet/JENIN	Jul 20
201.	Zaki Ali Halaika, 23	Shuyukh/KHALIL	Jul 20
200.	Nidal Rabbadi, 16	Old City/QUDS	Jul 19
199.	Jamal Jawdat AbdulKarim Qaddoumi, 29	Ein Beit Ma'/NABLUS	Jul 18
198.	Samir Sayeh, 13	NABLUS	Jul 14
197.	Amjad Khawaja, 17	NABLUS	Jul 13
196.	Hassan Ahmad Jabber 'Adis, 16	Anabta/NABLUS	Jul 11
195.	Faris Rashid Anabtawi, 17	NABLUS	Jul 11
194.	Zuhdi Mansour Zreiki, 17	Old Askar RC/NABLUS	Jul 10
193.	Fayek Sleiman Radwan Hussein, 25	Jabalya RC/GAZA	Jul 9
192.	Abdul Qader Qasem Dababat, 17	Tubas/JENIN	Jul 8
191.	Na'el Khameisa, 17	Zbuba/JENIN	Jul 2
190.	Fatmeh Yusef Sahwil, 26	Ibwein/RAMALLAH	Jul 1
189.	Arafat Ahmad Hanani, 16	Beit Furiq/NABLUS	Jun 30
188.	Ibrahim Ghassan Aranqi, 15	Taibe/RAMALLAH	Jun 29
187.	Taalat Khalil Zaqqout, 17	Rafah/GAZA	Jun 22
186.	Raed Khaled Haj Yusef, 17	Khan Yunis RC/ GAZA	Jun 18
185.	Taysir Hussein Blitat, 27	Beit Furiq/NABLUS	Jun 17
184.	Nidal Ibrahim Abu Hassan, 20	Battir/BETHLEHEM	Jun 15
183.	Deib Mahmud Hamad, 45	Ibwein/RAMALLAH	Jun 13
182.	Bassem Issa Sabbagh, 21	Jenin RC/JENIN	Jun 12
181.	Saed Moh'd Hayek, 18	EinSultan RC/JERICHO	Jun 12
180.	Imad Hussan Hawari, 16	Sebastia/NABLUS	Jun 9
179.	Mustafa Ahmad Odeh Halaika, 19	Shuyukh/KHALIL	Jun 3
178.	Moh'd Issa Ghanem, 26	Deir Ibzia'/RAMALLAH	Jun 3

#	Name, Age	Residence	Date
177.	In'am Rafiq Hamdan, 25	Jaba'/NABLUS	May 29
176.	Iyad Abdallah Shanaa', 16	Qalqilya/TULKARM	May 27
175.	Amin Rajab Abu Radaha, 14	Jalazon RC/RAMALLAH	May 27
174.	Moh'd Saadi Abu Lulu, 57	Breij RC/GAZA	May 24
173.	Kawthar Khaled Mohammad, 23	Tulkarm RC/TULKARM	May 21
172.	Majdi Mahmud Hillal,16	Ibwein/RAMALLAH	May 18
171.	Jihad Bassan Issi, 16	Jabalya RC/GAZA	May 16
170.	Ala'addin Moh'd Saleh, 15	Azmut/NABLUS	May 16
169.	Mahmud Abu Zeid, 33	Qabatya/JENIN	May 12
168.	Abdul Karim Raja Mu'ti, 21	Asakreh/BETHLEHEM	May 11
167.	Ibrahim Ahmad Hussein Odeh, 35	Dheishe RC/BETHLEHEM	May 9
166.	Judah Abdallah Taiyem, 28	Turmus Aya/RAMALLAH	May 5
165.	Jamal Mahmud Madhun, 20	Jabalya RC/GAZA	May 4
164.	Rizek Hussein Sabah, 16	Jabalya RC/GAZA	May 4
163.	Omar Moh'd Manasra, 18	Bani Naim/KHALIL	May 3
162.	Nidal Salem Balo, 19	Bani Naim/KHALIL	May 3
161.	Khaled Rafiq Umayrah, 25	Balata RC/NALBUS	May 3
160.	Naim Yusef AbuFarha, 22	Faqua/JENIN	May 1
159.	Sari Hillal Rustum, 35	Kfur Malek/RAMALLAH	Apr 28
158.	Arij Sleiman Daud aDik, 13	Kfur aDik/NABLUS	Apr 27
157.	Ahmad Hassan Salem, 27	Beit Arroush/KHALIL	Apr 24
156.	Moh'd Ibrahim Abu Zeid, 16	Qabatya/JENIN	Apr 23
155.	Moh'd Fayez Abu Ali, 25	Bani Suheila/GAZA	Apr 22
154.	Faraj Ismail Farrajallah, 23	Idna/KHALIL	Apr 22
153.	Moh'd Hassan Nassar, 22	Nuseirat RC/GAZA	Apr 20
152.	Ayda Othman Totah, 30	Zeitun/GAZA	Apr 18
151.	Ahmed Musa Zurub Abu Eiyeh, 20	Rafah/GAZA	Apr 18
150.	Nizar Ahmad Jaloudi, 26	Faqua/JENIN	Apr 18
149.	Iman Omar Abu Kamar, 22	Khan Yunis/GAZA	Apr 17
148.	Farid Ahmad Abu Darras, 25	Khan Yunis/GAZA	Apr 17
147.	Munir Ismail alTatari, 24	Jabalya/GAZA	Apr 16
146.	Jamal Hussein Shehadeh, 17	Breij RC/GAZA	Apr 16
145.	Taysin alBouji, 16	Rafah/GAZA	Apr 16
144.	Atwa Abu Arada Sha'er, 14	Rafah/GAZA	Apr 16
143.	Ayman Abu Amer, 22	Rafah/GAZA	Apr 16
142.	Abdul Muhsen Hanun, 19	Khan Yunis/GAZA	Apr 16
141.	Fikri Ibrahim alDaghmi, 22	Abasan/GAZA	Apr 16
140.	Bassam alHariri, 23	Jenin RC/JENIN	Apr 16
139.	Saadah Malek Sabah, 40	Jenin RC/JENIN	Apr 16
138.	Hilmi Abdallah Turukman, 22	JENIN	Apr 16
137.	Mihyi Addin Mawalha, 20	Qabatya/JENIN	Apr 16
136.	Hala Awad Amiri, 20	Habla/TULKARM	Apr 16
135.	Wael Hassan Taha, 25	NABLUS	Apr 14
134.	Nasser Hamed alLidawi, 22	NABLUS	Apr 14
133.	Jalal Yusef Milhem, 21	Kufr Rai/JENIN	Apr 11
132.	Moh'd Kamel AbdulQadr Yahia,20	Kufr Rai/JENIN	Apr 11
131.	Fuad Aziz Saleh Ashqar, 21	Kufr Rai/JENIN	Apr 11
130.	Yusef Rabi', 75	Deir Abu Mash'al/RAM	Apr 8
129.	Issam Abdul Halim Said, 16	Beita/NABLUS	Apr 7
128.	Musa Saleh Daud Bani Shamsa,22	Beita/NABLUS	Apr 6
127.	Hatem Fayez Ahmad alJabber, 22	Beita/NABLUS	Apr 6

#	Name, Age	Residence	Date
126.	Hamed Abdul Muhidi Ze'dat, 18	Bani N'eim/KHALIL	Apr 4
125.	Hamzeh Ibrahim AbuShab,20	Bani Sulheila/GAZA	Apr 4
124.	Ali Diab Abu Ali, 46	Yatta/KHALIL	Apr 3
123.	Salim Khalef Sha'er, 23	BETHLEHEM	Apr 2
122.	Jihad Mustafa 'Assi, 18	Beit Liqya/RAMALLAH	Apr 2
121.	Khamis Hassan Ahmad, 38	Deir Sudan/RAMALLAH	Apr 2
120.	Jamil Rashed Kurdi, 55	Sabra/GAZA	Apr 2
119.	Ahmad Khamis Kurdi, 42-father	Sabra/GAZA	Apr 2
118.	Ala' Ahmad Kurdi, 21-son	Sabra/GAZA	Apr 2
117.	Jamal Khalil Tumeizi, 22	Idna/KHALIL	Apr 1
116.	Ishaq Nimer Silmiyeh, 24	Idna/KHALIL	Apr 1
115.	Sleiman Ahmad Awwad Jneidi, 18	Yatta/KHALIL	Mar 31
114.	Moh'd Fares Hamed Ziben, 29	Yamun/JENIN	Mar 31
113.	Wajiha Yusef Rabi', 55	Deir AbuMash'al/RAM	Mar 30
112.	Shaker Ali Moh'd Shaker, 26	Deir Ibzia'/RAMALLAH	Mar 30
111.	Khaled Moh'd Qassem Salah,23	Burqa/NABLUS	Mar 30
110.	AbdulKarim Moh'd Halaika, 24	Shyukh/KHALIL	Mar 30
109.	Hussein Mahmud Hussein, 25	Yamoun/JENIN	Mar 30
108.	Ghassan Qassem Awad Mir'i,17	Maythaloun/JENIN	Mar 27
107.	Omar Mahmoud Hamad Rabai'ah,22	Maythaloun/JENIN	Mar 27
106.	Fahim Mah. Moh'd Nuseirat,27	Maythaloun/JENIN	Mar 27
105.	Yasser As'ad Ibrahim As'ad,15	Salfit/NABLUS	Mar 27
104.	Hussein Kamel Odeh, 19	Salfit/NABLUS	Mar 27
103.	Ayad Turki Salah(Khalil), 21	Zawateh/NABLUS	Mar 26
102.	Majed Hussein Deeb, 19	Kufr Thaleth/TULKARM	Mar 26
101.	Awad Qassem Ibrahim, 30	Kufr Thaleth/TULKARM	Mar 26
100.	Walid Abdul Fatah Fatafta, 18	Tarkumia/KHALIL	Mar 25
99.	Khaled Hassan Muraqtan, 18	Tarkumia/KHALIL	Mar 25
98.	Hikmat Daraghmeh, 26	Tubas/JENIN	Mar 24
97.	Majed Sawalmeh, 22	Balata RC/NABLUS	Mar 24
96.	Muhamed Ali Abu Zaru, 22	Balata RC/NABLUS	Mar 24
95.	Adel Ahmed Jaber, 18	Rafah/GAZA	Mar 21
94.	Nameq Hussein Milhem, 26	Kufr Dan/JENIN	Mar 20
93.	Khaled Moh'd Taher Hussein,23	Nazlit Issa/TULKARM	Mar 20
92.	Hani Ibrahim Abu Hammam, 23	Shati RC/GAZA	Mar 18
91.	Sabri Abu Sharar, 25	Khan Yunis/GAZA	Mar 17
90.	Hisham Daud aLushi, 31	Nazlit Issa/TULKARM	Mar 16
89.	Omar Yassin Hamarsheh, 27	Yaabad/JENIN	Mar 16
88.	Ashraf Mahmud Ibrahim, 22	Nur Shams RC/TULKARM	Mar 16
87.	Alam Said Nasrallah Sadaqa, 16	Anza/JENIN	Mar 15
86.	Arafat Abdul Aziz Hweih, 22	Ein Yabroud/RAMALLAH	Mar 15
85.	Yusef Ibrahim Ali Abu Eid, 22	Biddu/RAMALLAH	Mar 12
84.	Khader Mohammad Hamideh, 41	Mazraa Sharqiya/RAM	Mar 9
83.	Najeh Hassan Hijaz, 18	Turmus Aya/RAMALLAH	Mar 9
82.	Moh'd Othman Hamed, 17	Silwad/RAMALLAH	Mar 9
81.	Bassam Ibrahim Badarin, 18	Samou'/KHALIL	Mar 9
80.	Ayman Salim Ajaq, 17	Mazraa Sharqiya/RAM	Mar 6
79.	Rasem Mudhahi Khadirat Atlul,28	Dhahariyeh/KHALIL	Mar 5
78.	Mahel Musbah Waridat, 30	Dhahariyeh/KHALIL	Mar 5
77.	Mohammad Sa'afin, 22	Breij RC/GAZA	Mar 5
76.	Moh'd Ahmad Hussein Salah, 18	Khader/BETHLEHEM	Mar 4

#	Name, Age	Residence	Date
75.	Bakr Abdul Latif Shibani, 17	Araba/JENIN	Mar 4
74.	Yasser Daoud AbdulJabbar Abd,17	Borin/NABLUS	Feb 29
73.	Nihad AbdulGhaffar Khmour, 20	Aroub RC/KHALIL	Feb 27
72.	Baker Abdallah Bo, 17	Halhoul/KHALIL	Feb 27
71.	Majed Moh'd Atrash, 22	Halhoul/KHALIL	Feb 27
70.	Raed Mahmud Awad Barghuthi, 17	Aboud/RAMALLAH	Feb 27
69.	Ahmad Ibrahim Barghuthi, 21	Aboud/RAMALLAH	Feb 27
68.	Ahmad Dhiab Bitawi, 30	Jenin RC/JENIN	Feb 27
67.	Rashiqa Musleh Daraghmeh, 63	Tubas/JENIN	Feb 26
66.	Hassan Mohammad AbuKheiran, 22	Aroub RC/KHALIL	Feb 26
65.	Iyad alAshqar, 13	Jabalya RC/GAZA	Feb 26
64.	Issam Abu Khalifeh, 18	Jenin RC/JENIN	Feb 25
63.	Sami Ghaleb Dayeh, 19	NABLUS	Feb 25
62.	Mohammad Qassem Abu Zeid, 4	Qabatya/JENIN	Feb 24
61.	Rawda Lutfi Najib Hassan, 13	Baka Sharqiyeh/TULK	Feb 22
60.	Mahmud Nu'man Hushiyeh, 23	Yamun/JENIN	Feb 22
59.	Kamal Moh'd Darwish, 23	Deir Amaar/RAMALLAH	Feb 21
58.	Ragheb Sleiman Abu Ammara, 19	NABLUS	Feb 21
57.	Abdallah Atta Ataya, 19	Kufr Ni'meh/RAMALLAH	Feb 20
56.	Nasrallah AbdalQader Nasrallah, 12	Tulkarm RC/TULKARM	Feb 20
55.	Isma'il Halaiqa Mashni, 22	Shyukh/KHALIL	Feb 17
54.	Bashar Ahmad alMa'di, 20	NABLUS	Feb 12
53.	Basem Taysir alJitan, 14	NABLUS	Feb 12
52.	Ahmad Abu Sabil, 37	Tulkarm RC/TULKARM	Feb 11
51.	Imad Hamalawi, 20	Mghazi RC/GAZA	Feb 10
50.	Nabil Abu Khalil, 14	Attil/TULKARM	Feb 9
49.	Abdul Basset Juma', 27	Kufr Qaddum/NABLUS	Feb 8
48.	Imad Khader Sabarneh, 26	Beit Ommar/KHALIL	Feb 7
47.	Moh'd Ibrahim Shweiha Adi, 18	Beit Ommar/KHALIL	Feb 7
46.	Tayseer Abdallah Awad, 18	Beit Ommar/KHALIL	Feb 7
45.	Thamer Jalal Disuqi, 10	Burqa/NABLUS	Feb 6
44.	Ibrahim Mansour, 26	Balaa/TULKARM	Feb 3
43.	Asmaa Ibrahim Sabbubeh, 25	Anabta/TULKARM	Feb 2
42.	Murad Bassem Hamdallah, 17	Anabta/TULKARM	Feb 1
41.	Muaiyad Moh'd Sha'ar, 21	Anabta/TULKARM	Feb 1
40.	Ibrahim Abu Nahel, 31	Sheikh Radwan/GAZA	Jan 15
39.	Moh'd Ramadan Tubaza, 18	Nuseirat RC/GAZA	Jan 15
38.	Ahmad Ali Ibayyat Ta'amreh, 43	Cissan/BETHLEHEM	Jan 14
37.	Hussein Mustafa Ma'ali, 19	Kufr Ni'meh/RAMALLAH	Jan 13
36.	Ramadan Sobeih, 14	Beit Lahiya/GAZA	Jan 13
35.	Mohammad Yusef Yazuri, 30	Rafah/GAZA	Jan 12
34.	Bassel Yazuri, 23	Rafah RC/GAZA	Jan 11
33.	Mohammad Fayad, 20	Khan Yunis/GAZA	Jan 11
32.	Atta Mustafa Khdeir, 26	Khan Yunis/GAZA	Jan 11
31.	Rabeh Ghannam Hamed, 17	Bittin/RAMALLAH	Jan 11
30.	Touqan Misbeh, 32	Shuja'iyeh/GAZA	Jan 10
29.	Naji Hassan Ali (Kamil), 43	Qabatya/JENIN	Jan 10
28.	Bassam Khader Abu Musalem, 27	Khan Yunis RC/GAZA	Jan 9
27.	Khalil Isma'il Abu Luli, 54	Rafah/GAZA	Jan 9
26.	Khaled Awawdeh, 22	Briej RC/GAZA	Jan 8
25.	Mazen Ismail Musallam, 17	Maghazi RC/GAZA	Jan 7

#	Name, Age	Residence	Date
24.	Ali Moh'd Dahlan, 19	Khan Yunis RC/GAZA	Jan 5
23.	Haniyeh Ghazawneh, 25	Ram/JERUSALEM	Jan 3
22.	Mustafa alBeik, 19	Jabalya RC/GAZA	Dec 29
21.	Khaled Taleb Hameed, 20	Jabalya RC/GAZA	Dec 22
20.	Raed Shihadeh, 16	Shati RC/GAZA	Dec 21
19.	Nazek Ahmad Sawafta, 17	Tubas/JENIN	Dec 21
18.	Bassem Faisal Sawafta, 19	Tubas/JENIN	Dec 21
17.	Yusef Moh'd Ararawi, 24	Jenin RC/JENIN	Dec 21
16.	Mahmoud Qeisi, 19	Jenin RC/JENIN	Dec 21
15.	Abdul Salam Fteiha, 29	Breij RC/GAZA	Dec 18
14.	Maisara Hamdan Batniji, 26	Shuja'iyeh/GAZA	Dec 18
13.	Atwa Abu Samhadaneh, 20	Rafah/GAZA	Dec 16
12.	Abdul Malek Abu Hussein, 23	Khan Yunis RC/GAZA	Dec 15
11.	Khaled Abu Taqiyeh, 22	Jabalya RC/GAZA	Dec 15
10.	Ibrahim Mahmud Sakhleh, 25	Jabalya RC/GAZA	Dec 15
9.	Talal Hweiwi, 17	Beit Hanoun/GAZA	Dec 15
8.	Nafez AbuQteifan, 16	Deir Balah RC/GAZA	Dec 15
7.	Hassan Moh'd Jarghun, 22	Khan Yunis/GAZA	Dec 14
6.	Sahar Jirmi, 19	Balata RC/NABLUS	Dec 11
5.	Ali Isma'il Abdallah, 13	Balata RC/NABLUS	Dec 11
4.	Suhaila Ka'bi, 53	Balata RC/NABLUS	Dec 11
3.	Wahid Abu Salem, 13	Khan Yunis/GAZA	Dec 10
2.	Ibrahim Ekeik, 18	NABLUS	Dec 10
1.	Hatem Sissi, 15	Jabalya RC/GAZA	Dec 9

Palestinians Killed by Beating, Burning, Electrocution or Stoning

#	Name, Age	Residence	Date
37.	Marwan Salim Qaneiri, 27	Yaabad/KHALIL	Nov 23
36.	Ibrahim Yasser Matur, 32	Sair/KHALIL	Oct 19
35.	Ayman Ahmad Najar, 28	Shaboura/GAZA	Aug 31
34.	Hanni Shammi, 49	Jabalya/GAZA	Aug 22
33.	Maysara Ahmad Mattar, 25	Sheikh Radwan/GAZA	Aug 21
32.	Nabil Mustafa Bedah, 20	Beit Hanina/QUDS	Aug 16
31.	Nasim Ibrahim 'Abed, 26	Mghazi RC/GAZA	Aug 15
30.	Hisham Jamil Muqdad, 23	Shati RC/GAZA	Aug 14
29.	Atta Ahmad Ayyad, 21	Qalandya RC/QUDS	Aug 14
28.	Maher Darwish Maqqab, 28	Shati RC/GAZA	Aug 14
27.	Said Saleh 'Abed, 20	Tel Sultan/GAZA	Aug 11
26.	Khalil Mustafa 'Abadli, 41	Khan Yunis/GAZA	Aug 10
25.	Simone Elias Issa Ghannam, 17	Beit Sahour/BETHLEHEM	Jul 18
24.	Saber Faris Nimnim, 23	Shati RC/GAZA	Jul 16
23.	Hussein Juma' AbuJalaleh, 20	Jabalya RC/GAZA	Jun 7
22.	Ayad Abu Nadi, 25	Shati RC/GAZA	Jun 5
21.	Husni Moh'd Mahsiri, 41	Beit Jala/BETHLEHEM	May 16
20.	Ibrahim Abu Aishe, 71	KHALIL	May 15

#	Name, Age	Residence	Date
19.	Atiyeh Abu Risq, 19	Rafah/GAZA	Apr 21
18.	Suad Ahmed Yusef, 90	Zeitun/GAZA	Apr 12
17.	Ibrahim Mahmud Rai Zeid, 28	Qalqilya/TULKARM	Apr 11
16.	Khalil Khamzawi, 18	Askar RC/NABLUS	Apr 3
15.	Omar Hassan AbuMarahil, 27	Beit Lehiya/GAZA	Mar 21
14.	Moh'd Rahman Hamed, 24	Silwad/RAMALLAH	Mar 19
13.	Moh'd Mahmud Khaled, 19	EinBeitalMa RC/NABLUS	Mar 18
12.	Mohammad Skafi, 4	Shuja'iyeh/GAZA	Mar 12
11.	Kamleh Mahmud Sharaf, 60	Breij RC/GAZA	Mar 11
10.	Khaled Moh'd Ardha, 21	Old Askar/NABLUS	Mar 6
9.	Yusef Tawfiq Kilani, 21	Ya'abad/JENIN	Feb 25
8.	Anwar Amireh, 27	Bireh/RAMALLAH	Feb 23
7.	Moh'd Juma' Ra'i Shweideh, 68	Shujaiyeh/GAZA	Feb 14
6.	Khader Elias Tarazi, 19	Gaza City/GAZA	Feb 9
5.	Ayad Mohammad Aqel, 17	Breij RC/GAZA	Feb 7
4.	Rami Aklouk, 15	Deir Balah/GAZA	Feb 7
3.	Mohammad Mahmud Badran, 34	Jabalya/GAZA	Feb 4
2.	Mohammad Mahmoud Ibeid, 28	Ram/JERUSALEM	Jan 30
1.	Subhiyeh Darwish Hashash, 55	Balata RC/NABLUS	Jan 18

Palestinians Killed By Teargas

#	Name, Age	Residence	Date
66.	Ibrahim Mahmud Hamdiyeh, 80	Yamoun/JENIN	Dec 3
65.	Nasreen Jihad Nawajhah, 3	Khan Yunis/GAZA	Oct 26
64.	Qawqar Hamdallah Arrar, 17	Jaljuliya/TRIANGLE	Oct 15
63.	Moh'd Sharif Aza, 2	Qadoura/RAMALLAH	Sep 7
62.	Ala' Abu Ful, 12	Shatti/GAZA	Aug 23
61.	Khalil Yusef Ba'alushi, 52	Jabalya/GAZA	Aug 22
60.	Ghalia Ahmed Ali AbdulNabi, 31	Jabalya/GAZA	Aug 21
59.	Ansar Moh'd Heju, 65	Shatti/GAZA	Aug 16
58.	Thaer Adnan Badr, 25 days	Jabalya RC/GAZA	Jul 24
57.	Moh'd Khaled Sha'abilo, 35	Rafidiyeh/NABLUS	Jun 30
56.	Tawfiq Jaafer Malamha, 55	Qabatya/JENIN	Jun 30
55.	Abdallah Khaled Mubarak, ?	Ezzariyeh/BETHLEHEM	Jun 8
54.	Maisa Jaffal, 40 days	Dhahiriyeh/KHALIL	Jun 8
53.	Dina Munir aSawafri, 3	Zaitoun/GAZA	May 27
52.	Khaled Hasan Najar, 55	Shati RC/GAZA	May 4
51.	Naima Moh'd 'Adi, 55	Beit Ummar/KHALIL	Apr 24
50.	Moh'd Samhan AbdulQader Samhan, 52	RasKarkar/RAMALLAH	Apr 24
49.	Moh'd Musa Hamad, 30	Silwad/RAMALLAH	Apr 23
48.	Ismail Abu Sheikh, 50	Qalqilya/TULKARM	Apr 20
47.	Jamal Hussein Alqam, 3 days	Shu'fat	Apr 17
46.	Farid Tawfiq Amarneh, 11	Yaabad/JENIN	Apr 17
45.	Wadfa Faraj Allah, 70	Jabalya RC/GAZA	Apr 13
44.	Hassan Mahmud Qaud, 22	Shati RC/GAZA	Apr 12
43.	Subhiyeh Rashid Mankush, 60	Shati RC/GAZA	Apr 9
42.	Rajab Ahmad Slaibi, 75	Shati RC/GAZA	Apr 4

#	Name, Age	Residence	Date
41.	Hamid Abdallah Asmadi, 20 days	Qabatya/JENIN	Apr 2
40.	Shirin Ali Maniarawi, 1 mos.	Rafah RC/GAZA	Mar 29
39.	Nabila Ali Yajizi, 30	Sheikh Radwan/GAZA	Mar 26
38.	Hussein Fares Iqmeil, 70	Qabatya/JENIN	Mar 21
37.	Ola Omar Abu Sharifa, 4 mos.	Shati RC/GAZA	Mar 19
36.	Ali Moh'd Abu Hajjar, 70	Jabalya RC/GAZA	Mar 18
35.	Mustafa Froukh, 68	Shati RC/GAZA	Mar 18
34.	Salim al Yahia, 60	TULKARM	Mar 16
33.	Juma' Ibrahim alTukhi, 66	alAmari RC/RAMALLAH	Mar 16
32.	Yahia alMaghrabi, 2 mos.	Zeitun/GAZA	Mar 13
31.	Sanaar Samir Ebeid, 40 days	Khan Yunis RC/GAZA	Mar 9
30.	Yusef Hassuna, 3 mos.	Deir Balah RC/GAZA	Mar 8
29.	Khaled Mustafa Hawajreh, 2.5 mos.	Breij RC/GAZA	Mar 8
28.	Shirin AbdulMunem Elayan, 4 mos.	Deir Balah RC/GAZA	Mar 8
27.	Salahaddin Naqib, 33	Askar RC/NABLUS	Mar 7
26.	Salim Moh'd Musa Amer, 10 mos.	Khan Yunis/GAZA	May 7
25.	Khitam Sabri 'Aram, 8	Rafah/GAZA	Mar 3
24.	Salman Daher, 63	Baka Sharqiyeh/TULKARM	Mar 2
23.	Fuad Aiyub Sha'rawi, 48	KHALIL	Feb 26
22.	Ranin Yusef Sfair, 3 mos.	Rafah/GAZA	Feb 21
21.	Ahmad Sadek Abu Sahiyeh, 65	NABLUS	Feb 21
20.	Rana Mahmud Adwan, 3 mos.	Rafah RC/GAZA	Feb 17
19.	Arafat Moh'd Abu Rous, 6 mos.	Rafah RC/GAZA	Feb 17
18.	Fatima Salman, 57	Beit Safafa/BETHLEHEM	Jan 23
17.	Amneh Darwish, 72	GAZA	Jan 15
16.	Haitham Shqeiro, 4 mos.	Qalqilya/TULKARM	Jan 16
15.	Abdul Fattah Miskawi, 2 mos.	Qalqilya/TULKARM	Jan 16
14.	Samer Ali Juma'a Badaha, 5 mos.	Deir Amaar RC/RAMALLAH	Jan 14
13.	Imad Hamdi Abu Asi, 15 days	Zeitun Qtr/GAZA	Jan 14
12.	Moh'd Khaled Shahin, 75 days	Zeitun Qtr/GAZA	Jan 14
11.	Moh'd Ramadan Tubbaza, 17	Nuseirat RC/GAZA	Jan 14
10.	Fayrouz Ahmad Shobaki, 11	Deir Amaar RC/RAMALLAH	Jan 13
9.	Amira Askar, 35	abalya RC/GAZA	Jan 11
8.	Wijdan Faress, fetus	Khan Yunis/GAZA	Jan 10
7.	Mariam Abu Zahir, 81	Jabalya RC/GAZA	Jan 2
6.	Raed Obeid, 3 mos.	Jabalya RC/GAZA	Jan 1
5.	Amal Abdul Wahad Qseisa, 5days	Jabalya RC/GAZA	Dec 23
4.	Khaled alQidri, 14 days	Khan Yunis/GAZA	Dec 23
3.	Khalil Mahsiri, 76	Bireh/RAMALLAH	Dec 18
2.	Najwa Masri, 18	Beit Hanoun/GAZA	Dec 15
1.	Fatmeh alQidri, 1 day	Khan Yunis/GAZA	Dec 9

Palestinians Killed Under Suspicious Circumstances or Indirect Official Responsibility

#	Name, Age	Residence	Date
43.	Nawal Abu Thuriya, 52	Shati RC/GAZA	Nov 24
42.	Omar AbdulQader AbuSa'ker,	?	Nov 3
41.	Nimr Moh'd Mahmud Najjar, 17	Yatta/KHALIL	Oct 28
40.	Jawad Othman Amr, 44	KHALIL	Oct 19
39.	Rajeb Abu Rajeb Tamimi Moh'd Isma'il, 47	KHALIL	Oct 19
38.	Salem Mussah Naji Amr, 45	KHALIL	Oct 19
37.	Rami Madah, 13	Jaljuliya/TRIANGLE	Oct 14
36.	Riad Madah, 18	Jaljuliya/TRIANGLE	Oct 14
35.	Ibrahim Shamali, 47	Jabalya RC/GAZA	Oct 11
34.	Nasser Jamal Abu Thabet, 22	Balatta RC/NABLUS	Sep 29
33.	Inad Ahmad Mustafa Shalabi,43	Mazra'Sharqiyeh/RAMALLAH	Sep 22
32.	Salah Mustafa Kasab, 22	Sheja'iya/GAZA	Sep 11
31.	Miryam Yacoub Khouri, 65	Abboud/RAMALLAH	Aug 26
30.	Jalal Abu Khadijeh, 24	RAMALLAH	Aug 4
29.	Ribhi Barakat Kaid, 61	Columbus, OHIO, USA	Jul 30
28.	Moh'd Said Khaled Kitaneh, 25	Nazlit Issa/TULKARM	Jul 23
27.	Ma'azuz AbdulRahman Yamin, 25	Jeet/TULKARM	Jul 17
26.	Musa Omar, 45	Bouroqin/TULKARM	Jul 16
25.	Khadera Abdallah Awwad, 21	Turmos Aya/RAMALLAH	Jun 26
24.	Ahmed Tawfiq Sh'alan, 12	Dheishe RC/BETHLEHEM	Jun 12
23.	Rahi Moh'd alLahaliyeh, 41	Sa'ir/KHALIL	Jun 9
22.	Majdi Abu Safaka, 12	TULKARM	Jun 1
21.	Moh'd Saleh Qaadan, 35	Deir Ghusoun/TULKARM	May 21
20.	Shamseh Qaadan, 65	Deir Ghusoun/TULKARM	May 21
19.	Hassan Abdu Buhi, 80	EinBeitalMa/NABLUS	May 2
18.	Nidal Abu Shomar, 17	Beit Wazzan/NABLUS	May 1
17.	Badriyeh Sader Shahin, 55	NABLUS	Apr 15
16.	Ma'mun Jarad, 16	TULKARM	Apr 3
15.	Salah Khader Damuni, 60	Qabatya/JENIN	Mar ?
14.	Abdul Nasser Abu Shamaleh, 22	Deir Balah/GAZA	Mar 27
13.	Nawaf Abu Shamaleh, 24	Deir Balah/GAZA	Mar 27
12.	Abdul Wahab Abu Shamaleh, 25	Deir Balah/GAZA	Mar 27
11.	Nu'am Ibrahim Abed, 26	Deir Balah/GAZA	Mar 27
10.	Salah alAtaar, 22	Rafah RC/GAZA	Mar 15
9.	Atef Fayad, 30	Khan Yunis/GAZA	Feb 23
8.	Nabil Abu Orti, 25	Shati RC/GAZA	Feb 20
7.	Asmaa Moh'd Sharif, 18	Aroub RC/KHALIL	Feb 6
6.	Um Rabeh Hussein Hamed, ?	Bittin/RAMALLAH	Jan 11
5.	Abdallah Abdul Nabi, 70	Old Askar RC/NABLUS	Dec 25
4.	Issam Hamoudi, 29	Jabalya RC/GAZA	Dec 8
3.	Taleb Abu Zeid, 46	Mghazi RC/GAZA	Dec 8
2.	Ali Mahmud Isma'il, 31	Jabalya RC/GAZA	Dec 8
1.	Shaaban Nabhan, 26	Jabalya RC/GAZA	Dec 8

Appendix II

Communiques from the Unified National Leadership of the Uprising

Since the intifada began, its clandestine leadership has communicated with the people of the occupied West Bank and Gaza Strip by means of a series of nida' ("communiques," "appeal" or "call"). These are secretly printed and distributed inside the occupied territories and then broadcast by radio stations in Damascus and Baghdad. The first was issued on January 8, 1988. From no. 3 (January 18, 1988) onward, all the communiques have been signed by the "Palestine Liberation Organization—Unified National Leadership of the Palestinian Uprising in the Occupied Territories."

The source of almost all the communiques reproduced here—some of which we have excerpted—is the Foreign Broadcast Information Service, an arm of the Central Intelligence Agency which monitors radio stations worldwide and publishes translations of important broadcasts. Some of the communiques were monitored on the "Voice of the PLO" broadcasting from Baghdad, while others were monitored on "al-Quds Palestinian Arab Radio" in Damascus. The source makes a difference, because the Damascus station has been known to alter the text of the communiques it broadcasts in order to bring them into line with the positions of the Syrian government, which controls the station and is hostile to the current leadership of the PLO. By contrast, the Voice of the PLO in Baghdad has been much more consistent about broadcasting the communiques exactly as they were formulated by the Unified National Leadership.

Following communique no. 19, we have included a "Message to the Arab Summit," issued c. June 7, 1988 and directed to the conference of Arab heads of state about to convene in Algiers to discuss the uprising and its consequences.

We have also included an "Appeal to Israeli Voters" which the Unified National Leadership issued in late October 1988, shortly before Israel's general elections.

Aware of the effectiveness of the communiques, whose printing and distribution it has not been able to stop, the Israeli security service (Shin Bet) has at times resorted to putting out its own fake communiques in order to mislead and confuse the people of the occupied territories. We have included, following communique no.

26, an excerpt from one of these fake leaflets. This false version of no. 28, issued in anticipation of the convening of the Palestine National Council, was clearly designed to sow confusion and divide the Palestinians under occupation from the PLO leadership. It should be compared with the authentic text of communique no. 28 that follows it. The final communique included here is no. 29, issued after the PNC meeting in Algiers proclaimed the establishment of an independent State of Palestine.

Communique no. 1

January 8, 1988

In the name of God, the merciful, the compassionate.

Our people's glorious uprising continues. We affirm the need to express solidarity with our people wherever they are. We continue to be loyal to the pure blood of our martyrs and to our detained brothers. We also reiterate our rejection of the occupation and its policy of repression, represented in the policy of deportation, mass arrests, curfews, and the demolition of houses.

We reaffirm the need to achieve further cohesion with our revolution and our heroic masses. We also stress our abidance by the call of the PLO, the Palestinian people's legitimate and sole representative, and the need to pursue the bountiful offerings and the heroic uprising. For all these reasons, we address the following call:

All sectors of our heroic people in every location should abide by the call for a general and comprehensive strike until Wednesday evening, 13 January 1988. The strike covers all public and private trade utilities, the Palestinian workers and public transportation. Abidance by the comprehensive strike must be complete. The slogan of the strike will be: Down with occupation; long live Palestine as a free and Arab country.

Brother workers, your abidance by the strike by not going to work and to plants is real support for the glorious uprising, a sanctioning of the pure blood of our martyrs, a support for the call to liberate our prisoners, and an act that will help keep our brother deportees in their homeland.

Brother businessmen and grocers, you must fully abide by the call for a comprehensive strike during the period of the strike. Your abidance by previous strikes is one of the most splendid images of solidarity and sacrifice for the sake of rendering our heroic people's stand a success.

We will do our best to protect the interests of our honest businessmen against measures the Zionist occupation force may resort to against you. We warn against the consequences of becoming involved with some of the occupation authorities' henchmen who will seek to make you open your businesses. We promise you that we will punish such traitor businessmen in the not too distant future. Let us proceed united to forge victory.

Brother owners of taxi companies, we will not forget your honorable and splendid stand of supporting and implementing the comprehensive strike on the day of Palestinian steadfastness. We pin our hopes on you to support and make the comprehensive strike a success. We warn some bus companies against the consequences of not abiding by the call for the strike, as this will make them liable to revolutionary punishment.

Brother doctors and pharmacists, you must be on emergency status to offer assistance to those of our kinfolk who are ill. The brother pharmacists must carry out their duties normally. The brother doctors must place the doctor badge in a way that can be clearly identified.

General warning: We would like to warn people that walking in the streets will not be safe in view of the measures that will be taken to make the comprehensive strike a success. We warn that viscous material will be poured on main and secondary streets and everywhere, in addition to the roadblocks and the strike groups that will be deployed throughout the occupied homeland.

Circular: The struggler and brother members of the popular committees and the men of the uprising who are deployed in all the working locations should work to support and assist our people within the available means, particularly the needy families of our people. The strike groups and the popular uprising groups must completely abide by the working program, which is in their possession. Let us proceed united and loudly chant: Down with occupation; long live Palestine as a free and Arab country.

Communique no. 2

January 13, 1988

O masses of our great people. O people of martyrs, grandsons of al-Qassam. O brothers and comrades of Abu Sharar, Khalid Nazzal and Kanafani. O people of the uprising, which has been spreading from the roots of our homeland since 1936 and is escalating in a forceful way against the fascist occupation to scorch the land under the feet of its cowardly generals and soldiers. O heroes of the war of stones and Molotov cocktails: In escalation of our people's glorious uprising; out of loyalty to the pure blood of our people's martyrs; to promote the revolutionary epics written by the sons of Jabalya, Balata, 'Askar, al-Maghazi, al-Burayj, Qalandiya, al-Am'ari, Rafah, Khan Yunis, al-Shati', Tulkarm, and all the camps, towns, and villages of Palestine, which are united in the daily war and rose against repression, terrorism, and the policy of deportation, mass detention, poison gas, tracked vehicles and the closure of cities and camps; and to boost our firm and absolute cohesion with the PLO, the sole legitimate representative of our Palestinian people, the Unified National Command calls on all national action and popular committees to step up the successful popular uprising. They must also develop its forms, as we saw in last Monday's general comprehensive strike, by employing every means of revolutionary escalation. They must also declare Friday, 15 January 1988, a day of unity and solidarity in commemoration of the martyrs of the uprising. This is to be a day of prayer and symbolic funerals for our martyrs, and of tumultuous popular demonstrations. Let us chant in a single resounding voice: We sacrifice our souls and blood for you, O martyrs. Our souls and blood for Palestine.

O youth of Palestine, O throwers of incendiary stones, clearly the new fascists will be forced to admit the facts entrenched by your ferocious rebellion, which is charting a clear course toward a decisive form of national independence, enabling the flag of Palestine to flutter over the walls of holy Jerusalem.

O masses of the valiant Palestinian working class, let us take action so as to make the comprehensive general strike a success by stopping work on the designated days. Your pioneering proletarian role in our general uprising is the best answer to the threats and invective of the enemy authority and the best way to defeat its policy of racial discrimination and arbitrary action. You will thus declare your loyalty to the blood of the people's martyrs, which will compel the occupation authorities to reverse all their deportation orders and wrest the freedom of our heroic prisoners.

O valiant strugglers, owners of shops, the most important slogans of the uprising are represented by an intensified struggle to abrogate all tax laws and measures. This makes it incumbent upon you to continue the rebellion alongside every other sector of our people; workers, peasants, students and women. You should keep the national role you have played thus far at center stage. The people of the uprising will know how to protect honorable merchants, and when to severely punish anyone who seeks to trail behind the agents of the occupation authority.

O valiant sons of our people, drivers and owners of bus and taxi companies, your honorable national stand was clearly evident on the day of Palestinian steadfastness. We are confident that this position will be firm throughout the 3 days of the strike. We warn anyone who may break our spirit of unanimity that he will encounter the cubs of the uprising.

Communique no. 3

January 18, 1988

O masses of our great Palestinian people. O masses of the people of stones and Molotov cocktails. O soldiers of justice who are participating in our people's valiant uprising:

Blessed be your steel-hard arms. O heroes, blessed be your hands. O workers, blessed be your hands. O peasants, students, merchants, and women, blessed be your hands. O cubs of Palestine, who are tomorrow's generation:

A greeting of reverence and admiration to these great people who recorded the most splendid epics of struggle; a greeting to these people who fulfilled the call of duty and shook the earth under the Zionists' feet last week; a greeting of pride and glory to the masses of these resisting people; a greeting of reverence and admiration to the dear sacrifices being offered by our generous people and contemporary revolution; a greeting to you, O grandsons of al-Qassam; a greeting to this hand which is confronting the enemy soldiers in the alleys of the camps, villages, and towns throughout Palestine; a greeting to the wound which triumphs over the knife of Zionist terrorism and emerges lofty in the face of their war machine, tracked vehicles, and their asphyxiating and poisonous bombs.

A thousand greetings, all respect, admiration, glory, and immortality to you, O martyrs of our people, martyrs of the uprising, who watered the earth of the beloved homeland with your pure blood while hoisting the banners of freedom and independence. We repeat one million times: Blessed be your hands, O heroes in al-Shaykh Ridwan, Kafr Nu'man, Rafah, Jabalya, Qalqilya, and all camps, villages, streets and alleys. We repeat our pride in the people's masses, which chanted in one resounding voice: We redeem you with our souls and blood, O martyr; we redeem you with our souls and blood, O Palestine.

O masses of our great people, along the path of continuing and escalating the uprising and along the path of defeating occupation and realizing the slogans of the uprising, we call on all the national action committees and the popular committees to develop and escalate the success-ful popular uprising by declaring a comprehensive general strike from Tuesday, 19 January 1988, until Friday. Let prayers, symbolic funerals, and tumultuous popular demonstrations be renewed on Friday in memory of the martyrs of the uprising. Let the bells of churches ring in all villages and cities throughout Palestine.

O shopowners, who recorded honorable militant stands, who are facing the enemy's daily repression and arbitrary measures, who are firmly defying the closure orders, crowbars, and heavily-armed soldiers, and who are staging a commercial strike despite all the enemy measures: We greet you and your key role in our people's uprising and daily victories. We appeal to you to abide by the renewed general strike no matter how much the army presence is intensified and regardless of the measures adopted. We also call on you to continue to form and expand the merchants' committees in every street and city, every village and camp.

O masses of the Palestinian working class: Yes, the dark-skinned, steel-hard arms have succeeded in bringing the wheel of production in the Zionist factories and projects to a standstill through their large and effective participation in the general strike. Continue your strike against working in Zionist projects. Our hero workers, we have nothing to lose from our uprising but shackles, oppression and exploitation.

O masses of the valiant students, O you who have robbed the occupiers of their peace of mind throughout the years: Let us teach the enemy an unforgettable lesson. Let us teach the enemy that the policy of closing educational institutions, universities, institutes, and schools will only be disastrous for it. The Zionist authorities are shutting down all education institutions now. Let us send the large masses of our students in villages, camps, and cities to the school of revolution, the school of struggle in the streets, so that they can participate in shaking and scorching the earth under the Zionists' feet. Let us organize our ranks and utilize all the students' energies in the schools of struggle by continuing and escalating the uprising of our valiant people.

O brave sons of our people, O drivers of cars and buses, O owners of car and taxi companies: As you have done in the past, the Unified Leadership of the Uprising calls on you to bring traffic to a complete halt in all areas on the days of the strike with the exception of Friday.

To the sector of doctors and health services: We call on you to always be ready and to immediately join the medical committees which organize campaigns of medical aid to camps and besieged areas. We invite all doctors, pharmacists, nurses and laboratory technicians to participate in the aid campaigns because deteriorating health conditions and numerous diseases are prevailing in the camps as a result of the siege, starvation and use of poisonous gases.

To the owners of drug stores, drug factories, and pharmacies: We call on you to organize large-scale campaigns to donate drugs and provide free medicine to the medical and health committees which treat our wounded people.

To the owners of national capital and all financially capable people: We call on you to participate by donating goods, products and money to finance the camps and besieged areas. These donations should be handed to the competent national and popular committees and the supply committees in the various areas.

To the academics and professionals in various specialties: The uprising requires all your efforts. Participate in the national and popular committees and the specialized committees. Participate actively in the uprising whether by extending aid or through writings, songs, and slogans. Also participate in the information campaigns against the occupation policy.

Yes to our people's right to return, to self-determination and to building its independent state. Victory to our people's uprising, and down with the occupation. Glory and immortality to our righteous martyrs.

Communique no. 6

February 2, 1988

No voice can rise above the voice of the people of Palestine, the people of the Palestine Liberation Organization.

Let all efforts be united toward the continuation and escalation of the uprising!

O masses of our heroic people...you rebellious throngs in the camps, the villages and the cities of Palestine...you who by your will and your determination have triumphed over the policy of implanting the Zionist occupation, who have made the world hear your thundering voice, who have produced this wondrous and continually escalating uprising and seized the initiative from the rulers in Tel Aviv and put them into a situation of political siege and international condemnation...you whose struggle every day and every hour shows the way to victory, to the overthrow of the occupation and the establishment of the independent Palestinian state under the leadership of the PLO.

O masses of the uprising: at this very moment, American imperialism and its agents in the region are rushing about in an attempt to save the enemy entity from certain defeat, in a desperate effort to dissipate the tremendous national gains which you have achieved. American imperialism and its agents in the region are bent on plans and solutions which are designed to impose capitulation on us, for example Mubarak's liquidationist proposal and the US State Department's desperate efforts to dust off and resurrect a few of the embalmed local notables, in order to set up an "alternative leadership" in place of our sole legitimate leadership, the PLO. Behold, the upsurging salt of the earth acclaims the exclusive representativeness of the PLO and the right of the Palestinian people to return, to self-determination and to establish the independent state; it demands the isolation of these little yellowed leaves who go off on pilgrimage to meet with the representatives of the unholy trinity [Jordan, Egypt and the United States].

O masses of our great people: the Unified National Leadership, faithful to the blood of our martyrs and the torments of the thousands of wounded and imprisoned and in accordance with the program of the PLO, confirms its rejection of the Mubarak initiative and the efforts of the infamous Jordanian regime and its lackeys which seek to sneak through the capitulationist plans, whether the "division of functions" or any other plan which ignores our people's unchanging rights. It also affirms its rejection of the goals of the visit of the representative of American imperialism Philip Habib and likewise the anticipated visit of Murphy.

The masses of the uprising will remain on guard against anyone who tries to appoint himself over them and affirm that the fate of such as these will be defeat and total failure.

O sons of our people: Let us unify the efforts of all the forces, activities, organizations and popular and national committees in the struggle with a common will to implant and escalate the uprising and intensify its fury, and let us begin creating all sorts of appropriate organizational forms, committees and units in every village and city, and in every camp, so that they will link every neighborhood and street with the aim of paving the way toward total civil disobedience as a tremendous campaign of struggle.

The Unified National Leadership of the Uprising, in order to pave the way for this mission, calls on the masses of our people to:

1. Continue and escalate the general strike in Zionist enterprises and abstain from working in the settlements.

2. Call upon the municipal and local committees and the committees in the camps which have been appointed by the Zionist occupation authorities to resign immediately.

3. Complete the establishment of businessmen's committees in order to further the struggle to stop the payment of taxes immediately and to compel the occupation authorities to reconsider their thieving policy.

4. Call on the owners of property to follow the example of those who have refrained from collecting rents from shopkeepers as a result of the strike and in solidarity with those bulwarks of the glorious uprising, our brothers the merchants.

5. Demand that the families of detainees refrain completely from paying the unjust fines imposed on the detained heroes of the uprising by the Zionist courts.

6. Promote the national economy and locally-made national products, activate the household economy, and monitor and reduce consumption, in support of the uprising and as a step toward finding substitutes for Israeli products, which must be boycotted.

7. Respond in a revolutionary manner to the policy of beating and breaking by escalating the war of Molotov cocktails and stones.

O masses of our heroic people...

Broaden the base of confrontation, send forth mass demonstrations and marches and congregations, pray in the churches and the mosques, and carry out a general strike on Sunday and Monday (7-8 February 1988), on the occasion of the passing of two months since the flaring-up of the glorious uprising, in memory of the first squadron of our martyrs and in confirmation of the continuation and escalation of the uprising.

Let our national banner be raised, waving in the sky of Palestine. Let us affirm, today and every day, our determination and our perseverance to continue the struggle until we have achieved all our legitimate national rights, and foremost among them the right to return, self-determination and the establishment of the independent Palestinian state under the leadership of the PLO.

Glory to our people, eternal life to our righteous martyrs on the path to liberation.

We are winning!

Communique no. 7 or 8

c. February 18, 1988

In the name of God, the merciful, the compassionate. "You who believe. If you will aid the cause of God, he will aid you, and plant your feet firmly [Koranic verse]."

O our great people, your heroic uprising is frightening the enemies and adversaries. Your brave steadfastness has beaten all the barbaric Zionist means of repression, enjoyed the admiration of the whole world, and started to worry the defeatist regimes who fear the militant popular spirit will spread to the oppressed people who might topple them.

Thus an unholy alliance has been effected with the aim of extinguishing the fire of the blessed uprising. The best weapon they have been using is that of promises and illusions because their other weapons have failed. For days, they have been making many statements on opportunities for a solution which, according to them, will only begin once the uprising has ended.

Let them know our people and forces at home and abroad reject any phased solution short of an independent state. We will continue the uprising for months until we liberate our land. We will prove our ability to organize, to remain steadfast and to continue the uprising.

As a response to this, the nationalist forces, were able to establish connections inside the homeland and, based on their belief in the resourcefulness of our people, have been able to draw up a program of minimum requirements for the next six weeks. Committees and youths in every position are asked to understand and implement the program, and we are certain our people will carry out this program by their struggle and sacrifices. All of our struggling people are asked to implement the program and ensure the continuation of the uprising until it realizes its aims because if we retreat now, we will render all of our achievements useless and our retreat will be explained as an acceptance of autonomy. If we continue our uprising firmly, we will acheive our national rights.

1. Fridays will be official holidays for all. It is shameful for any Arab to work on Fridays in Zionist factories and farms. The movement of both public and private vehicles will stop and people, young and old, will go for prayers. Then, demonstrations will begin and proceed to the Zionist governor's headquarters, denouncing occupation and raising Palestinian flags.

2. Every Sunday there will be a total strike. Thus, workers will not go to work in Palestine on Fridays, Saturdays, and Sundays. Measures will be implemented every Sunday so committees and youths may carry out a continuous successful uprising.

3. Those whose living conditions force them to work can go to work provided they observe the following:

a. Only those over 25 years of age are allowed to go.

b. Only one member of a family is allowed to go.

c. The worker will use all his income to buy food which will be from Arab production. He will store foodstuffs for times of need.

d. Those who work will help their needy neighbors. All workers must be in their towns and villages on the evening of every Thursday and remain there until Monday morning. They should not spare any effort to destroy the Zionist factories and farms during their work and while they are spending the night inside these places.

4. Shops will be closed on Fridays and Saturdays. On other days they will be open for three hours a day, either from 0800 to 1100 or from 1700 to 2000 according to the need of every area.

5. Arab establishments, companies and farms must absorb the greatest number of the unemployed who refuse to work inside the Zionist entity. They will be compensated for any damages they sustain from their actions.

6. Our people and shopkeepers must boycott Zionist products. This is a daily struggle which everybody will carry out even if it is difficult for them.

7. Daily clashes and demonstrations with the Zionists will continue. Youths will bear the responsibility of holding the burning torch in all areas. Thus will we be able to organize our life and ensure the continuous uprising

for a long time until victory is realized, thanks to the heroism of our people and youth.

8. Popular committees will be organized to administer districts, make citizens' lives easier, and ensure the continuation of the uprising.

9. Women and old men will organize protest marches to the Red Cross headquarters and outside prisons and detention camps in every city, village and refugee camp at least once a week between Mondays and Thursdays.

10. Schoolgirls will daily go to school and will organize demonstrations from there. They will not observe orders to close schools.

11. We call on our people in the Galilee, the Triangle and the Negev to extend more and more support.

12. We call on Palestinian factions in the PLO to avenge the martyrs.

13. We call on our Arab nation and the Muslim world to organize effective and multifaceted support for our people's uprising.

14. We call on the world to pause a while and consider its role in our tragedy and in its continuation so far.

O our people, O our brothers, O our committees: Understand and observe this program as the minimum action to ensure the uprising's continuation. Escalate your action and your confrontation of the defeatists. By the continuing and raging uprising topple their capitulationist stands. No to occupation. No to capitulation. Long live Palestine, Arab and free. Long live our people's uprising. Glory and immortality to our good martyrs. Greetings to every elderly person, every youth, every child, every mother, every merchant, worker and driver among our heroic Palestinian Arab people. God be with us. Victory is near. Together along the path of liberating the land and man.

Communique no. 9

Late February, 1988

We pledge that the popular uprising will continue to escalate until the independent Palestinian state is established.

Our struggling people, your glorious uprising continues and your heroic confrontation of the enemy army and the Zionist settlers escalates, inflicting the heaviest losses on them and on their henchmen and scoring new achievements daily. Zionist murderer Rabin cannot but implicitly admit defeat. At last, he admitted that our people wage a civil war. Our heroes, the enemy has been defeated politically. Only US imperialism is seeking to save it from certain defeat. The enemy has been defeated economically. Its official figures about the direct losses it sustained in the stock exchange and productive enterprises have exceeded $2 billion as a result of our heroic workers' strike. The enemy was also defeated militarily.

You, the heroes of the uprising, are daily making the cost of occupation more prohibitive and are increasing its losses. You are proceeding with firm steps, determination and unfaltering will toward the establishment of your independent state. This is your decision, the decision of the masses of the uprising. It is the only decision on our Palestinian land.

We are united as one body and are nipping in the bud the conspiracy of US imperialism with Shultz as its hero. Shultz will only sustain a sweeping defeat in his attempt to market the Camp David goods which the Palestinian people had rejected. The agents of the reactionaries are hiding in their dens now that the uprising of the heroic people against the enemy and its agents has defeated them.

From the vanguard of the daily struggle and confrontation of the fascist Zionist enemy's tools of repression, we address our greetings to the comrades in the struggle on the occupied Golan Heights. We shake their hands which have inflicted painful and harsh blows on the Zionist enemy. More blows on the road to repulsing the Zionist enemy.

Heroes of the glorious uprising, brave student groups and academics, one of the pillars of the Zionist policy is to stultify our people and deprive them of one of the most basic rights acknowledged by international conventions and norms, the right to education. That's why the Zionist enemy has closed down all our educational institutions such as universities, higher institutes, and schools. By doing this, the enemy has deprived a third of a million students of receiving an education.

The Unified National Leadership of the Uprising has decided to confront the Zionist enemy's decisions by voiding them. It calls on the student masses, the teaching staff and the administrations of the educational institutions to carry out unified confrontation on all levels to defy the enemy's decision by organizing educational operations on a national basis and by foiling the stultification policy the enemy adopts against our masses. The Unified National Leadership also appeals to all international bodies and organizations to support our people's struggle for foiling this policy.

O businessmen, professional workers and craftsmen: Pursuant to and in line with the program of the uprising and the comprehensive popular revolution, let us sever one of the enemy's economic jugular veins and let us resoundingly proclaim our rejection of taxes in their various forms. Taxes are one of the lifelines which finance the enemy, including its tools of repression and its invader army.

Let us once again proclaim that the battle of taxes has begun. You are capable of waging this battle by organizing your rights and your collective unified stand. All the masses of the uprising will stand by your side in this battle. The accountants also have an important role in this battle.

Let March be the month during which our stolen funds will stop pouring into the enemy's coffers. We are confident that the unity of these sectors of our people and the unity of our people by abstaining from paying taxes will be another enemy defeat to be added to previous defeats.

Our masses, we are running the battle with you and through you. That's why the following has been decided:

1. The continued enforcement of the present arrangements with respect to the opening of businesses and shops from two to three hours daily in accordance with the circumstances of every area.

2. The need for our productive plants to operate at full capacity to enable the largest possible boycott of Zionist goods. These plants will suspend their activities only on the days of the general strikes announced by the Unified National Leadership.

3. With respect to industrial areas outside the cities which house shops, blacksmith workshops, garages and others, these areas will open for business from the morning until 1300 with the exception of the days of general strike during which they will be closed.

4. The need to keep open all clinics, dispensaries, and health centers all the time.

5. The nonpayment of fines imposed by the fascist Zionist military courts on our sons the detainees.

We urge property owners to demonstrate the ethics of our heroic people by reaching an understanding with their tenants on the amount of rent due to them for the last three months.

We urge our people in the cities, villages and camps to form collection funds under the supervision of national and popular committees in the various quarters of the cities, villages and camps to offer assistance and aid to those who need it in their respective locations. We also warn against responding to those who collect such assistance from outside these committees which you have formed.

The Unified National Leadership calls for exposing all the methods of sedition and sabotage to which the Zionist enemy resorts, such as setting cars on fire or disseminating rumors or statements to fragment our people's unity.

We address a militant greeting to the sons of Qabatya who have taught a lesson to those who betray their homeland and people. We call on those who work in the civil administration and the police departments to stop working there, to immediately resign and to join our people in their struggle and heroic uprising.

Sons of the independent state, while it praises your struggle and pledges to pursue the struggle with you and through you until the establishment of our independent state, the Unified National Leadership calls on the masses of the uprising and our children wherever they may be to carry out the following:

1. To use all means to topple the appointed municipal and rural committees which are the tools of the power-sharing capitulatory plan.

These committees stand in the trench that is hostile to our people, particularly after they refused to submit to the will of the masses of the uprising which have given them the chance to resign before it is too late. However, these committees insisted on continuing to betray their people and put themselves in the service of the enemy and its objectives.

2. The proclamation of 5 March 1988 as the day of the return to the land, working on it and cultivating it collectively.

3. The proclamation of Sunday, 6 March 1988, as the day of the Palestinian flag on which Palestinian flags will be flown on all locations and on every house. Flags will also be flown during the tumultuous demonstrations.

The Unified National Leadership also calls on the Palestinian and Arab masses throughout the Arab homeland and abroad to hold demonstrations on this day, and to fly Palestinian flags.

4. The teaching staff and students working or studying in educational institutions should proceed to these institutions, thus voiding the Zionist enemy's decision.

5. Let us escalate the war of attrition against the enemy, block the roads leading to the settlements, and put black paint over Hebrew inscriptions on walls, particularly inscriptions having a terrorist connotation.

6. The celebration on Tuesday of the 8 March anniversary, that of International Women's Day, by having Palestinian women go to the streets in tumultuous demonstrations announcing their rejection of the occupation and setting the most splendid examples of how to confront the Zionist army.

7. The proclamation of martyrs' day which falls on 9 March 1988 as a day of general strike and of mass demonstrations in the streets to celebrate the beginning of the fourth month of the glorious uprising and to commemorate the first group of martyrs of the popular uprising. Let this day become a new day of anger against the Zionists.

8. Holding tumultuous demonstrations starting from mosques and churches on Fridays and Saturdays.

Glory and praise to the martyrs of our heroic people. Ignominy and defeat to the US settlement plans. God is with us. Victory is close. Let us proceed to liberate the land and man.

Communique no. 12

c. April, 1988

In the name of God, the merciful, the compassionate. No voice can rise above the voice of the uprising; no voice can rise above the voice of the Palestinian people, the voice of the PLO. Call No. 12, [word indistinct] issued by the PLO-the Unified National Leadership...

O militant people, O people of al-Qassam and 'Abd al-Qadir al-Husayni. O people of struggle and sacrifices. Our triumphant uprising and popular revolution is in its fifth month. Our Palestinian masses are facing more than two-thirds of the Israeli army and all the herds of Zionist settlers whom the enemy sent to the streets of our camps, villages and towns to confront our unarmed people. This overwhelming revolution cannot be ended or liquidated by the breaking of bones, fascist killing and terrorism, mass arrests or economic harassment. Hundreds of thousands of Palestinians across our beloved homeland declare today there is no going back, that the revolution of stones will not stop before the establishment of our independent state. This was demonstrated in the immortal Land Day when two million Palestinians identified themselves with the united people. Now they are rising united behind the banner which will never fall, the banner of the PLO, the banner of the Unified National Leadership, the banner of liberation and the independent homeland. To raise this banner over the hills of Jerusalem, the Palestinians in all towns, villages, camps and streets are rising as one man.

O people of Palestine, O people of the PLO, O people of the Unified National Leadership. After its failure to put out the fires of the revolution through repression and terror, the occupation today is resorting to rumors and to spreading lies and forged statements allegedly signed by the Unified National Leadership in an attempt to cast doubt among our people, individuals and groups. The occupation is trying to sow the seeds of factionalism and sectarianism. It is spreading rumors about arresting the editors of the calls of the Unified National Leadership. All this is aimed at weakening the front of the burning uprising. The Unified National Leadership is certain that our people will be able to confront all the false rumors of the occupation. It affirms that the Unified National Leadership is the people of the uprising, represented by all its strata, groups and sectors...

While we are on the threshold of the fifth month of our glorious uprising and while we are hailing these days the fortieth anniversary of the battle of heroism and sacrifice—the Battle of al-Qastal and the commemoration of the martyrdom of heroic commander 'Abd al-Qadir al-Husayni—the Unified National Leadership affirms the following:

1. Denouncing the attempts to disrupt the convocation of the Arab summit in the first half of April. The summit should be held as soon as possible to back the struggle of the people of the uprising on the land of Palestine. We assure the Arab kings and presidents that we do not want funds. We would rather starve and remain destitute than bow down. We would rather die martyrs than concede our rights before final victory. However, we want the summit to abide in practice by its previous resolutions by asserting our people's inalienable rights to establish our independent state under the flag of the PLO, the leader of our struggle and our sole legitimate representative, and abide by an international conference with full powers with the participation of all parties, including the PLO in an equal and independent manner. We also call on the summit to close all Arab doors to the Shultz plot, which seeks to liquidate the uprising, by categorically rejecting it and closing Arab airports before his shuttle tours as well as to all other US envoys. Shultz and all those Arab regimes colluding with him should know that our only address is the PLO. It is the party concerned and the sole legitimate representative.

2. The Unified National Leadership and the masses of the uprising denounce the oppressive authorities' recent measures represented by isolating the West Bank and Gaza, imposing a curfew on Gaza for three days, and considering the West Bank a closed area to the movement of citizens and journalists in a desperate attempt to prevent the people of the uprising from commemorating immortal Land Day. We tell them that all these desperate attempts are doomed to miserable failure. The will of the revolution of the stones and the uprising shall triumph over all their fascist and Nazi methods.

3. Denouncing the occupation authorities' decision to consider the Youth Movement *[harakat al-shabiba]* illegal and to close a number of trade union offices and institutions and considering these measures as contrary to the most fundamental human rights and all international pacts and norms. The Unified National Leadership affirms that these measures will only make us more determined to continue the struggle.

4. The Unified National Leadership and the masses of the uprising appreciate the unified collective stand taken by merchants of the Ramallah area who pledged at a public meeting attended by thirty merchants not to pay taxes and who adhered to their pledge in practice. We consider this experiment an example that should be emulated by all merchants in all parts of the West Bank and Gaza.

5. The Unified National Leadership greets the stand taken by the members of the municipal and village committees who responded to the call for resignation by the Unified National Leadership and the masses of the uprising. The leadership announces the squandering of the blood and property of the chairmen and members of the committees who have not resigned. We tell them that the masses of the uprising will trample upon

whoever deviates from the stand of national unity and does not respond to the call and voice of the uprising.

6. The Unified National Leadership and the masses of the uprising esteem the mass resignation of the tax and customs departments in Gaza and calls on the employees of these departments in the West Bank to follow their example. The leadership also appreciates the mass resignation of the policemen who responded to the call of the uprising and calls on municipality members to immediately resign from their posts. The Unified National Leadership urges agricultural engineers, owners of plant nurseries, and those with experience and capabilities to give every support and guidance to the masses of peasants, farmers and striking workers to achieve maximum levels of self-sufficiency and to confront the measures of economic restriction used by the occupation authorities. Let us continue to reclaim and cultivate lands to meet our needs and support besieged areas. We should all realize that the task of all the masses of the uprising is to intensify their work and to increase their production during our long struggle. We must realize that strike does not mean not working. The Unified National Leadership, while continuing on the long and difficult road of defeating the occupation and establishing our independent state, calls on the masses of the uprising to entrench the following struggle activities:

a. Declaring Monday, 4 April, a general strike day as an expression of the uprising masses' rejection of the plot by George Shultz, the secretary of US imperialism. We reaffirm the PLO's stand and our determination to use the uprising to boycott any meetings with Shultz or any other US envoy.

b. Declaring Monday, Tuesday, and Wednesday, 4, 5, and 6 April, days of various struggle activities by the uprising, masses, committees, striking groups, and various national frameworks against Shultz' visit and in solidarity with the uprising and detainees and wounded, including sit-ins and various public and women's demonstrations.

c. Considering Tuesday, 5 April, a day of national action in which all national establishments and factories shall operate at full capacity in the interests of those affected by the uprising, such as the families of martyrs, wounded, detainees, besieged areas and workers who lost their jobs for ceasing to work in Zionist settlements and projects and also those who resigned in response to the call of the uprising. The national committees in every city, village, camp and quarter shall distribute the revenues of this day.

d. On the occasion of World Health Day on 7 April, the Unified National Leadership greets all doctors, pharmacists and nurses who have performed the duty of providing health care and relief work to the wounded of the uprising to work in the camps, villages, and cities. The leadership calls on all those employed in the health care field to receive more patients and provide more medical treatment.

e. Declaring Thursday, 7 April, the anniversary of the Battle of al-Qastal and the martyrdom of Palestinian commander 'Abd al-Qadir a day of violent clashes with the occupation forces and the cowardly settlers. Tumultuous demonstrations must come out in the streets and all our camps, villages and cities must turn into fortresses of confrontation and fortification for the uprising.

f. Declaring Saturday, 9 April, which is the anniversary of the martyrdom of the first group of martyrs in the uprising as well as the martyrs of the Dayr Yasin massacre, and the beginning of the fifth month of our uprising, a day of people's authority in which processions shall proceed to the graves of the martyrs, sit-ins shall be organized in municipalities and establishments, and demonstrations shall be staged everywhere. It should be declared a day of sweeping indignation against the occupation authorities and their oppressive measures. Let the ground erupt like a volcano under the feet of the invader occupiers.

g. Considering Friday and Sunday, 8 and 10 April, days of prayer for the repose of the souls of the uprising's martyrs. Processions and demonstrations shall be staged and sit-ins shall be organized in mosques and churches.

8. Monday, 11 April, shall be a day of general strike and of guiding the masses of our people on volunteer work for cultivating lands, developing Palestinian rural areas, and promoting developing Palestinian rural areas, and promoting environmental economy. O people of the uprising, continue to move forward. O cubs of the stones, march ahead. They shall not pass. The uprising shall triumph, shall triumph.

Communique no. 13

April 10, 1988

Our uprising is still going on and we must continue to ignite it, as the resultant climate should increase the factors of victory. We must consolidate these factors with tangible measures toward civil disobedience which we have initiated:

The civil administration institutions have begun to crumble. The majority and key employees of these institutions have tendered their resignations such as workers in the police, customs and income tax [departments]. A good number have quit their jobs. An overwhelming majority of our people has refused to pay taxes. There has been a tangible boycott of Zionist goods; our workers have stayed away from Zionist workplaces.

There have been other achievements including an enhancement of cooperation and solidarity among our people, a return to the land and its cultivation. There has also been a widespread increase in household economic activities and in popular committees around the occupied land. Our people have started building a new life system and boosting their national authority.

As we approach the blessed month of Ramadan, the month of sacrifice and cooperation, and as we approach the day of the Palestinian prisoner, the vanguard of our people in the front trench confronting the arbitrariness and oppression of occupation, the Unified National Leadership of the Uprising stresses the following:

Frontal attack against and denunciation of appointed municipal committees that have refused to respond to the national demand to step down. The Unified National Leadership of the Uprising calls upon our people to boycott these committees and not to pay license and professional or any other fees. The appointed committees are hereby warned once and for all to resign forthwith.

The Unified National Leadership of the Uprising hails our masses and economic institutions that have withheld taxes. It emphasizes the importance of sticking to this line and in the meantime warns all those who have paid taxes against the consequences of continuing to do so under any pretext. This applies to large factories and major economic establishments.

The Unified National Leadership salutes all the workers who resigned from the civil administration bodies, whether in the police force or the customs and income tax departments. It further calls upon the remainder of the police and income tax employees to quit and follow the example of their fellow workers.

The Unified National Leadership of the Uprising calls upon our heroic workforce to boycott employment in Israeli settlements on the occupied West Bank and Gaza Strip, given the paralyzing impact this will have on settlement building and their service sector. Furthermore, we call on our workers to form and expand worker committees in their workplaces and neighborhoods to organize themselves and enhance their militant role.

The Unified National Leadership of the Uprising calls on the national plants and productive establishments to double their turnout and take on additional workers and stresses the necessity of not deducting from wages on comprehensive strike days and not dismissing workers or reducing pay.

The Unified National Leadership of the Uprising praises the spirit of social and economic cooperation in our people and calls for setting up more popular, neighborhood and watch committees to run their affairs and set their roles in the uprising. It further calls on our masses to promote the notion of household economy in terms of tilling the land, keeping poultry, being frugal and boycotting Zionist goods, particularly during the blessed month of Ramadan.

The Unified National Leadership appeals to the Arab masses and the democratic forces wherever they are to escalate their struggle to support the uprising of the Palestinian people. It also hails Algeria's position and its role in holding the Arab summit conference and denounces some parties' attempts to postpone it.

The Unified National Leadership urges Syria to quickly redress its relation with the PLO, the leader of our people and their struggle, to confront imperialism and its plans and to serve the Arab liberation struggle. It also appeals to all the sons of our people and their professional sectors such as doctors, engineers, agricultural engineers, lawyers and teachers to participate in the uprising and relieve, support and serve the sons of our people.

The Unified National Leadership would like to warn the sons of our people of the enemy intelligence's attempts to betray our people by distorting the reputation of honorable people and harming their national reputation. Our people should seek accuracy in dealing with the rumors of the enemy and its agents. It also calls on our masses to be on guard against the enemy and its intelligence, which are trying to damage the property of the honorable people.

O our masses, O the makers of the free future, the Unified National Leadership, while marching with you on the path of long and difficult struggle to repulse the occupation and establish an independent Palestinian state, urges the masses of the continuing uprising to adhere to the following activities:

1. Challenging the enemy's decision to close shops in the morning. Let us confront this by insisting on opening our shops from 0800-1100. Regarding blessed Ramadan, the Unified National Leadership of the Uprising announces that shops will open from 1400-1700.

2. Friday, Sunday and Tuesday, 8, 10 and 12 April, 1988 are days of demonstrations and national activities.

3. Wednesday, 13 April, 1988, is a day of collecting donations and solidarity with the village of Beita. A one minute silence will be observed to honor the martyrs of the uprising at 1000.

4. Thursday and Saturday, 14 and 16 April, 1988, will be the days of a general strike in protest of mass arrests and the enemy's repressive and economic measures against our people.

5. Sunday, 17 April, 1988, is the day of the Palestinian prisoner. We call for staging a sit-in in the Red Cross and the Red Crescent offices and national institutions in solidarity with our sons in the fascist jails and for staging a hunger strike in these places.

6. Monday, 18 April, 1988, is the day of solidarity with the educational institutions. People will head toward them to show challenge and violate the decision to close them.

7. Tuesday, 19 April, 1988, is the day of solidarity with the families of the martyrs and prisoners. These families will be visited.

8. Wednesday, 20 April, is the day of national unity, the day of Algeria's unionist session, the day of national activities, and the day of national construction and promotion of agriculture and household economic activities.

9. Thursday, 21 April, is the day of the Palestinian Molotov in retaliation for the authorities' encouragement of the herds of settlers to open fire on the Molotov throwers. It is a day of general strike.

O the sons of our great people. Go ahead and confront the herds of settlers. Inflict more losses on the enemy. Let us continue to throw Molotovs and stones until we expel the occupation and achieve victory. Glory and immortality to our righteous martyrs. Victory is ours and death is for the Zionist occupiers.

Communique no. 14

April 20, 1988

In the name of God, the merciful, the compassionate. No voice can rise above the voice of the uprising, no voice can rise above the voice of the Palestinian people, the people of the PLO. Call of the martyr commander, teacher, and symbol Brother Khalil al-Wazir, Abu Jihad...

We pledge to you, O symbol of martyrs and teacher of generations, that we will be true to our vow and will continue to struggle and to fight until we realize all of our people's aims and aspirations. Your blood and the blood of our martyrs will never be in vain. Either we court martyrdom or we will raise the banner for which you devoted your life over holy Jerusalem, the capital of our independent Palestinian state. It will be the same pledge and vow until we realize victory or court martyrdom on the path of freedom and independence...

O our steadfast, persevering people, you are continuing your glorious, splendid march on the road of struggle and fighting with your great resources and escalating your brave, giant uprising. You are preparing the firm, unshakable ground to realize comprehensive civil disobedience. Through its extensive political moves, our great leadership is realizing great achievements and winning growing support for our people's revolution, with the creative support and joint moves of the friendly powers led by the political moves of the PLO and the friendly USSR on the road to convening a full-powered international conference in which Palestinians will be represented by an independent delegation to affirm our national legitimate rights to return, to have self-determination and to establish an independent Palestinian state as expounded by the majority of the world's states.

These achievements were the fruit of our glorious uprising. Therefore, escalate the struggle against the occupation, its bodies and its agents, particularly the appointed municipal committees. Expand and form new people's committees, strike forces and committees for areas, committees of guards and committees for supplies. Have more cohesion and unify national militant efforts in all areas. Improve the application of all the instructions mentioned in the uprising programs stipulated in previous statements. Continue to boycott Zionist products that can be replaced by local products and everything that you can do without.

Let the merchants commit themselves to boycotting Zionist goods. Continue to boycott the suckers of our blood, the customs and tax departments. Let those who have not resigned from the police and tax departments do so. We call on you to immediately join your colleagues. Do not cover yourselves by taking leave because the people are alert and their hand will reach all those who deviate from the march of the triumphant uprising.

O masses of our glorious uprising, in tune with the uprising program, we ask you to observe the following:

1. We stress the importance of full commitment to the decision not to pay taxes to the suckers of our people's blood.

2. We appreciate the role of our people, our agricultural and popular committees and area committees, for their response to the call of the land by practicing planting at home and in plots through agricultural cooperatives. We call on all of our committees and people to expand and entrench agriculture and cooperatives until they encompass all areas in our beloved land.

3. We call on our masses and people to continue to practice rationalization and to reduce their spending during the blessed month of Ramadan, the month of sacrifice and cooperation.

4. We call on our workers to completely boycott the Zionist settlements.

5. We call for allowing room for action for all the health committees, extending assistance to our people in all areas and increasing the number of training courses for first aid, preventive medicine, and health education. We ask the brother doctors to reduce their charges in support of our uprising masses.

6. Out of our commitment to the PLO Executive Committee decision to support those who resign from the police and tax departments and our brave workers who boycott the Zionist settlements, the popular and other committees will extend assistance to all of them.

7. We salute the brave masses of the Golan Heights, affirm our joint struggle, and greet the Palestinian and Arab masses inside the Zionist entity

and in the Arab states for their support to our uprising. Let us all move against occupation and injustice. We call on the Arab governments to release the Palestinian and Arab detainees in their prisons to serve our people's uprising.

8. We call for the immediate resignation of the active directors of the Civil Administration Department in the Gaza Strip.

9. We stress the need for the ICRC and UNRWA to shoulder their responsibilities in providing food and medicine to the besieged cities, villages, and camps subjected to curfews...

We pledge to our martyr Abu Jihad and all of our honest martyrs that the day will come when our Kalashnikovs will sing in every area of Palestine and in every village, camp and city to mark the end of Zionist fascism and to enable our people to reap as fruits their legitimate national rights under the PLO leadership. The pledge and vow will be the same: Either victory or martyrdom for the sake of a free, independent Palestine. We will emerge victorious...

Communique no. 15

April 30, 1988

Despite all the oppression, isolation, the besieging of camps and villages, starvation, killing, detention, the crime of assassinating commander Abu Jihad, terrorism, deportation, and the psychological warfare being waged by the Zionist enemy's apparatus with the aim of aborting the uprising, our people have not reneged and will not renege on their objectives.

Through the use of their creative energies, they are creating new means of confrontation in reply to the escalation measures being employed by the enemy, adapting themselves to a protracted phase of struggle until the occupiers are expelled and the independent state is established.

Contrary to all the calls for capitulation being voiced by the occupiers, our people view the daily accomplishments they are scoring as a solid basis for continuing and developing the uprising.

The uprising has brought about a new pattern for our daily economic and social life, a pattern based on the fact that the uprising is a protracted and continuous revolutionary process—a process that cannot be free of hardships, victims and difficult living conditions.

However, the uprising is replete with accomplishments which have entrenched national unity among all sectors of our people and their national forces—a unity embodied by the great cooperation being shown by the popular committees, the strike forces and the guard committees and also by the extensive cultivation of land, the formation of cooperatives and the unprecedented social integration.

The accomplishments scored by the uprisings are not only restricted to thwarting the US-reactionary conspiratorial schemes and the dreams harbored by the Zionists of perpetuating their hegemony over the occupied territories.

These accomplishments go beyond this to win further international support for our just objectives and bring about a suitable atmosphere—now more than ever—in view of the joint Soviet-Palestinian agreement to render successful the convening of an international conference with full powers based on the legitimate national rights of our people and to force the Zionist enemy and its ally, US imperialism, to succumb to the will of the international community which is voicing further support day by day for our people's objectives.

This was clearly shown in UN Security Council Resolution 605 which stressed the need for recognizing the legitimate national rights of the Palestinian people.

Due to the clear effects of the uprising, and also of the Palestinian, Algerian, Libyan and Soviet efforts, the Syrian-Palestinian relationship is proceeding in the right direction.

This relationship was crowned by the meeting between a Palestinian delegation led by Brother Abu Ammar [Yasir Arafat], PLO Executive Committee chairman, and Syrian President Hafiz al-Asad.

We urge Syria to manifest a relationship of militant alliance with the PLO based on respecting the independence of Palestinian national decision-making. The nationalist Arab states are urged to establish a new steadfast, militant base whose list of priorities should include the convening of an Arab summit conference to support the uprising and the embodiment of an Arab political stand vis-a-vis the US imperialist schemes, headed by the Shultz plan.

The effects of the uprising were felt by the sons of our steadfast people in the Lebanese arena in a way allowing the expansion of their struggle and ending their suffering.

Moreover, this development has allowed the return of the Palestinian factions still outside the PLO so they will join the PLO's bodies on the basis of the program of the eighteenth PNC session.

The uprising has brought about a qualitative leap in the international balance of power in favor of our people's national rights to repatriation, self-determination, and the establishment of an independent Palestinian state under the PLO's leadership...

O masses of our great people. The issuance of Communique no. 15 coincides with 1 May, International Workers' Day. On this militant day which is celebrated by the world's workers, our Palestinian people take pride in the revolutionary role being played by our workers and their union organizations and also by all the Palestinian proletariat and other sectors of our people.

We also pay tribute to the great sacrifices they are offering in defense of our people's national cause. We take pride in the struggle being waged by our valiant workers; they are suffering because of their continuation of the uprising.

We call upon international bodies and international labor organizations to show solidarity with the Palestinian labor movement against the deportation, detention and harassment decisions taken against unionists and against the decisions to close, storm and ban the activities of labor unions.

On 1 May, we salute our valiant workers with greetings and pride in their militant role and urge them to effect a comprehensive boycott of work in Zionist settlements.

We also urge them to adhere to work inside the occupied territories. We ask them to move to the cultivation of the land and to miss no opportunity allowing them to do away with work behind the so-called green line.

On this occasion, we call upon our valiant workers to offer further bountiful offerings in embodiment of the unified Palestinian will. We also call for forming unified labor committees and for working to unify the ranks of the labor and union movement.

We greet and appreciate the merchants' firm and honorable stand. We also greet the merchants in the heroic city of Jerusalem who rejected the Zionist enemy's orders.

We urge all merchants not to respond to any Zionist calls to open their shops in violation of the national stand. We stress the importance of full abidance by all sectors not to pay taxes.

We also stress the importance of not increasing commodities' prices. Boycotting work in Zionist settlements and Zionist products will inevitably lead to fragmenting the economic and social structure of the Zionist entity.

We greet the masses of our people in the Gaza Strip and its heroic besieged camps for their heroic steadfastness. We call on our people in the al-Shati', Dayr al-Balah and other camps to foil the Zionist enemy's plan to hold citizens' identity cards with the objective of aborting the uprising.

We appeal to international bodies and the UNRWA to restore full supplies to all camps of Gaza Strip residents immediately to bolster their valiant steadfastness in the face of the fascist Zionist measures.

We urge the masses of our people to deal the strongest blows to workers in the police apparatus and the appointed municipal and village councils who deviated from the will of our people, headed by al-Zir, al-Tawil, Khalil Musa and Jamil Sabir Khalaf.

The Unified National Leadership of the Uprising affirms that the measures that have been taken against them thus far were only a warning.

Out of a commitment to the recommendations of our valiant merchants committees and to our citizens, we call for opening shops for three hours, from 0900-1200, in all areas.

This applies to gas stations with the possibility of having only one Arab gas station on duty. The industrial areas shall abide by the set opening hours of 0800-1300.

O masses of our struggler people, on the road to achieving civil disobedience and out of a commitment to the militant program of the Unified National Leadership, the militant arm of the PLO, we urge our national key figures and our struggler masses to observe the following:

1. To consider 1 May a general national day. This day shall be turned into a day of confrontation with the enemy's fascist forces and a day of popular demonstrations in villages and cities during which Palestinian flags shall be hoisted and slogans denouncing the Zionist enemy shall be raised.

We call on institutions, factories, and companies to abide by making this day a paid holiday for their workers.

2. To consider 4 May a day of comprehensive strike and a day for national development during which all activities and various committees shall be devoted to cultivating land and rebuilding demolished houses.

3. To consider 5 May a day for breaking the enemy's decision closing academic institutions. We stress the importance of academic institutions abiding by duty hours from 0900-1200.

4. To consider 7 May a day for solidarity with our valiant merchants where everyone opens shops through the support of our people and the strike forces.

5. To consider 9 and 10 May days for a comprehensive strike during which all facilities and transportation shall stop to greet the first galaxy of the uprising's martyrs.

On the occasion that the uprising has entered its sixth month, the people's will shall be embodied through striking at the forces and agents of the Zionist enemy and all militant activities and energies shall be exploited to escalate the uprising against the fascist Zionist enemy.

The days from 2 May until 11 May shall be considered days of intensified activities and the anger of Palestine. Sundays and Fridays shall be considered days to perform prayers for the souls of the martyrs.

The Unified National Leadership calls on all popular and national committees to name streets and institutions after martyrs of the uprising to keep them alive in our generations' memories.

Mammoth demonstrations shall be staged from mosques and churches against the usurper enemy and its settlers.

The road to civil disobedience requires the further formation of popular, neighborhood, educational, guard, agricultural, information, and solidarity committees. O masses of our people, who offer continuous sacrifices, continue to develop your means of daily struggle.

Intensify the use of popular means against all enemies beginning with the holy stones and ending with the incendiary Molotov cocktails. O our people and the youths and girls of Palestine, further strike force, further sacrifices for the sake of Palestine.

Every hit to our enemy's body will bring us closer to the great victory. The blood of our righteous martyrs will not be wasted uselessly. We will continue with you to achieve our objectives of freedom and independence.

We affirm that the PLO is the only party with which any dialogue can be held concerning our legitimate national rights.

Greeting to our steadfast citizens and to all national, Arab, and international efforts that support our triumphant uprising. We will continue together on the road of the glorious uprising. We will triumph.

Communique no. 17

May 24, 1988

No voice can rise above the voice of the uprising. No voice can rise above the voice of the people of Palestine.

Communique no. 17, the call of the children of the stones and RPGs [rocket-propelled grenades]...

O masses of our heroic people. Our people's contributions and their march of struggle are growing with time. You have given a true revolutionary response to the June defeat, the defeat of the Arab regimes and their programs. You have detonated the mighty revolution of our people. There has been the legendary steadfastness of the fighters of our revolution and their allies in the Lebanese national movement. With the will to fight, the alliance of guns, and the unity of blood they have defeated and humiliated the 'invincible' army during the Zionist invasion of Arab Lebanon and the repeated aggression against Lebanon. They did so despite that army's military and technological superiority. And then there has been the glorious, continuing and escalating uprising which has proven once again there can be no coexistence with neo-Nazism and its artificial Zionist entity. The uprising has also confirmed that their is no alternative to struggle and to a protracted people's war as the way to regain our rights to repatriation and self-determination, and to establish an independent Palestinian state under the leadership of the PLO, the sole legitimate representative of our people.

As it stands on the threshold of total civil disobedience, the Unified National Leadership of the Uprising calls on all friends throughout the world to show solidarity and to seek to achieve the demands of the victorious uprising as a prelude to imposing a comprehensive and just solution to our people's sacred cause.

1. To provide international protection for our people under the yoke of occupation, and to annul Zionist violations and laws that conflict with the 1949 Fourth Geneva Convention, including the cessation of the collection of illegal taxes, settlement, amendments to the laws that were in force prior to the occupation and the treatment of our prisoners as prisoners of war.

2. The Palestinian people accept Resolution 605 unanimously adopted by the UN Security Council—a resolution that approaches our people's cause as the cause of a people who have a legitimate right to live in their own land, thus rescinding all resolutions that do not approach our cause as the cause of a people who have legitimate national rights in their own homeland.

3. To release all the valiant detainees and prisoners of our revolution and our people's uprising immediately, close down all Nazi detention camps, and desist from the policy of expulsion and deportation from the homeland, the demolition of homes and persecution of our people.

4. To withdraw the army from residential areas, stop turning the camps into ghettos, and end violations of mosques and holy places.

The Unified Leadership affirms the need to meet these urgent demands by our uprising. While doing so, it also affirms that our Palestinian people's struggle will continue and escalate until our legitimate rights to repatriation, self-determination and the establishment of an independent state with Jerusalem as its capital under the leadership of the PLO are achieved. This call coincides with the summit meeting between Gorbachev and Reagan. Our people's masses attach special importance to this meeting. They call on the summit to agree regarding the establishment of our people's legitimate and human demands to achieve their national independence, self-deter-mination, and return to their usurped homeland. The Soviet-Palestinian agreement, supported by all friends of the people and by an international consensus on our people's legitimate national rights, is a just, irreplaceable basis for any comprehensive political solution to the Middle East problem.

O masses of our great people, the Arab summit comes after a long waiting period and amid the uprising's lofty escalation as well as the climax of fascist Zionist repression against our Palestinian Arab people. While affirming the need to extend all forms of unified Arab support and solidarity to the sons of our people, we, on behalf of our masses, children, old men, women, prisoners, and the strugglers of our gigantic revolution, call on the summit:

1. To reject the Shultz' initiative firmly and explicitly and not to receive him, and to foil all imperialist and Zionist plots and schemes against our people and their cause.

2. We affirm that the PLO is the sole legitimate representative of our people and the quarter which has the right to speak on behalf of them in all forums with an independent Palestinian will. We condemn all attempts to circumvent this representation and our people's legitimate rights by some Arab sides.

3. To provide democratic liberties for the Arab masses and to allow them to exercise their natural right to solidarity and cohesion with the masses of the triumphant uprising, to set free all political detainees, and to open all fronts for fedayin activity against the Zionist entity.

4. We stress our people's rejection of all suspect plans, especially the Camp David accords, resolutions 242 and 338, the Shultz initiative, and "division of functions."

5. We stress the importance of and need for a unified political stand adopting our legitimate national rights to repatriation, self-determination and the establishment of an independent Palestinian state with Jerusalem as capital under the PLO leadership before the entire world.

O masses of our valiant people, while stressing all previous decisions, the Unified National Leadership calls on our masses to further escalate their boycott of the occupation authorities' departments and taxes, appointed municipal and village councils, and work inside settlements. It also calls on our masses to deal painful blows to those violating our people's will and to the Zionist enemy and the herds of settlers. You are called upon to work more, offer further sacrifices, deal further blows, form further general and specialized committees and strike forces, and to hurl further stones and Molotov cocktails.

While we are at the threshold of comprehensive civil disobedience, we call on you to observe the following:

1. The immediate resignation of the employees of the departments of traffic, licensing, organization, housing, identity cards, and labor offices.

2. To completely stop paying taxes and going to the tax department to obtain clearance.

3. The comprehensive and complete boycott of Israeli products. We also stress the need for the merchants in Jerusalem and elsewhere to work for marketing agricultural products and the national Arab-made industries as an alternative to Zionist industrial products.

4. The removal of merchandise displayed by sidewalk vendors and selling at houses, particularly at the al-Ram area, and abidance by selling at the set hours.

5. We call on all students working at academic institutions to go to their schools and educational institutions and to adhere to school hours until 1200, and we call on our people to abide by continuing and reinforcing popular education.

We call on our struggling masses to further boycott and confront those who deviated from our people's will. The past and current decisions of boycotting the occupation circles are a contribution to the limited civil disobedience which paved the way for the comprehensive civil disobedience which will be announced after the completion of the necessary conditions. Based on this, we call on you to carry out the following militant program and activities:

1. To consider tomorrow, 25 May, the passage of forty days after the martyrdom of the national leader and struggler brother Abu Jihad, a day for staging a comprehensive strike and escalating violent struggle. We also call on our masses and our national frameworks to hold commemorative celebrations and mammoth demonstrations. We also call on the national figures to effectively participate in the required activities to honor our symbolic martyr Abu Jihad and all the martyrs of the triumphant Palestinian revolution.

2. To consider the days of 29 and 30 May days for staging a comprehensive strike and escalating the distinguished struggle on the occasion of the convocation of the Reagan-Gorbachev summit.

3. To consider 1 June, International Children's Day, a day of our Palestinian children, during which we shall hold children's parades and present gifts to the children of our righteous martyrs, detainees, and valiant deportees.

4. To consider the days from 3-7 June days for a comprehensive strike in reply to the Zionist Shultz' visit, and on the anniversary of the invasion of Lebanon and the defeat of the Arab regimes. During these days, our strike forces should deal the most painful blows to the occupation soldiers, the herds of settlers and those who deviated from our people's will. These days shall be considered distinguished days of struggle that require a high level of popular participation.

5. To devote the rest of the days for reinforcing popular education and for forming more popular committees, strike forces, family solidarity committees, and other specialized committees.

O our great people, march steadily and resolutely with a spirit of unlimited and great sacrifices, unified struggle, and strong will to make the dawn of the free and independent Palestine. We will achieve victory. God is with us and victory is near. We are together on the path of liberating man and land.

Communique no. 18

May 28, 1988

O masses of our heroic people, who have destroyed the illusions of occupation in more than twenty years, who have refuted the claims about our people's coexistence with occupation, and who have destroyed all attempts to create feeble alternatives to our people's sole legitimate representative, the PLO, through destroying alternatives to the right to repatriation, to self-determination, and to an independent national state: You continue to proceed on the road through your suffering, through the huge sacrifices, and through the constant flow of blood, on the road to achieving freedom and independence for our militant people.

Here is the victorious uprising destroying the apparatus and tools of the fascist occupation, which were established to serve the occupation's interests and to link the interests of our people's masses with the occupation. On the ruins of these tools you are building the apparatus of the heroic people's authority through the popular committees with their various tasks.

Here is the uprising restoring to our national cause its natural stature as the cause of a people who are struggling for the sake of their legitimate national rights. This cause has thus become an important topic on the agenda of the Moscow summit as well as the major topic at the "summit of the uprising" in Algiers.

O our heroic Palestinian people, while marking these days—the twenty-first anniversary of the Arab regimes' defeat and of the occupation of the remainder of our dear homeland, amid the convening of the Moscow summit and the Arab summit and also in view of George Shultz' attempts to resume the conspiracy aimed at aborting the uprising—our people's masses are daily escalating their victorious uprising. There will be no return nor will there be any retreat until occupation is removed and an independent Palestinian state is established under the PLO's leadership.

Our masses know their path through revolution to obtain their rights. It is the path of persistent struggle. More than twenty years of coercion, persecution, oppression, and attempts to liquidate our identity and our people's national cause have created the generation of the uprising—the generation of freedom, independence, and of building an independent national state on its sacred national soil. This generation is determined to make the occupation pay a dear price for desecrating our land and holy places. It is also determined to turn occupation into a hell that will burn the occupying soldiers and settlers.

The Unified National Leadership of the Uprising calls on our masses to further escalate the delivery of painful blows to the neo-Nazis and to further entrench and organize the generation of the uprising and its specialized committees and strike teams along the path of carrying out a comprehensive civil disobedience and fulfilling the slogans and just demands of the uprising as a basic introduction to wrest our people's national legitimate rights to repatriation, self-determination, and the establishment of an independent state.

These slogans and demands include the need to implement the four Geneva Conventions; dispatch international observers to provide the necessary protection for the sons of our people; withdraw the army from the cities, villages, and camps; lift the siege clamped on them; release the detainees; return deportees to their homeland; cancel the taxes and other laws and legislations enacted by the occupation authorities; hold democratic elections for the municipal and village councils; and remove restrictions imposed on our national production to allow for the building and developing of the industrial, agricultural, and services sectors.

The PLO—the Unified National Leadership, along with our people's masses, while waging a tough struggle within a firmly established national unity, calls on the Arab summit leaders to shoulder their responsibilities before their peoples and history by supporting this Palestinian struggle not through denunciation, condemnation, and verbal backing, but by:

1. Adopting a clear and unified political stand before the whole world in support of the PLO and the soleness and legitimacy of its representation of our people and providing all means of support enabling our people to continue their struggle.

2. Rejecting all liquidationist solutions, headed by the Shultz initiative, and insisting on the need to hold a fully empowered international conference with the participation of the PLO in an independent delegation just like the other parties.

3. Releasing political prisoners from Arab prisons, giving democratic freedoms to the Arab masses so they can act in solidarity and cohesion with our people's triumphant uprising, and allowing for fedayin action across Arab borders in the direction of occupied Palestine.

Along the path of implementing a comprehensive civil disobedience, the PLO—Unified National Leadership of the Uprising emphasizes the following:

The need for the immediate resignation of workers in traffic and licensing departments, organization and housing departments, and identity card and registration offices. After the occupation authorities have been forced to reopen schools, it is essential to reprogram the curriculum to compensate the students for what they missed, especially secondary school students in their final year. We trust that schools will continue to be the strong citadels of the uprising. Popular education should play a complementary role in raising our students' efficacy.

Total withholding of cooperation seeks to restrict the movement of the population by boycotting certifications of good conduct and relevant official documents and refusing to have dealings with defeatists; and appointed agent municipal committees in every location are called upon to mobilize the population for a commitment to this patriotic stand.

Banning the payment of all kinds of taxes, boycotting Zionist goods—industrial or agricultural—and completely withholding labor from Zionist settlements.

Refusal by our sons in the [Gaza] Strip to receive the new identity cards. The popular committees are called upon to play a mobilizing role toward that end to consolidate the boycott and in compliance with resolutions of the Unified Leadership of the Uprising.

An intensification of the formation and organization of popular committees, neighborhood committees, health committees, sentry committees, agricultural committees, mobilization guidance committees, information committees, and strike forces—the militant arm of the Unified National Leadership of the Uprising—as well as the economic committees, and encouraging, developing, and entrenching household agriculture and rationalized consumption and spending.

Directing and intensifying blows to dissenters from the will of our people in the appointed village and city council committees, customs offices, and police and intensifying the use of the means of popular struggle beginning with the stone and ending with the gasoline bomb against all the enemies.

O masses of our struggling people, the PLO—the Unified National Leadership—calls on all segments of our people to mark the following days with sweeping mass anger coinciding with forthcoming political events by executing and implementing the following militant activities:

First, dedicating 28 and 29 May to massive marches and rallies involving all national cadres, organizations, and personalities so our voice—the voice of the uprising—may be heard loud and clear by the superpower leaders in Moscow.

Second, dedicating 30 May to an all-out strike and raising the pitch of the militant struggle to mark the Gorbachev-Reagan summit and increasing the writing of nationalist slogans and raising flags in all villages, cities and camps.

Third, dedicating 1 June—International Children's Day—to children's demonstrations raising Palestinian slogans and flags. In the meantime, various committees, especially committees of solidarity with victims of our people, will distribute gifts to the children of the martyrs, the wounded, detainees, and deportees.

Fourth, dedicating 3,4,5, and 6 June to full-scale strikes to mark the visit of Shultz, the Lebanese invasion, and the twenty-first anniversary of the Zionist occupation. In the meantime, our masses and strike forces will stage demonstrations and confrontations with occupiers and their agents. May the land scorch the feet of the usurping occupiers and their agents.

Communique no. 19

c. June 6, 1988

No voice can rise above the voice of the uprising. No voice can rise above the voice of the people of Palestine.

Communique no. 19, the call of the detainees of the uprising.

O masses of our great people, you are fully adhering to the march of your escalating popular uprising. You are adhering to our people's legitimate national rights—including the right to repatriation, self-determination and the establishment of an independent state—and you are firmly rallying around the PLO, your sole legitimate representative, declaring your decisive reply to all plots, projects and options aimed at harming our national rights and liquidating our cause through Camp David and Shultz' initiative.

O masses of our brave people. As the Reagan-Gorbachev summit has failed to reach an agreement on the Middle East crisis and its central issue, the Palestine question, as a result of the intransigent US position and its hostility to our people's aspirations and legitimate national rights, we hail the Soviet support for our cause and we stress our categorical rejection of Shultz' initiative and his tours of the region, which represent a new link in his desperate attempts to abort your glorious uprising. They also represent an additional attempt to exercise US pressures on some Arab sides to affect the Arab summit's political resolutions and spread Shultz' initiative and unilateral solutions in harmony with US imperialist plans in the region.

The meetings, which were and are being held between Rabin, Zionist war minister and terrorist, and some agents who have departed from our people's victorious march and their national will, are no more than attempts to create weak alternatives to represent our people and ignore our sole legitimate representative.

The suspect activity of the agent newspaper *al-Nahar* to establish a research center and its attempt to spread poison through its pages, as well as the suspect activity of its officials, are only an attempt to mislead our people and spread confusion and division among their ranks to divert them from the sound national course. The popular and national committees of the uprising stress their firm condemnation of any meetings with any US and Zionist politicians. They also stress that any talks with our people should take place through our sole legitimate representative.

O masses of our struggling people, through the unity of your will, sacrifices and the escalation of the uprising, you epitomize the decisive reply to your enemies' claim that the uprising is fading away and that your struggle has weakened.

Despite all means of fascist repression and persecution, which are being stepped up by the enemy forces against the masses of the victorious uprising, the uprising is achieving day after day more goals in regaining our freedom and liberation through escalating your boycott of the occupation organs, such as the growing resignations from the Civil Administration Department, not paying taxes to the suckers of our people's blood, boycotting Zionist products, supporting national industries, boycotting work in settlements, effectively cultivating our lands, breeding animals, rationalizing consumption, storing basic items, achieving family and social solidarity, reinforcing the organs of the people's authority, escalating struggle against the fascist occupation forces and the deviationists, and fully abiding by the militant program and resolutions of the uprising's popular and national committees.

This great achievement puts the accelerating march of the uprising on the threshold of a new phase of the struggle—the phase of full-scale civil disobedience. An announcement on this will be made as the requirements for its implementation become available, with completing the construction of institutions of the people's authority in all of the Palestinian cities, villages and camps topping the list. As the uprising's popular and national committees salute the steadfastness of our heroic detainees in the camps of neo-Nazism in the Negev, al-Zahiriya, 'Atlit, Ansar, Megiddo, and al-Fara, as well as all the other detention centers, they stress the need for the resignation forthwith of the appointed village and municipal councils; policemen; customs and tax officers; traffic policemen; and housing, identity card, and birth registration bureau personnel. The uprising's popular and national committees urge a boycott of Zionist goods, clean bills of payment, and withholding of tax payments.

We applaud the attitude of those who have heeded the uprising's call to resign from the above-mentioned agencies and departments, especially those who quit the traffic department. We applaud the heroic resistance to the repressive occupation measures and the scheme of changing identity cards by our masses in the Gaza Strip. We applaud our courageous merchants for abiding by the commercial strike and organizing the opening of their stores until 1200. We caution our people against propaganda and psychological war waged by enemy agencies and agents through media organs or phony leaflets. One of the novel tactics resorted to by Zionist intelligence in spying on people's activities and making arrests is driving cars with West Bank and Gaza Strip license plates and wearing Palestinian folk dress.

We applaud the influential role of our courageous student population in the uprising. As we emphasize that resumption of classes marked an achievement of the uprising and an expression of the enemy's predicament, we urge our children, teachers and academic institutions to regularly hold classes and make up for lost days by going to school on official holidays. We urge total observance of full-scale strike days and office hours until 1200 on normal days. We also urge intensifying popular classes to raise the standard of our pupils' education and so they can make up days missed.

We also call on our pupils to continue to join the uprising's activities and stage demonstrations, rallies and sit-ins in solidarity with fellow detainees. We call upon our heroic laborers to set up further unified worker committees and join existing trade union frameworks to further their rights and their national struggle. We emphasize that working hours should not be increased or any deductions made from any worker's pay on account of the days of full-scale strike. We stress the need to do away with [word indistinct], as it is a departure from the practice of opening commercial stores. We warn all of those who promote Zionist products under Arab names and call on the striking forces to enforce this.

O masses of our valiant uprising, as we congratulate you on your uprising's entering its seventh month with all vigor, we salute your determination to carry it forward on the road of our people's rights to repatriation, self-determination, and statehood. We likewise salute the steadfastness of our heroic kinfolk under siege and our strugglers in the detention centers, our wounded, and the relatives of our martyrs and deportees.

We call upon you to implement the following program of struggle:

1. The 9th of June will be a day of general strike to mark the beginning of the uprising's 7th month and the fall of the first of the uprising's martyrs.

2. The 11th of June will be a day of solidarity with our heroic detainees. Sit-ins, marches, and demonstrations will be held on that day under the supervision of the committees for solidarity with detainees at Red Cross centers.

3. The 13th of June will be a day for strengthening the building of the power of the people, on which our masses will strengthen the formation and the spreading of popular and specialized committees in all areas.

4. The 15th of June will be a day of general strike in solidarity with students and detainees and to bolster popular education.

5. The 16th of June will be a day for storing food and medical supplies, fuel, and other essential supplies.

6. The 18th of June will be a day of intensive mass escalation under the slogan of rallying around the PLO and insisting on our people's rights to repatriation, self-determination and a national state. On that day blows will be dealt to those who do not comply with our people's will.

7. The 19th of June will be a day for a complete boycott of the Civil Administration departments to boost mass resignations and the laws of the people's power.

8. The 20th of June will be the day of the martyred Palestinian child on which children's marches and visits to the parents of our martyred children will be organized.

9. The 22nd of June will be a day of general strike, a day for turning to the land, reclaiming and cultivating it, and destroying and burning the enemy's industrial and agricultural property.

10. Fridays and Sundays will be days for prayers for the souls of our martyrs and days for tumultuous marches and demonstrations.

O our people, let there be further escalation and confrontation of the enemy forces and settlers by resorting to all methods of popular resistance, including the sacred stone and the incendiary Molotov cocktail. We will follow the martyrs' will in our resistance. God is with us. Victory is near. Together along the path of liberating land and man.

Message to the Arab Summit

c. June, 1988

Brother Arab League Secretary General Chedli Klibi, Your Excellency President Chadli Benjedid, chairman of the Arab summit conference, esteemed kings and presidents of the Arab countries: From the main arena of conflict with our nation's enemies and from the heart of holy Jerusalem, the cradle of religions, we address you to acquaint you with the sufferings of our steadfast people, of martyrs and the hundreds of women who suffered miscarriages from poisonous gases.

Our entire people appeal to you to shoulder your pan-Arab responsibilities by supporting them and extending actual assistance to them, to confront attempts to ignore them and harm their political entity the PLO, the leader of their struggle and their sole legitimate representative, and the Unified National Leadership of the Uprising, their struggling arm in the occupied territories. Our people are determined to offer every sacrifice for the sake of their freedom and their legitimate national rights, foremost of which are the right to repatriation, self-determination and the establishment of an independent state under the PLO.

We are confident the Arab nations will not disappoint the militant people of Palestine and will not refrain from supporting them with all means. We are also confident that our glorious nation's resources will deter the usurping enemy if some of these capabilities are used to support our struggle. Our people and the masses of the uprising expect your esteemed conference to shoulder the pan-Arab responsibility of supporting our heroic uprising and the leader of the Palestinian people's struggle, the PLO, our sole legitimate representative, politically, materially, diplomatically, and morally.

We expect you to lend this support to enable them to achieve their goals, by defending our sanctities and the honor of Arabism, and to enable them to live in freedom on their national soil. While we expect your conference to take a clear-cut policy and support our struggle and our sole, legitimate representative, we pledge to you in the name of our masses in the occupied homeland and the masses of the uprising to continue struggle to achieve the following:

1. Secure international protection for our masses from the crimes of the Zionist occupation to pave the way to end the occupation and achieve our people's freedom and independence.

2. Cancel emergency laws and achieve the withdrawal of the Zionist army from the cities, villages and camps.

3. Foil all the suspected plans which deny our people's rights. These plans include autonomy, Camp David, and Shultz' initiative.

4. Convene an international conference with full powers to be attended by the permanent Security Council member states as well as by the PLO independently and on an equal footing with all other parties, considering this conference as the only way to bring about a lasting, just and comprehensive peace.

5. Establish an independent national state under the PLO, its sole legitimate representative.

While we hope your conference will realize its cherished aims, we ask that your governments approve the following:

1. Persevere in carrying out a large-scale media campaign to expose the occupation authorities' practices against our people.

2. Effect permanent and continuous coordination with our sole legitimate representative, the PLO, based on equality and independence.

3. Release Palestinian detainees in some Arab jails.

4. Allow Palestinian communities in the host Arab countries to establish their institutions and unions to be devoted to permanent participation in the struggle against the Zionist enemy.

5. Establish permanent supporting funds for the PLO and funnel all Arab assistance through them.

6. Open Arab frontiers to the fighters of the Palestinian revolution and establish military training camps.

As Palestinian people, our seventy years of struggle have been crowned with the present uprising. Our struggle has realized great achievements for our people and all of the Arab peoples, preserving the dignity of all of us and consecrating our persistent struggle to win our legitimate aspirations to live with honor. Your support for our struggle to establish an independent state is an essential factor for uniting the glorious Arab nation.

Long live the glorious Arab people. Long live our heroic Palestinian people. Long live the PLO, our sole legitimate representative.

Communique no. 20

June 22, 1988

In the name of God, the merciful, the compassionate. Call, call, call. No voice can rise above the voice of the uprising. No voice can rise above the voice of the people of Palestine, the people of the PLO.

Communique no. 20 issued by the PLO—Unified National Leadership of the Uprising. The call of Jerusalem.

O masses of our great people. O masses of the mighty uprising with its popular and national committees. O strike forces of the uprising which deal blows to the occupation remnants with stones, incendiary Molotov cocktails, and all popular resistance means, the tumultuous popular uprising has neither subsided nor has its blaze simmered down as the occupation leaders have been deluding themselves. It intensified, scoring one achievement after the other, and constituted a substantial moral nourishment for pursuing the march of the mighty uprising. Our people observe with evident pride the achievements the uprising has imposed on the international and Arab state of affairs.

The resolutions adopted by the uprising summit in Algiers have come to confirm the changes the uprising has imposed on the Arab world and which have restored self-esteem to the Palestinian people and their cause. The Algiers summit political resolutions are in line with the slogans of the uprising. They have dealt a harsh blow to US policy in the region and have blocked the way to Shultz' attempts to peddle his plan. They have also reaffirmed our people's legitimate national rights to repatriation, self-determination and the establishment of an independent Palestinian state, as well as the fact that the PLO is the sole representative of our people wherever we live. These resolutions have also reaffirmed the need to hold an international conference which enjoys full prerogatives with the participation of the PLO on an equal footing with other parties, as well as the provision of international protection for the sons of our people in the occupied territories.

While we praise the Algerian efforts, in the person of President Chadli Benjedid, in convening this summit and rendering it a success, we call on its leaders to abide by its resolutions and to seriously and effectively work for implementing these resolutions.

O masses of our heroic people, by pursuing its militant march and dismissing any retreat, the uprising brings our people day after day closer to the attainment of its direct objectives on the road to attaining the Palestinian people's national objectives of liberation and independence. Therefore, the Unified National Leadership emphasizes its transient objectives. These are securing international protection for our people in the occupied territories, sending international observers to supervise the implementation of UN laws, holding municipal elections under international supervision, implementing the fourth Geneva convention on the protection of civilians during war, withdrawing the army from residential areas, releasing detainees, closing the Nazi detention centers, repatriating deportees, suspending the deportation policy and respecting human rights.

O masses of our great people, the occupiers believed that their announcement of their annexation of Jerusalem on 28 June 1967 would enable them to impose a *fait accompli* on our people and would contribute to making the world think Jerusalem had become united under the administration of the occupation. However, the effective and active participation of our masses in Jerusalem has foiled the calculations of the occupiers and has entrenched our masses' clinging to the capital of our aspired state with its holy places and civilized heritage.

The Unified National Leadership affirms the following:

The need to pursue the students' struggle to obtain the release of their detained colleagues. The Unified National Leadership calls for the enhancement of popular education for all students, particularly the tawjihi [final scholastic year] students. It reiterates its call to the student body and to its unified committees to work for the protection of the education process by abiding only by the Unified National Leadership's decisions. It calls on officials in universities and institutes to work for the organization of academic life. It also appeals to local, Arab, and world universities to accept the detained tawjihi students who have obtained the first semester diploma and calls on the higher education council to adopt this demand and work for its realization.

The Unified National Leadership greets the heroic merchants who are subjected to surprise tax raids, who are committed to the nonpayment of taxes, and who are determined to pursue the march with our people. It also stresses the need to bolster the confrontation with respect to the nonpayment of all types of taxes, particularly taxes levied on factories. It calls on our heroic merchants to organize sit-ins in protest against the measures the occupation takes against them.

We praise our struggling masses in the Gaza Strip for their confrontation of the occupation authorities' fascist measures, particularly in the al-Burayj camp, in light of the resignation of its local council. We warn our masses in Dayr al-Balah against financial blackmail, which is made by some suspects under national cover. The Unified National Leadership stresses the need to ignore the authorities' instructions to remove national slogans from walls and the need to form committees to secure the process of holding secondary examinations.

The Unified National Leadership affirms its call to all employees in the departments of planning and housing, and the offices of residents' registration and traffic, to resign immediately from their posts to achieve total separation in our masses' relations with enemy institutions. It calls on the strike forces to strengthen their blows against the appointed municipal and village committees and against those who have not resigned from the organs of police and tax.

We call on our doctors to reduce their examination charges and we call on the owners of properties to reduce the rent of properties for those who cannot pay for those affected by the uprising.

We call on Arab countries to grant democratic liberties and to release Arab and Palestinian detainees from prisons.

O masses of the uprising, while the uprising is passing through its seventh month with characteristic escalation and vigor, the Unified National Leadership asserts that for the period of this call its program is dedicated to Jerusalem to express our people's adherence to its Arab character. The program is as follows:

1. June 24 is a day for solidarity with our heroic merchants and for protest against confiscation of properties and identification cards and against the issuing of summonses. During this day blows will be dealt to tax offices and those working in them.

2. June 25 is a day of struggle against apartheid and of solidarity with South Africa. On that day our people will unite in solidarity with all peoples subjected to racial discrimination. It will be a day of struggle under the slogan: Freedom for peoples, death for racists.

3. June 26 is a day of people's authority. On that day blows will be dealt against those who deviated from our people's will and centers of the appointed municipal committees will be attacked.

4. June 28, the day on which the occupation authorities announced their decision to annex Jerusalem, is a day of general strike to assert its Arab character.

5. June 27 and 29 are days of escalation of masses' activity and for massive demonstrations in all areas, and particularly in Jerusalem, under the slogan: Jerusalem is the capital of our Palestinian state.

6. June 30 is a day of national construction. Our masses will unite in solidarity with owners of destroyed and closed houses. All committees will offer help in reconstructing destroyed houses.

7. July 1 is a day of Palestinian heritage. On that day seminars, exhibitions, and other activities will be held to show the civil image of our national heritage and to preserve it from the attempts of deformation and extinction.

8. July 2, the eighteenth anniversary of the heroic strike by detainees in Ashkelon detention center, is a day of solidarity with all detainees and their giant struggles.

9. July 3 is a day of national health. On that day medical personnel and health committees will conduct medical activities.

10. July 4 is a day to strengthen the formation of popular committees and strike forces and a day of storing and popular education.

11. July 5 is a day of general strike. On that day all civil administration departments will be boycotted. On that day Palestinian names will be given to schools and institutions with non-Palestinian names.

O masses of our heroic people, more strikes against fascist occupiers and the herds of settlers; more strike forces, the struggling arm of the Unified National Leadership; more strengthening of the use of popular struggle methods; more destruction of our fascist enemy's property everywhere.

Glory be to our heroic people. Immortality to our virtuous martyrs. We will inevitably triumph.

Communique no. 22

July 21, 1988

O masses of our great people: Your triumphant uprising is escalating day after day, achieving further accomplishments and forging its way ahead with a relentless will and a strong militant unity based on the constants of Palestinian national action represented by our people's national rights to repatriation, self-determination and the establishment of an independent state on national soil with Arab Jerusalem as its capital.

The PLO—the Unified National Leadership, while congratulating our masses, our resisting people's masses, and the Islamic nation on the occasion of the blessed 'Id al-Adha, calls for further unity of ranks and consolidation of the militant national unity of all the national and religious forces to employ all the people's energies in resisting the fascist occupation because the enemy is our common enemy, who does not distinguish between one citizen and another, and there is no room for opening gaps among the ranks of our masses at a time when we are in dire need of the unity of militant efforts and intensification of painful blows to the decaying fabric of occupation that is gradually falling apart.

Our people's masses have succeeded in gaining large-scale world support for our people's rights and our national cause, in disrupting several occupation organs, in increasing contradictions within the Zionist entity, in splitting its political, economic, military and popular institutions, in promoting and entrenching the people's national authority, and in foiling all frail alternatives to the PLO as our people's sole legitimate representative. The new and evolving patterns of our masses' lives and the forms and methods of their confrontation of the occupation authorities' repressive policies are only an indication that the uprising has entered a qualitatively new stage.

O struggling masses of our people, what is happening in the Lebanese arena against our people's masses and the struggling Palestinian rifle is a link in the American scheme aimed at liquidating the militant Palestinian presence in the Lebanese arena.

What the dissident clique, led by Abu Musa [Sa'id Musa Muragha], has perpetrated against our revolution and the PLO and our kinfolk in Lebanon was a stab in the back of our people's blessed uprising.

We call on Syria to immediately stop the scheme of liquidation and spare the Sidon area from what happened in the valiant Burj al-Barajina and Shatila camps. We call on all the revolution factions and the friendly Lebanese forces to stand up like one man to defend our people's rights in the camps of steadfastness in Lebanon.

The Unified National Leadership, while greeting the legendary confrontation demonstrated by the Jerusalem masses in defense of our sanctuaries and the attempts to desecrate and destroy them, calls on our people's masses to protect our holy places and to firmly confront with blood and fire the Zionist Ministry of Interior's decision to resume excavations under the blessed Al-Aqsa Mosque.

The Unified National Leadership, while praising the heroic epics scored by our masses in rebelling Bayt Sahur, steadfast Qalqilya, and all besieged and burning areas, emphasizes the following:

Full adherence to all the previous calls for resignations, boycotts and organization of citizens' lives. The importance of continuing to set up popular committees and support them by rallying around them, seeking their help in solving all problems, and backing their implementation of their programs considering them the people's alternative authority to the occupation authority's organs and appointed committees.

Bolstering and intensifying popular education programs to counter the occupation authorities' stultification policy of closing schools and other institutions. The academic program of the tawjihi students should be intensified and the release of detained students should be demanded so they can take their examinations.

Commending our people's sons in the occupied territories who responded to the calls of the Unified National Leadership to destroy enemy property and to deal blows to its forces. We call on them to actualize their support for our people's uprising and ask them not to respond to the occupation authorities' attempts to recruit them in its organs and departments in the West Bank and Gaza Strip. They should foil the attempt to involve them in this dirty scheme.

Commending the stand taken by the government hospitals—administrations, doctors, and staff—for refusing to obey the authorities' unfair instructions on the rendering of medical services to our people.

The abidance of government department employees, with the exception of the health apparatus, by the days of general strikes.

The firm and collective confrontation of the tax authority and refraining from yielding to its blackmail. The steadfastness of Bayt Sahur should be taken as an example in confronting the tax collection men.

Prohibiting the payment of fines and bail money.

Caution should be taken against the intelligence methods of using men pretending to be newsmen and news agency correspondents and using local public and private cars in surveillance and arrest operations. Caution, all caution against poisonous rumors disseminated by enemy organs, intelligence and agents.

Commendation of our kinfolk's struggle in Jericho and al-'Awja'. We call on them not to be carried away by the tendentious rumors being disseminated by the occupation authorities to split our masses' unity. Such rumors should be firmly confronted.

Total boycott of Israeli centers of tourism and recreation as a contribution to besieging the Zionist economy.

On the occasion of the blessed 'Id al-Adha, the Unified National Leadership announces that shops shall open on Friday and Saturday morning, 22 and 23 July, until 1900. On the 'Id days they will open until 1400. It stresses the need to cancel all celebrations on the 'Id days; these will be confined to religious rituals. There shall be economic expenditures and the 'Id sermon should be devoted to the uprising and the dangers posed to the holy places.

In confirmation of the Unified National Leadership's decision, factories can work with full production capacity for any time they deem fit in coordination with the labor committees, while preserving the workers' rights, especially when working additional hours. Moreover, public vehicles' working time is not confined to certain hours as is the case with the commercial sector. It should be stressed, however, that general strikes should be observed.

The Unified National Leadership, while greeting the striking teams for their effective role in confronting the occupation forces and their organs and departments and those violating our masses' will, calls on them to strike with an iron fist all those who did not resign. They are required to close the streets on the days of general strikes and allow only doctors' cars to pass. They should also write unified national slogans that should be signed only by the Unified National Leadership. Flags should be hoisted, demonstrations organized, tires burned, and stones and Molotov cocktails thrown.

While making a pledge to our revolution, righteous martyrs and the PLO, the leader of our struggle, that it will continue the path of struggle and escalate the uprising along the road of freedom and independence, the Unified National Leadership calls on our masses to carry out the following militant activities:

1. Celebrating the 'Id days by organizing mass processions to visit the martyrs' tombs and place wreaths of flowers and Palestinian flags on them, staging mammoth demonstrations and visiting the families of martyrs, wounded, detainees and deportees.

2. Saying prayers for the souls of martyrs on Fridays and Sundays. Demonstrations and marches will be staged in protest against the occupation authorities' practices against our Islamic and Christian holy places.

3. On 29 July there will be a day of general strike in solidarity with the Palestinian female detainees and in protest against the oppression and harassment to which they are exposed.

4. On 1 and 2 August there will be days of a general strike in solidarity with the deportees and in denunciation of the arbitrary deportation orders.

5. On 21 July-5 August there will be militant activities and mammoth mass confrontations as well as consecration of the people's authority, consolidation of the popular committees, enhancement of popular education, and performance of distinguished activities in solidarity with those harmed by the triumphant uprising.

It is according to the will of the martyrs that we proceed and resist and we will triumph.

Communique no. 23

c. August 5, 1988

In the name of God, the merciful, the compassionate. No voice can rise above that of the uprising. No voice can rise above the voice of the Palestinian people, the people of the PLO.

O masses of our struggling Palestinian people. O masses of the victorious uprising: These days, your uprising is entering its ninth month while it makes more and more achievements on the long and hard path of struggle toward freedom and independence and toward realizing our people's legitimate national hopes and aspirations for repatriation, self-determination, and establishment of their independent state with Jerusalem as its capital.

The latest Jordanian measures to disengage legal and administrative ties with the West Bank came as one of the most important achievements of the great popular uprising. These measures also came as a practical step to implement the Algiers summit resolutions and to bolster the status of the PLO and the exclusivity of its representation of our people as the only party authorized to shoulder all responsibilities toward our people in the homeland and in the diaspora.

Jordan, and all Arab states, are requested to provide the necessary facilities to our people wherever they may be, particularly in the occupied territories, to enable them to continue their struggle and uprising.

This achievement comes to add to your previous achievements, where you made the enemy lose more than $2 billion in the economic sector and where you obtained three resolutions from the UN Security Council. For the first time, these resolutions talk about the occupied Palestinian territories.

You have exposed before the whole world the racist and fascist face of the occupation. You have confirmed our people's national legitimate rights in the uprising's summit in Algiers. You have covered a tangible distance on the path of dismantling the military rule's organs and departments and on the path of building the people's solemn national authority, represented by the national popular committees. You have laid the foundations for a new lifestyle based on cooperation and self-reliance. We all should be proud of these achievements. We must always be ready to preserve and develop them.

The visit by US envoy Murphy to the Middle East region is only a continuation of Shultz' plan and an attempt to breathe life into it after it was foiled by the uprising.

Therefore, the uprising's leadership calls for a continuation in the boycott of the US envoy, or any other envoy of the US administration, as long as this administration continues its denial of our people's national rights and our sole legitimate representative—the PLO.

The leadership calls on our people to receive Murphy with crowded demonstrations and fierce clashes with the occupation troops.

The Unified National Leadership and the masses of the uprising welcome Iran's acceptance of Security Council Resolution 598 on the Gulf war. They consider it a positive step to put an end to this destructive war, which squandered the material and human resources of both countries, and to expel the US fleets from the Gulf. The stopping of this war will offer a great service to our people's uprising and national struggle, especially since Iraq is scoring these glorious victories in defense of our Arab nation's eastern gate.

In the name of the masses of the occupied land, the Unified National Leadership conveys its greetings to the leaders of our revolution and people who are meeting in Baghdad within the framework of the PLO Central Council's meetings. They praise their efforts to achieve resolutions that will support our people's uprising, that will entrench the national unity within the framework of the PLO, based on collective leadership and the resolutions of the eighteenth session of the PNC, and that will affirm the need to convene an effective international conference, with the attendance of the PLO as the sole legitimate representative on an equal footing with other sides to achieve our people's national rights of repatriation, self-determination and the establishment of the independent Palestinian state on our national soil.

You, O sons of our heroic people, the Zionist enemy, through deporting many of you from your homeland, deludes itself into believing it is capable of checking the ongoing uprising. Over the past eight months, you have proved that the measures being perpetrated by the enemy—namely, the deportations, the house demolitions, the terrorizing of citizens, the economic measures and the war it has been waging on the popular nationalist committees, its closure of nationalist institutions, and the claims it has been propagating through the mass media and agents to the effect that the uprising has ended and that its momentum has been weakened—all this and more will fail in the face of your burning flame and the high degree of your readiness to make sacrifices and offer bountiful offerings.

On this road, the Unified National Leadership calls for confronting the enemy and its organs through stressing the following:

Pursuing the enemy's collaborators, those who have not tendered their resignations, those who promote the enemy's products, and those who propagate tendentious rumors. Besides, it must be stressed that people must boycott work in Jewish settlements and must also refrain from paying taxes, fines, and financial bails.

Enhancing and bolstering the activities carried out in a show of solidarity with the male and female detainees jailed in enemy prisons and detention centers, especially those detained in the Ansar III detention center. The women's committees and bodies must shoulder a special responsibility in organizing sit-ins and other appropriate activities.

The Unified National Leadership of the Uprising salutes the peoples who are struggling for the sake of attaining freedom and independence in Namibia, South Africa and Chile and calls upon those with a living conscience throughout the world to work toward releasing the prisoners of freedom and conscience, headed by freedom fighter Nelson Mandela.

Greetings to the Jerusalem masses for their defense of the capital of their independent Palestinian state. They are called upon to maintain a continuous presence around the Al-Aqsa Mosque area to prevent the authorities from carrying out diggings and to confront any danger to our Islamic and Christian holy places.

Deepening and expanding the manifestations of disobedience to the orders issued by the occupation authorities regarding wiping out patriotic graffiti, and summonses, bringing down Palestinian flags, and removing roadblocks and barricades.

Demonstrating collective confrontation of the detention campaigns, the tax-collection campaigns, and the campaigns of demolishing houses, a manifestation of which occurred in the heroic town of Bayt Furik.

Beware of the occupation authorities' attempts to break the unified stand of our merchants by tempting some of them rather than all, such as exempting some from paying taxes in return for renewing their vehicle licenses with the aim of maintaining dealings with the enemy's organs.

We would like to pay tribute to the EEC member states' stand which took the form of failing to approve the renewal of the economic agreement with Israel. We require the Palestinian farmers to refrain from exporting their products through the Israeli Agrexco Company. Beware of some suspect local parties and figures and their relations with the Agrexco Company. We also ask them to form national exporting and marketing institutions.

Also, the Unified National Leadership requires the popular committees to market local agricultural products, to form marketing committees and to support the existing marketing committees with the aim of supporting the Palestinian farmer and aborting enemy attempts to prevent some areas from exporting their products.

The Unified National Leadership affirms that the authorities' closure of universities and higher institutes of learning and termination of the school year before its set date clearly indicate that the occupation seeks to prevent the sons of our people from receiving education.

Consequently, we have no choice but to depend on ourselves to educate ourselves and our sons through organizing and developing popular education. We also ask our universities and our lecturers to find ways to resume university education, especially for students in the final years of study. We also call upon the Higher Educational Council to shoulder its responsibilities in this regard and demand that the universities and higher institutes be reopened.

The Unified National Leadership of the Uprising hails the Jewish doctors who rejected the occupation measures regarding not treating the uprising's wounded, the journalists who are being exposed to repression because they have raised their voices high against the occupation, and all those who are being tortured because they support our people's national rights.

It calls on them to bolster their support for our just struggle and to enlighten the Israeli street about our just rights. This is because any human being who accepts persecution of another cannot be free.

The Unified National Leadership of the Uprising calls on the national and progressive forces behind the green line to discard their differences, stop their mutual propaganda campaigns, and close their ranks and unify their potential to serve our people's triumphant uprising and to attain their legitimate national rights.

The Unified National Leadership of the Uprising, while it is proud of the marches of the strike forces that are wrapped with the colors of the Palestinian flag in the old city in Nablus, and while it appreciates the role of our masses in the camps in Gaza in confronting the enemy's repressive policy, and also in Nablus, Jenin, 'Azzun, and the camps of Jalazun, al-Am'ari, Duhaysha, Jabalyah, al-Shati', and al-Burayj, and all our people's concentrations, also calls for promoting the level of popular committees, the specialized committees, and the strike forces.

It calls on all positions to escalate their uprising and implement the following activities:

1. The day of 8 August 1988 shall be a day for expressing solidarity with the Palestinian detainees, particularly in Ansar II. During this day solidarity activities should be carried out and women's organizations should also perform their duties in this regard.

3. This day of 10 August shall be a news media day to explain the demands of the uprising and its achievements on popular and world levels. Journalists should play a prominent role in this regard.

4. The day of 13 August shall be a day on which the popular and national committees should assess their role to promote and enhance their performance and organization and to set the required programs to develop the uprising.

5. The day of 17 August, the day of Jerusalem, shall be a day of a comprehensive strike to glorify the capital of our great Palestinian state and to protest the arrest and repression campaigns against its righteous sons.

6. The day of 21 August, the twentieth anniversary of the Zionist burning of the blessed Al-Aqsa Mosque, shall be a day of demonstrations and confrontations with the occupiers in condemnation of this hideous crime and of attempts to desecrate and destroy the holy places thorough excavations. This day shall be considered the day of the Al-Aqsa Mosque.

7. The day of 22 August shall be a day for a comprehensive strike to protest the tax authorities' practices against the valiant merchants and to express solidarity with their struggle.

Let us further escalate confrontations against the occupation's soldiers, organs, and agents. Let us have further cohesion and revolutionary vigilance. We will inevitably achieve victory.

General order: No one shall be allowed to speak for, make a statement, or issue a communique in the name of the Unified National Leadership of the Uprising without its prior knowledge or an authorization from it. Let us be cautious against press statements and calls attributed to the Unified National Leadership of the Uprising.

Communique no. 24

c. August 22, 1988

No voice rises above that of the uprising; no voice rises above that of the people of Palestine. Brothers: Here are the most important points of Communique no. 24—the call of the martyrs of the uprising behind bars, issued by the popular and nationalist committees.

The uprising will carry on until national independence in the face of all challenges.

Masses of the giant uprising: Your uprising is tirelessly entering its thirty-sixth week with full momentum and generosity, declaring to the whole world that there is no going back on our people's accomplishments on the road to the establishment of an independent state on our national soil.

Our people: In an attempt to quell the uprising, extinguish its mounting flames and rein it in, and in light of the key role of the popular committees in solidifying the independent authority of the people and dismantling that of the occupation, the terrorist Rabin and his fascist government made a law warning the popular committees and threatening their members with imprisonment and banishment. The popular committees are innovations of our people in the uprising and natural outgrowths of their struggle.

If Rabin thinks that mass expulsions and long prison sentences can kill the uprising, he is facing a disappointment. Just as our people aborted his decision banning the popular committees and shutting down corporations, societies and unions, so will they abort this decision. Our people's response will be decisive and clear. It will be to set up additional committees in all the villages, camps, cities, and neighborhoods; our entire people are popular committees. They are their lungs, which they will never relinquish.

Rabin's expulsion of a number of our people's cadres on the pretext of their membership and leadership of popular committees is but an application of the "transfer" policy, previously proposed by fascist political parties. Does Rabin think that this policy will extinguish the torch of the uprising? For every banished struggler, dozens will appear. Just as banishments failed in the past, so will they fail this time. Indeed, our people's response will be to intensify the uprising, stoke its fires and develop it.

Our people, strugglers who have experienced the bitterness of expulsion orders, know that their stay outside the homeland will not be long and that the day is not far off when they will return to their homeland and an independent Palestinian state, whose outlines are on the horizon. The whole world now realizes more than ever before the importance of settling regional conflicts. Just as the racist occupiers were defeated, so will the occupiers be kicked out of our land so we can build our independent state with Jerusalem as its capital.

Our striving people, our people in the valiant Gaza Strip: The occupation authorities' recourse to a curfew on the entire Gaza Strip and a ban on journalists and reporters from the area are but failed attempts to extinguish the fires of the uprising in its first den. Our people's response in the Strip was resolute, with thousands of Gazans turning out to confront the machines of the occupiers with their bodies and denounce the crime against three of our laborers. The world has learned about what is happening in the closed Gaza Strip in defiance of the occupiers. This response of yours is a true example of disobeying the orders of the occupiers and a prelude to total civil disobedience.

Our people in Ansar and all the Zionist detention centers: Glory is yours. You are raising defiance armed with nothing except your faith in your people and their just cause. Glory to the martyrs of the uprising behind bars—the two martyrs of Ansar III and the two martyrs of torture in the cells of al-Muskubiya and al-Zahiriya. The enemy's recourse to rounding up strugglers unveils the hysteria that grips it in the face of the mounting uprising. Your people in the occupied homeland—that large prison—and in the diaspora are firmly convinced that you will pursue confrontation of the plans of liquidation and humiliation being practiced against you. Yours is part of your people's struggle for their legitimate rights and national independence.

Free people of the world: In the name of our people under curfews and in prisons, the bereaved, children, women, and the elderly who are suffering from the repressive measures of occupation, the command of the uprising's popular and nationalist committees appeals to world public opinion and all human rights groups to stand alongside our striving people and bring pressure to bear on the Zionist authorities to halt mass expulsions, shut down the desert Ansar III detention center, and release more than 3,000 Palestinian strugglers held in this facility, which is very much like a Nazi concentration camp.

The command of the popular and nationalist committees warns the Zionist man in the street against the consequences of the policy of oppression and repression espoused by Shamir, Rabin and Peres against our Palestinian people. This policy will bring you harm if it continues.

Our masses behind the green line: The command of the popular and nationalist committees of the uprising appeals to you once again to set aside your marginal differences, halt information campaigns and close ranks to confront the policy of repressing and smothering the Palestinian Arab identity, pursued by the Zionist authorities. It further calls on you to abort the feverish reactionary efforts against your leaders.

Our valiant masses: The command of the popular and nationalist committees of the uprising—as it salutes our striving masses in Tulkarm, Qabatya, 'Assun, Till, Barqa, Nablus, Kafr Malik, al-Jalazun, al-Am'ari, Balata, Qalandiya, Duhaysha, Bethlehem, Bayt Jala, Bayt Sahur, Bani Nu'aym, al-Zahiriya, al-'Arrub, al-Fawwar, and all the camps and our people's population centers in the heroic [Gaza] Strip—likewise bows in awe and respect for the martyrs of the uprising behind bars.

It appeals to our people to emphasize the following constants in the daily struggle:

Popular education: The leadership of the popular and national committees of the uprising urges all secondary school and university teachers and students to be recruited to render the popular education campaign a success on 1 September, particularly the education of the elementary classes. It also urges them to foil the authority's policy of closing down schools and depriving our sons of education. Popular education is a national responsibility to which everyone must adhere.

Tendentious rumors and statements: The leadership of the popular and national committees of the uprising appeals to our people to abide by its central calls issued in the territories and to be cautious against tendentious statements. In this regard, we warn against the enemy's attempts to sow discord between the national religious forces as recently happened in the Gaza Strip when the enemy tried to set fire to a car belonging to a person from the Islamic complex.

We also warn against defaming the honorable citizens and fabricating family differences in the name of the national cause as happened in the Gaza Strip and Tulkarm. We also ask our people to guard their property and be cautious against the thieves sent by the enemy in a futile attempt to convince our people of the need for a police apparatus.

National agricultural products: We stress the need to boycott Zionist agricultural products and purchase national agricultural products only. Greengrocers and sidewalk vendors should also abide by these instructions.

Winter crops: The leadership of the popular and national committees of the uprising appeals to all our masses to continue promoting and reclaiming the land in preparation for the coming winter and also to plant on this land cereals and legumes such as lentils, chickpeas, broad beans, garlic, wheat and other crops that can be stored.

Medical treatment charges: We ask our private hospitals and doctors to take into account the difficult situation our people are experiencing by reducing fees for medical treatment by a tangible percentage.

Positive initiatives: The leadership of the popular and national committees of the uprising lauds the numerous positive initiatives by the popular and national committees in the territories in a way that conforms with the program of escalating the uprising, such as declaring the car strike in the Gaza Strip and distributing forms among merchants in their shops to count the Zionist goods to support our people in boycotting these goods. Another example is the distribution of treatment cards among the afflicted families in Hebron so that they can receive medical treatment at reduced fees.

O our revolutionary masses, the leadership of the popular and national committees of the uprising, while taking pride in the growing spirit of confrontation enjoyed by our masses as well as the successive attacks carried out by the strike forces against the enemy's forces, apparatus, and settlers, urges the masses of the uprising to promote their confrontation of the Zionist presence and carry out the following militant priorities:

23 August will be a day for deportees, a day of Molotov cocktails. On this day, our masses will rise up in denunciation of the deportation policy.

24 and 25 August will be days for comprehensive strikes in honor of the anniversary of the uprising's martyrs behind bars.

26 August, the anniversary of the 1929 al-Buraq uprising, we ask our masses to mark this anniversary by various militant activities.

On 27 August the strike forces will deal blows to those who were asked to resign, but have not yet done so.

On 30 August a comprehensive strike will be observed in solidarity with the deportees.

On 31 August a comprehensive strike will be observed to protest the burning by the fascists of three of our Palestinian workers in Tel Aviv.

On 1 September detainees will stage a hunger strike to protest the conditions of their arrest. Our masses will also stage sit-ins at the headquarters of international bodies.

The first week of September will be a week for the popular committees devoted to promoting them and forming more of them.

Fridays and Sundays will be devoted to prayers for the souls of the uprising's martyrs.

Further unity, solidarity, and escalation on the path of our people's victorious uprising until national independence is realized. God is with us and victory is close. Let us proceed together on the path of liberating land and man.

Communique no. 26

c. September 26, 1988

No voice rises above the voice of the uprising. No voice rises above the voice of the Palestinian people. Communique no. 26, the Call of Palestine. O masses of our struggling people, your uprising, in its tenth month, is achieving new developments, represented by the nonaligned countries' meeting, which affirmed your just demands and called for a total Zionist withdrawal from the occupied territories and their placement under temporary international supervision in preparation for our people's achieving their right to self-determination.

The Zionist enemy is admitting anew, this time through Shamir, that it is impossible to put an end to the uprising militarily and by force. O sons of our heroic people, your continuation in the popular uprising guarantees the destruction of the US administration's belligerence. It will lead it to give up its arrogance and impossible conditions, which it is attempting to impose on our legitimate representative, the PLO.

Let American imperialism, which supports our enemy with all its power, know that it is the one obliged to bend to our people and not the other way around. Let it recognize the PLO as the sole and legitimate representative of our Palestinian people and their rights to repatriation, to self-determination and to establish an independent state on their national soil with Jerusalem as capital.

Let the Zionist entity know its might and satellites are not more powerful than our stones and will not be able to extinguish the rays of hope shining through the eyes of our children. The Zionist entity is not stronger than the United States nor are our people weaker than the people of Vietnam.

O masses of the uprising, we are a free and struggling nation. The glorious uprising has taught us that through it; through our sacrifices and struggles; through our inflicting great political and economic losses on the enemy; through reversing the winning equation of the occupation, turning its financial gains into losses; and through effecting a true change in the local and international balance of power, we can wrest from the enemy even more achievements along the path of freedom and independence.

Your uprising has come as the most powerful voice of protest. You have declared it loudly and resonantly: No to the occupation, yes and a thousand yeses to liberty and independence. From the depths of this roaring voice, the popular and national committees have structured thorough their repeated calls your specific and general political demands.

The masses of our people ask the UN General Assembly in its forty-second session to assert the national rights of our people, take all measures guaranteeing their implementation and force the Zionist entity to adhere to them. This we ask for along with the following:

1. The Zionist entity's withdrawal from the Palestinian and Arab territories occupied in 1967, including Arab Jerusalem.

2. Canceling all annexation measures and removing the settlements built in the occupied territories.

3. Placing the occupied Palestinian territories under UN supervision and providing protection to our people's masses for a period not exceeding a few months to pave the way for the Palestinian people's free exercise of their right to self-determination.

Work should be done to commit the Zionist entity to the following:

A. Immediately implementing UN Security Council Resolutions 605, 607 and 608.

B. Canceling the 1945 emergency regulations as well as all the domestic and international legislation and military orders.

C. Withdrawing the army from populated Palestinian areas.

D. Releasing the uprising's detainees and repatriating the deportees.

E. Holding free elections for municipal and village councils under UN supervision.

F. Implementing the Fourth Geneva Convention of 1949 as well as all international agreements that regulate the occupation's relationship with the occupied territories.

G. Halting the annihilation measures against our people in terms of economic siege, killings, demolition of houses, torture, deportations, administrative detentions and building of settlements.

O masses of our militant people, the only way to realize these legitimate demands and compel our arrogant enemy to recognize them is through further struggle on all levels, through escalating the uprising and promoting it to higher levels, and though maintaining the uprising's momentum. Moreover, we should always take the initiative. Proceeding on this path, we urge adherence to the following guidelines:

The occupation's onslaught: Anticipating the occupation's onslaught by massive popular action; enhancing the strike committees, the guard duty committees, and the popular committees; consolidating the phenomenon of secretiveness and discretion as well as closing ranks of the internal front; taking to the streets following the example of free Nablus whose masked youths took to the streets in an organized march, thereby marking the takeoff of the esteemed Palestinian popular army. Greetings, all greetings to them and to the uprising's masses in the heroic besieged areas in Qalqilya, Tulkarm, 'Anabta, Kafr Malik and the Gaza Strip whose merchants refused to yield to the enemy's demand to write their names and addresses on the doors of their shops.

The uprising initiative: Taking the uprising initiative; escalating the struggle against the appointed municipal and village committees boycotting the civil administration as well as its bodies and its Arab employees by the masses; striking at and liquidating the agents following the example of the heroic actions carried out against them in Gaza, Nablus, Jenin, Yatta, Sinjil, and other areas; and boycotting and alienating the agents.

Popular education: The aim of popular education is not only the completion of the school curriculum, but also the elimination of illiteracy and the urging of all educational institutions to play their role in defining ways of evaluation and promotion of those who study in the popular education classes. Our slogan is: "Education for resistance."

The workers: We urge our workers to continue their refusal to go to work on days of comprehensive strike and to reject the Zionist demand that workers stay overnight within the green line on the eves of comprehensive strike days so they can avoid revenge. Three of our workers faced such revenge.

The merchants, the factories, and the workshops: The popular and national committees reiterate the need not to pay taxes. The merchants' committees should follow up this issue and reinforce the boycott of Zionist goods which have local alternatives, by publishing lists of them, guaranteeing ways not to raise prices, reducing the prices of national products, fixing prices for the citizens, urging the employers to pay wages and salaries on time as they were doing on the eve of defining the opening and closure hours of the shops, and paying for the days of comprehensive strike.

Agricultural work and cooperatives: The popular and national committees call for mass effort to reap and squeeze out olive fruits and encourage food storage and cooperative work so we can benefit from every Palestinian olive tree. We also urge farmers and oil merchants to sell their products in the local market at reasonable prices because it is our oil and we will use it locally if we cannot export it.

Unity of the internal front: The popular and national committees stress the importance of reinforcing the unity of our internal front, whose rock has crushed all forms of repression and terrorism. We urge our masses to combat all forms of sectarian conflict, which the enemy and its agents are trying to stir up. We also affirm that pumping up some people to show them as if they are rivals of the popular and national committees will fail.

People who are sought for arrest: The popular and national committees salute the sons of our people who have rejected arrest orders. The committees urge the masses to support and assist them.

O the masses of our generous people: The popular and national committees highly appreciate our brave masses in steadfast Qalqilya, which has inspired fear in the hearts of the brutal settlers with its stones, Molotov cocktails, and nails; shaken the entity of the repressive Zionist generals; and replied to the repressive measures by escalating its struggle.

The committees also highly appreciate the Khan Yunis revolutionary masses, which resolutely confront the terrorist Rabin, the minister of repression, and his entourage. They also urge the specialized committees and the strike teams to define a militant timetable in accordance with the circumstances of each center to implement the following combat operations:

1. Escalating the daily confrontations of the Zionist forces and settlers and destroying the enemy's property.

2. Continuing the process of clearing the internal front of the desecration of the enemies.

3. Stepping up voluntary work to help the farmers during olive harvesting season.

4. Showing solidarity with the besieged places by revolutionizing and activating them so no place can be singled out, by sending medical and supply materials to them, and by taking care of the agricultural crops.

5. Showing solidarity with those harmed by the uprising, including captives, wounded, martyrs' families, deportees, the owners of demolished houses, and those who were expelled from work by staging strikes and sit-ins and by assisting them.

6. Monday, 3 October, 1988 will be a day of comprehensive strike to protest the enemy's measure to continue the closure of schools and educational institutions. Sunday, 9 October, 1988 will also be a day of comprehensive strike on the occasion of the eleventh month of the uprising.

Appeal to Israeli Voters

Late October, 1988

To the Israeli public, to the lovers of a just and honorable peace, to all people in the region:

During the past twenty-one years of the Israeli occupation of the West Bank and Gaza, the issue of the occupation and peace has never until now been the center of your daily and electoral concerns. You were never this concerned about what our Palestinian people want, and about what our coming emergency PNC session—the session of the popular uprising—will decide. We are now witnessing historic times in which the international community is experiencing a period of openness and desire to solve regional conflicts by peaceful means. This is a time in which our people are more determined than ever to obtain their just and legitimate rights and accomplish a comprehensive and lasting peace for all the peoples of this area.

But instead of your leaders stating the clear truth, they block every initiative aimed at solving our bloody conflict in an honorable and just way. Your leaders consciously distort our blessed popular uprising, its goals and its democratic and peaceful means by increasing their oppressive measures, violating the most basic human rights and international principles which are aimed at protecting women, children and the aged. Your leaders are working on the illusion that they can demoralize and exhaust our people and therefore crush the uprising. We approach you from a position of confidence that the way of repression and terror which your army and government practice against our unarmed people is proving to be a failure because our people's uprising is accelerating. Your leaders' action will not produce any sign of peaceful coexistence between the occupation authorities and the victims. Therefore, the only guaranteed way to peace is by granting the Palestinian people their legitimate right of self-determination, the right of return, and to establish the independent Palestinian state in the West Bank and Gaza. [Peace will be accomplished] by guarantees of mutual security for all the people in the area.

And contrary to what your government leaders are accusing us of, we declare to you in a clear way and in the name of our people that the blessed uprising came as an expression of our people's refusal of occupation and insistence on living in freedom, liberty and honor just like all the countries of the free world which are able to exercise sovereignty. This has been our continuous search, for a just peace and security for all. The slogan of the uprising has also been clear: the need for Israel to withdraw from the territories occupied in 1967 so that we can create our Palestinian state on them ...

The uprising has proven the failure of the military expansionist policies, the threats of "transfer," and the other options that could be imposed on our people, such as "autonomy" and the "condominium" plan. We have shown that no option exists except the Palestinian option represented by the PLO, our sole and legitimate representative, within the context of an international conference with full authority. In the same way that our people don't impose the personality or the identity of the representatives of Israel at this conference, we insist on our right to choose by ourselves who represents us. And in this context our choice is the PLO as the sole and legitimate representative of all our people inside and outside. The search for alternatives to the PLO will not produce results and is counter-productive. Attempts to separate our people from their brethren outside will also fail.

The PLO/Unified Leadership feels that the clarity of the uprising's slogans and its peaceful and democratic nature are a vivid expression of the Palestinians' desire for a just peace and security. It approaches Israelis in order to create the kind of atmosphere necessary to accomplish this just peace which will give security to all people of the area. This includes the Palestinian state and Israel. For this it calls on the Israelis to vote for peace, for withdrawal, for an effective international conference, for recognition of and negotiations with the PLO.

The Unified Leadership commends all Israeli progressive and peace forces for their courage and applauds all who denounce Israeli terror in the occupied territories.

The PLO/Unified Leadership, in the name of the people of the uprising, calls on our Arab brethren inside to vote for the lists that support the legitimate rights of our Palestinian people, led by the PLO, and the convening of an effective international conference with the participation of the PLO in order to create the Palestinian state under its leadership.

The Unified Leadership of the Uprising addresses the minds and consciences of every Israeli so that they can seize this historic opportunity to reach a just peace. This appeal is made with the Unified Leadership recognizing its historic responsibility, and its determination to continue the uprising until complete Israeli withdrawal from Jerusalem, the West Bank and Gaza is accomplished and the Palestinian people are able to enjoy their right to self-determination, the right to return and to establish the independent Palestinian state...

Fake Communique no. 28

O great people of the uprising!

O great people for independence!

We salute the conferences which were held in Aqaba and Baghdad, with Husni Mubarak, the president of the biggest Arab country; Saddam Hussein of Iraq, the eastern gate of the Arab world; and King Hussein of Jordan, the door to hope in the battle for victory.

The meetings of our three most influential friends in the area confused Israel and put it in a corner because of this peace assault which came as the result of the uprising.

The Israelis were so upset by the meetings that they bombed the camps in Lebanon and intensified their attacks in the occupied territories...

The Unified National Leadership of the Uprising, with the masses behind it, declares that if the PNC does not adopt resolutions that fit with its aspirations, the Unified National Leadership of the Uprising will prove its ability to take its future into its own hands, to achieve independence and self-determination, and to change the struggle from being a revolt against occupation into a struggle to defend a state on its homeland...

Communique no. 28

October 30, 1988

In the name of God, the merciful, the compassionate. No voice rises above the voice of the uprising. No voice rises above the voice of the Palestinian people, the people of the PLO. Communique no. 28 issued by the PLO, the Unified National Leadership of the Uprising, the call of independence.

O masses of our great people, your uprising is on the verge of entering its twelfth month after all the barbaric Zionist measures of repression have failed. These measures consist of killings, arrests, deportation, and demolition of properties to abort and snuff out the flame of the tumultuous revolution which flows from your sacred chests as you, the heroes of the strike forces, the popular committees and all the sectors of our militant masses have decided through your heroic persistence to pursue the blessed popular revolution and to offer the costly sacrifices it requires on the road to freedom, independence and the repulsion of occupation. The world at large now testifies to the bravery of your strikes, which inflicted successive political defeats on the Zionist machine of repression and the fascist executioners in Tel Aviv.

At this time in particular, and while our children in 'Anabta and the Tulkarm, Khan Yunis, and Rafah camps are falling as a result of the unjust Zionist bullets in the battles of honor, heroism and sacrifice, our PNC prepares to hold its nineteenth extraordinary session, the uprising martyrs' session and that of the symbol martyr Abu Jihad, in the country of the million martyrs to transform the achievements of our heroic and ever-escalating uprising into political gains on the road to freedom, independence and national liberation, and to formulate a realistic and well-defined political program that will honor the blood of our martyrs, the groans of our wounded and the sufferings of our prisoners in enemy jails.

O masses of our heroic people, the Unified National Leadership renews the pledge to you and to the leaders of our revolution, headed by the father symbol Abu Ammar [Yasir Arafat], that it will proceed forward with the popular uprising until the attainment of all our firm national objectives, chief among which is the right to repatriation, self-determination and the establishment of an independent state with Arab Jerusalem as its eternal capital.

Our people's victorious uprising, which continues to push ahead with legendary pride and a vigor unprecedented in the history of human civilization, daily scores one victory after another, leaving our enemy and all the organs of repression it possesses to founder and to be perplexed after our great masses succeeded in exercising their sacred slogan that there can be no going back, no retraction, and no submission no matter the cost we will pay and in spite of the convoys of martyrs who are daily falling on the altar of national independence. The honorable righteous blood of our martyrs and their spirits that hover in the sky of our beloved homeland, Palestine, will crown our PNC session with laurels and slogans for the continuation of both the revolution and the uprising, God willing.

O masses of our struggling people, the Unified National Leadership, which is the striking arm of the PLO, the sole legitimate representative of our people everywhere, salutes, in your name, the leaders of our revolution who will take part in the session of martyrs and national independence and urges them to work seriously for crystallizing a clear and definitive political program that secures the firm and inalienable national rights of our people and is in line with the requirements of the current stage. The program should also be able to deal with the world community on the basis of our people's adherence to the achievement of a just peace in the region and an honorable solution to our cause.

Within this framework, the Unified National Leadership stresses to Israeli public opinion that our blessed uprising, which our people exploded with the blood of their beloved sons on 9 December, was not out of a desire to shed Palestinian or Jewish blood. Rather, it was a revolution against the injustice, oppression and fascism of the occupation and a national determination to establish just peace in our region. Such a peace cannot be attained unless a Palestinian state is established on our national soil.

As we call on our PNC to adopt realistic resolutions and political programs for the sake of our people and to end the occupation and establish our independent state, we also take the opportunity to emphasize the call that the PLO—the Unified National Leadership—has recently issued to Israeli public opinion and which called on Arab and Israeli voters to vote for the forces of peace that support our people's right to self-determination and the establishment of their independent state on the soil of their homeland.

O all of our kinfolk: The Unified National Leadership salutes the UN General Assembly session which will be convened especially to discuss the blessed uprising of our people, to support our just cause, and to accentuate the right of the Palestinian people to self-determination and the establishment of an independent state on their soil.

The Unified National Leadership calls on the General Assembly member states to expedite the placement of the occupied territories under international supervision and the protection of our defenseless people against the acts of oppression, murder and forced expulsion by the occupation forces. The Unified National Leadership hopes the distinguished General Assembly will move beyond protest and condemnation of the enemy's tyrannical operations to action to put an end to the violations of Palestinian human rights and safeguard the present and future of the Palestinians, so they may perform their cultural role and contribute to the march of humanity in the service of the just causes in the world.

The Unified Leadership appeals to the UN Security Council, the international community, and all freedom- and peace-loving nations to denounce the savage, barbaric bombings of our people's camps in Lebanon by the Zionist air force. The gradual annihilation of our people in Lebanon coincides with the oppression, physical liquidation and mass arrests practiced by occupation forces against our heroic people in the occupied land, where they are seeking to ignite the situation on the eve of Israel's elections in order to secure votes.

We appeal to the UN General Assembly to bring pressure to bear on the occupation authorities to reopen higher education establishments and fight the Zionist policy of making illiterates of our people. The Unified National Leadership condemns suspect moves by certain quarters in Lebanon that every now and then attempt to destroy the Palestinian presence there. It urges all nationalist efforts in Lebanon to join hands in resisting Zionist occupation and confronting its arrogant acts against our people and the heroic Lebanese people and their nationalist forces supportive of and allied with the PLO, the sole legitimate representative of our people.

Our great masses: The UN General Assembly session which was called to debate the uprising on the Palestinian day coincides with the 1974 appearance of the symbol leader Abu Ammar for the first time at the United Nations, where he gave Palestine's historic speech. The leader of the Palestinian march then waved an olive branch in one hand as a symbol of peace and a gun as a symbol of struggle in the other. Inspired by the speech, our people in the occupied land hold the olive branch in one hand and the sacred stone in the other.

These days mark the anniversary of the PLO being recognized as a UN member with observer status despite attempts by American imperialism to have this recognition withdrawn or [word indistinct]. The Unified National Leadership urges our people, their strike forces and popular committees to intensify daily action by way of demonstrations and stone throwing at occupation forces to mark the occasion Palestinian-style, whose distinctiveness we all know.

Our great masses: The Unified National Leadership would like to call the following points to your attention:

1. We would stress the importance of strict observance of the days of general strike called by the Unified National Leadership in its official statements instructing the strike forces to see to its implementation.

2. The Unified National Leadership would like to remind you that the partial strike hours run between 0800 and 1200.

3. The Unified National Leadership urges the submersion of marginal and side differences that may disrupt our blessed militant march.

4. It stresses the common aim and destiny of all sectors of our people and national factions of establishing an independent state and of self-determination. We call for closure of ranks and directing all energies to defeating occupation.

5. We stress the importance of popular education and the need to undertake the required efforts to make it a success, given the shutdown of educational institutions by occupation authorities.

6. The need to keep the schools open in Jerusalem and Gaza and not to give further justifications to the occupation authorities to close them again.

7. We urge popular committees and strike forces to organize voluntary work and join assistance groups to help poor farmers reap their olive harvests in all areas.

8. The Unified National Leadership stresses what was mentioned in its previous statements, the importance of commitment to boycotting the occupation's circles as much as possible, and implementation of the instructions of the local leadership of the Unified National Leadership in this regard.

O masses of the sacred uprising. The Unified National Leadership urges you to carry out the militant missions and activities as follows:

Tuesday, 1 November, is the day of the martyred child.

Wednesday, 2 November, is the day of overall strike on the occasion of the ill-starred Balfour Declaration, and the day of overall escalation.

Friday, 4 November, the day for harvesting the olive crop and on which assistance groups and the social work and voluntary committees will help our farmers to harvest the olive crop.

Sunday, 6 November, is the day of solidarity with Ansar III detainees and all our detainees.

Monday, 7 November, is the day of education on which denunciation cables will be sent regarding the continuation of the policy of making our people illiterate. Sit-ins and protest marches will also be staged against the continued closure of education institutions.

Wednesday, 9 November, is the day of comprehensive strike to mark the passage of twelve months of our uprising. Marches will be held and visits to martyrs' tombs and the families of detainees will take place.

Friday, 11 November, is the day of family and social cooperation. Needy families will be assisted and social visits will be exchanged.

Saturday, 12 November, is the day of the PNC. Festivals, meetings, and conferences will be held. Marches will be organized and militant cables will be sent to the PNC on the occasion of its session. The days of the PNC session will be days for special escalation. Throw more Molotov cocktails, firebombs and stones. Let us burn the ground under the feet of the Zionist invaders.

Tuesday, 15 November, is the day of national independence on which the masses of our Palestinian people everywhere will center their attention on Algiers pending the national independence declaration. It will be a day of comprehensive celebrations, whose activities include:

A. Raising Palestinian flags over every house and place and writing national slogans in the name of the Unified National Leadership.

B. Visiting the tombs of the martyrs who sacrificed their souls for the sake of freedom and independence.

C. Organizing rallies in which national songs are sung and strike forces and scouts march.

D. All the masses of our people will take to the streets at 1600 on 15 November. They will use loudspeakers and chant: My country, my country, my country: My love and heart are for you. These activities will continue for three days.

Saturday, 19 November, is the day of comprehensive strike on the anniversary of the martyrdom of the exemplary leader 'Izz al-Din al-Qassam.

Fridays and Sundays are days of prayer for the souls of the martyrs. Sweeping demonstrations will be held in support of the extraordinary PNC session's decisions.

O our masses, O sons of al-Qassam, O brothers of martyr Abu Jihad and all our righteous martyrs: Make more sacrifices, throw more Molotov cocktails, and achieve more unity. We will continue to resist together on the martyrs' path. Long live the PLO, the sole legitimate representative of our people wherever they may be. Long live 15 November, the day of national independence. Long live the brave uprising of our people.

Communique no. 29

November 20, 1988

To the masses of our people:

May you enjoy your well-deserved celebrations, for you are the hosts of these festivities and the joy of the independent state. Congratulations on all the resolutions of the Palestine National Council in its Session of the Uprising! Congratulations on the declaration of an independent Palestinian state! Congratulations to the mother of the martyr, for she has celebrated only twice: when she gave her son, and when the state was declared. Felicitations to the wounded who smiled and forgot their pain only after hearing the declaration of independence! Congratulations to the prisoners behind bars, whom, after the declaration of independence, no force will be able to demoralize!

Congratulations to all our women, men, children, and the old! The declaration is your stone, affirming the oneness of your struggle with the will of our sole legitimate representative. This stone, which has penetrated the most far-flung corners of the earth, has frightened our enemies and increased their isolation and fear. Our friends, on the other hand, have been celebrating with us, and news agencies continue to bring news of their recognition of our right to a state.

To the People of the Uprising:

In the name of the people of the occupied territories, the Unified National Leadership of the Uprising sends greetings to the PNC and to the Executive Committee of the PLO, our sole legitimate representative. The Unified National Leadership of the Uprising wishes to express its appreciation for the responsible way in which the PLO interacted with the uprising; this was reflected in the ratification of the declaration of independence and the independent Palestinian state, and in the adoption of a clear political program taking advantage of the historic opportunity presented to our people to gain its rights. These rights are the right to return, to self-determination and the establishment of an independent state.

The decisions of the PNC have measured up to the intensity of our uprising, and have provided it with increased momentum. These decisions reflect the strength of national unity both inside and outside the occupied territories. Our leadership has demonstrated its ability to take decisive steps at this most critical juncture in the struggle of our people. This historic opportunity has come about as a result of the sustained struggle of our people, most recently during the uprising.

The declaration of the independent Palestinian state affirms the Palestinian identity of our occupied land as well as the sovereignty of the Palestinian people over this land. The declaration affirms that it is impossible to retreat from the goal of national independence, whatever the difficulties and no matter how great the sacrifice. It has foreclosed all the suspect "alternatives" and "options" proposed over the years by forces hostile to our people, and has underlined the fact that only one option, the Palestinian choice, will survive.

The PNC in its Session of the Uprising, the Session of Martyr Abu Jihad, has called for the convening of an effective international conference under United Nations auspices to be attended by the five permanent members of the UN Security Council, all parties to the conflict, and the PLO on an equal footing with other parties. The PNC has called for the convening of an international conference based on UN Resolutions 242 and 338, at the same time affirming the right of the Palestinian people to self-determination. This position demonstrates our people's desire for a just and comprehensive peace, and reflects the Palestinians' stance towards the resolution of regional conflicts based on international legitimacy.

The decisions of the PNC cannot be considered as concessions given *gratis,* as has been claimed by some. They are rather realistic, responsible and revolutionary resolutions meant to put an end to the Zionist lies about the goals of our revolution, and to place limits upon the suffering of our people under occupation. Our state is the state of all the Palestinians.

The Unified National Leadership of the Uprising appeals to certain fundamentalist quarters to place the national interest above their factional concerns and interests, and to correct the negative attitudes which, whether intended or not, serve only the enemy. These quarters are called upon to draw the correct conclusions from the joyous mass celebrations which reflect the deep roots of the Palestine Liberation Organization in our society. The opportunity is still there to unite all sincere efforts in the framework of the uprising under the leadership of the Unified National Leadership of the Uprising.

The Unified National Leadership of the Uprising calls upon all Arab states to match their words with deeds by exploiting their energies and resources in making the declaration of an independent state a reality; we call upon them to exert pressure upon the United States and the Western nations for the convening of an international conference and the realization of our inalienable national rights. The true measure of Arab solidarity is the achievement of this goal, which is the goal of our people as well as that of all the people in the Arab world.

To the Masses of Our People:

The Unified National Leadership of the Uprising wishes to underline the following:

1. We affirm that all segments of the people of the occupied Palestinian state support and endorse the declaration of independence and all other resolutions taken at the nineteenth session of the PNC. As a demonstration of this fact, the United National Leadership of the Uprising calls upon the striking forces to escalate their confrontations with the occupation authorities.

2. We denounce all suspect communiques and statements, especially those which malign individuals and accuse them of embezzlement. We also denounce any statement which defames a national organization with the aim of creating schisms within our ranks. We warn our people to beware of collaborators who threaten anyone raising his voice in support of the decisions of the PNC. We call upon you to make the Palestinian voice heard loud and clear all over the world. The continuation of the independence celebrations is the answer to those collaborators who have tried without success to silence some nationalist figures. The United National Leadership of the Uprising warns all collaborators to beware.

3. We call upon you to strengthen popular committees, and to support national industries while at the same time guaranteeing the rights of our workers and working towards employing more laborers in national enterprises.

4. We encourage our people to form cooperatives for the marketing of agricultural produce, and to support Palestinian farmers in their struggle against the restrictions placed on them by the occupation authorities.

5. We call upon you to continue the struggle to reopen educational institutions, to expand popular education and to combat the occupier's designs to keep our people ignorant.

6. In view of the decisions taken at the nineteenth session of the PNC, the United National Leadership of the Uprising blesses the statement issued by nationalist institutions and professional associations on November 15, Independence Day, in which they announced that their unions, societies and institutions were now independent Palestinian bodies. We invite all Pales-

tinian institutions and sectors to lay the foundation for the new structure, the framework for the struggle for independence.

The Unified National Leadership of the Uprising calls upon you to continue the celebrations of the feast of independence, and invites our people to observe the following:

1. To devote November 21 to paying visits to the wounded and to families of prisoners and martyrs.

2. To stage marches on November 22, to strike at collaborators, and to increase pressure on appointed municipal councils to resign from their posts.

3. To observe a general strike on November 23 in solidarity with deportees, and to call for the rescinding of standing deportation orders.

4. To devote November 24 to political mobilization and to hold seminars clarifying the significance and ramifications of the resolutions of the PNC.

5. To mount attacks against the occupation and its collaborators on November 25 and 26.

6. To observe a general strike on November 28 in solidarity with prisoners and to call for their immediate release.

7. To mark the Day of Solidarity with the People of Palestine on November 29, when our leader Yasir Arafat will address the General Assembly of the United Nations. The flag of our independent state will be raised on this day, and demonstrations and confrontations with the army will be launched.

8. To devote the period from November 30 to December 4 to escalating support for our state and for the PLO's standing in the United Nations. November 30 shall be considered a day of national solidarity when popular committees will organize campaign to provide supplies and winter clothing to needy families.

9. To observe a general strike on December 6 in solidarity with prisoners at the Ansar III prison.

May our unity be strengthened!

More stones and molotovs against the enemy and its collaborators!

On the path of the martyr Abu Jihad, we continue and resist!

Proclamation of the Independent Palestinian State

Issued by the Nineteenth Session of the Palestine National Council, held in Algiers, November 15, 1988

In the name of God, the Compassionate, the Merciful.

Palestine, the land of the three monotheistic faiths, is where the Palestinian Arab people was born, on which it grew, developed and excelled. The Palestinian people was never separated from or diminished in its integral bonds with Palestine. Thus the Palestinian Arab people ensured for itself an everlasting union between itself, its land and its history.

Resolute throughout that history, the Palestinian Arab people forged its national identity, rising even to unimagined levels in its defense as invasion, the designs of others, and the appeal special to Palestine's ancient and luminous place on that eminence where powers and civilizations are joined...all this intervened thereby to deprive the people of its political independence. Yet the undying connection between Palestine and its people secured for the land its character and for the people its national genius.

Nourished by an unfolding series of civilizations and cultures, inspired by a heritage rich in variety and kind, the Palestinian Arab people added to its stature by consolidating a union between itself and its patrimonial land. The call went out from temple, church and mosque to praise the Creator, to celebrate compassion, and peace was indeed the message of Palestine. And in generation after generation, the Palestinian Arab people gave of itself unsparingly in the valiant battle for liberation and homeland. For what has been the unbroken chain of our people's rebellions but the heroic embodiment of our will for national independence? And so the people were sustained in the struggle to stay and to prevail.

When in the course of modern times a new order of values was declared with norms and values fair for all, it was the Palestinian Arab people that had been excluded from the destiny of all other peoples by a hostile array of local and foreign powers. Yet again has unaided justice been revealed as insufficient to drive the world's history along its preferred course.

And it was the Palestinian people, already wounded in its body, that was submitted to yet another type of occupation over which floated the falsehood that "Palestine was a land without people." This notion was foisted upon some in the world, whereas in Article 22 of the Covenant of the League of Nations (1919) and in the Treaty of Lausanne (1923), the community of nations had recognized that all the Arab territories, including Palestine, of the formerly Ottoman provinces were to have granted to them their freedom as provisionally independent nations.

Despite the historical injustice inflicted on the Palestinian Arab people resulting in their dispersion and depriving them of their right to self-determination, following upon UN General Assembly Resolution 181 (1947), which partitioned Palestine into two states, one Arab, one Jewish, yet it is this resolution that still provides those conditions of international legitimacy that ensure the right of the Palestine Arab people to sovereignty and national independence.

By stages, the occupation of Palestine and parts of other Arab territories by Israeli forces, and the deliberate dispossession and expulsion from their ancestral homes of the majority of Palestine's civilian inhabitants, was achieved by organized terror; those Palestinians who remained, as a vestige subjugated in their homeland, were persecuted and forced to endure the destruction of their national life.

Thus were principles of international legitimacy violated. Thus were the Charter of the United Nations and its resolutions disfigured, for they had recognized the Palestinian Arab people's national rights, including the right of return, the right to independence, the right to sovereignty over territory and homeland.

In Palestine and on its perimeters, in exile distant and near, the Palestinian Arab people never faltered and never abandoned its conviction in its rights of return and independence. Occupation, massacres and dispersion achieved no gain in the unabated Palestinian consciousness of self and political identity, as Palestinians went forward with their destiny, undeterred and unbowed. And from out of the long years of trial in every mounting struggle, the Palestinian political identity emerged further consolidated and confirmed. And the collective Palestinian national will forged itself in a political embodiment, the Palestine Liberation Organization, its sole legitimate representative, recognized by the world community as a whole as well as by related regional and international institutions. Standing on the very rock of conviction in the Palestinian people's inalienable rights, and on the ground of Arab national consensus, and of international legitimacy, the PLO led the campaigns of its great people, molded into unity and powerful resolve, one and indivisible in the triumphs, even as it suffered massacres and confinement within and without its home. And so Palestinian resistance was clarified and raised into the forefront of Arab and world awareness, as the struggle of the Palestinian Arab people achieved unique prominence among the world's liberation movements in the modern era.

The massive national uprising, the intifada, now intensifying in cumulative scope and power on occupied Palestinian territories, as well as the unflinching resistance of the refugee camps outside the homeland, have elevated consciousness of the Palestinian truth and right into still higher realms of comprehension and actuality. Now at last the curtain has been dropped around a whole epoch of prevarication and negation. The intifada has set siege to the mind of official Israel, which has for too long relied exclusively upon myth and terror to deny Palestinian existence altogether. Because of the intifada and its irreversible revolutionary impulse, the history of Palestine has therefore arrived at a decisive juncture.

Whereas the Palestinian people reaffirm most definitely its inalienable rights in the land of its patrimony:

Now by virtue of natural, historical and legal rights and the sacrifices of successive generations who gave of themselves in defense of the freedom and independence of their homeland;

In pursuance of resolutions adopted by Arab summit conferences and relying on the authority bestowed by international legitimacy as embodied in the resolutions of the United Nations Organization since 1947; and in exercise by the Palestinian Arab people of its rights to self-determination, political independence and sovereignty over its territory;

The Palestine National Council, in the name of God, and in the name of the Palestinian Arab people, hereby proclaims the establishment of the State of Palestine on our Palestinian territory with its capital Jerusalem (al-Quds al-Sharif).

The State of Palestine is the state of Palestinians wherever they may be. The state is for them to enjoy in it their collective national and cultural identity, theirs to pursue in it a complete equality of rights. In it will be safeguarded their political and religious convictions and their human dignity by means of a parliamentary democratic system of governance, itself based on freedom of expression and the freedom to form parties. The rights of minorities will be duly respected by the majority, as minorities must abide by decisions of the majority. Governance will be based on principles of social justice, equality and nondiscrimination in public rights on grounds of race, religion, color or sex under the aegis of a constitution which ensures the role of law, and on an independent judiciary. Thus shall these principles allow no departure from Palestine's age-old spiritual and civilizational heritage of tolerance and religious co-existence.

The State of Palestine is an Arab state, an integral and indivisible part of the Arab nation, at one with that nation in heritage and civilization, with it also in its aspiration for liberation, progress, democracy and unity. The State of Palestine affirms its obligation to abide by the Charter of the League of Arab States, whereby the coordination of the Arab states with each other shall be strengthened. It calls upon Arab compatriots to consolidate and enhance the emergence in reality of our State, to mobilize their potential, and to intensify efforts whose goal is to end Israeli occupation.

The State of Palestine proclaims its commitment to the principles and purposes of the United Nations, and to the Universal Declaration of Human Rights. It proclaims its commitment as well to the principles and policies of the Non-Aligned Movement.

It further announces itself to be a peace-loving state, in adherence to the principles of peaceful co-existence. It will join with all states and peoples in order to assure a permanent peace based upon justice and the respect of rights so that humanity's potential for well-being may be assured, an earnest competition for excellence be maintained, and in which confidence in the future will eliminate fear for those who are just and for whom justice is the only recourse.

In the context of its struggle for peace in the land of love and peace, the State of Palestine calls upon the United Nations to bear special responsibility for the Palestinian Arab people and its homeland. It calls upon all peace- and freedom-loving peoples and states to assist it in the attainment of its objectives, to provide it with security, to alleviate the tragedy of its people and to help to terminate Israel's occupation of Palestinian territories.

The State of Palestine herewith declares that it believes in the settlement of regional and international disputes by peaceful means, in accordance with the UN Charter and resolutions. Without prejudice to its natural right to defend its territorial integrity and independence, it therefore rejects the threat or use of force, violence and terrorism against its territorial integrity or political independence, as it also rejects their use against the territorial integrity of other states.

Therefore, on this day unlike all others, 15 November 1988, as we stand at the threshold of a new dawn, in all honor and modesty we humbly bow to the sacred spirits of our fallen ones, Palestinian and Arab, by the purity of whose sacrifice for the homeland our sky has been illuminated and our land given life. Our hearts are lifted up and irradiated by the light emanating from the much-blessed intifada, from those who have endured and have fought the fight of the camps, of dispersion, of exile, from those who have borne the standard of freedom, our children, our aged, our youth, our prisoners, detainees and wounded, all those whose ties to our sacred soil are confirmed in camp, village and town. We render special tribute to the brave Palestinian woman, guardian of sustenance and life, keeper of our people's perennial flame. To the souls of our sainted martyrs, to the whole of our Palestinian Arab people, to all free and honorable peoples everywhere, we pledge that our struggle shall be continued until the occupation ends, and the foundation of our sovereignty and independence shall be fortified accordingly.

Therefore, we call upon our great people to rally to the banner of Palestine, to cherish and defend it, so that it may forever be the symbol of our freedom and dignity in that homeland, which is a homeland for the free, now and always.

In the name of God, the Compassionate, the Merciful.

Say: "O God, Master of the Kingdom, Thou givest the Kingdom to whom Thou wilt, and seizest the Kingdom from whom Thou wilt. Thou exaltest whom thou wilt, and Thou abasest whom Thou wilt; in Thy hand is the good; Thou art powerful over everything."

Palestine National Council "Political Communique"

Issued by the Nineteenth Session of the Palestine National Council, held in Algiers, November 15, 1988

In the name of God, the Compassionate, the Merciful.

In the valiant land of Algeria, hosted by its people and its President Chedli Benjedid, the Palestine National Council held its nineteenth extraordinary session—the session of the intifada and independence, the session of the martyred hero Abu Jihad—in the period between 12 and 15 November 1988.

This session culminated in the announcement of the rise of the Palestinian state in our Palestinian land, the natural climax of a daring and tenacious popular struggle that started more than seventy years ago and was baptized in the immense sacrifices offered by our people in our homeland, along its borders, and in the camps and other sites of our diaspora.

The session was also distinguished by its focus on the great Palestinian intifada as one of the major milestones in the contemporary history of the Palestinian people's revolution, on a par with the legendary steadfastness of our people in their camps in our occupied land and outside it.

The primary features of our great people's intifada were obvious from its inception and have become clearer in the twelve months since then during which it has continued unabated: It is a total popular revolution that embodies the consensus of an entire nation—women and men, old and young, in the camps, in the villages and in the cities—on the rejection of the occupation and on the determination to struggle until the occupation is defeated and terminated.

This glorious intifada has demonstrated our people's deeply rooted national unity and their full adherence to the Palestine Liberation Organization, the sole legitimate representative of our people, all our people, wherever they congregate—in our homeland or outside it. This was manifested by the participation of the Palestinian masses—the unions, their vocational organizations, their students, their workers, their farmers, their women, their merchants, their landlords, their artisans, their academics—in the intifada through its Unified National Command and the popular committees that were formed in the urban neighborhoods, the villages and the camps.

This, our people's revolutionary furnace and their blessed intifada, along with the cumulative impact of our innovative and continuous revolution inside and outside of our homeland, have destroyed the illusion our people's enemies have harbored that they can turn the occupation of Palestinian land into a permanent *fait accompli* and consign the Palestinian issue to oblivion. For our generations have been weaned on the goals and principles of the Palestinian revolution and have lived all its battles since its birth in 1965—including the heroic resistance against the Zionist invasion of 1982 and the steadfastness of the revolution's camps as they endured siege and starvation in Lebanon. Those generations—the children of the revolution and of the Palestine Liberation Organization—rose to demonstrate the dynamism and continuity of the revolution, detonating the land under the feet of its occupiers and proving that our people's reserves of resistance are inexhaustible and their faith is too deep to uproot.

Thus did the struggle of the children of the RPGs outside our homeland and the struggle of the children of the sacred stones inside it blend into a single revolutionary melody.

Our people have stood fast against all the attempts of our enemy's authorities to end our revolution, and those authorities have tried everything at their disposal: they have used terrorism, they have imprisoned us, they have sent us into exile, they have desecrated our holy places and restricted our religious freedoms, they have demolished our homes, they have killed us indiscriminately and premeditatedly, they have sent bands of armed settlers into our villages and camps, they have burned our crops, they have cut off our water and power supplies, they have beaten our women and children, they have used toxic gases that have caused many deaths and abortions, and they have waged a war of ignorance against us by closing our schools and universities.

Our people's heroic steadfastness has cost them hundreds of martyrs and tens of thousands of casualties, prisoners and exiles. But our people's genius was always at hand, ready in their darkest hours to innovate the means and formulas of struggle that stiffened their resistance, bolstered their steadfastness and enabled them to confront the crimes and measures of the enemy and carry on with their heroic, tenacious struggle.

By standing firm, continuing their revolution and escalating their intifada, our people have proven their determination to press ahead regardless of the sacrifices, armed with the great heritage of struggle, an indomitable revolutionary will, a deeply entrenched national unity that has been rendered even stronger by the intifada and its attendant struggles inside and outside our homeland, and total adherence to the nationalist principles of the Palestine Liberation Organization and its goals of ending the Israeli occupation and achieving the Palestinian people's inalienable right to repatriation, self-determination and the establishment of the independent Palestinian state.

In all this, our people relied on the sustenance of the masses and forces of our Arab nation, which have stood by us and backed us, as demonstrated by the wide popular support for the intifada and by the consensus and resolutions that emerged at the Arab summit in Algiers—all of which goes to confirm that our people do not stand alone as they face the fascist, racist assault. This precludes any possibility of the Israeli aggressors isolating our people and cutting them off from the support of their Arab nation.

In addition to this Arab solidarity, our people's revolution and their blessed intifada have attracted widespread worldwide solidarity, as seen in the increased understanding of the Palestinian people's cause, the growing support of our just struggle by the peoples and states of the world, and the corresponding condemnation of Israeli occupation and the crimes it is committing, which has helped to expose Israel and increase its isolation and the isolation of its supporters.

Security Council Resolutions 605, 607 and 608, and the resolutions of the General Assembly against the expulsion of the Palestinians from their land and against the repression and terrorism with which Israel is lashing the Palestinian people in the occupied Palestinian territories—these are strong manifestations of the growing support of international opinion, public and official, for our people and their representative, the Palestine Liberation Organization, and of the mounting international rejection of Israeli occupation with all the fascist, racist practices it entails.

The UN General Assembly's Resolution 21L/43/1 of 11 April 1988, which was adopted in the session dedicated to the intifada, is another sign of the stand the peoples and states of the world in their majority are taking against the occupation and with the just struggle of the Palestinian people and their firm right to liberation and independence. The crimes of the occupation and its savage, inhuman practices have exposed the Zionist lie about the democracy of the Zionist entity that has managed to deceive the world for forty years, revealing Israel in its true light—a fascist, racist, colonialist state built on the usurpation of the Palestinian land and the annihilation of the Palestinian people, a state that threatens and undertakes attacks and expansion into neighboring Arab lands.

It has thus been demonstrated that the occupation cannot continue to reap the fruits of its actions at the expense of the Palestinian people's rights without paying a price—either on the ground or in terms of international public opinion.

In addition to the rejection of the occupation and the condemnation of its repressive measures by the democratic and progressive Israeli forces, Jewish groups all over the world are no longer able to continue their defense of Israel or maintain their silence about its crimes against the Palestinian people. Many voices have risen among those groups to demand an end to these crimes and call for Israel's withdrawal from the occupied territories in order to allow the Palestinian people to exercise their right to self-determination.

The fruits that our people's revolution and their blessed intifada have borne on the local, Arab and international levels have established the soundness and realism of the Palestine Liberation Organization's national program, a program aimed at the termination of the occupation and the achievement of our people's right to return, self-determination, and statehood. Those results have also confirmed that the struggle of our people is the decisive factor in the effort to snatch our national rights from the jaws of the occupation. It is the authority of our people, as represented in the popular committees, that controls the situation as we challenge the authority of the occupation's crumbling agencies.

The international community is now more prepared than ever before to strive for a political settlement of the Middle East crisis and its root cause, the question of Palestine. The Israeli occupation authorities, and the American administration that stands behind them, cannot continue to ignore the national will, which is now unanimous on the necessity of holding an international peace conference on the Middle East and enabling the Palestinian people to gain their national rights, foremost among which is their right to self-determination and national independence on their own national soil.

In the light of this, and toward the reinforcement of the steadfastness and blessed intifada of our people, and in accordance with the will of our masses in and outside of our homeland, and in fidelity to those of our people that have been martyred, wounded or taken captive, the Palestine National Council resolves:

First: On the Escalation
and Continuity of the Intifada

A. To provide all the means and capabilities needed to escalate our people's intifada in various ways and on various levels to guarantee its continuation and intensification.

B. To support the popular institutions and organizations in the occupied Palestinian territories.

C. To bolster and develop the popular committees and other specialized popular and trade union bodies, including the attack groups and the popular army, with a view to expanding their role and increasing their effectiveness.

D. To consolidate the national unity that emerged and developed during the intifada.

E. To intensify efforts on the international level for the release of detainees, the return of those expelled, and termination of the organized, official acts of repression and terrorism against our children, our women, our men and our institutions.

F. To call on the United Nations to place the occupied Palestinian land under international supervision for the protection of our people and the termination of the Israeli occupation.

G. To call on the Palestinian people outside our homeland to intensify and increase their support, and to expand the family-assistance program.

H. To call on the Arab nation, its people, forces, institutions and governments, to increase their political, material, and informational support for the intifada.

I. To call on all free and honorable people worldwide to stand by our people, our revolution, our intifada against the Israeli occupation, the repression, and the organized, fascist official terrorism to which the occupation forces and the fanatical armed settlers are subjecting our people, our universities, our institutions, our national economy, and our Islamic and Christian holy places.

Second: In the Political Arena

Proceeding from the above, the Palestine National Council, being responsible to the Palestinian people, their national rights and their desire for peace as expressed in the Declaration of Independence issued on 15 November 1988; and in response to the humanitarian quest for international detente, nuclear disarmament, and the settlement of the Arab-Israeli conflict and its core, which is the question of Palestine, within the framework of the United Nations Charter, the principles and provision of international legality, the norms of international law, and the resolutions of the United Nations, the test of which are Security Council Resolutions 605, 607 and 608, and the resolutions of the Arab summits, in such a manner that safeguards the Palestinian Arab people's rights to return, to self-determination, and the establishment of their independent national state on their national soil, and institutes arrangements for the security and peace of all states in the region.

Toward the achievement of this, the Palestine National Council affirms:

1. The necessity of convening the effective international conference on the issue of the Middle East and its core, the question of Palestine, under the auspices of the United Nations and with the participation of the permanent members of the Security Council and all parties to the conflict in the region including the Palestine Liberation Organization, the sole legitimate representative of the Palestinian people, on an equal footing, and by considering that the international peace conference be convened on the basis of United Nations Security Council resolutions 242 and 338 and the attainment of the legitimate national rights of the Palestinian people, foremost among which is the right to self-determination and in accordance with the principles and provisions of the United Nations Charter concerning the right of peoples to self-determination, and by the inadmissibility of the acquisition of the territory of others by force or military conquest, and in accordance with the relevant United Nations resolutions on the question of Palestine.

2. The withdrawal of Israel from all the Palestinian and Arab territories it occupied in 1967, including Arab Jerusalem.

3. The annulment of all measures of annexation and appropriation and the removal of settlements established by Israel in the Palestinian and Arab territories since 1967.

4. Endeavoring to place the occupied Palestinian territories, including Arab Jerusalem, under the auspices of the United Nations for a limited period in order to protect our people and afford the appropriate atmosphere for the success of the proceeding of the international conference toward the attainment of a comprehensive political settlement and the attainment of peace and security for all on the basis of mutual acquiescence and consent, and to enable the Palestinian state to exercise its effective authority in these territories.

5. The settlement of the question of the Palestinian refugees in accordance with the relevant United Nations resolutions.

6. Guaranteeing freedom of worship and religious practice for all faiths in the holy places in Palestine.

7. The Security Council is to formulate and guarantee arrangements for security and peace between all the states concerned in the region, including the Palestinian state.

The Palestine National Council affirms its previous resolutions concerning the distinctive relationship between the Jordanian and Palestinian peoples, and affirms that the future relationship between the two states of Palestine and Jordan should be on a confederal basis as a result of the free and voluntary choice of the two fraternal peoples in order to strengthen the historical bonds and the vital interests they hold in common.

The National Council also renews its commitment to the United Nations resolutions that affirm the right of peoples to resist foreign occupation, colonialism and racial discrimination, and their right to struggle for their independence, and reiterates its rejection of terrorism in all its forms, including state terrorism, affirming its commitment to previous resolutions in this respect and the resolution of the Arab summit in Algiers in 1988, and to UN Resolutions 42/195 of 1987 and 40/61 of 1985, and that contained in the Cairo declaration of 1985 in this respect.

Third: In the Arab and International Arenas

The Palestine National Council emphasizes the importance of the unity of Lebanon in its territory, its people and its institutions, and stands firmly against the attempt to partition the land and disintegrate the fraternal people of Lebanon. It further emphasizes the importance of the joint Arab effort to participate in a settlement of the Lebanese crisis that helps crystalize and implement solutions that preserve Lebanese unity. The Council also stresses the importance of consecrating the right of the Palestinians in Lebanon to engage in political and informational activity and to enjoy security and protection; and of working against all the forms of conspiracy and aggression that target them and their right to work and live; and of the need to secure the conditions that assure them the ability to defend themselves and provide them with security and protection.

The Palestine National Council affirms its solidarity with the Lebanese nationalist Islamic forces in their struggle against the Israeli occupation and its agents in the Lebanese south; expresses its pride in the allied struggle of the Lebanese and Palestinian peoples against the aggression and toward the termination of the Israeli occupation of parts of the south; and underscores the importance of bolstering this kinship between our peoples and the fraternal, resistant people of Lebanon.

And on this occasion, the Council addresses a reverent salute to the long-suffering people in our camps in Lebanon and its south, who are enduring the aggression, murder, starvation, destruction, air raids, bombardments, and sieges perpetrated against the Palestinian camps and Lebanese villages by the Israeli army, air force and navy, aided and abetted by hireling forces in the region; and it rejects the resettlement conspiracy, for the Palestinian's homeland is Palestine.

The Council emphasizes the importance of the Iraq-Iran cease-fire resolution for the establishment of a permanent peace between the two countries and in the Gulf region, and calls for an intensification of the efforts being exerted to ensure the success of the negotiations for the establishment of peace on stable and firm foundations; affirming, on this occasion, the pride of the Palestinian Arab people and the Arab nation as a whole in the steadfastness and triumphs of fraternal Iraq as it defended the eastern gate of the Arab nation.

The National Council also expresses its deep pride in the stand taken by the peoples of our Arab nation in support of our Palestinian Arab people and of the Palestine Liberation Organization and of our people's intifada in the occupied homeland; and emphasizes the importance of fortifying the bonds of resistance among the forces, parties and organizations in the Arab national liberation movement, in defense of the right of the Arab nation and its peoples to liberation, democracy and unity. The Council calls for the adoption of all measures needed to reinforce the unity of struggle among all members of the Arab national liberation movement.

The Palestine National Council, as it hails the Arab states and thanks them for their support of our people's struggle, calls on them to honor the commitments they approved at the summit conference in Algiers in support of the Palestinian people and their blessed intifada. The Council, in issuing this appeal, expresses its great confidence that the leaders of the Arab nation will remain, as we have known them, a bulwark of support for Palestine and its people.

The Palestine National Council reiterates the desire of the Palestine Liberation Organization for Arab solidarity as the framework within which the Arab nation and its states organize themselves to confront Israel's aggression and within which Arab prestige can be enhanced and the Arab role strengthened to the point of influencing international policies to the benefit of Arab rights and causes.

The Palestinian National Council expresses its deep gratitude to all the states and international forces and organizations that support the national rights of the Palestinians, and affirms its desire to strengthen the bonds of friendship and cooperation with the Soviet Union, the People's Republic of China, the other socialist countries, the non-aligned states, the Latin American states and the other friendly states, and notes with satisfaction the signs of positive evolution in the position of some West European states and Japan in the direction of support for the rights of the Palestinian people, applauds this development, and urges intensified efforts to increase it.

The National Council affirms the fraternal solidarity of the Palestinian people and the Palestine Liberation Organization with the struggle of the peoples of Asia, Africa and Latin America for their liberation and reinforcement of their independence; and condemns all American attempts that threaten the independence of the states of Central America and interfere in their affairs.

The Palestine National Council expresses the support of the Palestine Liberation Organization for the national liberation movements in South Africa and Namibia under the leadership of SWAPO with a special salute to our brother combatant, Nelson Mandela, against the racist regime of Pretoria; demands that the people of the two countries be enabled to attain their liberty and independence; and also expresses its support for the African confrontation states and its condemnation of the racist South Africa regime's aggression against them.

The Council notes with considerable concern the growth of the Israeli forces of fascism and extremism and the escalation of their open calls for the implementation of their policy of annihilation and individual and mass expulsion of our people from their homeland, and calls for intensified efforts in all arenas to confront this fascist peril. The Council at the same time expresses its appreciation of the role and courage of the Israeli peace forces as they resist and expose the forces of fascism, racism and aggression; support our people's struggle and their valiant intifada; and back our people's right to self-determination and the establishment of an independent state. The Council confirms its past resolutions regarding the reinforcement and development of relations with these democratic forces.

The Palestine National Council also addresses itself to the American people, calling on them all to strive to put an end to the American policy that denies the Palestinian people's national rights, including their sacred right to self-determination, and urging them to work toward the adoption of policies that conform with the Human Rights Charter and the international conventions and resolutions and serve the quest for peace in the Middle East and security for all peoples, including the Palestinian people.

The Council charges the Executive Committee with the task of completing the formation of the Committee for the Perpetuation of the Memory of the Martyr Abu Jihad, which shall initiate its work immediately upon the adjournment of the Council.

The Council sends its greeting to the United Nations Committee on the Exercise of the Inalienable Rights of the Palestinian People, and to the fraternal and friendly international and non-governmental institutions and organizations, and to the journalists and media that have stood and still stand by our people's struggle and intifada.

The National Council expresses deep pain at the continued detention of hundreds of combatants from amongst our people in a number of Arab countries, strongly condemns their continued detention, and calls upon these countries to put an end to these abnormal conditions and release those fighters to play their role in the struggle.

In conclusion, the Palestine National Council affirms its complete confidence that the justice of the Palestinian cause and of the demands for which the Palestinian people are struggling will continue to draw increasing support from honorable and free people around the world; and also affirms its complete confidence in victory on the road to Jerusalem, the capital of our independent Palestinian state.

Intifada and Independence

1. See, for example, Robert I. Friedman's article in *Mother Jones* (June 1988).

The West Bank Rises Up

1. *New York Times*, December 20, 1987.

2. *Jerusalem Post*, February 26, 1988.

3. In his 1987 report, Benvenisti notes a "new trend in Palestinian resistance" in the ratio between "planned violent acts involving firearms, perpetrated by organized cells" and spontaneous rock throwing and violent demonstrations, what he calls "terrorist/spontaneous" acts, from 1:11 between 1977-84 to 1:18 in 1986-87. Benvenisti fails to relate these to other forms of resistance, such as the sit-ins, marches, demonstrations and commercial strikes that characterized the "mini-uprising" of the spring of 1986, and the slow development of community-based mobilization and grassroots committees since about 1980.

4. Although, interestingly, not its politics. "Official" statements, anyway, continue to stress an independent state, rather than the politics of return.

5. Meron Benvenisti, *The West Bank Data Base Project 1987 Report.*

6. *Jerusalem Post*, December 16, 1987.

7. *New York Times*, January 1, 1988; *Jerusalem Post*, December 28, 1987.

8. *Jerusalem Post*, December 25, 1987.

9. *Ibid.*

10. *Jerusalem Post*, January 20, 1988.

11. *Ibid.*

12. *Jerusalem Post*, February 18, 1988.

13. *Jerusalem Post*, February 15, 1988.

14. *Jerusalem Post*, February 19, 1988.

Beita

1. One effect of the intifada has been to weaken the sway of the Palestinian clan over local politics. The military authorities have been able in the past, for example, to exploit intrafamilial rivalries to their advantage; this is no longer possible. Participation in local committees in the uprising crosses family lines and blurs them; loyalty to the nascent state is replacing the older feudal subjection.

The Palestinian People

1. For some of the author's analyses of these political changes, see Rashid Khalidi, "Palestinian Politics After the Exodus from Beirut," in Robert Freedman (ed.), *The Middle East After Camp David* (Syracuse: Syracuse University Press, 1986); "Policy-Making in the Palestinian Polity," in Harold Saunders (ed.), *New Directions in Foreign Relations: The United States in a Changing Middle East* (Washington, DC: American Enterprise Institute, forthcoming); and "The PLO as Representative of the Palestinian People," in R. Norton and M. Greenberg (eds.), *The International Relations of the PLO* (Carbondale, IL: Southern Illinois University Press, forthcoming). For the Lebanese political context for these changes, see Rashid Khalidi, *Under Siege: PLO Decisionmaking During the 1982 War* (New York: Columbia University Press, 1986), chapter 1. See also "The Uprising and the Palestinian Question," *World Policy Journal,* vol. 5, no. 3 (Summer 1988), pp. 497-517.

2. For a discussion of the literature on this subject see Zachary Lockman, "Original Sin," in this volume, and Rashid Khalidi, "Revisionist Views of the Modern History of Palestine: 1948," *Arab Studies Quarterly,* vol. 10, no. 4 (Fall 1988), pp. 49-57.

3. For the full text of the Political Statement, see the appendix.

What the Uprising Means

1. See Peter Demant, "Israeli Settlement Policy Today," *MERIP Reports,* 116 (July-August 1983).

Palestinian Women

1. G. al-Khalili, *The Palestinian Women and the Revolution* (Acre: Dar al-Aswar, 1981; in Arabic), and Julie Peteet, "Women and the Palestinian Movement: No Going Back," *MERIP Middle East Report,* 138 (January-February 1986), pp. 20-24.

2. See Jayawardena Kumari, *Feminism and Nationalism in the Third World* (London: Zed Press, 1986), and Miranda Davis, *Third World, Second Sex* (London: Zed Press, 1983).

3. Most of the premises of In'ash al-Usra were closed down by the military authorities for a period of two years on June 20, 1988.

4. *The Atlantic,* June 1988.

5. For a critique of this perspective see Amal Rassam, "Toward a Theoretical Framework for Women's Studies": "To begin an inquiry into the subject by taking the public/private scheme as a 'given' is to run the risk of distorting data by forcing them into one or the other of the two categories, and more important, it draws attention away from the central fact that Arab men and women live in one world, no matter how much it seems to be separated into two domains."

6. Al-Haq, *Punishing a Nation* (Boston: South End Press, 1989, forthcoming).

7. Rosemary Sayigh, "Looking Across the Mediterranean," *MERIP Middle East Report,* 124 (June 1984).

8. B. Lipman, *Israel: The Embattled Land: Israeli and Palestinian Women Talk About Their Lives* (London, 1988), p. 153.

9. Popular committees, which often include representatives of the different PLO factions, have guided the uprising on a community level, while neighborhood committees took on the tasks of survival and community development: alternative teaching, home gardening, protection of the neighborhood, food storage, first aid and health. Sometimes a single committee handles

all these functions, but often they are separate. At their peak of public activity, neighborhood committees were most widespread in the towns, particularly Ramallah, Beit Sahur and Nablus.

10. In Palestinian society men can have authority over women even if there is no material base for it; for example a younger brother may have authority over a sister who is supporting him. This authority is sometimes understood as deriving from the *shari'a* (Islamic law) which makes men the guardians of women.

11. Rosemary Sayigh, "Looking Across the Mediterranean," p. 23.

12. *The Jerusalem Post*, August 19, 1988.

13. Michele Barret, *Women's Oppression Today: Problems in Marxist-Feminist Analysis* (London: Verso, 1980), p. 4.

The Islamic Resistance Movement

1. For a survey of Palestinian Islamist groups, including the Muslim Brothers, see Jean-Francecois Legrain, "Islamistes et Lutte Nationale Palestinienne dans les Territoires Occupés par Israel," *Revue Francaise de Science Politique*, vol. 36, no. 2 (April 1986), pp. 227-247; and Sa'id al-Ghazali, "An Introduction to Islamic Parties and Programmes," *Al-Fajr Weekly*, June 29, 1984, pp. 8-9.

2. Israeli journalist Yehuda Litani has claimed as much: "Until [a] few years ago, some Israeli officials thought that the best way to fight the PLO was to encourage the Moslem fundamentalists in the territories. Some of the fundamentalist groups did receive help and encouragement from the Israeli authorities..." *The Jerusalem Post*, September 8, 1988.

3. In contrast to pre-uprising Muslim Brothers positions regarding the PLO, the Hamas Charter considers the PLO as "the closest of intimates." And until such time as the PLO adopts an Islamist outlook, Hamas' attitude toward it will be that of "a father to his son or a brother to his brother."

Original Sin

1. Benny Morris, *The Birth of the Palestinian Refugee Problem* (Cambridge: Cambridge University Press, 1988), p. 207.

2. (New York: The Free Press, 1986).

3. At Deir Yassin, a village near Jerusalem, military forces from Begin's Etzel (known to US citizens as the "Irgun") and Yitzhak Shamir's Lehi massacred 250 Palestinian civilians on April 9-10, 1948.

4. Tom Segev, *1949: The First Israelis* (New York: Free Press, 1986), p. 89.

5. *A History of the Israeli Army* (New York: MacMillan, 1985), p. 40.

6. See Peretz Kidron, "Truth Whereby Nations Live," in Edward Said and Christopher Hitchens (eds.), *Blaming the Victims: Spurious Scholarship and the Palestinian Question* (New York: Verso, 1988).

7. Originally published in *The Spectator* of May 12, 1961, "The Other Exodus" has been reprinted in Walter Laqueur and Barry Rubin (eds.), *The Israel-Arab Reader* (New York: Penguin, 1984), and in Walid Khalidi (ed.), *From Haven to Conquest* (Washington, DC: Institute for Palestine Studies, 1987).

8. See "The Wordless Wish: From Citizens to Refugees," in Ibrahim Abu-Lughod (ed.), *The Transformation of Palestine* (Evanston, IL: Northwestern University Press, 1971).

9. See, for example, Nafez Nazzal, *The Palestinian Exodus from Galilee, 1948* (Washington, DC: Institute for Palestine Studies, 1978).

10. In a few cases, expulsions were fortuitously averted. A few days after the depopulation of Lydda and Ramle, for example, the IDF commander responsible for Nazareth, just conquered, was ordered to expel its inhabitants. He refused to carry out the order, which was eventually rescinded by the high command. However, as Flapan notes (p. 101), the fact that the order was given suggests "the existence of a definite pattern of expulsion."

11. Simha Flapan, *The Birth of Israel: Myths and Realities* (New York: Pantheon, 1987), pp. 3-4.

12. Flapan, *Ibid.,* p. 10.

13. Flapan, *Ibid.,* p. 116.

14. Flapan, *Ibid.,* p. 241.

15. Segev, *op cit.,* p. vii.

16. Segev, *op cit.,* pp. 322-323.

17. Now available in English as *Israel's Fateful Decisions* (New York: Harper and Row, 1988).

From Land Day to Peace Day

1. Israel includes the approximately 125,000 Arabs of annexed East Jerusalem among its "non-Jewish" residents. They are omitted here because, while they may apply for Israeli citizenship, very few have actually done so. The legal status of those who have not is ambiguous; they may vote (but usually do not) in municipal elections, but not in Knesset elections.

2. The Triangle consists of twenty-seven Arab villages along Israel's pre-1967 border with Jordan, many of which were ceded by Jordan to Israel during the 1949 armistice talks.

3. As reported in the *Jerusalem Post International Edition,* November 26, 1988.

4. *The Conditions and Status of the Arabs in Israel: Abstracts of papers presented as part of a research project under the direction of Professor Henry Rosenfeld with the support of the Ford Foundation* (Tel Aviv, June 1988). Only this summary and one of the five monographs (Majid al-Haj and Henry Rosenfeld, *Arab Local Government in Israel*) are currently available. The International Center for Peace in the Middle East is seeking an American publisher for all the monographs.

5. *Ibid.*

6. Tirzah Agassi, "Hashem Mahameed: Living Among the Jews," *New Outlook,* July 1988, p. 21.

7. *Ibid.*

8. Interviews with laid-off teachers during the Nazareth work camp, July 21, 1987.

9. This account of the origins of the NCALC is based on al-Haj and Rosenfeld, *Arab Local Government in Israel,* pp. 141 ff.

10. In 1965 the Communist Party of Israel split. The mainly Jewish group, which kept the party name, dissolved in 1972. The second, mainly Arab group took the name "New Communist List" (Rakah), but has now reclaimed the party name.

11. *Yedi'ot Abronot,* April 19, 20, 1976; *Jerusalem Post,* April 22, 23, 1976; al-Haj and Rosenfeld, *Arab Local Government in Israel,* p. 146.

12. According to Table 2, the DFPE's share of the 1977 Arab vote was 49.4 percent. But if estimates of the vote in the mixed cities are included, the DFPE's share of the Arab vote may have been as high as 50.8 percent.

13. *Jerusalem Post International Edition,* November 12, 1988.

14. See Shammas' articles in *The New York Review of Books,* March 31, 1988 and September 29, 1988 and the exchange of letters, November 24, 1988.

15. *Hadashot,* April 5, 1988; *Ha'aretz,* June 8, 1988.

16. *al-Sinara,* November 25, 1988. The symposium was held at the Institute for Arab Studies at Giv'at Chaviva, an institution operated by Mapam's kibbutz movement.

The Uprising's Impact on Israel

1. *Yedi'ot Ahronot,* March 7 and 13, 1988.

2. *Ha'aretz,* August 18, 1988.

3. *Ha'aretz,* August 24, 1988.

4. Dan Margalit, *Ha'aretz,* August 28, 1988.

5. Akiva Eldad, *Ha'aretz,* July 4, 1988.

6. Interview with Shamir, *Ha'aretz,* March 11, 1988.

7. Ya'ir Sheli, *Ha'aretz* supplement, August 15, 1988.

8. *Ha'aretz,* October 18, 1988.

9. *Yedi'ot Ahronot,* October 26, 1988.

10. *Ha'aretz,* April 7, 1988.

11. Dr. Gidon Biger, *Ha'aretz,* November 15, 1988.

12. *Ha'aretz,* May 6, 1988. See also Mapam's program.

13. CRM program.

14. *Ha'aretz,* June 12 and 24, 1988; September 11, 1988. Y. Harkabi, *Hachra'ot Goraliot* [Fateful Decisions] (Tel Aviv, 1986), pp. 49-78.

15. *Yerushalayim,* October 7, 1988.

16. *Ha'aretz,* June 24, 1988.

17. *Ha'aretz,* June 8 and August 14, 1988.

18. Shlomo Gazit, *Hagezer vehamakel* [The Carrot and the Stick] (Tel Aviv, 1985), pp. 150, 179, 182.

19. Dan Sagir series in *Ha'aretz,* April 20-May 3, 1988.

20. *Ibid.*

21. *Ha'aretz,* April 25, 1988.

22. *Judea, Samaria and Gaza Area Statistics,* March 1987.

23. Tzvi Timor, *Al Hamishmar,* January 1, 1988.

24. According to Bruno: 1) There was no significant drop in Israeli exports to the territories, except for textiles which depend on workshops in the territories; 2) The number of workers from the territories coming to work in Israel decreased by 20 percent, affecting mainly the agricultural and construction sectors but generally not at the macroeconomic level; 3) Increased military expenditures (estimated at $65 million) were not considered real expenses because they were moved from one line item to another in the military budget, though increasing the number of troops would lead to additional expenses; 4) Tourism had not been affected, but a drop was expected in April. *Ha'aretz,* March 11, 1988; *Hadashot,* March 13, 1988.

25. *Davar,* May 5, 1988.

26. *Davar,* March 15, 1988.

27. *Ha'aretz,* August 31, 1988.

28. *Ha'aretz,* July 27, 1988.

29. *Ha'aretz,* November 29, 1988.

30. *Ha'aretz,* June 28, 1988.

31. Lecture in a meeting with contractors. *Hadashot* and *Davar,* May 4, 1988.

32. *Ha'aretz,* April 1, 1988.

33. The drop is not only the result of the boycott; customs taxes on foreign cigarettes were lowered as well.

34. Data given by officer for agricultural affairs, *Ha'aretz,* May 27, 1988.

35. *Yedi'ot Ahronot,* June 2, 1988.

36. *Ha'aretz,* June 24, 1988.

37. *Ha'aretz,* August 23, 1988.

38. *Ha'aretz,* April 11, 1988.

39. *Ha'aretz,* August 2, 1988.

40. *Davar,* May 5, 1988; *Yedi'ot Ahronot,* October 17, 1988.

41. *Yedi'ot Ahronot,* June 13, 1988.

42. *Ha'aretz,* May 5, 1988; *The West Bank Data Base Project 1987 Report,* p. 30.

43. *Ha'aretz,* November 7, 1988.

44. *Ma'ariv* business supplement, December 16, 1988.

45. Eliyahu Slefter, *Ha'aretz,* March 10, 1988.

46. *Yedi'ot Ahronot,* December 23, 1988.

The Protest Movement in Israel

1. Yesh Gvul leaflet, March 1986.

2. Benny Morris, *Jerusalem Post,* June 3, 1988. The author of this article subsequently served time in a military prison for refusing to perform reserve duty in the occupied territories.

3. S. Slutski, *Al Hamishmar,* July 12, 1988.

4. Tuvia Baskind, *Al Hamishmar,* July 20, 1988.

5. Avi Biniyahu, *Al Hamishmar,* July 25, 1988.

6. *Ha'aretz,* June 16, 1988.

7. Newsletter of the Twenty-First Year, June 1988.

8. Advertisement, *Hadashot,* January 29, 1988.

9. Lili Galili, *Ha'aretz,* June 15, 1988.

10. Peace Now advertisement, *Kol Ha'ir,* December 18, 1987.

11. Peace Now advertisement, *Ha'aretz,* January 14, 1988.

12. Peace Now advertisement, *Jerusalem Post,* February 12, 1988.

13. Peace Now advertisement, *Jerusalem Post,* August 5, 1988.

Israel's Role in US Foreign Policy

1. Speaking for the governing Likud bloc in 1984, Knesset member Roni Milo announced that "we have never said that we renounce our right to [the State of Jordan], though in the context of negotiations with Jordan we might agree to certain concessions in Eastern Transjordan" (*Ma'ariv,* January 3, 1984). In February 1988, the Platform Committee of Herut reiterated that the right of the Jewish people to the Land of Israel, including Jordan, is "permanent and not subject to any appeal," though they do not "propose to go to war on Amman" (Dorit Gefen, *Al-Hamishmar,* February 29, 1988). The same position had long been held by the Ahduth Avodah movement, which played a decisive role under the Golda Meir government; see Yossi Beilin, *Mehiro shel Ihud* (Revivim, 1985). The ideological principles of LEHI (the Stern group), headed by current Prime Minister Yitzhak Shamir, were republished by its members in 1958 and do not appear to have been withdrawn. They fix the Land of Israel as extending from the Nile to the Euphrates, "where the entire Hebrew nation will reside in security," and declare the right of the Jews to this territory as "incontestable: it did not expire and never can expire." They declare "an eternal war against all those who satanically stand in the way of the realization [of our] aims" and call for "the re-establishment of the monarchy," "the construction of the Third Temple as a symbol in the process of Total Redemption," and solution of "the problem of the aliens" through "population exchanges" (meaning expulsion). Ya'ir (Avraham Stern), "Principles of Renais-

sance, 1940-1, reprinted in Ya'akov Banai, *Hayalim Almonim* ("Unknown Soldiers") (Tel Aviv, 1958). The mainstream Zionist leadership traditionally regarded partition as a temporary expedient to be overcome by further expansion. See my *Fateful Triangle* (South End Press, 1983, chapter 4, sec. 9.1) and references cited there; also Shabtai Tevet, *Ben-Gurion and the Palestinian Arabs* (Oxford, 1985); Tom Segev, *1949* (MacMillan, 1986); Simha Flapan, *The Birth of Israel* (Pantheon, 1986).

2. AP, April 8; Elaine Sciolino, *New York Times,* April 6, 8, 1988.

3. Fouad Moughrabi, Occasional Paper no. 4, *American Public Opinion and the Palestine Question,* International Center for Research in Public Policy, 1987.

4. See *Fateful Triangle,* pp. 77-8, and references cited, including Shmuel Segev, *Ma'ariv,* March 2, 1983, who notes the re-endorsement of this position at the PLO National Council meeting in February 1983.

5. Harkabi, *Ikarey Hasichsuch bein Yisrael le'Arav* (Pirsumei Mediniyut 22, January 1988, Jerusalem).

6. Yoav Karni, *Yediot Ahronot,* Nov. 27, 1984.

7. For a recent review of the early efforts to deal with the problem, see Benny Morris, *The Birth of the Palestinian Refugee Problem: 1947-1949* (Cambridge University Press, 1988, chapter 9). Morris concludes that both sides treated the refugees as "a political weapon," noting that "Arab policy on this score was bolstered by a genuine economic inability to properly absorb hundreds of thousands of refugees and by fear of the refugees as a major potential subversive element *vis-à-vis* their own regimes" while Israel also held that "returning refugees would constitute a Fifth Column" and that repatriation would be economically and socially unfeasible.

8. For further background on these matters, see my *Towards a New Cold War* (Pantheon, 1982), *Turning the Tide* (South End Press, 1985), *On Power and Ideology* (South End Press, 1987), *The Culture of Terrorism* (South End Press, 1988), and sources cited.

9. See sources cited in note 9 for explicit references and quotes, here and below.

10. For references and further discussion, here and below, see *Towards a New Cold War;* also Aaron David Miller, *Search for Security* (University of North Carolina Press, 1980); Irvine Anderson, *Aramco, the United States and Saudi Arabia* (Princeton University Press, 1981); Michael Stoff, *Oil, War and American Security* (Yale University Press, 1980). Eisenhower cited in Steven Spiegel, *The Other Arab-Israeli Conflict* (Chicago, 1985, p.51).

11. Cited by Bruce Cumings, *World Policy Journal,* Winter 1987-88; see also *Towards a New Cold War,* pp. 97-8.

12. See Michael Bar-Zohar, *Ben-Gurion: A Biography* (New York, 1978, p. 261f.).

13. For details, see *Fateful Triangle* and *The Culture of Terrorism.*

14. Glenn Frankel, *Washington Post,* November 19, 1986.

15. *Ha'aretz,* November 11, 1983.

16. Glick, *The Triangular Connection: America, Israel and American Jews* (Allen & Unwin, London, 1982, p. 113f.); Michael Oreskes, *New York Times,* May 16, 1985. The *Times* article was occasioned by the concern that unions might sell Israel bonds as a consequence of strikebreaking activities by El Al at a New York airport.

17. *Ot,* March 9, 1972, cited by Amnon Kapeliouk, *Le monde diplomatique,* October 1977.

18. For extensive evidence, see *Towards a New Cold War,* chapter 6.

19. Schiff, "The Spectre of Civil War in Israel," *Middle East Journal,* Spring 1985.

20. *Jerusalem Post,* November 27, 1987.

21. Beilin, *op. cit.,* pp. 147, 139.

22. For additional discussion, see the valuable study by Amnon Kapeliouk, *Israel: la fin des mythes* (Paris, 1975), translation from the Hebrew original.

23. Beilin, *op. cit.,* pp. 42-3.

24. Yosef Heller, *Bama'vak lamdina,* Jewish Agency protocols, May 19-20, 1936.

25. Beilin, *op. cit.,* p. 20.

26. Norman Kempster, *Los Angeles Times,* January 23, 1988.

27. See, e.g., Avner Yaniv, who observes that the effect of the "Egyptian defection" was that "Israel would be free to sustain military operations against the PLO in Lebanon as well as settlement activity on the West Bank;" *Dilemmas of Security* (Oxford, 1987, p. 70).

28. *Jerusalem Post,* November 13, 1981.

29. James Markham, *New York Times,* December 3, 1975.

30. For documentation, see my *Pirates and Emperors* (Claremont, 1986; Amana, 1988), and *Fateful Triangle.*

31. *New York Times,* March 21, 1977.

32. David Hirst, *Manchester Guardian Weekly,* August 7, 1977.

33. *Dilemmas of Security,* p. 88.

34. *Washington Post,* July 26, 1981.

35. *Op. cit.,* p. 105.

36. *Ha'aretz,* June 25, 1982.

37. *Op. cit.,* [pp. 52-3, 67ff., 100-1. Yaniv criticizes the "anti-Zionist" conception that "the war in Lebanon was inspired by Begin's ideologically motivated desire to liquidate the PLO and thus consolidate Israel's own claim upon the West Bank," apparently unaware that this is essentially his own analysis, often in virtually the same terms (p. 20; cf. p. 23).]

38. *Nouvel Observateur*(Paris), May 4, 1984; *Observer*(London), April 29, 1984; *Jerusalem Post,* May 16, 1984; *San Francisco Examiner,* May 5, 1984; *Washington Post,* July 8, 1984.

39. *New York Times,* March 17, 21 and June 2, 1985.

40. Yitzhak Ben-Horin, *Ma'ariv,* Dec. 4; *Ma'ariv,* December 5; Eyal Ehrlich, *Ha'aretz,* December 19, 1986.

41. *Hadashot,* Jan. 7, 1988; *Ha'aretz,* December 31, 1987.

42. Interview, *Nouvel Observateur,* January 7, 1988.

43. AP, January 15; *Toronto Globe & Mail,* January 15, 1987; also published prominently in several small local newspapers in the United States.

44. *New York Review of Books,* June 25, 1987. UN English translation, quoted in *The Other Israel,* Newsletter of the Israeli Council for Israeli-Palestinian Peace, November-December 1987.

45. *New York Times,* March 12, 1988.

46. *Ha'aretz,* April 12; *Jerusalem Post,* April 13; *Ha'aretz,* April 7; *Toronto Globe & Mail,* April 26; Tony Banks, *Jane's Defence Weekly,* May 7.

47. Joel Brinkley, *New York Times,* June 22, 1988.

48. *In These Times,* June 22, distributed several days earlier; *New York Times,* June 22, 1988. In subsequent weeks, there were continued indications of controversy within the PLO over the Abu Sharif initiative.

49. *New York Times,* December 20, 1987; *Washington Post,* January 25, 1988; *New York Times,* January 26, 1988; *New York Times,* January 17, 1988; *Boston Globe,* January 13, 1988; *Yediot Ahronot,* March 2, 1988.

The Conflict and the US Peace Movement

1. The positions of the anti-intervention caucus are best expressed in Michael Albert and David Dellinger (eds.), *Beyond Survival: New Directions for the Disarmament Movement* (Boston: South End Press, 1983).

2. A transcript of the original conference was published in 1983 by the New England Regional Office of AFSC. An enlarged edition was later published as Joseph Gerson (ed.), *The Deadly Connection: Nuclear War and US Intervention* (Philadelphia: New Society, 1986).

3. After nearly a week of negotiations on the exact wording of PLO statements, Arafat had met virtually every condition the US administration could think up. Finally, in exasperation, he asked at a Geneva news conference if he would have to do a strip-tease next.

The Road Ahead

1. AIPAC, *Near East Report*, March 13, 1989.

2. *Building for Peace: An American Strategy for the Middle East* (Washington Institute for Near East Policy, 1988), p. 77.

3. *Ibid.*, pp. 12, 33.

4. Jaffee Center for Strategic Studies, *Israel, the West Bank and Gaza: Toward a Solution* (Tel Aviv, 1989), pp. 20, 22. These recommendations, "conceived and written on an entirely independent Israeli basis," were published separately from a larger study, *The West Bank and Gaza: Israel's Options for Peace,* which was sponsored largely by the American Jewish Congress and B'nai Brith.

5. *Washington Post*, March 15, 1989.

6. *Washington Jewish Week*, March 16, 1989.

About the Contributors

Dan Almagor is one of Israel's preeminent songwriters, playwrights and theatrical and television producers. For decades a solidly establishment figure, in 1988 he broke with the national consensus in response to the intifada. The poem printed in this collection was first published in *Middle East Report* 157 (March-April 1989).

George Azar has covered Middle East developments as a photojournalist for more than 10 years. A book of his photos from Lebanon and Palestine, *Palestine through Arab Eyes,* will be published by the University of California Press in 1991.

Hussein Barghouti is a Palestinian songwriter. "A Song For Childhood" was recorded as part of a cassette tape entitled *Mawt al-Nabi* by the musical group Sabreen. It was released in Palestine in 1988.

Melissa Baumann is a free-lance journalist based in Cambridge, MA. Her contribution first appeared in *Middle East Report* 152 (May-June 1988) and is based on a visit to the occupied territories in January-February 1988 sponsored by Grassroots International.

Joel Beinin teaches Middle East history at Stanford University. He is an editor of *Middle East Report* and co-author (with Zachary Lockman) of *Workers on the Nile: Nationalism, Communism, Islam, and the Egyptian Working Class, 1882-1954.* An earlier version of "From Land Day to Peace Day" appeared in *Middle East Report* 150 (January-February 1988).

Azmy Bishara is a Palestinian Arab citizen of Israel currently living in Jerusalem and teaching at Birzeit University. His contribution first appeared in *Middle East Report* 157 (March-April 1989).

Peter Boullata, born in Jerusalem, is a creative writing student at Concordia University in Montreal, Canada.

Ellen Cantarow is a free-lance journalist living in Cambridge, MA and associate editor of *The Women's Review of Books.* Her work has appeared regularly in *Middle East Report.* Another version of her essay in this book was published in the April 1989 issue of *Grand Street.*

Noam Chomsky is professor of linguistics at the Massachusetts Institute of Technology and a contributing editor of *Middle East Report.* His books include *The Fateful Triangle: The United States, Israel and the Palestinians; Pirates & Emperors: International Terrorism in the Real World;* and, most recently, *Necessary Illusions: Thought Control in Democratic Societies.*

Mahmoud Darwish, born in Palestine in 1942, is perhaps the best-known and most popular Palestinian poet. He has received the International Lotus Prize for Poetry and the Lenin Peace Prize. The poem printed in this collection is translated from the *Jerusalem Post,* April 2, 1988. It sparked an unprecedented furor in the Israeli Knesset and press.

Beshara Doumani is a Ph.D. candidate at Georgetown University and teaches Middle East history at the University of Pennsylvania. He is a contributing editor of *Middle East Report,* where his chapter first appeared in issue 157 (March-April 1989).

Rita Giacaman is an instructor at Birzeit University.

Lisa Hajjar is a doctoral candidate in sociology at American University. During 1987-88 she was an editorial assistant for *Middle East Report.* An earlier version of "Palestine and the Arab-Israeli Conflict for Beginners" appeared in *Middle East Report* 154 (September-October 1988).

Joost Hiltermann lives in Ramallah and works for the human rights monitoring organization, al-Haq/Law in the Service of Man, the West Bank affiliate of the International Commission of Jurists.

Ibn al-Jabal ("Son of the Mountain") is the pseudonym of a Palestinian activist who wrote this poem in June 1988 while imprisoned in Ansar III. It was translated by Barbara Harlow and Makram Copty.

Todd Jailer is an activist on Middle East and Central America issues and is a member of the South End Press collective.

Penny Johnson lives in Ramallah, works in the public relations department of Birzeit University and is a contributing editor of *Middle East Report.* "The West Bank Rises Up" first appeared in *Middle East Report* 152 (May-June 1988).

Reuven Kaminer, a member of Shasi (Israeli Socialist Left), is one of four Israelis convicted of participating in a delegation that met with representatives of the PLO in Rumania in November 1986. The case is currently under appeal to the Supreme Court of Israel.

Rashid Khalidi is associate professor of Middle East history at the University of Chicago, an editor of *Middle East Report* and author of *Under Siege: PLO Decisionmaking During the 1982 War.* An earlier version of his contribution appeared in *Middle East Report* 146 (May-June 1987).

Zachary Lockman is associate professor of Middle East history at Harvard University, an editor of *Middle East Report* and co-author (with Joel Beinin) of *Workers on the Nile: Nationalism, Communism, Islam, and the Egyptian Working Class, 1882-1954.* An earlier version of "Original Sin" appeared in *Middle East Report* 152 (May-June 1988).

Melani McAlister is a former Middle East staffperson for Boston Mobilization for Survival and is currently a member of the staff of the Jefferson Park Writing Project in Cambridge, MA.

Hanan Mikha'il-Ashrawi, born in Nablus, is Dean of the Arts Faculty at Birzeit University. Her poem, included in this collection, first appeared in Kamal Boullata's *Women of the Fertile Crescent: Modern Poetry by Arab Women.*

Lee O'Brien lives in Ramallah, works in the public relations department of Birzeit University and is a contributing editor of *Middle East Report.*

Nizar Qabbani, born in Syria in 1932, is one of the Arab world's leading poets. He has published over 25 collections of poetry. The poem included in this collection was translated by Sherif al-Musa and appeared in *Middle East Report* 152 (May-June, 1988).

Mouin Rabbani interned with *Middle East Report* during 1987-88. He researched and wrote the centerfold for issue 152 (May-June 1988), parts of which have been integrated into "Palestine and the Arab-Israeli Conflict for Beginners."

Rick Reinhard is a documentary photographer based in Washington, DC. He traveled in Palestine and Israel in 1988 with *Middle East Report* editors Joe Stork and Jim Paul.

Edward W. Said is Parr Professor of English and Comparative Literature at Columbia University, a member of the Palestine National Council and a contributing editor of *Middle East Report.* His books include *Orientalism, The Question of Palestine* and *After The Last Sky: Palestinian Lives.* A version of his introduction to this book also appeared in *Social Text.*

Joe Stork is the editor of *Middle East Report.* His contribution, based on a visit to the occupied territories in June 1988, first appeared in *Middle East Report* 154 (September-October 1988).

Salim Tamari teaches sociology at Birzeit University and is a contributing editor of *Middle East Report.* His contribution originally appeared in *Middle East Report* 152 (May-June 1988).

Lisa Taraki lives in Ramallah and teaches sociology at Birzeit University. Her contribution previously appeared in *Middle East Report* 156 (January-February 1989).

John Tordai works as a photographer with Select Agency in London and other agencies. A collection of his Palestine photos will be published in early 1991 in London.

Anita Vitullo is a journalist living in Jerusalem and a contributing editor of *Middle East Report.* An earlier version of her chapter appeared in *Middle East Report* 152 (May-June 1988).

About South End Press

South End Press is a nonprofit, collectively run book publisher with over 150 titles in print. Since our founding in 1977, we have tried to meet the needs of readers who are exploring or are already committed to the politics of fundamental social change. Our goal is to publish books that encourage critical thinking and constructive action on the key political, cultural, social, economic and ecological issues shaping life in the United States and in the world. In this way, we hope to give expression to a wide diversity of democratic social movements and to provide an alternative to the products of corporate publishing.

If you would like to receive a free catalog of South End Press books or get information on our membership program—which, for $40, offers two free books of your choice and a 40% discount on all other titles—please write us at South End Press, 116 Saint Botolph Street, Boston, MA 02115.

Other Books of Interest Available from South End Press

*Punishing a Nation: Israeli Human Rights Violations
During the Palestinian Uprising*
Al-Haq/Law in the Service of Man

The Fateful Triangle: The United States, Israel, and the Palestinians
Noam Chomsky

Israeli Foreign Policy: South Africa and Central America
Jane Hunter

My War Diary: Lebanon June 5-July 1, 1982
Dov Yermiya

The Battle of Beirut: Why Israel Invaded Lebanon
Michael Jansen

The Real Terror Network: Terrorism in Fact and Propoganda
Edward S. Herman

*US Imperialism: From the Spanish-American War
to the Iranian Revolution*
Mansour Farhang